Inducing Intimacy

Kennedy presents a new way of evaluating the regulation of deceptively induced intimacy, that is, sex and sexual/romantic relationships, based on an innovative genealogy of legal responses to this conduct. This book traces the development of a range of civil and criminal laws across c. 250 years, showing how using deception to induce intimacy has been legally understood, compensated and punished. It offers an original interpretation of the form and function of these laws by situating them in their social and cultural contexts. It argues that prevailing notions of what makes intimacy valuable, including the role it plays in self-construction, have shaped and constrained the laws' operation. It shows how deceptively induced sex has come to be treated more seriously while the opposite is true of deceptively induced relationships and concludes by presenting a new framework for deciding whether and when deceptively induced intimacy should be regulated by law today.

Chloë Kennedy is Professor of Law and History at the School of Law, University of Edinburgh. She has published widely in the areas of criminal law, legal history, legal theory, and law and gender. She is the co-editor of two books – *Scottish Feminist Judgments: (Re)Creating Law from the Outside In* (Hart, 2019) and *Leading Works in Criminal Law* (Routledge, 2023). *Inducing Intimacy: Deception, Consent and the Law* is the product of a research fellowship Chloë was awarded by the Arts and Humanities Research Council.

Law in Context

Series editors
Professor Kenneth Armstrong
University of Cambridge
Professor Maksymilian Del Mar
Queen Mary, University of London
Professor Sally Sheldon
University of Bristol and University of Technology Sydney

Editorial advisory board
Professor Bronwen Morgan
University of New South Wales
Emeritus Professor William Twining
University College London

Since 1970, the Law in Context series has been at the forefront of a movement to broaden the study of law. The series is a vehicle for the publication of innovative monographs and texts that treat law and legal phenomena critically in their cultural, social, political, technological, environmental and economic contexts. A contextual approach involves treating legal subjects broadly, using materials from other humanities and social sciences, and from any other discipline that helps to explain the operation in practice of the particular legal field or legal phenomena under investigation. It is intended that this orientation is at once more stimulating and more revealing than the bare exposition of legal rules. The series includes original research monographs, coursebooks and textbooks that foreground contextual approaches and methods. The series includes and welcomes books on the study of law in all its contexts, including domestic legal systems, European and international law, transnational and global legal processes, and comparative law.

Books in the Series
Acosta: *The National versus the Foreigner in South America: 200 Years of Migration and Citizenship Law*
Alaattinoğlu: *Grievance Formation, Rights and Remedies*
Ali: *Modern Challenges to Islamic Law*
Alyagon Darr: *Plausible Crime Stories: The Legal History of Sexual Offences in Mandate Palestine*
Anderson, Schum & Twining: *Analysis of Evidence, 2nd Edition*
Ashworth: *Sentencing and Criminal Justice, 6th Edition*
Barton & Douglas: *Law and Parenthood*
Baxi, McCrudden & Paliwala: *Law's Ethical, Global and Theoretical Contexts: Essays in Honour of William Twining*
Beecher-Monas: *Evaluating Scientific Evidence: An Interdisciplinary Framework for Intellectual Due Process*
Bell: *French Legal Cultures*
Bercusson: *European Labour Law, 2nd Edition*

Birkinshaw: *European Public Law*
Birkinshaw: *Freedom of Information: The Law, the Practice and the Ideal, 4th Edition*
Blick: *Electrified Democracy: The Internet and the United Kingdom Parliament in History*
Broderick & Ferri: *International and European Disability Law and Policy: Text, Cases and Materials*
Brownsword & Goodwin: *Law and the Technologies of the Twenty-First Century: Text and Materials*
Cane & Goudkamp: *Atiyah's Accidents, Compensation and the Law, 9th Edition*
Clarke: *Principles of Property Law*
Clarke & Kohler: *Property Law: Commentary and Materials*
Collins: *The Law of Contract, 4th Edition*
Collins, Ewing & McColgan: *Labour Law, 2nd Edition*
Cowan: *Housing Law and Policy*
Cranston: *Making Commercial Law Through Practice 1830–1970*
Cranston: *Legal Foundations of the Welfare State*
Darian-Smith: *Laws and Societies in Global Contexts: Contemporary Approaches*
Dauvergne: *Making People Illegal: What Globalisation Means for Immigration and Law*
David: *Kinship, Law and Politics: An Anatomy of Belonging*
Davies: *Perspectives on Labour Law, 2nd Edition*
Dembour: *Who Believes in Human Rights?: Reflections on the European Convention*
de Sousa Santos: *Toward a New Legal Common Sense: Law, Globalization, and Emancipation*
Diduck: *Law's Families*
Douglas-Scott: *Brexit, Union, and Disunion: The Evolution of British Constitutional Unsettlement*
Dowdle: *Transnational Law: A Framework for Analysis*
Dupret: *Positive Law from the Muslim World: Jurisprudence, History, Practices*
Emon: *Jurisdictional Exceptionalisms: Islamic Law, International Law, and Parental Child Abduction*
Estella: *Legal Foundations of EU Economic Governance*
Fortin: *Children's Rights and the Developing Law, 3rd Edition*
Garnsey: *The Justice of Visual Art: Creative State-Building in Times of Political Transition*
Garton, Probert & Bean: *Moffat's Trusts Law: Text and Materials, 7th Edition*
Ghai & Woodman: *Practising Self-Government: A Comparative Study of Autonomous Regions*
Glover-Thomas: *Reconstructing Mental Health Law and Policy*
Gobert & Punch: *Rethinking Corporate Crime*
Goldman: *Globalisation and the Western Legal Tradition: Recurring Patterns of Law and Authority*
Haack: *Evidence Matters: Science, Proof, and Truth in the Law*
Harlow & Rawlings: *Law and Administration, 4th Edition*
Harris: *An Introduction to Law, 8th Edition*
Harris, Campbell & Halson: *Remedies in Contract and Tort, 2nd Edition*
Harvey: *Seeking Asylum in the UK: Problems and Prospects*
Herring: *Law and the Relational Self*
Hervey & McHale: *European Union Health Law: Themes and Implications*
Hervey & McHale: *Health Law and the European Union*
Holder & Lee: *Environmental Protection, Law and Policy: Text and Materials, 2nd Edition*

Jackson & Summers: *The Internationalisation of Criminal Evidence: Beyond the Common Law and Civil Law Traditions*
Jeutner: *The Reasonable Person: A Legal Biography*
Kennedy: *Inducing Intimacy: Deception, Consent and the Law*
Kostakopoulou: *The Future Governance of Citizenship*
Kreiczer-Levy: *Destabilized Property: Property Law in the Sharing Economy*
Kubal: *Immigration and Refugee Law in Russia: Socio-Legal Perspectives*
Lewis: *Choice and the Legal Order: Rising above Politics*
Likosky: *Law, Infrastructure and Human Rights*
Likosky: *Transnational Legal Processes: Globalisation and Power Disparities*
Lixinski: *Legalized Identities: Cultural Heritage Law and the Shaping of Transitional Justice*
Loughnan: *Self, Others and the State: Relations of Criminal Responsibility*
Lunney: *A History of Australian Tort Law 1901–1945: England's Obedient Servant?*
Maughan & Webb: *Lawyering Skills and the Legal Process, 2nd Edition*
McGaughey: *Principles of Enterprise Law*
McGlynn: *Families and the European Union: Law, Politics and Pluralism*
Mertens: *A Philosophical Introduction to Human Rights*
Miller: *An Introduction to German Law and Legal Culture: Text and Materials*
Moffat: *Trusts Law: Text and Materials*
Monti: *EC Competition Law*
Morgan: *Contract Law Minimalism: A Formalist Restatement of Commercial Contract Law*
Morgan & Yeung: *An Introduction to Law and Regulation: Text and Materials*
Nash: *British Islam and English Law: A Classical Pluralist Perspective*
Ng: *Political Censorship in British Hong Kong: Freedom of Expression and the Law (1842–1997)*
Nicola & Davies: *EU Law Stories: Contextual and Critical Histories of European Jurisprudence*
Norrie: *Crime, Reason and History: A Critical Introduction to Criminal Law, 3rd Edition*
O'Dair: *Legal Ethics: Text and Materials*
Oliver: *Common Values and the Public–Private Divide*
Oliver & Drewry: *The Law and Parliament*
Palmer & Roberts: *Dispute Processes: ADR and the Primary Forms of Decision-Making, 1st Edition*
Palmer & Roberts: *Dispute Processes: ADR and the Primary Forms of Decision-Making, 3rd Edition*
Picciotto: *International Business Taxation*
Pieraccini: *Regulating the Sea: A Socio-Legal Analysis of English Marine Protected Areas*
Probert: *The Changing Legal Regulation of Cohabitation, 1600–2010: From Fornicators to Family, 1600–2010*
Radi: *Rules and Practices of International Investment Law and Arbitration*
Reed: *Internet Law: Text and Materials*
Richardson: *Law, Process and Custody*
Roberts & Palmer: *Dispute Processes: ADR and the Primary Forms of Decision-Making, 2nd Edition*
Rowbottom: *Democracy Distorted: Wealth, Influence and Democratic Politics*
Sauter: *Public Services in EU Law*
Scott & Black: *Cranston's Consumers and the Law*

Seneviratne: *Ombudsmen: Public Services and Administrative Justice*
Seppänen: *Ideological Conflict and the Rule of Law in Contemporary China: Useful Paradoxes*
Siems: *Comparative Law, 3rd Edition*
Stapleton: *Product Liability*
Stewart: *Gender, Law and Justice in a Global Market*
Tamanaha: *Law as a Means to an End: Threat to the Rule of Law*
Taylor: *Fortin's Children's Rights and the Developing Law, 4th Edition*
Tuori: *Properties of Law: Modern Law and After*
Turpin & Tomkins: *British Government and the Constitution: Text and Materials, 7th Edition*
Twining: *General Jurisprudence: Understanding Law from a Global Perspective*
Twining: *Globalisation and Legal Theory*
Twining: *Human Rights, Southern Voices: Francis Deng, Abdullahi An-Na'im, Yash Ghai and Upendra Baxi*
Twining: *Jurist in Context: A Memoir*
Twining: *Karl Llewellyn and the Realist Movement, 2nd Edition*
Twining: *Rethinking Evidence: Exploratory Essays, 2nd Edition*
Twining & Miers: *How to Do Things with Rules, 5th Edition*
Wan: *Film and Constitutional Controversy: Visualizing Hong Kong Identity in the Age of 'One Country, Two Systems'*
Ward: *A Critical Introduction to European Law, 3rd Edition*
Ward: *Law, Text, Terror*
Ward: *Shakespeare and Legal Imagination*
Watt: *The Making Sense of Politics, Media, and Law: Rhetorical Performance as Invention, Creation, Production*
Wells & Quick: *Lacey, Wells and Quick: Reconstructing Criminal Law: Text and Materials, 4th Edition*
Woodhead: *Caring for Cultural Heritage: An Integrated Approach to Legal and Ethical Initiatives in the United Kingdom*
Yeung and Ranchordás: *An Introduction to Law and Regulation: Text and Materials, 2nd edition*
Young: *Turpin and Tomkins' British Government and the Constitution: Text and Materials, 8th Edition*
Zander: *Cases and Materials on the English Legal System, 10th Edition*
Zander: *The Law-Making Process, 6th Edition*

International Journal of Law in Context: A Global Forum for Interdisciplinary Legal Studies

The *International Journal of Law in Context* is the companion journal to the Law in Context book series and provides a forum for interdisciplinary legal studies and offers intellectual space for ground-breaking critical research. It publishes contextual work about law and its relationship with other disciplines including but not limited to science, literature, humanities, philosophy, sociology, psychology, ethics, history and geography. More information about the journal and how to submit an article can be found at http://journals.cambridge.org/ijc

Inducing Intimacy

Deception, Consent and the Law

CHLOË KENNEDY
University of Edinburgh

CAMBRIDGE
UNIVERSITY PRESS

Shaftesbury Road, Cambridge CB2 8EA, United Kingdom

One Liberty Plaza, 20th Floor, New York, NY 10006, USA

477 Williamstown Road, Port Melbourne, VIC 3207, Australia

314–321, 3rd Floor, Plot 3, Splendor Forum, Jasola District Centre, New Delhi – 110025, India

103 Penang Road, #05–06/07, Visioncrest Commercial, Singapore 238467

Cambridge University Press is part of Cambridge University Press & Assessment, a department of the University of Cambridge.

We share the University's mission to contribute to society through the pursuit of education, learning and research at the highest international levels of excellence.

www.cambridge.org
Information on this title: www.cambridge.org/9781009361057

DOI: 10.1017/9781009361095

© Chloë Kennedy 2024

This publication is in copyright. Subject to statutory exception and to the provisions of relevant collective licensing agreements, no reproduction of any part may take place without the written permission of Cambridge University Press & Assessment.

First published 2024
First paperback edition 2025

A catalogue record for this publication is available from the British Library

Library of Congress Cataloging-in-Publication data
Names: Kennedy, Chloë, author.
Title: Inducing intimacy : deception, consent, and the law / Chloë Kennedy.
Description: Cambridge, United Kingdom ; New York, NY : Cambridge University Press, 2024. | Series: Law in context | Includes bibliographical references and index.
Identifiers: LCCN 2024014769 (print) | LCCN 2024014770 (ebook) | ISBN 9781009361101 (hardback) | ISBN 9781009361095 (ebook)
Subjects: LCSH: Sex and law. | Sexual consent. | Sexual ethics. | Sex crimes – Law and legislation.
| Intimacy. | Prostitution – Law and legislation.
Classification: LCC K5194 .K46 2024 (print) | LCC K5194 (ebook) | DDC 346.01/62–dc23/eng/20240402
LC record available at https://lccn.loc.gov/2024014769
LC ebook record available at https://lccn.loc.gov/2024014770

ISBN   978-1-009-36110-1   Hardback
ISBN   978-1-009-36105-7   Paperback

Cambridge University Press & Assessment has no responsibility for the persistence or accuracy of URLs for external or third-party internet websites referred to in this publication and does not guarantee that any content on such websites is, or will remain, accurate or appropriate.

Contents

Acknowledgements		*page* x
Table of Cases		xii
Table of Statutes		xxviii
1	Inducing Intimacy: An Introduction	1
	Part I Marriage	
2	Making Marriage	29
3	Promising Marriage	64
4	Faking Marriage	88
	Part II Sex	
5	Eliciting Sex	121
6	Procuring Sex	144
7	Imposing Sex	169
8	Inducing Intimacy: A Conclusion	199
	Bibliography	220
	Index	238

Acknowledgements

Much of this book was researched and written during an Arts and Humanities Research Council (AHRC) early career research leader fellowship, which ran from January 2020 to January 2022 (AH/S013180/1) and a subsequent year of research leave. I would therefore like to begin by thanking the AHRC and the University of Edinburgh School of Law for the time and resources needed to complete this work. Special thanks go to Shauna Thompson, Head of the Research, Knowledge Exchange and Impact Office at the School of Law, for her encouragement and expert guidance in applying for the fellowship. I am also grateful to the School of Law for supplementing the funding for this project via the Research and Impact Facilitation Fund on more than one occasion.

Embarking on a major research project during a global pandemic presented various challenges, including limited or no access to archival materials and the cessation of face-to-face conferences and exchanges with colleagues. I was lucky, in these circumstances, to benefit from the knowledge and expertise of staff at National Records of Scotland, the Advocates Library and the Signet Library. In particular, James Hamilton, Research Principal of the Society of Writers to the Signet, and Helen Robinson, Reader Services Librarian at the Advocates Library, were enormously helpful. David Brown, Collection and Access Services Senior Library Assistant at the Advocates Library, was also very generous with his time, giving me a tour of the library's holdings and helping me navigate the process of obtaining access. Fergus Smith was also kind enough to share his expertise regarding the Sheriff Court holdings at National Records Scotland.

Throughout the period of research leave, I was fortunate to be invited to speak about some of the ideas and arguments that made their way into this book at various events, including seminars hosted by the Political Turn in Criminal Law Thinking (later, Theory) group, the Oxford Criminal Law Discussion Group and the Oxford Jurisprudence Discussion Group. On top of this, I benefitted from a series of seminars on the themes of identity and trust, organised by Lindsay Farmer and myself, and a two-day symposium on modern histories of consent, which Laura Lammasniemi and I arranged.

Beyond these events, many people helped me stay focussed on, and enthusiastic about, this book. First and foremost, Lindsay Farmer has been a huge support from the inception of this project right through to its end, dedicating precious time and energy to reading drafts of funding applications, helping me with the proposal that led to this book, scheduling regular catch ups, providing feedback on chapters and, finally, putting together a workshop to discuss the bulk of the manuscript. I would like to offer my sincere thanks to those who participated in this workshop, including the commentators – Alan Brown, Stephen Bogle, Antony Duff, Lindsay Farmer, Nicola Lacey, Laura Lammasniemi and Anat Rosenberg – and everyone else who attended – James Chalmers, Kajsa Dinesson, JP Fassnidge, Alice Krzanich, Arlie Loughnan, Sandra Marshall, Robbie Reid, Neil Walker and Gabrielle Watson. Many other colleagues read portions of this book, providing me with helpful comments and much-needed reassurance when I (frequently) strayed outside my comfort zone. I would particularly like to thank Katie Barclay, Gillian Black, Dan Carr, Henrique Carvalho, Andrew Cornford, Matt Dyson, Maebh Harding, Max Kiener, Laura MacGregor, Hector MacQueen, Rebecca Probert, Lorna Richardson and Tanya Serisier. Finally, Emily Postan and Rachel Clement Tolley both provided inspiration for the arguments in this book through discussions about identity construction and deceptive sex, respectively.

There are lots of other people who helped shape this book whom I would like to thank. Kelly-Ann Couzens worked with me as a postdoctoral research assistant for over a year, and we had many illuminating discussions during this time. Kit Baston was also a postdoctoral research assistant during the project's early phases, bringing enthusiasm and acumen to the role, and Alice Krzanich did a fantastic job during the month I benefitted from her research assistance. Kate Harvey assisted in writing the policy paper that was included in the Criminal Law Reform Now Network's consultation paper on reforming the English criminal law on deception, mistake and sexual consent; her expertise greatly improved the text. Lastly, during Jamie Crewe's year-long artistic residency, which was partly funded by the AHRC fellowship, we had regular discussions about the themes of the project, often joined by Julie-Ann Delaney and Liv Laumenech of the University of Edinburgh's Art Collection. I enjoyed these talks and am pleased to see that the artwork that was produced during the residency, *False Wife*, has been positively received.

At Cambridge University Press, I would like to thank the editors with whom I worked, Tom Randall, Marianna Nield and Tobias Ginsberg. I am also grateful to the *Law in Context* general editors Kenneth Armstrong, Maks del Mar and Sally Sheldon for giving me the opportunity to be part of this series. Kate McIntosh compiled the index and Rob Gibson drew up the bibliography and tables, so thank you to them. Parts of the final chapter of this book draw substantially on material within the article 'Criminalising Deceptive Sex: Sex, Identity and Recognition' (2021) 41(1) *Legal Studies* 91–110. I thank the publishers for permitting me to use this material.

Finally, I would like to thank my partner, family and friends. Though the support and care they provided throughout my writing this book is just one small reason I am grateful for their love, it deserves acknowledgement.

Table of Cases

Case Reports

A v. B 2007 WL 919500, 62
A v. M (1865) 4 Scot L Mag & Sheriff Ct Rep 1, 90
AB v. CB (1884) 11 R 1060, 52, 53
AB v. CB (1885) 22 SLR 461, 53
AB v. CB (1906) 42 SLR 411; (1906) 8 F 603, 52, 53
AB v. CD ('Glasgow Sheriff Court', *The Glasgow Herald*, 1 April 1865, p. 5), 134
Ackerman v. Blackburn 2000 Fam LR 35, 11
Alexander v. Alexander 1920 SC 327, 47
Allardyce v. Allardyce 1954 SLT 334, 52
Armstrong v. Thomson (1894) 2 SLT 70, 136
Assange v. Sweden 2001 WL 5077784, 189, 190
Attorney-General's Reference (No. 1 of 1975) [1975] QB 773, 151
Baird v. Hard (1859) NRS CS228/B/21/32, 52
Bell v. Graham (1859) 15 ER 91, 97
Bell, John (1777) NRS JC7/39, 130
Bern v. Montrose Lunatic Asylum, Montrose (1893) 20 R 859, 128
Borthwick v. Borthwick (1896–1897) 4 SLT 130, 128
Boyd v. Eadie (1917) 33 Scot L Rev 1, 134
Boyd v. Swan (1898) 14 Scot L Rev 230, 132, 135, 138
Brady v. Murray 1933 SLT 534, 98
Brown v. Harvey 1907 SC 588, 136, 138, 139, 140
Browne v. Burns (1843) 5 D 1288, 97
Bruce v. Bruce (1919) NRS CS46/1919/4/71, 42
Buchanan v. Macnab (1785) Mor 13918, 133
Buchanan v. Pocock (1979) NRS SC21/6/1979/6, 72
Burke v. Burke 1983 SLT 331, 32, 33
Cameron v. Cameron (1813) NRS CC8/6/1501, 134
Cameron v. Malcolm (1756) Mor 12680; NRS CS271/69676, 101
Campbell v. Cochran (1747) Mor 10456, 94–96
Campbell v. Honyman (1830) Fac Dec 838 (see also list below), 105, 106
Campbell v. Sassen (1826) 2 W & S 309 (see also list below, Sassen v. Campbell (1824)), 35, 97

Cathcart *v.* Brown (1905) 7 F 951, 132, 134, 140
Cattanach *v.* Robertson (1864) 2 M 839, 85
Charleson *v.* Stewart (1899) NRS CS240/C/19/4, 83
Craigie *v.* Hoggan (1838) 16 S 584, 97–98
Crossan *v.* Cumming (1963) NRS SC58/22/1963/1, 68, 78
D *v.* A (1845) 1 Rob Ecc 279, 51
Dalrymple *v.* Dalrymple (1811) 161 ER 665, 93, 96, 97
Davidson *v.* Davidson 1921 SC 341, 100, 102
Dewar *v.* Dewar 1995 SLT 467, 11
Duguid *v.* Duguid (1909) NRS CS256/176, 32, 52, 53
Duran *v.* Duran (1904) 7 F 87, 98
EA (AP) *v.* GN (A) [2015] CSIH 26, 142
Elder *v.* M'Lean 1829 8 S 56, 11
Elliot *v.* Parkinson (1905) 12 SLT 710, 100
Evett, Edward Pratt (1882) NRS AD14/82/41, 180
F *v.* F 1945 SC 202, 53–55
Fleming *v.* Corbet (1859) 21 D 1034, 98
Fletcher *v.* Grant (1878) 6 R 59 (see also list below), 82
Forbes *v.* Countess of Strathmore [1750] 1 Elchies 365; (1751) 6 Paton 684, 99
Forbes *v.* Wilson (1868) 6 M 770, 107
Forster *v.* Forster (1869) 6 SLR 519; (1870–75) LR 2 Sc 244, 98
FRB *v.* DCA [2019] EWHC 2816 (Fam), 63
G *v.* G (1922) 60 SLR 125, 52
G *v.* HM Advocate 2016 SLT 282, 62
Gardner *v.* Gardner (1919) NRS CS46/1919/9/7, 47
Gibson *v.* Morrison (1891) NRS CS46/1891/12/47, 53
Gordon *v.* Merricks (1885) NRS CS46/1885/5/65, 52
Gourlay *v.* Gourlay (1890) NRS CS46/1890/9/33, 53
Gow *v.* Lord Advocate 1993 SLT 275, 11
Grahame and Erskine *v.* Burn (1685) Mor 8472, 66
Gray *v.* Brown (1878) 5 R 971, 134
Gray *v.* Millar (1901) 39 SLR 256, 136, 138–140
Gray *v.* The Criminal Injuries Compensation Board 1999 SC 137, 156
Greig *v.* Robertson (1891) NRS CS247/2272, 129
Grey *v.* Criminal Injuries Compensation Board 1999 SC 137, 195
Guest *v.* Lauder (1909) NRS CS46/1909/10/8, 52
Hamilton *v.* Hamilton (1839) 2 D 89; (1842) 1 Bell App 736, 98
Hardie *v.* Boog (1931) SLT 198, 109
Harthan *v.* Harthan [1949] P 115, 54
Harvie *v.* Inglis (1837) 15 S 964; (1839) 14 Fac Dec 608 (see also list below), 92
Hegarty *v.* Shine (1878) 14 Cox CC 145, 184–187
Hill *v.* Wilson (1871) 8 SLR 340, 130
Hislop *v.* Ker (1696) Mor 13908, 132
HM Advocate *v.* Charles Kelly (1885) 5 Coup 722, 126

HM Advocate *v.* Charles Sweenie (1858) 3 Irvine 109, 173
HM Advocate *v.* Montgomery 1926 JC 2, 173
HM Advocate *v.* William Fraser (1847) NRS JC26/1847/592; William Fraser (1847) Ark 280, 150, 156, 162–163, 165, 166, 173, 180, 194
Hoggan *v.* Craigie (1839) MacL & Rob 942, 97–98
Holmes *v.* McMurrich [1920] SLR 523, 139
Hussain *v.* Houston 1995 SLT 1060, 181
Hutchison *v.* Brand (1793) NRS CC8/6/913, 92
Imrie *v.* Imrie (1891) 19 R 185, 98, 105
Jamieson *v.* Jeffrey (1783) NRS CC8/6/684, 32, 42–44
Johnston *v.* Pasley (1770) Mor 13916; (1769) NRS CC8/6/459 (see also list below), 75
Jolly *v.* McGregor (1828) 3 W & S 85, 96, 101, 102
Kello *v.* Taylor (1787) 3 Paton 56 (see also Kello *v.* Taylor (1787)), 101
L *v.* L 1931 SC 477, 52, 54
Lang *v.* Lang 1921 SC 44, 46–48, 79
Lendrum *v.* Chakravarti 1929 SLT 96, 35–37
Leslie *v.* Leslie (1860) 22 D 993, 98, 107
Lindsay *v.* Lindsay 1927 SC 395, 109
Linning *v.* Hamilton (1748) Mor 13909 (see also list below), 125, 132, 137
Lockyer *v.* Sinclair (1846) 8 D 582, 97, 101, 102
Longworth *v.* Yelverton (1862) 1 M 161 (see also Yelverton *v.* Longworth (1864)), 97, 107–108
M *v.* Y (1934) SLT 187, 108
M'Arthur *v.* Lawson (1877) 4 R 1134, 69
M'Leod *v.* Adams 1920 1 SLT 229, 40–41
MacAlister *v.* Dun (1759) 2 Paton 29, 99
MacDonald *v.* MacDonald (1863) 1 M 854, 99
MacDougall *v.* Chitnavis 1937 SC 40; 1937 SC 390, 36–37
Mackenzie *v.* Macfarlane (1889) NRS CS241/2527, 32, 33
Mackenzie *v.* Stewart (1848) 10 D 611, 106
MacLauchlan *v.* Couper & Stark (1808) NRS CS271/55559, 95
MacLauchlan *v.* Dobson (1796) Mor 12693, 101
MacLeod *v.* MacAskill 1920 SC 72, 136, 138–140
Maloy and other *v.* Macadam and others (1885) 12 R 431, 108
McCormack *v.* Shrimpton (1840) NRS CS46/1840/3/1, 32, 33
McCulloch *v.* McCulloch (1919) NRS CS255/1310, 47
McGahan *v.* Allison (1946) NRS SC58/22/1946/7, 130, 140
McIntyre *v.* Smith (1957) NRS SC1/11/1957/14, 78
McLauchline *v.* McDonald (1782) NRS CC8/6/668, 92
McLellan *v.* Miller (1828) NRS CC8/6/2116, 92
McNeill *v.* Wilson (1797) NRS CS271/4258, 133–135
Mendal *v.* Mendal [2007] EWCA Civ 437, 32
Miles *v.* Sim (1830) Fac Dec 84 (see also list below, Sim *v.* Miles (1829)), 106

Mills and Another *v.* Findlay and Another 1994 SCLR 397, 69
Moar *v.* Glass (1924) 49 Scot L Rev 237, 125, 134
Monteith *v.* Robb (1844) 6 D 934 (see also list below, Robb *v.* Monteith (1842–1844)), 105
Morgan *v.* Morgan [1959] P 92, 54
Morison *v.* Ferguson (1859–1860) 2 Scot LJ 1 109, 75
Morrison *v.* Dobson (1869) 8 M 347, 108
Moss *v.* Moss [1897] P 263, 45, 46
Murray *v.* Fraser 1914 SLT 200; 1916 1 SLT 300, 126, 127, 134, 139, 140
Murray *v.* Napier (1861) 23 D 1243, 74, 76, 107
N *v.* C 1933 SC 492, 108, 109
Nicol *v.* Bell 1954 SLT 314, 11
Orlandi *v.* Castelli 1961 SLT 118, 101, 102
P *v.* B [2001] 1 FLR 1041, 62
Papadimitropoulos *v.* The Queen (1957) 98 CLR 249, 174, 194
Paterson *v.* Cumming (1815) NRS CC/8/6/1572, 32, 33, 52
Pennycook and Grinton *v.* Grinton and Graite (1752) Mor 12677 (see also list below), 96, 106
Petrie *v.* Petrie's Executrix and Another 1911 SC 360, 98, 99
Pithie *v.* Walker (1920) NRS SC23/23/1920/8, 82, 83
Polack *v.* Shiels 1912 2 SLT 329, 32
Purves, James (1848) J. Shaw 124, 111
Quinn *v.* McAskill (1952) NRS SC36/9/1952/19, 134, 135
R *v.* B [2007] 1 WLR 1567, 188
R *v.* B [2013] 2 Cr App R 29, 177, 183
R *v.* Barrow (1865–72) LR 1 CCR 156, 171
R *v.* Bennett (1866) 176 ER 925, 183
R *v.* Bongab [1971–72] PNGLR 433, 174, 175
R *v.* Broadfoot (1977) 64 Cr App R 71, 151
R *v.* Cairns [1997] Cr App R (S) 118, 114
R *v.* Camplin (1845) 169 ER 163, 172
R *v.* Carter (1968) 52 Cr App R 117, 193
R *v.* Case (1850) 169 ER 381, 179
R *v.* Chapman [1959] 1 QB 100, 154
R *v.* Christian and Another (1913) 23 Cox CC 541, 149
R *v.* Clarence (1888) 22 QBD 23, 174, 184–187, 207
R *v.* Dee (1884) 15 Cox CC 579, 172–174, 194
R *v.* Devonald [2008] EWCA Crim 527, 177
R *v.* Dica [2004] QB 1257, 165, 187, 188
R *v.* Elbekkay [1994] EWCA Crim 1, 160, 175
R *v.* Flattery (1877) QBD 410, 144, 161–162, 172, 179
R *v.* Fletcher (1859) 8 Cox CC 131, 172
R *v.* Green [2002] EWCA Crim 1501, 181
R *v.* Jackson (1822) 168 ER 911, 163, 166, 171

R v. Jheeta [2007] EWCA Crim 1699, 177, 183
R v. Johnson [1964] 2 QB 404, 152
R v. Kirkpatrick 2022 SCC 33, 189
R v. Konzani [2005] 2 Cr App R 14, 187
R v. Lawrance [2020] EWCA Crim 971; [2020] 1 WLR 5025, 167, 188, 191–192, 212
R v. Linekar [1995] QB 250, 160, 185
R v. M [2001] EWCA Crim 1563, 185
R v. Mackenzie and Higginson (1911) 6 Cr App R 64, 148, 152
R v. McNally [2014] QB 593, 177–178, 188
R v. Millward (1994) 158 JP 1091, 151
R v. Moon, Frederick; R v. Moon, Emily [1910] 1 KB 818, 130
R v. O'Shay (1898) 19 Cox CC 76, 161–162
R v. Piper [2007] EWCA Crim 2151, 185
R v. Richardson [1999] QB 444, 181
R v. Saunders (1838) 173 ER 488, 171
R v. Sinclair (1867) 13 Cox CC 28, 184
R v. Stanton (1844) 174 ER 872, 179
R v. Tabassum [2000] 2 Cr App R 328, 181
R v. Williams (1838) 173 ER 497, 171
R v. Williams (1898) 62 JP 310, 148, 150
R v. Williams [1923] 1 KB 340, 162, 181
R (F) v. Director of Public Prosecutions [2014] QB 581, 190–191
R (Monica) v. Director of Public Prosecutions [2019] QB 1019, 152–153, 160, 168, 177, 178, 191, 209
Ramage v. Mackintosh (1811) NRS CC8/6/1452, 32, 34
Rampal v. Rampal [2001] 3 WLR 795, 57
Reid v. Laing (1819) NRS CS234/L/10/1; (1823) 1 Shaw 440, 105, 106, 109
Reid v. MacFarlane (1919) 2 SLT 24, 136, 138, 139, 140
Reid v. Reid (1879) NRS CS247/5174, 52
Reids v. Mill (1879) 16 SLR 338, 45
Robertson v. Henderson (1833) 12 S 70, 134
Robertson v. Steuart (1874) 11 SLR 427, 100–102, 107
Robinson v. Walker (1900) NRS CS46/1900/2/27, 53
Ross v. MacLeod (1861) 23 D 972, 106–107
Scott v. Stewart [1870] SLR 8 44, 76, 133
SG v. WG 1933 SC 728, 54
SH v. HK 2003 SLT 515; 2006 SC 129, 101–103
Shields v. Crossroads (Orkney) [2013] CSOH 144, 142
Sinclair v. Rowan (1861) 23 D 1365, 74
Sinclair v. Smith (1860) D 1475 (see also list below), 71
Smail v. McNeil (1908) NRS CS250/6564, 81
Soutar v. Peters 1912 SLT 111, 130
Spiers v. Hunt [1908] 1 KB 720, 72

Spiers *v.* Spiers (1895) NRS CS46/1895/2/103, 52, 53
S-T (formerly J) *v.* J [1998] Fam 103, 56–58
Stein *v.* Stein 1914 SC 903, 46–48
Steuart *v.* Robertson (1875) 2 R (HL) 80 (see also Robertson *v.* Steuart (1874)), 100
Stewart *v.* Lindsay (1817) Fac Dec 380 (see also list below), 104, 105
Stewart *v.* Menzies (1833) 12 S 179; (1837) 15 S 1198, 98, 133
Stroyen *v.* McWhirter (1901) NRS CS240/S/24/2, 81
Sullivan *v.* Sullivan (1818) 161 ER 728, 43
Sutherland *v.* Hamilton Hart (1880) NRS CS46/1880/11/50, 136
Syme *v.* Pirie (1909) NRS CS46/1909/6/66, 53
Taylor *v.* Kello (1786) Mor 12687 (see also Taylor *v.* Kello (1786)), 101, 102
Thomson *v.* Thomson (1914) NRS CS255/487, 52
Thomson *v.* Wright (1767) Mor 13915; NRS CS271/63713, 79
Thomson, Robert, 1907 (JC26/1907/133; AD15/07/16), 173
Todd *v.* Taylor (1909) CS46/1909/3/58, 50
Tucker *v.* Aitchison (1846) 9 D 21, 68, 75
Turpy *v.* McCandie (1825) NRS CC8/6/1983 (see also list below), 133, 134
Walker *v.* Colquhoun (1828) NRS CS271/67308, 125, 127, 132–135
Walker *v.* M'Isaac (1857) 19 D 340, 130
Wheelock *v.* Cameron (1889) NRS CS46/1889/12/17, 52
Whiston *v.* Whiston [1995] Fam 198, 57
Wilkie *v.* Wilkie (1907) NRS CS46/1907/5/89, 53
Wilson *v.* Horn (1904) 11 SLT 702; NRS CS46/1904/3/25, 39–41, 44
Wright *v.* Sharp (1880) 17 SLR 293, 34
X *v.* Y (1921) SLT 79, 109
X *v.* Y [2015] 3 WLUK 1062, 62
Yelverton *v.* Longworth (1864) 2 M (HL) 49 (see also Longworth *v.* Yelverton (1862)), 107, 109
Young *v.* Young (1892) NRS CS46/1892/5/86, 32, 52, 53

Other Named Cases and Alternative Reports

Abraham *v.* McLetchy ('Glasgow Breach of Promise Case', *The Aberdeen Weekly Journal*, 18 July 1885, p. 8), 75
Adams *v.* Adams ('Court of Session', *The Glasgow Herald*, 19 December 1895, p. 4), 32
Alexander *v.* Alexander (1920) General Collection, Paper 44, 47
Allan *v.* Aitken ('Local Breach of Promise Action', *The Glasgow Herald*, 12 July 1882, p. 9), 82
Allan *v.* Henderson ('Glasgow Sheriff Court', *The Glasgow Herald*, 20 December 1880, p. 6), 83
Anderson *v.* Currie ('Abandonment of Action for Alleged Seduction', *Edinburgh Evening News*, 20 July 1882, p. 2), 72

Armstrong *v.* Thomson ('Court of Session', *The Glasgow Herald*, 14 November 1894, p. 4), 136

Asher *v.* Rennie ('The Asher-Rennie Breach of Promise Case', *The Glasgow Herald*, 27 December 1871, p. 4), 76

AV *v.* CD ('Glasgow Sheriff Court', *The Glasgow Herald*, 1 April 1865, p. 5), 129

Bagan *v.* Clark ('Couple Not Allowed to Walk Out Together', *The Evening Telegraph*, 23 March 1910, p. 3), 79

Bain *v.* Gray ('Breach of Promise Case against a Married Man', *The Aberdeen Weekly Journal*, 20 July 1898, p. 6; 'The Glasgow Breach of Promise Case', *Dundee Advertiser*, 14 October 1898, p. 10), 134, 135

Bain, Elspeth ('High Court of Justiciary', *Edinburgh Evening News*, 8 November 1880, p. 3), 112

Barclay *v.* Christie ('Settlement of an Aberdeenshire Breach of Promise', *The Aberdeen Journal*, 20 March 1886, p. 5), 79

Barron, Isaac ('Manchester Assizes', *Manchester Times*, 29 January 1887, p. 3), 194

Beachey *v.* Brown ('English Cases' (1860) 4(42) *Journal of Jurisprudence*, p. 321), 81

Bedford *v.* McKowl ('Court of Common Pleas', *Caledonian Mercury*, 3 March 1800, p. 2), 72

Beever, John ('Circuit Court of Justiciary at Perth', *Fife Herald, and Kinross, Strathearn, and Clackmannan Advertiser*, April 28 1853, p. 3), 111

Bell *v.* Bell ('Cardenden Miner Gets His Marriage Annulled', *Dundee Courier*, 20 March 1920, p. 7), 47

Bennet *v.* Ninian (1807) Hume Collection, vol. 99, Paper 49, 133, 134

Black *v.* Cotton ('Aberdeen Sheriff Court', *The Aberdeen Journal*, 24 October 1889, p. 3; 'Serious Charges against an Aberdeen Photographer', *Dundee Courier*, 17 December 1889, p. 3), 136

Booth, George ('Circuit Court of Justiciary', *The Aberdeen Herald*, 27 April 1844, p. 3), 111

Bowie *v.* Beaton ('The Cuminestown Breach of Promise Case', *The Aberdeen Journal*, 22 March 1893, p. 8), 138

Bray *v.* Ross ('Aberdeen Pantomime Sequel', *The Aberdeen Journal*, 12 January 1918, p. 4), 78

Brennan *v.* Jeffs ('Breach of Promise of Marriage', *Caledonian Mercury*, 14 February 1862, p. 2), 67

Brett *v.* Stewart ('A Simple Young Lad', *Dundee Courier*, 4 May 1904, p. 4), 139

Brodie *v.* Carmichael ('Breach of Promise Cases', *Dundee Courier*, 22 February 1879, p. 3), 83

Brownlee *v.* Wharrie ('Perthshire Breach of Promise Case', *The Evening Telegraph*, 9 January 1886, p. 3; 'Breach of Promise Case in Edinburgh', *Edinburgh Evening News*, 9 January 1886, p. 3), 135

Burns *v.* McNair ('Decision in the Paisley Breach of Promise Case', *Dundee Courier*, 22 February 1878, p. 6; 'Paisley', *The Glasgow Herald*, 21 March 1878, p. 3), 107, 128

Bush v. Reith ('A Boyish Attachment', The *Evening Telegraph*, 3 December 1919, p. 5), 68

Campbell v. Beveridge ('Judgment in the Cardross Case', *Fife Herald, and Kinross, Strathearn, and Clackmannan Advertiser*, 25 July 1861, p. 2), 128

Campbell v. Cochran (1747) Kilkerran Collection, vol. 14, Paper 1; (1747–1751) Arniston Collection, vol. 31, Paper 1, 94–96

Campbell v. Honyman (1827–1830) General Collection, Paper 509 (see also case reports), 105–107

Campbell, Colin ('Circuit Court of Justiciary', *Inverness Courier*, 24 April 1844, p. 3), 111

Cattanach v. Robertson (1864) General Collection, Paper 149, 85

Cavan v. Saunders ('A Vanman Sued for Damages', *Dundee Courier*, 25 December 1896, p. 4; '£500 Damages for Seduction', *Dundee Courier*, 15 January 1897, p. 4), 139

Chapman v. Niven ('Court of Session', *The Glasgow Herald*, 17 January 1898, p. 9), 101

Christie v. Fraser ('Scotch News', *Fife Herald*, 4 June 1863, p. 4), 80

Clark v. Fairweather (1727) (F. P. Walton (ed.), *Lord Hermand's Consistorial Decisions, 1684–1777* (Edinburgh: The Stair Society, 1940), p. 68), 32, 33

Coleman v. Storm ('A Falkirk Seduction Case', *Dundee Courier*, 30 January 1878, p. 3), 72

Couper v. Cullen ('Court of Session', *The Glasgow Herald*, 1 April 1874, p. 4), 76, 77

Craig v. Langlands ('The Glasgow Breach of Promise Case', *Edinburgh Evening News*, 22 August 1881, p. 2), 72

Craig v. Todd ('Another Edinburgh Breach of Promise Case', *Edinburgh Evening News*, 20 June 1884, p. 3), 83

Craig, Alexander ('Perth Circuit Court of Justiciary', *Fife Herald, and Kinross, Strathearn, and Clackmannan Advertiser*, 3 May 1838, p. 4), 111

Croall v. Hutchison ('Breach of Promise of Marriage', *Fife Herald*, 1 August 1844, p. 4), 80

Cutts v. Shepherd ('Court of Queen's Bench', *John Bull* (Vol XXXVII), 6 February 1858, p. 96), 155

Danks, Charles ('Curious Case of Bigamy', *Birmingham Daily Post*, 4 August 1886, p. 7), 194

Davidson, Christina and Gillespie, William ('Sheriff Criminal Court', *The Glasgow Herald*, 13 February 1883, p. 3), 112

Davies, Brynley George ('Bigamist Gets Three Years', *Chelmsford Chronicle*, 10 February 1950, p. 12), 193

Day, William ('Bogus Millionaire – Remarkable Career of a Bigamist', *Daily Record*, 25 April 1917, p. 6), 193

Donald v. Lawrie ('Male Pursuer in Aberdeen Breach Case', *Dundee Courier*, 23 October 1908, p. 7), 67

Dow v. Macleod ('Affection Lost', *Dundee Courier*, 8 November 1905, p. 4), 85

Ellis v. Kerr ('The Aberdeen Breach of Promise Case', *Dundee Courier*, 1 August 1889, p. 3), 78

Ellison, Joseph ('Glasgow Bigamy Cases', *Edinburgh Evening News*, 26 March 1915, p. 5), 111

Evanton v. Ross ('Ross-Shire Breach of Promise Case', *Aberdeen Press and Journal*, 1 February 1899, p. 6), 68

Farquharson v. Anderson (1800), discussed in Leneman, *Promises, Promises*, pp. 124, 129, 134

Fawcett, Thomas ('Alleged Use of a Drugged Cigarette', *The Evening Telegraph*, 9 April 1923, p. 1), 111

Fletcher v. Grant (1878) General Collection, Paper 22 (see also case reports), 76, 82

Forbes v. Brown ('The Perth Breach of Promise Case', *The Glasgow Herald*, 13 June 1870, p. 4), 67

Forbes v. Countess of Strathmore (1749–1750) Drummore Collection, vol. 10, Paper 49; (1754–1756) Campbell Collection, vol. 4, Paper 5, 99

Forbes v. Simpson ('The Elgin Breach of Promise Case', *The Aberdeen Journal*, 25 January 1887, p. 6; 'Elgin – Settlement of the Breach of Promise Case', *The Aberdeen Journal*, 1 March 1887, p. 7), 83

Fulton v. Anderson ('Alleged Seduction Case in Banchory', *Aberdeen Press and Journal*, 12 November 1892, p. 7; 'The Girl's Action against a Married Man', *Dundee Courier*, 26 December 1892, p. 2), 138

Georgeson v. Walterson ('A Shetland Breach of Promise Case', *The Glasgow Herald*, 22 October 1894, p. 9), 78

Gomm, Frederick Douglas ('Bigamy Sentences – Judge's Comment to Barrow "Bus Driver"', *Lancashire Evening Post*, 18 January 1844, p. 4), 193

Greenwood, Harry ('Judge on Bigamy – Leniency in Leicester Assize Case', *Nottingham Evening Post*, 27 October 1942, p. 9), 193

Grey v. Criminal Injuries Compensation Board (1999) General Collection, Paper 15, 195

Hall v. Bryce ('A Heartless Breach of Promise Case', *Dundee Courier*, 6 March 1877, p. 3), 71

Hall, Austin, discussed in McLaren, *Trials of Masculinity*, ch. 9, 159

Halliday v. Miller ('Glasgow Sheriff Court', *The Glasgow Herald*, 27 May 1871, p. 2), 134

Handley v. Halket ('Breach of Promise Case', *The Glasgow Herald*, 12 December 1871, p. 3), 79

Hare v. Scott ('Lanarkshire Sheriff Court', *The Glasgow Herald*, 30 August 1870), p. 2, 67

Harkins v. McKechnie ('Glasgow Sheriff Court', *The Glasgow Herald*, 25 May 1864, p. 6), 85

Harris v. Norval ('Breach of Promise Case', *The Glasgow Herald*, 18 March 1870, p. 6), 82

Harris, Joseph ('Extraordinary Bigamy Case', *Birmingham Mail*, 29 January 1886, p. 2), 193

Harvie *v.* Inglis (1834–1837) General Collection, Paper 238 (see also case reports), 105, 106

Hatch (1859), discussed in Wiener, Men of Blood, pp. 115–116, 181

Henderson *v.* Allan ('£100 Claim', *The Evening Telegraph*, 30 May 1924, p. 8), 82

Henderson *v.* O'Donnell ('Sheriff Small Debt Court', *The Glasgow Herald*, 16 October 1866, p. 3), 80

Hendley, Charles ('High Court of Justiciary', *The Scotsman*, 15 December 1841, p. 3), 111

Hewat *v.* Bennet ('Breach of Promise of Marriage in Perth', *Fife Herald*, 7 January 1858, p. 4), 67, 76

Hill *v.* Wilson ('Court of Session', *The Glasgow Herald*, 6 February 1871, p. 6), 130

Hislop *v.* Affleck ('An Edinburgh Breach of Promise', *Edinburgh Evening News*, 6 May 1874, p. 2), 72

Hogg *v.* Gow (1812) Faculty Collection, Paper 16; 'Court of Session' (1812) *Scots Magazine and Edinburgh Library Miscellany* 721–724, 66–69, 75

Hoggan *v.* Craigie (1838) General Collection, Paper 135, 97–98

Hollis, William ('The Criminal Law Amendment Act Inadequate', *Leeds Mercury*, 11 May 1887, p. 2), 148

Horas, Theodore and Horas, Laura ('Charges against "Mental Scientists"', *Sheffield Daily Telegraph*, 11 October 1901, p. 7), 157, 161

Hughes ('The Charge of Bigamy against a Clergyman', *Leamington Spa Courier*, 17 November 1883, p. 3), 180, 193

Hunter, David ('Lamberton Toll', *Kelso Chronicle*, 27 April 1849, p. 7), 193

Hutton *v.* Peters ('The Arbroath Breach of Promise', *Dundee Courier*, 22 June 1901, p. 4), 69, 75

Hyne, Arthur ('The Trial of Arthur Hyne', *The Aberdeen Journal*, 14 February 1908, p. 6), 193

Imrie *v.* Imrie ('Court of Session', *The Scotsman*, 21 October 1903, p. 7), 32

Irvine *v.* Hamilton of Grange (1706), discussed in Walton (ed.), *Consistorial Decisions*, p. 67, 132

Jenkins ('Assizes', *The Examiner*, 17 August 1828, p. 13), 174

Johnston *v.* Pasley (1770), discussed in Blackie, 'Unity in Diversity: The History of Personality Rights in Scots Law' in Whitty and Zimmermann (eds.), *Rights of Personality in Scots Law*, pp. 125, 127 (see also case reports), 66, 69

Kand *v.* Forsyth ('A Fife Breach of Promise Case', *Dundee Courier*, 29 October 1887, p. 3), 69

Kerr *v.* Moore ('Amusing Breach of Promise Case', *Paisley Herald and Renfrewshire Advertiser*, 6 February 1865, p. 2), 67, 75

Kidd *v.* Vogel ('Girl Sues Cupar Butcher', *The Evening Telegraph and Post*, 25 February 1926, p. 6; 'Girl's Action Against Cupar Butcher', *The Evening Telegraph*, 17 May 1926, p. 3), 129, 137

Kinder *v.* Andrew ('Glasgow Man Sued for Breach of Promise', *Dundee Courier*, 12 December 1903, p. 4), 82

King *v.* McVey ('An Airdrie Breach of Promise Case', *The Glasgow Herald*, 1 January 1894, p. 9), 68, 74

Laidlaw *v.* Reid ('Innerleithen Widow's Breach of Promise Action', *Edinburgh Evening News*, 13 May 1898, p. 3), 135

Langlands *v.* Wright ('The Wright Breach of Promise', *The Aberdeen Journal*, 27 July 1888, p. 7), 139

Lennie *v.* Burnside ('Edinburgh Man's Breach of Promise Case', *Edinburgh Evening News*, 22 June 1893, p. 2), 80

Linning *v.* Hamilton (1748), discussed in Fergusson, *Consistorial Law*, p. 121 (see also case reports), 137

Longmore *v.* Massie (1883), discussed in Guthrie, *Select Cases Decided in the Sheriff Courts of Scotland* (vol. 2), pp. 450–453, 68

Low v Allardice (1791–1797), discussed in Leneman, *Promises Promises*, pp. 21–25, 106

Low *v.* Allardice (1794) Dreghorn Collection, vol. 79, Paper 11, 92, 105, 106

M'Auley *v.* Pollok ('The Action against Sir Hew Craurford Pollok, Bart', *The Aberdeen Weekly Journal*, 14 September 1878, p. 6), 134

Macdonald *v.* Cameron ('An Elgin Breach of Promise', *Dundee Courier*, 21 May 1878, p. 2), 68

MacDonald *v.* Campbell ('The Ross-Shire Breach of Promise Case', *The Aberdeen Journal*, 9 December 1898, p. 6), 80

MacGregor, Frederick ('Inverness Justiciary Court', *The Elgin Courier*, 16 April 1847, p.3), 111

Mackay *v.* Scott ('Blairgowrie Man's Breach', *The Evening Telegraph*, 13 December 1904, p. 5), 67

MacKellar *v.* Hamilton ('Breach of Promise Case at Greenock', *The Glasgow Herald*, 30 December 1875, p. 4), 82

Mackenzie *v.* Hughes ('Aberdeen Breach of Promise', *The Aberdeen Journal*, 29 March 1881, p. 4), 83

MacLachlan *v.* Curle ('Glasgow Breach of Promise Case', *The Glasgow Herald*, 1 February 1893, p. 10; 'The Glasgow Breach of Promise Case', *The Glasgow Herald*, 21 February 1893, p. 3), 83

MacPherson *v.* Moir ('The Turiff Breach of Promise Case', *The Aberdeen Journal*, 7 February 1900, p. 4), 83

Mair *v.* Taylor ('A Portsoy Breach of Promise Case', *Aberdeen Press and Journal*, 27 March 1879, p. 3), 70

Marshall *v.* Linton ('Glasgow Sheriff Court', *The Glasgow Herald*, 7 November 1860, p. 6), 135

McConnachie *v.* Kilgour ('Huntly Photographer Sued', *Aberdeen Daily Journal*, 22 October 1915, p. 7), 138

McGowan *v.* Fisher (1797) Campbell Collection, vol. 85, Paper 41, 125, 128, 130, 133

McIntyre v. Brewster ('Perthshire Breach of Promise and Seduction Case', *The Evening Telegraph*, 14 March 1889, p. 3), 136

McIntyre, John ('Court of Justiciary, Aberdeen', *Montrose, Arbroath, and Brechin Review*, 25 April 1856, p. 3), 111

McKean v. Kessack ('An Inverness Breach of Promise Case', *The Glasgow Herald*, 22 November 1883, p. 5; 'Inverness Breach of Promise Case', *Edinburgh Evening News*, 22 March 1884), 83

McKenzie v. Brander ('Local News', *Elgin Courier*, 20 February 1863, p. 5), 82

McLean v. MacKay ('Breach of Promise', *Dundee Courier*, 26 December 1878, p. 3), 82

McLeod v. Miller ('Local Intelligence', *The John o'Groat Journal*, 17 February 1843, p. 2), 68, 79

McLeod v. Robertson ('Married Man Makes Love to a Servant', *The Courier*, 14 April 1911, p. 8), 72

McLeod, John ('Circuit Court of Justiciary', *Caledonian Mercury*, 27 September 1834, p. 4), 111

McPhail, Thomas ('Glasgow Bigamist Gets 18 Months', *Dundee Evening Telegraph*, 15 February 1923, p. 6), 111

McPhedran v. Campbell ('Inveraray Sheriff Court', *The Glasgow Herald*, 20 July 1860, p. 7), 83

McVey v. Savage ('Scotch News', *Fife Herald*, 19 May 1859, p. 2), 83

Mearns v. Fraser ('The Kintore Breach of Promise Case', *The Aberdeen Journal*, 21 February 1893, p. 6), 85

Mears and Chalk ('Southampton Borough Sessions', *Southampton Herald*, 11 January 1851, p. 6; 'Law Courts', *The Examiner*, 25 January 1851, p. 10), 151

Meikle v. McGhie (1819–1822), discussed in Leneman, *Promises Promises*, pp. 124–125, 132

Millar v. Copeland ('Amusing Breach of Promise Case', *Dundee Courier*, 5 May 1873, p. 3), 80

Milne v. Craik ('The Forfar Breach of Promise Case', *The Glasgow Herald*, 27 February 1874, p. 4), 85

Mitchell v. Stirling (1798) Hermand Collection, vol. 27, Paper 2, 133

Mitches v. Walker ('Aberdeen, Wednesday, Oct. 29, 1890', *The Aberdeen Journal*, 29 October 1890, p. 4), 68

Morison v. Dunlop (1756) (Walton (ed.), *Consistorial Decisions*, pp. 93–95), 32

Morrison v. McIntyre ('Sheriff Court – Monday', *The Glasgow Herald*, 26 April 1864, p. 3), 82

Morrison v. Sinclair ('Monikie', *The Courier and Argus*, 17 October 1907, p. 6), 140

Morrison v. Tait (1888), discussed in Prior, *Fond Hopes Destroyed: Breach of Promise Cases in Shetland*, pp. 66–67, 80

Morse, Charles Stanley ('"One of the Worst Cases of Bigamy"', *Dundee Evening Telegraph*, 4 March 1941, p. 3), 112

Mouat v. Nisbet (1826), discussed in Prior, *Fond Hopes Destroyed: Breach of Promise Cases in Shetland*, pp. 24–28, 70

Muir, James ('Paisley – Sheriff Court', *The Glasgow Herald*, 27 April 1883 p. 6), 111

Munro v. Munro ('An Unhappy Cromarty Wedding', *Aberdeen Journal*, 15 July 1916, p. 4), 47

Mushet v. Murray ('Breach of Promise Case at Lanark', *Edinburgh Evening News*, 18 June 1902, p. 2), 82

Neill v. Cassidy ('Scots Girl Wins "Breach" Case', *Dundee Courier*, 24 November 1932, p. 7), 68

Nicol v. Robertson ('Court of Session', *The Glasgow Herald*, 24 June 1880, p. 3), 134

Oxley, Maurice ('Miner Fined £100', *Nottingham Evening Post*, 1 December 1965, p. 6), 152

Pateman v. Watson ('Court of Session', *The Glasgow Herald*, 17 February 1876, p. 7), 85

Peffers v. McKean ('Sheriff Small Debt Court – Yesterday', *The Glasgow Herald*, 20 September 1860, p. 3), 82

Pennycook v. Grinton (1752) Pitfour Collection, Paper 16, 96

Pennycook v. Grinton and Graite (1755) in Fergusson, *Consistorial Law*, p. 105 (see also case reports), 105, 106

Petrie v. Ross ('Court of Session', *The Glasgow Herald*, 10 June 1896, p. 9), 32

Prior, John Walden ('Three Years for Bigamy', *Aberdeen Journal*, 24 July 1917, p. 6), 112

R v. Barker, discussed in Derry, 'Sustained Identity Deceptions' in CLRNN, *Reforming the Relationship* (2021), pp. 15–23, 177

R v. Cutts ('Singular Action', *Bell's Life in London and Sporting Chronicle*, 15 March 1857, p. 7), 155

R v. Pearson, discussed in Wiener, *Men of Blood*, p. 117, 171

R v. Rackstraw, discussed in Wiener, *Men of Blood*, p. 117, 171

R v. Williams ('Procuring' (1898–1899) 6 SLT 158) (see also case reports), 148

Reekie v. McKinven ('"Something Died Within Me"', *Dundee Courier*, 20 May 1921, p. 5), 84

Reid v. Reid ('The Reid Breach of Promise Case', *The Aberdeen Journal*, 20 January 1909, p. 3), 68

Reid v. Smith ('Dundee Breach of Promise Case', *Dundee Courier*, 3 May 1878, p. 3), 85

Ritchie v. Robertson ('The Altyre Breach of Promise Case', *The Aberdeen Journal*, 7 January 1905, p. 7), 84

Robb v. Monteith (1842–1844) General Collection, Paper 128 (see also case reports, Monteith v. Robb (1844)), 96, 105, 107

Robertson v. Henderson (1833), General Collection, Paper 25, 134

Rodger v. McKenzie ('Singular Breach of Promise Case', *Dundee Courier*, 20 May 1875, p. 3), 82

Rolls, John Thomas ('Airman's "Base Deception" – Bigamous Marriage at Hoole Methodist Church', *Cheshire Observer*, 4 March 1944, p. 3), 193

Table of Cases

Rose, Henry ('Dundee Circuit Court of Justiciary', *The Dundee Advertiser*, 12 September 1866, p. 3), 111

Ross *v.* Reid ('Claim to Wifehood Fails', *The Courier*, 23 December 1921, p. 5), 109

Sandilands *v.* King ('Jury Trials – Friday', *Caledonian Mercury*, 3 April 1858, p. 2), (1858) General Collection, Paper 187, 82

Sassen *v.* Campbell (1824) General Collection, Paper 114, 35

Sbano (2007) ('Pilot "Raped Woman in Herpes Treatment Con"', Press Association Regional Newswire – London, 24 April 2007; 'Rape Case against Pilot Collapses', Press Association Regional Newswire – London, 1 May 2007), 182

Scott *v.* Harvey ('Lochgelly Spirit Merchant Sued for £500', *Dundee Courier*, 2 April 1910, p.6), 136

Scott *v.* Love ('Scotch Breach of Promise Case', *The Aberdeen Journal*, 28 March 1885, p. 8), 128

Scott *v.* Rae ('Breach of Promise of Marriage', *John o'Groat Journal*, 12 February 1863, p. 4), 68

Scott *v.* Stewart ('The Pitlochry Breach of Promise Case', *The Glasgow Herald*, 3 January 1870, p. 5), 76

Scrimgeour *v.* Bell ('Dundee Seduction Case', *The Evening Telegraph*, 10 March 1898, p. 4), 138

Shaw *v.* Campbell ('Amusing Breach of Promise Case in Elgin', *The Aberdeen Journal*, 22 February 1884, p. 7), 68

Sheriff *v.* Potter ('The Nurse and the Colonel', *Edinburgh Evening News*, 10 November 1896, p. 4), 130

Sim *v.* Miles (1829) General Collection, Paper 27 (see also case reports, Miles *v.* Sim (1830)), 105–107

Simes, Giles ('County Bench', *Berkshire Chronicle*, 7 March 1863, p. 5; 'Western Circuit', *Reading Mercury*, 7 March 1863, p. 6), 171

Simpson *v.* Jack ('Forfarshire Minister's Breach of Promise', *The Evening Telegraph*, 31 May 1888, p. 2), 70, 84

Simpson *v.* Logan ('An Aberdeenshire Breach of Promise', *The Aberdeen Weekly Journal*, 18 October 1876, p. 8), 76

Sinclair *v.* Smith ('Law Intelligence', *The Caledonian Mercury*, 18 July 1860, p. 4) (see also case reports), 69

Skinner *v.* Greig ('Action for Breach of Promise and Seduction', *Fife Herald, and Kinross, Strathearn, and Clackmannan Advertiser*, 12 December 1861, p. 3), 131, 135

Smith and Holdsworth ('West-Riding Michaelmas Sessions', *Leeds Times*, 22 October 1853, p. 3; 'West Riding Michaelmas Sessions', *Leeds Intelligencer*, 22 October 1853, p. 8), 149

Smith *v.* Grierson (1753–1755) Campbell Collection, vol. 2, Paper 34; (1755) in Fergusson, *Consistorial Law*, p. 137, 104–106

Smith *v.* Saddler ('An Alyth Breach of Promise of Marriage Case', *Dundee Courier*, 15 April 1864, p. 4), 82

Smyth and Taylor ('Central Criminal Court, April 10', *The Morning Post*, 11 April 1851, p. 7), 146

Spalding *v.* Oman ('Small Debt Court', *Dundee Courier*, 7 January 1861, p. 3), 67, 75

Steele *v.* Steele ('Court of Session', *The Glasgow Herald*, 4 November 1893, p. 4), 32

Steen, Ramon Moir ('"Girls Not Safe from You", Judge Tells Man', *Hull Daily Mail*, 15 May 1962, p. 1), 157

Stephenson, Thomas ('Bigamy', *Shields Daily News*, 30 October 1882, p. 3), 193

Stewart *v.* Ferguson ('Breach of Promise Case at Portree', *The Evening Telegraph*, 25 April 1890, p. 2), 129

Stewart *v.* Jackson ('Heartless Breach of Promise Case', *Edinburgh Evening News*, 22 December 1886, p. 2), 72

Stewart *v.* Lindsay (1816–1817) Hume Collection, vol. 126, Paper 53, 104–106

Stewart *v.* White ('Perth Breach of Promise Case', *The Aberdeen Journal*, 24 March 1905, p. 3), 82

Stroyen *v.* McWhirter ('The Farmer's Daughter's Breach of Promise Case', *Edinburgh Evening News*, 24 July 1902, p. 3), 81

Stuart *v.* Robertson ('The Dunfermline Breach of Promise Case', *Dundee Courier*, 16 April 1897, p. 5), 78

Sword *v.* Fullerton ('Breach of Promise Suit', *Dundee Courier*, 17 July 1907, p. 5), 140

Tait *v.* Edgar ('Glasgow Breach of Promise Case', *Edinburgh Evening News*, 21 July 1902, p. 3), 71

Tasker *v.* McGregor ('Comrie Baker Wins Appeal', *The Evening Telegraph*, 8 June 1923, p. 1), 80

Taylor, William ('Central Criminal Court', *Reynolds's Newspaper*, 11 January 1863, p. 6), 193

Taylor, William Gregory ('Police Intelligence', *The Standard*, 26 January 1891, p.2; 'The Alleged Sham Curate', *Lloyd's Illustrated Newspaper*, 1 February 1891, p. 4), 155

Thomson *v.* Walkingshaw ('A Glasgow Breach of Promise Case', *Edinburgh Evening News*, 5 October 1883, p. 2), 83

Thomson, Robert Reid Storrar Balmain ('Too Many Soldier-Bigamists', *Dundee Courier*, 22 March 1941, p. 2), 112

Thornton *v.* Rodger ('Forfar – £40 Damages for Breach of Promise', *The Aberdeen Journal*, 6 February 1885, p. 6), 82

Thorpe *v.* Currie ('Glasgow Sheriff Court', *The Glasgow Herald*, 13 July 1859, p. 3), 71

Torrance *v.* Muir ('Court of Session', *The Glasgow Herald*, 20 June 1888, p. 9), 83

Tosh *v.* Hall ('Action for Breach of Promise', *The Aberdeen Journal*, 14 August 1886, p. 5), 81

Toutt *v.* Mitchell ('Master and Servant', *Dundee Courier*, 30 March 1905, p. 6; 'Remarkable Dundee Case', *The Evening Telegraph and Post*, 13 June 1905, p. 4; 'A Dundee Scandal', *Edinburgh Evening News*, 31 January 1906, p. 2), 137

Turpy *v.* McCandie (1824–1826), General Collection, Paper 339 (see also case reports), 129, 133

Urquhart *v.* Ashforth ('Breach of Promise Case', *Aberdeen Press and Journal*, 25 August 1877, p. 6), 70

Verney, Edmund Hope ('The Charge against Captain Verney', *The Belfast Newsletter*, 7 May 1891, p. 5), 148

Wallace *v.* Brown ('Dundee Breach of Promise', *Dundee Courier*, 28 January 1904, p. 3), 82

Wallace *v.* Gossland ('Widow Suing for Breach of Promise', *The Evening Telegraph*, 17 September 1879, p. 2), 129

Watson *v.* Allan ('The Stanley Breach of Promise Case', *Aberdeen Press and Journal*, 1 April 1882, p. 2; 'Stanley Breach of Promise Case', *The Evening Telegraph*, 12 April 1882, p. 4;), 78

Watson *v.* Anderson ('News of the Day', *Dundee Courier*, 31 October 1888, p. 3), 72

Watson *v.* Kirkland ('Peculiar Breach of Promise Case', *The Glasgow Herald*, 19 July 1888, p. 2; 'The Glasgow Breach of Promise Case', *The Glasgow Herald*, 23 July 1888, p. 4), 81

Watson *v.* Milne ('An Aberdeenshire Breach of Promise Case', *Edinburgh Evening News*, 28 April 1876, p. 2), 76

Webster, William ('Dundee Circuit Court', *Dundee Courier*, 13 September 1867, p. 2), 111

White *v.* Dickson (1808–1809), discussed in Leneman, *Promises, Promises*, pp. 120, 126, 129

Wilkie *v.* Wilkie ('Court of Session', *The Scotsman*, 15 June 1918, p. 3), 47

Wilson ('"Salvationist Convicted of Bigamy"', *Dundee Evening Telegraph*, 15 February 1889, p 3), 193

Wilson *v.* Young ('The Ayrshire Breach of Promise Case', *Edinburgh Evening News*, 16 July 1896, p. 7), 71

Wilson, Chris ('Sex Fraud Woman Put on Probation', BBC News, 9 April 2013), 165

Wyllie *v.* McCreath ('Court of Session', *The Glasgow Herald*, 22 March 1889, p. 9), 75

Xavier, Duarte, discussed in Derry, 'Sustained Identity Deceptions' in CLRNN, *Reforming the Relationship* (2021), pp. 15–23, 165

Table of Statutes

Children Act 1908
   s. 17, 130
Civil Partnership Act 2004, 58
   s. 3(1)(b), 31
   s. 50, 48
   s. 50(b), 50
   s. 50(e), 58–59
   s. 51, 48, 50, 58–59
   s. 86(1)(d), 31
   s. 100(1), 115
   s. 123(2)(a), 35
   s. 123(2)(b), 37
Civil Partnership (Opposite-Sex Couples) Regulations (The) 2019, 58
Civil Partnership (Scotland) Act 2020, 58
Clandestine Marriages Act 1753, 10
Crime and Punishment (Scotland) Act 1997
   sched. 3, 156
Crimes Act 1900 (New South Wales), 189
Criminal Justice and Public Order Act 1994, 159
   s. 142, 159
   sched. 11, paragraph 1, 159
Criminal Law Amendment Act 1885, 138, 146, 147, 149–151, 154, 155, 157–159, 161, 163, 193–194
   Part I, 153
   s. 2(1), 147, 148, 154–155
   s. 2(2), 147
   s. 2(3), 147
   s. 2(4), 147
   s. 3, 148, 155–157, 159, 161, 162
   s. 3(1), 147
   s. 3(2), 147, 149–150, 156, 161
   s. 3(3), 147
   s. 4, 161, 173

s. 5(1), 126–127
s. 11, 158–159
Criminal Law (Consolidation) (Scotland) Act 1995
   s. 7(3), 173
Divorce (Scotland) Act 1938, 48
Domestic Abuse (Scotland) Act 2018, 26
Evidence Act 1851, 74
Evidence (Scotland) Act 1853, 74
   s. 4, 74
Evidence Further Amendment Act 1869, 74
Evidence Law Amendment (Scotland) Act 1874, 74, 94
   s. 3, 104, 107
Family Law (Scotland) Act 1985
   s. 17, 30
Family Law (Scotland) Act 2006, 103
   s. 3, 10
   s. 21, 60
Fraud Act 2006, 210
Immigration Act 1971
   s. 24A, 103
Immigration and Asylum Act 1999, 103
Jury Courts Abolition Act 1830, 121
Larceny Act 1916, 157
Law Reform (Contributory Negligence) Act 1945, 33
Law Reform (Husband and Wife) (Scotland) Act 1984
   s. 1, 86
Law Reform (Miscellaneous Provisions) Act 1970
   s. 1, 86
   s. 5, 142
Marriage (Same Sex Couples) Act 2013, 58
Marriage (Scotland) Act 1916
   s. 2, 31
Marriage (Scotland) Act 1939, 10
Marriage (Scotland) Act 1977
   s. 5(4), 31
   s. 20A(4), 103
   s. 20A(5)(a), 35
   s. 20A(5)(b), 37
   s. 24 (A1), 115
Marriage and Civil Partnership (Scotland) Act 2014, 58
   s. 5(1), 51
   s. 28(3), 115
Marriage Notice (Scotland) Act 1878
   s. 14, 31

Matrimonial Causes Act 1860, 49
Matrimonial Causes Act 1907
   s. 1, 34
Matrimonial Causes Act 1937, 48–49
   s. 7(1), 48, 49
   s. 7(1)(b) and (c), 49–50
   s. 12, 48
   s. 12(1)(c), 61
   s. 13, 48
Matrimonial Causes Act 1965, 50
   s. 9(1)(b)(ii), 50
   s. 9(2), 50
Matrimonial Causes Act 1973, 50–51
   s. 11(b), 31
   s. 11(c), 56
   s. 12(1)(d), 50
   s. 12(1)(h), 58–59
   s. 13, 58–59
Mental Deficiency Acts 1913 to 1927, 49
Mental Health Act 1959, 50
Nullity of Marriage Act 1971, 50
   s. 1(c), 56
Offences Against the Person Act 1837, 171
Offences Against the Person Act 1861, 147, 155
   s. 20, 184
   s. 47, 184
   s. 49, 147, 152
Perjury Act 1911
   s. 3, 31
Protection of Women Act 1849, 146–149, 151, 153, 155
   s. 1, 146–147
Registration of Births, Deaths and Marriages (Scotland) Act 1854
   s. 60, 31
Requirements of Writing (Scotland) Act 1995
   s. 11, 104
Sexual Offences Act 1956
   s. 1(2), 173
   s. 3, 151, 152–153, 159–160, 164–166
Sexual Offences Act 2003, 165, 183, 191, 208
   s. 4, 165
   s. 26, 145
   ss. 34–37, 145
   s. 74, 178

Table of Statutes

    s. 76, 182
    s. 76(2)(a), 182
    s. 76(2)(b), 175, 209
Sexual Offences (Scotland) Act 1976
    s. 2(1)(b), 151, 156
    s. 2(2), 173
Sexual Offences (Scotland) Act 2009, 145, 208
    s. 4, 165
    s. 12, 178
    s. 13(2)(d), 182
    s. 13(2)(e), 176
Theft Act 1968, 157

1

Inducing Intimacy
An Introduction

1.1 Intimacy, Trust and Law

Both sex and intimate relationships are shot through with expectations of trust. We tend to hope that our sexual and romantic partners will be honest, open and reliable, and it matters to us when they are not.[1] At the same time, we tend to think of sex and intimate relationships as distinctively private and personal. With some important exceptions, such as the prosecution of certain kinds of abuse, these forms of intimacy are typically considered no one else's business, least of all that of the state.[2] The idea that law, especially criminal law, might have a role to play in securing these expectations of trust, and offering redress when they are violated, therefore seems doubtful. Nevertheless, in recent decades, academics, legal practitioners and cultural commentators have begun to take this idea seriously and consider whether and when one form of untrustworthy conduct – deceptive sex – merits criminal punishment.

There is now a sizeable body of academic literature aimed at working out what is wrong with sex like this, which archetypically takes place when one person is operating under a false belief that has been caused by their sexual partner's deception,[3] and how law should respond to it. Despite some important disagreements, there is a general consensus that sexual autonomy – the idea that we should have control over with whom we have sex, what kind of sex we have and under what conditions[4] – is important and deserves robust protection. As a result, there is a default assumption that criminalisation is

---

[1] Dennis J. Fortenberry, 'Trust, Sexual Trust and Sexual Health: An Interrogative Review' (2019) 56(4–5) *The Journal of Sex Research* 425–439; Ken J. Rotenberg and Pamela Qualter, '50 Shades of Trust', *Psychology Today*, 24 February 2014, www.psychologytoday.com/us/blog/matter-trust/201402/50-shades-trust.

[2] Jean L. Cohen, *Regulating Intimacy: A New Legal Paradigm* (Princeton: Princeton University Press, 2002). See Peter Goodrich, *Law in the Courts of Love: Literature and Other Minor Jurisprudences* (London: Routledge, 1996) and Elizabeth Brake, 'Love and the Law' in Christopher Grau and Aaron Smuts (eds.), *The Oxford Handbook of Philosophy of Love* (New York: Oxford University Press, 2017) for some critiques of this view.

[3] Stuart P. Green, *Criminalizing Sex: A Unified Liberal Theory* (New York: Oxford University Press, 2020), p. 101.

[4] On the rise of sexual autonomy, see Lindsay Farmer, *Making the Modern Criminal Law: Criminalization and Civil Order* (Oxford: Oxford University Press, 2016), ch. 9.

an appropriate response to almost any conduct that interferes with sexual autonomy. Yet because the potential consequences of this, which in the context of this book include the possibility that many instances of deceptive sex might amount to a crime, most likely a sex crime, are undesirable to many, this default assumption has generated ambivalence. While some support expansive criminalisation,[5] others reject this but struggle to find a satisfactory and persuasive basis on which to do so.[6]

A similar situation has arisen within legal practice where prosecutions for deceptive sex across the world have increased and come to encompass a greater number of the deceptions that typically occur within 'ordinary' relationships, such as deceptions about ethnicity, HIV status, gender, relationship intentions and the use of contraception.[7] Since these deceptions threaten sexual autonomy, they appear plausible candidates for punishment. Yet deceptive sex that occurs within these 'ordinary' relationships does not typically involve the abuse of power or trust that characterises deceptive sex in other kinds of relationships, such as between doctors and patients or teachers and pupils,[8] and in circumstances involving adults with mental impairments.[9] The case for a criminal law response is accordingly weaker.[10] On top of this, these prosecutions embody the threat (or promise, depending on your point of view) of expansive criminalisation, which has generated some pushback within the legal profession. In England and Wales, for example, judges have clung to doctrines that limit the range of deceptions that can lead to criminal liability, but, in doing so, they have produced judgments whose consistency and adherence to the relevant legislation are questionable.[11]

Beyond the courtroom and academy, reflections on the ethics and legality of deceptive sex have cropped up in mainstream publications[12] and popular entertainment.[13] Here, too, the focus tends to be the kind of deceptions that arise

---

[5] For example, Jonathan Herring, 'Mistaken Sex' [2005] *Criminal Law Review* 511–524.
[6] This challenge has led Jed Rubenfeld to argue that sexual autonomy is not the proper foundation for rape laws; see Jed Rubenfeld, 'The Riddle of Rape by Deception and the Myth of Sexual Autonomy' (2013) 122(6) *The Yale Law Journal* 1372–1443.
[7] See Chloë Kennedy, 'Criminalising Deceptive Sex: Sex, Identity and Recognition' (2021) 41(1) *Legal Studies* 91–110.
[8] Of course, deception can sometimes be used to gain power, and men and women in 'ordinary' relationships do not, even nowadays, meet on exactly equal ground; see bell hooks, *All about Love: New Visions* (New York: William Morrow, 2003), ch. 3.
[9] Home Office, *Setting the Boundaries: Reforming the Law on Sex Offences* (London: Home Office Communication Directorate, 2000), Paragraphs 2.18.7, 4.10.1–4.10.2.
[10] Cf. deceptive sex in relationships of trust or authority; see Patricia J. Falk, 'Rape by Fraud and Rape by Coercion' (1998) 64(1) *Brooklyn Law Journal* 39–180 at 131.
[11] David Ormerod, 'Rape and Deception (Again)' [2020] 10 *Criminal Law Review* 877–881; see Chapter 7.
[12] For example, Neil McArthur, 'Is Lying to Get Laid a Form of Sexual Assault?', *Vice*, 5 September 2016; Abby Ellin, 'Is Sex by Deception a Form of Rape?', *The New York Times*, 23 April 2019; Roseanna Sommers, 'You Were Duped into Saying Yes. Is It Still Consent?', *The New York Times*, 5 March 2021.
[13] For example, Michaela Coel's HBO-BBC series 'I May Destroy You' (2020).

within 'ordinary' relationships between adults with full capacity, and opinion is divided on how best to respond to, or even describe, this kind of conduct.[14] The widespread interest these questions have generated suggests that the challenge of how to understand and deal with deceptive sex is not merely a case of 'doctrinal theory in search of a problem'.[15] Furthermore, the contention surrounding deceptive sex within 'ordinary' relationships suggests that the questions of whether, when and why a legal response, particularly punishment, is warranted in this context demand independent and sustained treatment.[16]

This book is a response to that demand. It aims to provide an account of how and why 'ordinary' cases of deceptive sex have come to appear as a problem that deserves a serious, punitive response and to develop a new way of thinking about, and answering, the question of whether such a response is justifiable and desirable. I go about pursuing these two aims by constructing a genealogy of legal responses to deceptive sex across the modern period (c. 1750 to the present), which locates these responses within the landscape of civil and criminal law responses to a wider, related set of practices.[17] These practices, which I refer to as 'inducing intimacy', extend beyond deceptive sex to include deceptively induced sexual and/or romantic relationships. Though sex and these relationships do not exhaust the terrain of intimacy – both traditional and queer models of intimacy would include friendships, biological and non-biological family relations and other asexual and aromantic relationships[18] – they are often related to one another in the 'Western' cultural imaginary.[19] As I show in the rest of this book, they are often related in law, too, such that sex is definitionally significant to a number of the legal actions examined. The association between sex and romantic relationships is also one of the reasons why, for better or worse, I do not focus extensively on commercial sex in this book – this is a category of sexual exchange that has traditionally been distinguished from sex with a perceived affective dimension.[20] That said, although sex and intimate relationships

---

[14] One term in circulation is 'consent theft'; see Katie Tobin, 'What Is 'Consent Theft' and Why Aren't We Talking about It?', *Restless*, 31 March 2021.

[15] Joseph J. Fischel, *Sex and Harm in the Age of Consent* (Minneapolis: University of Minnesota Press, 2016), p. 206, mostly disagreeing with the quotation.

[16] For an exposition of the different treatment of lies in intimate and non-intimate contexts in US law, see Jill Hasday, *Intimate Lies and the Law* (New York: Oxford University Press, 2019).

[17] I draw on Amia Srinivasan's approach to genealogy that focuses on how representational systems sustain certain practices and exclude certain possibilities; see Amia Srinivasan, 'Genealogy, Epistemology and Worldmaking' (2019) 119(2) *Proceedings of the Aristotelian Society* 127–156.

[18] Phillip L. Hammack, David M. Frost and Sam D. Hughes, 'Queer Intimacies: A New Paradigm for the Study of Relationship Diversity' (2019) 56(4–5) *The Journal of Sex Research* 556–592; Luke Brunning and Natasha McKeever, 'Asexuality' (2021) 38(3) *Journal of Applied Philosophy* 497–517.

[19] Lynn Jamieson, 'Personal Relationships, Intimacy and the Self in a Mediated and Global Digital Age' in Kate Orton-Johnson and Nick Prior (eds.), *Digital Sociology: Critical Perspectives* (London: Palgrave Macmillan, 2013), pp. 13–33; Brake, 'Love and the Law'.

[20] Andrew Gilbert, *British Conservatism and the Legal Regulation of Intimate Relationships* (Portland: Hart Publishing, 2018), p. 6. Where sex work is relevant to the development of the legal actions with which I am concerned, I discuss it.

are related, it is important to study them on their own terms, since they are not wholly reducible to one another either culturally or in law.[21]

The first core argument of this book is that examining legal responses to deceptively induced sex and intimate relationships together and mapping how they have changed over time reveals that these responses have reflected prevailing ideas about what makes these two forms of intimacy valuable. More specifically, I argue that they have reflected cultural shifts in the way that selfhood and intimacy are related and in the way that sex and intimate relationships are held in esteem. I set out these shifts later in this chapter, in Sections 1.3 and 1.4, and explore their relationship to legal responses to inducing intimacy in the chapters that follow, but, in a nutshell, my analysis shows that for much of the past couple of hundred years, this cultural framework structured the law and limited its scope. In more recent decades, however, this framework has largely been superseded by a thin conception of autonomy that tends to value choice for choice's sake. This has had important consequences for legal responses to inducing intimacy, including an increased and more punitive reliance on criminal law and the eclipse of legal responses focusing on intimate relationships by legal responses that focus on sex.

Though these developments make sense in light of the historical contexts within which they occurred, they have created certain problems. I introduce these problems in more detail in Section 1.5 before more fully engaging with them in Chapter 8, but, put simply, they boil down to two issues. First, the scope of sexual offence laws has become nebulous and potentially vast. Second, sexual offence laws cannot capture everything that is wrongful and harmful about inducing intimacy, even if we focus only on the wrongs and harms it might be desirable (and feasible) for law to address.

In response to these problems, the second core argument of this book, which I outline briefly in Section 1.5 and expand upon in Chapter 8, is that a culturally embedded account of what makes intimacy valuable has the potential to better structure and constrain legal responses to inducing intimacy under contemporary conditions. This, I argue, would provide a way of responding to deceptive sex, and indeed deceptive intimate relationships, which takes seriously the impetus behind the current dominance of sexual autonomy – that is, a concern for respecting agency and individual choice in intimate contexts – while ameliorating some of its most serious deficiencies.

1.2 Scope and Approach

To help orient the rest of this book, in this section I delineate the scope of the analysis I undertake in Chapters 2–7 and outline the approach I adopt in undertaking it. I begin by introducing the range of legal actions with which

---

[21] Claire Langhamer, 'Love and Courtship in Mid-Twentieth-Century England' (2007) 50(1) *The Historical Journal* 173–196; Laura A. Rosenbury and Jennifer E. Rothman, 'Sex In and Out of Intimacy' (2010) 59(4) *Emory Law Journal* 809–868.

1.2 Scope and Approach

I am concerned, explaining their significant features and how they align with the book's overarching questions and themes. While doing so, I explain why I chose to focus on particular jurisdictions and time periods, and I indicate the sources on which I relied. Following this, I give a sense of my methodological commitments and how these have shaped my approach, concentrating on my decision to look at both civil and criminal law responses to inducing intimacy and sharing my views on how historically informed research can be relevant and useful to critical and evaluative legal scholarship with a contemporary focus. Here, I gesture towards how the insights generated by my analysis underpin the critically reflective and reform-oriented discussion in the concluding sections of Chapters 2–7 and throughout Chapter 8.

The historical, and to some extent ongoing, special status that marriage has attracted means that a number of the legal actions I examine relate to the constitution of this kind of intimate relationship. So, for example, I consider the law relating to the formation of marriage alongside actions of declarator of marriage, which were brought to try to establish the existence of a contested marriage, and I consider the law of nullity of marriage alongside actions of declarator of nullity, which were brought to try to show that that what appeared to be a valid marriage was in fact not. Where relevant, I also touch upon laws regulating the distribution of assets upon a court finding that a purported marriage is null and the civil wrongs of deceit, fraud and intentional infliction of emotional distress. The other civil wrongs I discuss in more detail are breach of promise of marriage – that is, the unjustifiable termination of an engagement – and seduction, a somewhat amorphous delict (and tort) which included, among other things, persuading a woman to engage in sexual intercourse by falsely promising her marriage. On the criminal law side, the main offences I consider are bigamy, the offence of 'marrying' another despite being part of a subsisting prior marriage; a selection of procuring offences that involved using deception to persuade a woman to engage in unlawful forms of sex; and rape by deception, the crime of engaging in deceptive conduct that, by law, precludes or vitiates sexual consent.

Some of these areas of law have been examined in existing scholarship more than others. For example, the Scottish action of seduction and the more recent history of breach of promise of marriage have been noticeably under-explored.[22] The contribution of this book to the historiography on the discrete actions discussed is therefore considerable, especially in relation to more neglected areas of law. Even where I discuss areas of law that are more familiar, however, I analyse them in a new way by showing how they have constituted legal responses to inducing intimacy. In doing so, I focus on both the structure and substance of legal actions. With respect to structure, I rely on a broad conception of deception that encompasses lies, misrepresentations,

---

[22] The existing literature is cited, where relevant, in Chapters 3 and 5.

other ways of misleading and failures to disclose information,[23] and I attend to the different ways deception has been held to affect the existence or validity of consent. I take a similarly expansive view when it comes to identifying other relevant features of these actions, remaining alive to the possibility that an intention to deceive and proof of reliance might be unnecessary.[24] I point out these features in each of the chapters that follow, and I draw out some general reflections about them in Chapter 8.

With respect to substance, I am interested in the wrongs and potential harms that have been attributed to inducing intimacy, paying attention to how these can extend beyond the deceived person(s) to incorporate the communicative environment in which intimate relations occur and background levels of trust,[25] as well as specific social and legal institutions. The question of which topics have been singled out as significant is crucial, revealing how these laws have settled the so-called line-drawing problem, that is, how to determine which deceptions merit a legal response. In addition to tracing changes in the range of qualifying deceptions, I draw out the connections between these deceptions and the interests and institutions they were, or are, considered to threaten. In other words, I show how the objects of the law's protection relate to the substance of the deceptions that have elicited a legal response. Again, I offer some general reflections on these points in Chapter 8 as well as commenting on them in each of the chapters that follow.

Even though my focus is deception, broadly construed, some of the actions I consider, such as breach of promise of marriage, the procuring offences and rape by deception, could potentially provide redress for the failure to honour promises, even in the absence of deception. For example, if someone made a good faith promise to marry and disclosed their decision not go ahead with the marriage as soon as possible, they might nevertheless be liable for damages via an action of breach of promise of marriage. In such circumstances, there would have been no deception at the outset because a genuine intention to marry existed, and it could not even be said that deception crept into the relationship via an undisclosed change of heart. With this in mind, the actions I discuss can best be understood as legal responses to untrustworthiness in the context of sex and relationships; beyond cases of clear-cut deception, they are concerned with keeping promises, both explicit and implicit, and abstaining from certain communicative practices.[26] Nevertheless, within this wider category of conduct, the possibility of deception is ubiquitous in part because of the way that failing to honour a promise throws doubt on the

---

[23] Gregory Klass, 'Meaning, Purpose, and Cause in the Law of Deception' (2012) 100 *Georgetown Law Journal* 449–496 at 450.

[24] Gregory Klass, 'The Law of Deception: A Research Agenda' (2018) 89 *University of Colorado Law Review* 707–740 at 726, 729–730; cf. Larry Alexander and Emily Sherwin, 'Deception in Law and Morality' (2003) 22 *Law and Philosophy* 393–450 at 433.

[25] Klass, 'The Law of Deception' at 709; Klass, 'Meaning, Purpose, and Cause' at 451, 481.

[26] Jan Philipp Reemtsma, *Trust and Violence: An Essay on a Modern Relationship* (Princeton: Princeton University Press, 2012), p. 14.

sincerity of the initial commitment.[27] Furthermore, when deception has been detected it has been treated as significant in law, often aggravating the case.

As should now be clear, the range of laws I analyse is extensive, which is a consequence of my desire to understand how legal responses to a particular kind of conduct have developed, as opposed to examining any discrete area of law.[28] The temporal scope of this book is similarly ambitious, spanning twenty-five decades. Again, the decision of where to set the temporal boundaries of the analysis was driven by my motivating questions. Apart from witnessing fundamental changes in the cultural meanings of intimacy, which I outline in Sections 1.3 and 1.4, the modern era saw big changes in the law relating to inducing intimacy. At least as importantly, and as I explain in a little more detail later in this section, the legal responses that existed during this period are in many ways the correlates, or predecessors, of the laws that now exist. Adopting a wide-ranging perspective in terms of both legal doctrine and time period was therefore necessary to achieve the aims of this book.

Partly to manage the task of analysing such a vast amount of material – which I sourced from legal treatises, law reform reports, reported and unreported cases, newspaper stories, contemporaneous journals and archival holdings – in the majority of Chapters 2–7 I focus primarily on a single legal system – Scotland. I chose the relevant treatises and law reform reports because they are the most prominent of those concerning the areas of law I examine, and I located the majority of the reported cases via searches of major legal databases. I found the unreported cases, which make up the majority of those relating to areas of law with few reported decisions, such as bigamy, seduction and breach of promise of marriage, via searches of newspaper archives and journals from the time. These journals also supplied valuable commentary on legal cases and developments. The archival records I consulted include court papers relating to Sheriff Court, Court of Session and Justiciary Court trials[29] held by National Records Scotland and the Signet Library as well as Session Papers – pleading papers and interlocutors (short records of case outcomes) – held by the Advocates Library.[30]

Despite the emphasis on Scotland, I refer to developments elsewhere, particularly in England and the United States, to highlight important points of confluence and divergence and I cast the net wider again where I discuss contemporary developments so as to identify recent and emerging trends. Furthermore, much of the discussion in Chapter 6 and some of the discussion

---

[27] Joseph Raz, *The Morality of Freedom* (Oxford: Clarendon Press, 1988), p. 384.
[28] For some reflections on the value and limitations of thinking in terms of areas of law, see Tarunabh Khaitan and Sandy Steel, 'Areas of Law: Three Questions in Special Jurisprudence' (2023) 43(1) *Oxford Journal of Legal Studies* 76–96. I set out the benefits of my approach in greater detail in Chapter 8.
[29] On these courts, see *Stair Memorial Encyclopaedia* (reissue, 2016), Paragraphs 49–88; 89–138; 139–199.
[30] Angus Stewart, 'The Session Papers in the Advocates Library' in Hector L. MacQueen (ed.), *Miscellany Four* (Edinburgh: The Stair Society, 2002), pp. 199–221.

in Chapter 7 relates to laws which applied, or apply, to both Scotland and England and Wales, and much of the litigation I mention in those chapters occurred in England. In these chapters, a different focus was necessary to appreciate the relevant legal developments, that is, those relating to the procuring offences and rape by deception. As the main case study of Chapters 2–5, however, Scotland is particularly appropriate due to its relatively small size and some of its legal idiosyncrasies.

For example, the law of what is called irregular marriage survived for longer in Scotland than it did in other European nations,[31] where abolition occurred much earlier.[32] Unlike regular marriages, which were conducted by authorised celebrants and were similar to marriages as we know them today, irregular marriage did not involve formal solemnisation.[33] Instead, there were three ways irregular marriage could be constituted or proved according to Scots law: expressing mutual consent to marriage; promising marriage then engaging in sexual intercourse; and cohabiting as, and being reputed to be, spouses.[34] Crucially, all three forms of irregular marriage depended, at least in theory, on nothing more than the valid marital consent of the parties.[35] Assuming such

---

[31] Eleanor Gordon, 'Irregular Marriage and Cohabitation in Scotland, 1855–1939: Official Policy and Popular Practice' (2015) 58(4) *The Historical Journal* 1059–1079 at 1060. For a very general outline of the development of marriage law in Scotland, see Eric Clive, *The Law of Husband and Wife in Scotland*, 4th ed. (Edinburgh: W. Green & Sons, 1997), and for accounts of marriage formation in early modern Scotland, see Leah Leneman, *Promises, Promises: Marriage Litigation in Scotland, 1698–1830* (Edinburgh: National Museums of Scotland, 2003); Katie Barclay, 'Marriage, Sex, and the Church of Scotland: Exploring Non-Conformity amongst the Lower Orders' (2019) 43(2) *Journal of Religious History* 163–179; and Katie Barclay, 'Doing the Paperwork: The Emotional World of Wedding Certificates' (2020) 17(3) *Cultural and Social History* 315–332.

[32] For example, by the Clandestine Marriages Act 1753 in England; see Rebecca Probert, *Marriage Law and Practice in the Long Eighteenth Century: A Reassessment* (Cambridge: Cambridge University Press, 2009).

[33] In addition to regular and irregular marriage, clandestine marriage – marriage that was constituted by a religious ceremony but not otherwise regular – is sometimes referred to as a third mode of contracting marriage; see Brian Dempsey, 'The Marriage (Scotland) Bill 1755' in Hector L. MacQueen (ed.), *Miscellany Six* (Edinburgh: Stair Society, 2009), pp. 77–78.

[34] Rebecca Probert, Maebh Harding and Brian Dempsey, 'A Uniform Law of Marriage? The 1868 Royal Commission Reconsidered' (2018) 30(3) *Child and Family Law Quarterly* 217–237; Clive, *Husband and Wife*, Paragraph 05.001. The first two forms of irregular marriage were formally abolished by the Marriage (Scotland) Act 1939 and the latter survived until 2006; see Family Law (Scotland) Act 2006, s. 3. On the history of irregular marriage in Scotland, see Eleanor Gordon, 'Irregular Marriage: Myth and Reality' (2013) 47(2) *Journal of Social History* 507–525. On marriage registration, see Gordon, 'Myth and Reality' and Anne Cameron, 'The Establishment of Civil Registration in Scotland' (2007) 50(2) *The Historical Journal* 377–395.

[35] James Dalrymple Stair; John S. More (ed.), *Institutions of the Law of Scotland, Deduced from Its Originals, and Collated with the Civil, Canon, and Feudal Laws, and with the Customs of Neighbouring Nations* (Edinburgh: Bell & Bradfute, 1832), p. 32; John Erskine, *An Institute of the Law of Scotland* (Edinburgh: John Bell, 1773), p. 84 and subsequent editions; G. Campbell H. Paton (ed.), *Baron Hume's Lectures, 1786–1822* (Edinburgh: J. Skinner & Co. Ltd., 1939), p. 22; James Fergusson, *A Treatise on the Present State of the Consistorial Law in Scotland, with Reports of Decided Cases* (Edinburgh: Bell & Bradfute, 1829), p. 105; Maurice

marital consent could be proved, according to the rules of evidence, the court could issue a legal declaration of the parties' married status.[36]

Given this relative laxity in the formation of marriage and the primacy of consent, there is a wealth of litigation, much of which concerns the complexities of determining the existence, and legal efficacy, of consent – topics that lie at the heart of this book. Furthermore, the two forms of irregular marriage on which I concentrate most – marriage constituted by present consent and by promise of marriage followed by sex – provided ample opportunities for deceptively induced intimacy. By offering insincere (or, at any rate, unfulfilled) promises of marriage or behaving in a way that implied the existence of marital consent a man (and it was almost always a man) could lure a woman into a false sense of security. To be sure, marriage by habit and repute also created opportunities for duplicitous conduct; it allowed a man to induce a woman to enter an 'illicit, or equivocal' cohabitation in the hope it might 'merge into matrimony'[37] and then, by his circumspect behaviour, leave her marital status uncertain. In practice, however, the number of cases of marriage by habit and repute appears to have been comparatively small.[38] More importantly, in the cases that were litigated the discussion tends to centre on the impression the man's conduct made on the world at large;[39] there are relatively few cases which focus on the impression such a man's conduct made on his would-be spouse.[40] By contrast, and as I explore in Chapter 4, the impression created on the mind of a trusting 'wife' was central to cases of purported marriage by present consent or promise of marriage and sex.

Beyond marriage, the Scottish delict of seduction was, unlike its Anglo-American counterpart, always available to the woman whose sexual consent

---

Lothian, *The Law, Practice and Styles Peculiar to the Consistorial Actions Transferred to the Court of Session, by Act 1, Gul. IV. c. 69* (Edinburgh: Adam Black, 1830), pp. 25–26; Patrick Fraser, *Treatise on the Law of Scotland as Applicable to the Personal and Domestic Relations* (Edinburgh: T. & T. Clark, 1846), p. 87 and *Treatise on Husband and Wife: According to the Law of Scotland* (Edinburgh: T. & T. Clark, 1876), p. 415; Frederick Parker Walton, *A Handbook of Husband and Wife* (Edinburgh: W. Green & Sons, 1893), p. 2 and subsequent edition (Frederick Parker Walton, *A Handbook of Husband and Wife according to the Law of Scotland* (Edinburgh: W. Green & Sons, 1922)).

[36] Around the middle of the nineteenth century, a semi-formalised system of registering irregular marriages emerged (Gordon, 'Myth and Reality', especially at 515–516), but litigation to establish the existence of irregular marriages continued.

[37] *Report of the Royal Commission on the Laws of Marriage* (London: George E. Eyre & William Spottiswoode, 1868), p. 82.

[38] According to evidence given to the 1868 Royal Commission on the Laws of Marriage, it was 'extremely rare' for marriage to be established on this ground alone; see *Report of the Royal Commission*, p. xxxiii. My own research suggests that the two other modes of constituting irregular marriage were more frequently litigated.

[39] There do not appear to be many cases like this, but see *Dewar* v. *Dewar* 1995 SLT 467 and *Gow* v. *Lord Advocate* 1993 SLT 275, which, unusually, involves a woman defender. This focus on the impression of the world at large is also a feature of cohabitation with habit and repute cases where the defender claimed that neither party intended marriage; see, for example, *Elder* v. *M'Lean* 1829 8 S 56; *Ackerman* v. *Blackburn* 2000 Fam LR 35.

[40] *Nicol* v. *Bell* 1954 SLT 314 is the clearest example.

was compromised by false promises of marriage. This underexplored action can therefore be seen as a civil law analogue to the laws criminalising deceptive sex that developed thereafter and so it is worth examining in conjunction with these more recent laws. A further feature of the civil law actions I consider, which underscores the value of comparing them to these criminal laws, is what might loosely be described as their quasi-punitive functions. By quasi-punitive functions I mean the meting out of burdensome impositions that aim to give material force to accountability for wrongdoing[41] in the service of vindicatory, deterrent, communicative (sometimes censorious) and/or retributive ends. Punitive damages are the most obvious example, but compensatory damages often fulfil one or more of these functions even if that is not their main purpose.[42] In particular, damages for dignitarian or emotional injuries – the kind of damages frequently awarded via the actions considered in this book – tend to blur the line between compensation and punishment most profoundly. As some authors have argued, punitive damages can be considered compensation for the additional dignitarian and emotional injuries caused by particularly culpable wrongdoing.[43] But even when dignitarian or emotional damages are awarded for the underlying wrong, rather than the malice or other culpable attitude that accompanies it, it can be hard to distinguish these damages functionally from criminal punishment when the latter is conceived as remedying the injury to the victim's honour.[44] It is particularly difficult to draw this distinction when emotional injuries are presumed[45] because this places the emphasis of the action on the wrongdoer's conduct.[46] As I discuss further in Section 1.5, a focus on the wrongdoer's conduct is a hallmark of criminal law.

Perhaps more surprisingly, actions brought to establish the existence of marriage could serve punitive or quasi-punitive functions too. For example, a controversial rule that prevented defenders from relying on their misleading

---

[41] R. A. Duff, 'Torts, Crimes and Vindication: Whose Wrong Is It?' in Matthew Dyson (ed.), *Unravelling Tort and Crime* (Cambridge: Cambridge University Press, 2014), pp. 146–173, pp. 150–152; Marc Galanter and David Luban, 'Poetic Justice: Punitive Damages and Legal Pluralism' (1993) 42(4) *American University Law Review* 1394–1463 at 1397.

[42] John C. P. Goldberg and Benjamin C. Zipursky, *Recognizing Wrongs* (Cambridge, MA: Harvard University Press, 2020); Galanter and Luban, 'Poetic Justice'; Findlay Stark, 'Tort Law, Expression and Duplicative Wrongs' in Paul B. Miller and John Oberdiek (eds.), *Civil Wrongs and Justice in Private Law* (New York: Oxford University Press, 2020), pp. 441–462.

[43] Marc O. DeGirolami, 'Reconstructing Malice in the Law of Punitive Damages' (2021) 14(1) *The Journal of Tort Law* 193–240 at 231–232.

[44] Galanter and Luban, 'Poetic Justice' at 1432–1433.

[45] Eric Descheemaker, 'Rationalising Recovery for Emotional Harm in Tort Law' (2018) 134 *Law Quarterly Review* 602–626 at 608, 624–625; Niall R. Whitty, 'Overview of Rights of Personality in Scots Law' in Niall R. Whitty and Reinhard Zimmermann (eds.), *Rights of Personality in Scots Law: A Comparative Perspective* (Edinburgh: Edinburgh University Press, 2009), pp. 147–246, pp. 207–208.

[46] For more reflections on all these points, see Chloë Kennedy, 'Comparing Criminal and Civil Responsibility: Contextualising Claims to Distinctiveness' in Thomas Crofts, Louise Kennefick and Arlie Loughnan (eds.), *Routledge International Handbook on Criminal Responsibility* (Routledge, forthcoming 2025).

1.2 Scope and Approach

conduct made it harder for a man to escape the conclusion that he was married to a woman when he had (mis)led her to believe this was the nature of their relationship. Similarly, controversial rules facilitating proof of a defender's marital consent played a comparable role. If a defender's behaviour signalled an intention to wed, a court might find he was married to the pursuer even if he denied that this was his intention.

The first rule, which can be interpreted as a species of personal bar (known elsewhere as estoppel),[47] might plausibly be described as an example of forfeiture by insincere act. As such, it constitutes a forced change in rights and duties based on the defender's culpable wrongdoing.[48] Indeed, the use of personal bar has been described as not only 'preventing' but 'penalising' inconsistent conduct.[49] The second rule is less clearly an example of personal bar[50] but imputing consent where it does not subjectively exist, or at least where it is denied, can also be considered a forced change in rights and duties.[51] The use of these doctrines to effectively force marriage signals an additional layer of punitiveness because, as other studies have shown, coercing marriage – an enduring status that entailed serious economic and behavioural obligations – was punishment in everything but name.[52]

Identifying an element of punitiveness across both civil and criminal law responses to inducing intimacy assists the critical and evaluative ambitions of this book in two ways, both of which are underpinned by my views on the roles historically informed scholarship can perform. In short,[53] I believe that this kind of research can play a generative as well as constraining role in evaluating legal developments and cautiously suggesting ideas for reform. In other words, on top of providing a reality check on ideal theorising, by warning against potential unintended consequences and pointing out the degree of contingency that marks out all human-made laws and institutions, historically informed scholarship might help articulate alternative normative bases for laws and legal systems, predicated on features of human behaviour and institutions observed over time. Since this approach is rooted in empirical studies of 'real world' phenomena yet aspires towards a foundation that is not entirely reducible to any

---

[47] Elspeth Reid, 'Personal Bar: Case-Law in Search of Principle' (2003) 7(3) *Edinburgh Law Review* 340–366.
[48] Kimberly Kessler Ferzan, 'Losing the Right to Assert You've Been Wronged: A Study in Conceptual Chaos?' in Miller and Oberdiek (eds.), *Civil Wrongs and Justice*, pp. 111–130, pp. 117–118.
[49] Reid, 'Personal Bar' at 344 and 350.
[50] Elspeth Reid, 'Protecting Legitimate Expectations and Estoppel in Scots Law' (2006) *Electronic Journal of Comparative Law*, www.ejcl.org/103/art103-11.pdf at 9.
[51] Ferzan, 'Losing the Right', pp. 113–114, 118.
[52] Melissa Murray, 'Marriage as Punishment' (2012) 112(1) *Columbia Law Review* 1–65.
[53] For more detail, see Chloë Kennedy, 'Immanence and Transcendence: History's Roles in Normative Legal Theory' (2017) 8(3) *Jurisprudence* 557–579 and Chloë Kennedy, 'Sociology of Law and Legal History' in Jiří Přibáň (ed.), *Research Handbook on the Sociology of Law* (Northampton: Edward Elgar, 2020), pp. 31–42. See also Philip Selznick, *The Moral Commonwealth: Social Theory and the Promise of Community* (Berkeley: University of California Press, 1992).

given moment in time, it rejects the absolutism that is sometimes attributed to the so-called is/ought distinction. Furthermore, since it aims to provide both a deep understanding of contemporary predicaments and new ways to respond to these, this approach can be used as a basis for both critique – an enriched sense of the complexity of the problem – and criticism – potential ways forward.

In light of this, the two ways in which identifying an element of punitiveness across the criminal and civil laws examined is valuable are, first, that a shift towards *increased* punitiveness over time becomes clear and, second, a previously unappreciated foundation for these laws emerges. Starting with the first point, though the range of actions I study has a longstanding association with punishment, broadly construed (which is the crux of what I suggest by identifying instances of civil law quasi-punitiveness), the shift from private to public law responses has certain ramifications which, as I explain further in Section 1.5 and Chapter 8, should be considered when appraising the form and function of existing and prospective legal responses to inducing intimacy. But the fact that the practices of inducing intimacy have attracted a punitive or quasi-punitive response across the modern period shows that there is something enduring about the idea that they are wrongful and warrant censure and deterrence. More importantly, the fact that there is a plausible substantive continuity across these legal responses that is rooted in the relationship between selfhood and intimacy suggests that this link constitutes something like the normatively significant core of these actions.[54] The way this link, and its instantiation in law, has been shaped by different historical dynamics acts as a reminder that it can be underpinned by sensibilities that would not appeal to many contemporary societies. At the same time, the longstanding status of the association suggests this is an important foundation on which an alternative way forward, based on a re-worked version of this association, might be grounded.[55] I explore this possibility in more detail in Chapter 8.

1.3 Selfhood and Intimacy

To begin to substantiate the claim that there is plausible continuity of the kind just described it is necessary to say more about the links between selfhood and intimacy and how these have changed over time. In this section I therefore set out how, broadly speaking, general shifts in conceptions of selfhood have been reflected in changing expectations of intimate relationships before going on, in the next section, to show how these changes can also be detected in the value that is ascribed to sex.[56]

---

[54] On identifying such a core, despite considerable change, see Maksymilian Del Mar, 'Philosophical Analysis and Historical Inquiry' in Markus D. Dubber and Christopher Tomlins (eds.), *The Oxford Handbook of Legal History* (Oxford: Oxford University Press, 2018), pp. 3–21.

[55] See also Alan Norrie, 'Criminal Law and Ethics: Beyond Normative Assertion and Its Critique' (2017) 80(5) *Modern Law Review* 955–973.

[56] These sections support the assertion that 'intimacy is important in the construction of the self, and ideas of selfhood shape our intimate interactions'; see George Morris, 'Intimacy in Modern British History' (2021) 64(3) *The Historical Journal* 796–811 at 806.

1.3 Selfhood and Intimacy

One typical characteristic of modern conceptions of selfhood is that they are predicated on the belief that individuals necessarily participate actively in their own self-construction. As Christine Korsgaard has put it, '[c]arving out a personal identity for which we are responsible is one of the inescapable tasks of human life'.[57] This is in contrast to earlier conceptions of selfhood, according to which the self was conceived of as largely given, having mostly been fixed by powerful, often hierarchical, societal or cosmic orders.[58]

In late modernity, however, this process of self-construction has become reflexive in new and increasingly demanding ways. Under late modern conditions, self-construction has come to involve continually constructing and maintaining a biographical narrative that is composed via myriad choices, filtered through abstract systems.[59] As might be expected given the importance of generating and sustaining this life narrative, the late modern self is to a large extent considered to be inwardly generated.[60] External referents, such as social and cultural institutions, figure as significant but they tend to appear as such because of the way they support or hinder the inward, reflexive process of self-construction.[61]

Before moving on from this point I first want to foreground a distinction that I come back to towards the end of this chapter and in Chapter 8, that is, between different ways of construing this relationship between internal and external. The distinction is exemplified by two similar, but importantly different, ways of thinking about modern selfhood: autonomy and authenticity. These two ideals are similar in the way they prioritise generating and acting on one's own reasons; they are both agent-centred in that regard. But whereas autonomy emphasises the importance of deliberation and choice that is free from external referents, such as social institutions, cultural norms and even other people, authenticity tends to present external referents in a more positive light. Put differently, while autonomy valorises an ideal of freedom that is maximally self-determining, authenticity emphasises the importance of deciding in accordance with one's values but recognises the significance of external horizons of meaning, including for the ability to hold these values at all.[62] Though

---

[57] Christine M. Korsgaard, *Self-Constitution: Agency, Identity, and Integrity* (Oxford: Oxford University Press, 2009), p. 24.

[58] Jerrold Seigel, *The Idea of the Self: Thought and Experience in Western Europe Since the Seventeenth Century* (Cambridge: Cambridge University Press, 2005), p. 43. See also Charles Taylor, *Sources of the Self: The Making of Modern Identity* (Cambridge, MA: Harvard University Press, 1989).

[59] Anthony Giddens, *Modernity and Self-Identity: Self and Society in the Late Modern Age* (Cambridge: Polity Press, 1991). The idea of narrative self-construction is much older; see Thomas Ahnert and Susan Manning, 'Introduction' in Thomas Ahnert and Susan Manning (eds.), *Character, Self, and Sociability in the Scottish Enlightenment* (New York: Palgrave Macmillan, 2011), pp. 1–30.

[60] See also Dror Wahrman, *The Making of the Modern Self: Identity and Culture in Eighteenth-Century England* (New Haven: Yale University Press, 2004).

[61] Giddens, *Modernity and Self-Identity*, p. 75.

[62] Somogy Varga and Charles Guignon, 'Authenticity', *The Stanford Encyclopedia of Philosophy*, Spring 2020 Edition, Edward N. Zalta (ed.), https://plato.stanford.edu/archives/

these ideals tend to shade into one another, they have different implications for how concepts that aim to protect freedom, such as consent, are fleshed out,[63] as I show more fully in Chapter 8.

Returning to modern conceptions of selfhood and their link with intimate relationships, historically speaking marital status was the key to this association. For centuries, marriage bestowed prestige and respectability on its participants, particularly women, at the same time as it imposed obligations. Anyone who 'failed' to marry would be held in correspondingly low esteem, but women, especially mothers, had most to lose in reputational (and material) terms through remaining unmarried.[64] Though these positively and negatively inflected relationships between selfhood and marital status endured for much of the modern period, several important changes across this time have oriented marriage, and intimate relationships more generally, towards the kind of concern for individual choice and self-fulfilment that is characteristic of late modern selfhood. These changes are clustered around waves of liberalisation that took place in the late eighteenth century, the late nineteenth century, and across the twentieth century (in the 1920s, 1970s and during the last couple of decades) that have, essentially, three dimensions.

First, each wave has increased the extent to which love is considered an appropriate motive for entering and staying in marriage, sometimes to the exclusion of other considerations,[65] with the result that marriage has lost much of its hegemonic status. Almost as soon as the core aspirations of marriage were reconfigured from political and economic advantage to love and companionship, conservatives warned that these new ambitions would undermine the institution they were meant to protect. The fear, which proved well-founded, was that marriage would be rendered optional. With love as the bedrock of marriage, a dearth of love could 'excuse' those who remained unmarried or left their spouse and the presence of love could elevate non-marital intimate relationships, making it harder to disparage them as inferior or deficient.[66] Though it would take post-war social security innovations and the growth in paid work for women for marriage rates to decline, since then single person and single

---

spr2020/entries/authenticity; Charles Taylor, *The Ethics of Authenticity* (Cambridge, MA: Harvard University Press, 1991), pp. 28, 36–39; Selznick, *The Moral Commonwealth*, pp. 12, 65, 71.

[63] Maiken Umbach and Mathew Humphrey, 'Introduction' in Maiken Umbach and Mathew Humphrey (eds.), *Authenticity: The Cultural History of a Political Concept* (Cham: Springer International Publishing, 2018), pp. 1–12, p. 3; Fred M. Frohock, 'Liberal Maps of Consent' (1989) 22(2) *Polity* 231–252.

[64] Katherine Holden, Amy Froide and June Hannam, 'Introduction' (2008) 17(3) *Women's History Review* 313–326.

[65] Stephanie Coontz, *Marriage, a History: How Love Conquered Marriage* (New York: Penguin Books, 2006); Katie Barclay, *Love, Intimacy and Power: Marriage and Patriarchy in Scotland, 1650-1850* (Manchester: Manchester University Press, 2011), pp. 60, 88, 94; Claire Langhamer, 'Love, Selfhood and Authenticity in Post-War Britain' (2012) 9(2) *Cultural and Social History* 277–297.

[66] Coontz, *Marriage, A History*, p. 175; Langhamer, 'Love, Selfhood and Authenticity'.

parent households have proliferated[67] and sophisticated calls for the abolition of state-recognised marriage have appeared.[68]

Second, parties to intimate relationships now expect to have greater choice over their partner and more control over the terms of their relationship. Again, almost as soon as the transition towards love-based marriage began it started to appear inappropriate for anyone but the potential spouses to decide on the suitability of the match.[69] Importantly, this also changed ideas about what criteria should be used in making that decision, with a greater range of personal, and more personalised, characteristics supplementing (and sometimes supplanting) general attributes like rank or wealth.[70] The notion that people should be able, or even required, to set the terms of their relationships developed later but it has gained traction in recent decades.[71] Reflecting the increased reflexivity of late modernity, some of these terms are reviewed and renegotiated throughout the course of the relationship[72] and in keeping with the way relationships continue to play a role in self-construction, the phrase 'relational orientation' has emerged to refer to the kind(s) of intimate relationship in which one participates.[73]

Third, it is now expected that marriages, and intimate relationships more generally, should be easy to end when they are no longer satisfying[74] – that liberty both to enter and exit relationships should be maximised – and that they should do more to satisfy us. Over the course of the last few centuries the expectations placed on intimate relationships have multiplied to include emotional and, later, sexual satisfaction, as well as affection, fidelity, honesty, respect, temperamental and intellectual compatibility, and intimacy,[75] which

[67] www.ons.gov.uk/peoplepopulationandcommunity/birthsdeathsandmarriages/families/bulletins/familiesandhouseholds/2018.
[68] For example, Clare Chambers, *Against Marriage: An Egalitarian Defence of the Marriage-Free State* (Oxford: Oxford University Press, 2017).
[69] Note, however, that social conformity remained important in some communities, such as working-class ones, even as expectations of marriage changed; see Andrea Thomson, '"The Best of Both Worlds"? Young Women, Family and Marriage in 1970s Scotland' in Katie Barclay, Jeffrey Meek and Andrea Thomson (eds.), *Courtship, Marriage and Marriage Breakdown: Approaches from the History of Emotion* (New York: Routledge, 2019), pp. 127–143.
[70] Barclay, *Love, Intimacy and Power*, p. 110; Coontz, *Marriage, A History*, p. 243; Lawrence Stone, *Uncertain Unions: Marriage in England, 1660–1753* (Oxford: Oxford University Press, 1992), p. 8.
[71] Pamela Haag, *Marriage Confidential: Love in the Post-Romantic Age* (New York: Harper Perennial, 2011).
[72] Coontz, *Marriage, A History*, p. 282; Giddens, *Modernity and Self-Identity*, p. 90.
[73] Amber K. Stephens and Tara M. Emmers-Sommer, 'Adults' Identities, Attitudes, and Orientations Concerning Consensual Non-Monogamy' (2020) 17 *Sexuality Research and Social Policy* 469–485; Margaret Robinson, 'Polyamory and Monogamy as Strategic Identities' (2013) 13(1) *Journal of Bisexuality* 21–38.
[74] Giddens, *Modernity and Self-Identity*, p. 90; Anthony Giddens, *The Transformation of Intimacy: Sexuality, Love and Eroticism in Modern Societies* (Newark: Polity Press, 1992), p. 137. See also Benedict Douglas, 'Love and Human Rights' (2023) 43(2) *Oxford Journal of Legal Studies* 273–297 and Brian L. Frye and Maybell Romero, 'The Right to Unmarry: A Proposal' (2020) 69(1) *Cleveland State Law Journal* 89 104.
[75] Coontz, *Marriage, A History*, pp. 8, 20, 23, 177, 259, 271; Tanya Cheadle, *Sexual Progressives: Reimagining Intimacy in Scotland, 1880–1914* (Manchester: Manchester University Press, 2020), pp. 2, 17; Langhamer, 'Love, Selfhood and Authenticity' at 280, 293.

has come to mean providing access to one's private self, feelings and dissatisfactions.[76] In some respects, these contemporary ideals have increased the overlap between intimate relationships and friendships, with both characterised by an emphasis on choice and self-individualisation,[77] but there remain important distinctions, such as general expectations of exclusivity within intimate relationships and the conventional and legal priority that is still afforded intimate relationships.[78] In this context, the additional expectations placed on intimate relationships have charged them with the burden of meeting a remarkable number of complex and sometimes competing needs,[79] and it is now more likely that one or more of these will not be met.

Pausing on the expectations of honesty and intimacy, both of which are obviously relevant to the subject of this book, these have been transformed by changes in the way people meet and communicate. For example, dating apps and digitally mediated communications present new opportunities for deception in intimate contexts but they also provide new ways of potentially regulating such deceptions.[80] At a more profound level, however, the move to love-based relationships has complicated what it might mean to be honest with an intimate partner on account of changes in the way love has been understood. Across the nineteenth century, the idea that love could develop from, or even be created out of, feelings of respect and appreciation of good character came under threat from the belief that love could not be willed or reasoned into existence. As love came to be seen as a spontaneous and uncontrollable force lying beyond the grasp of reason[81] it became harder to identify feelings of true love in other people and oneself.[82] Yet because the ideal marital relationship was supposed to be grounded in true love, the tasks of conveying and detecting genuine emotions could not be easily dismissed.

---

[76] Barclay, *Love, Intimacy and Power*, p. 135; Coontz, *Marriage, A History*, pp. 20–21.

[77] On friendship, see Arlie Loughnan, *Self, Others and the State: Relations of Criminal Responsibility* (Cambridge: Cambridge University Press, 2020), p. 219.

[78] Rhaina Cohen, 'What If Friendship, Not Marriage, Was at the Center of Life?', *The Atlantic*, 20 October 2020.

[79] As Barbara Rosenwein points out, the modern idea of 'obligation free' love is arguably a source of more onerous obligations – stemming from the obligation to meet these needs out of love – than earlier ideals about love; see *Love: A History in Five Fantasies* (Cambridge: Polity Press, 2022), p. 65.

[80] Robert Sparrow and Lauren Karas, 'Teledildonics and Rape by Deception' (2020) 12(1) *Law, Innovation and Technology* 175–204; Stefanie Duguay, 'Dressing Up Tinderella: Interrogating Authenticity Claims on the Mobile Dating App Tinder' (2017) 20(3) *Information, Communication & Society* 351–367; Gayle Brewer, 'Deceiving for and during Sex'; Catalina L. Toma, James Alex Bonus and Lyn M. Van Swol, 'Lying Online: Examining the Production, Detection, and Popular Beliefs Surrounding Interpersonal Deception in Technologically-Mediated Environments' in Tony Docan-Morgan (ed.), *The Palgrave Handbook of Deceptive Communication* (Cham: Springer International Publishing, 2019), pp. 551–556 and pp. 583–602.

[81] Coontz, *Marriage, A History*, pp. 178, 184; Barclay, *Love, Intimacy and Power*, pp. 109, 111.

[82] Barclay, *Love, Intimacy and Power*, p. 111; Claire Langhamer, 'Trust, Authenticity and Bigamy in Twentieth-Century England' in Barclay, Meek and Thomson (eds.), *Courtship, Marriage and Marriage Breakdown*, pp. 160–174.

Indeed, the expectation that marriage should be grounded in true love meant it could be considered immoral to marry for any other reason[83] and immoral to marry without it.[84]

If there is a neat, one-word way of summarising these transformations in intimate relationships and selfhood across the modern period it might be this: tension. Intimate relationships matter as much as they ever have, perhaps more, because they are a potentially stable source and site of self-construction in a world where other external referents are neither given nor standardly perceived as welcome. At the same time, they are harder to secure and sustain. The desire for transparency in intimate relationships has reached new heights, as has the range of information over which we want control, but this desire is easily frustrated, not least because one of the central planks of the intimate relationship – its emotional connection – is not verifiable in a straightforward way. Finally, intimate relationships are still expected to be secure but they are also expected to be dispensable. This desire for easy egress effectively rules out, or at least makes less appealing, any effort to protect against untrustworthy conduct that would simultaneously make it harder to leave the relationship. Furthermore, if Katherine Hawley is correct in suggesting that trust in intimate relationships, unlike trust more generally, is motive sensitive,[85] then an intimate relationship where *either* party feels compelled to stay is likely to be unattractive to *both* parties. Thinking about the still-popular views that intimate relationships should be based on love and that true love is spontaneous[86] it becomes clear why a relationship that lacks this quality, irrespective of whose love is untrue in this sense, is likely to be undesirable.

In Part I, I argue that each of the changes outlined in this section, and the tensions to which they give rise, is evident in the laws and legal actions examined there. As I argue in Chapters 2 and 3, the range of deceptions that might render marital consent invalid and promises of marriage non-binding has in many ways mirrored anxieties about, and expectations of, marriage and spouses. Furthermore, the various attempts to extend this range and efforts to make emotional authenticity matter to the law of breach of promise of marriage largely coincided with the periods of liberalisation outlined above. In terms of the perceived harms and wrongs of these two areas of law, they were very clearly rooted in the gendered significance of marital status. This is a feature they shared with the rules governing the formation of marriage I discuss in Chapter 4, which provided redress for women who had been misled about their marital status alongside the crime of bigamy, which for much of the modern period was conceived as a crime against the deceived spouse.

---

[83] Coontz, *Marriage, A History*, pp. 178–179.   [84] Barclay, *Love, Intimacy and Power*, p. 61.
[85] Katherine Hawley, *How to Be Trustworthy* (Oxford: Oxford University Press, 2019), p. 24.
[86] Work by Mikko Salmela confirms that, according to mainstream thinking, spontaneity is considered the hallmark of authentic emotions; see 'What Is Emotional Authenticity?' (2005) 35(3) *The Journal for the Theory of Social Behaviour* 209–230.

The shift away from this understanding of bigamy towards its reconfiguration as one of several crimes that damaged the state's ability to monitor the existence of valid marriage and the legal benefits this bestows was ironically facilitated by a greater concern with individual choice and happiness. As the deceived spouse's decision-making powers and happiness came to matter more, the possibility that they might wish to forgive and remain with their partner, despite the deception, also came to matter more. A relatively similar narrative helps explain the formalisation of the process of constituting marriage and the difficulty in using marriage as a form of punishment for deceptive conduct aimed at the would-be spouse. As the state's interest in effectively managing this relationship for its own benefit – that is, to avoid the 'misuse' of marriage by couples looking to 'cheat' the state – grew, the capacity of this area of law to function as a form of individual redress declined. Finally, the decline and eventual demise of the action of breach of promise of marriage owes much to the liberalisation of marriage and the sense that compelled marriage is not only an affront to the institution but also to the individuals who enter it.

Overall, in addition to strengthening the overarching argument that cultural conceptions of selfhood and intimacy are reflected in, and shore up, legal responses to deceptively induced intimacy, these changes mean that various instances of inducing intimacy that were formerly censured, either directly or indirectly, are no longer recognised as wrongful via law. Yet developments regarding the law of nullity elsewhere in the world and the innovative use of other civil wrongs suggest that there is still a desire for legal responses to this kind of conduct. These developments therefore indicate that there remains a sense in which trying to obtain formal censure for this kind of untrustworthy conduct is tantalising; they also underscore the reality that liberalisation does not necessarily go hand in hand with a reduced role for law, a point that is especially clear in legal developments concerning sex.

1.4 Sex and Marriage

As this section highlights, the value now generally ascribed to sex reflects the emphasis on individual choice and control that characterises contemporary conceptions of selfhood. In other words, as I suggested at the start of the previous section, ideas and experiences of selfhood seem to have shaped the way this form of intimacy is understood. This suggestion appears even more plausible when the changing relationship between sex and marriage is considered. While these two forms of intimacy have historically been intertwined, across the modern period they have come to acquire independent (though overlapping) significance and, eventually, value. Crucially, just as the changes outlined in Section 1.3 have shaped legal responses to inducing intimacy, the changes outlined in this section have, I argue, been similarly consequential for law.

1.4 Sex and Marriage

The idea that sex and marriage might be related but unevenly valued is part of a distinctively 'Western tradition' that bears the imprint of Christian thinking and reform. In other cultural settings, the notion that sexual desire and romantic love are in tension, with the latter acting to tame the former, did not take root; instead, sex was celebrated in and of itself and thought capable of creating powerful, even spiritual, connections between humans.[87] According to beliefs that dominated in the 'West', however, marriage – ideally marriage based on love – for a long time constituted the sole context within which sex was considered permissible or even civilised. It also provided the institutional setting through which sex could purportedly be rendered benign.[88]

Since any effort to contain sexual desire within the confines of marriage necessarily acknowledges the existence (and threat) of sex outside marriage there is an important sense in which sex and marriage have always had independent significance, even according to the peculiarly Christian ethic that has prioritised marriage. What is significant about the modern period is the way sex has become associated with a potentially freestanding cultural artefact, that is, sexuality, and accordingly valued more positively both within and outside marriage. Temporally speaking, sexuality – the idea that sexual desire and pleasure is rooted in a constitutive feature of human personality – and the closely related concept of sexual identity, which refers to the way we define ourselves by reference to sexuality, are generally considered to have gained prominence throughout the nineteenth century and come most fully to the fore during the early twentieth century.[89] At this time, this new aspect of personhood could at least in principle be decoupled from phenomena like eroticism, intimacy and love, with which sex was traditionally associated,[90] and valued discretely on independent grounds.[91]

That said, the emergence of the concept of sexuality did not, at least in the early stages, coincide neatly with any significant move towards what might now be called sex positivism.[92] Instead, the late Victorian era is notable for

---

[87] William M. Reddy, *The Making of Romantic Love: Longing and Sexuality in Europe, South Asia and Japan, 900–1200 CE* (Chicago: University of Chicago Press, 2012), ch. 1, discussing sexual practices in South Asian and Japanese regions, and Joseph E. David, *Kinship, Law and Politics: An Anatomy of Belonging* (Cambridge: Cambridge University Press, 2020), p. 28, discussing sacramental and trans-substantive interpretations of corporeal union.
[88] Coontz, *Marriage, A History*, p. 9; Cheadle, *Sexual Progressives*, pp. 15, 22; Pat Moloney, 'Savages in the Scottish Enlightenment's History of Desire' (2005) 14(3) *Journal of the History of Sexuality* 237–265; Barclay, 'Marriage, Sex and the Church of Scotland'.
[89] David M. Halperin, 'Is There a History of Sexuality?' (1989) 28(3) *History and Theory* 257–274; Farmer, *Making the Modern Criminal Law*, p. 282.
[90] Halperin, 'History of Sexuality?', especially at 259.
[91] Timothy Willem Jones and Alana Harris, 'Introduction: Historicizing "Modern" Love and Romance' in Alana Harris and Timothy Jones (eds.), *Love and Romance in Britain, 1918–1970* (London: Palgrave Macmillan, 2015), pp. 1–19.
[92] Leigh Ann Wheeler, 'Inventing Sexuality: Ideologies, Identities and Practices in the Gilded Age and Progressive Era' in Christopher McKnight Nichols and Nancy C. Unger (eds.), *A Companion to the Gilded Age and Progressive Era* (Chichester: Wiley-Blackwell, 2017), pp. 102–115.

the social purity movements which, among other things, were directed at more tightly regulating sex so as to protect women and girls from exploitation.[93] Furthermore, despite changes in marriage expectations, marital sex essentially remained the only culturally valued form of sex until well into the twentieth century. Even in the face of growing egalitarian relationship ideals, increased sex education and greater availability of contraceptives, any new, more positive attitudes to sex were confined to its role within marriage until the 1970s when non-marital heterosexual sex (of some kinds) started to enjoy some mainstream esteem.[94] Since this time, although there have been many important changes in attitudes towards sex it would be fair to say that by and large the value now ascribed to sex is in many ways a function of the value that is ascribed to ideals of autonomy and individual liberty more generally.[95] The desire to discipline certain forms of sex has therefore certainly not abated.[96] Instead, in line with changing expectations of intimate relationships, marriage no longer exerts the same disciplinary force it once did[97] and it cannot provide a normatively compelling framework for other areas of law, either.

In Part II, I argue that for much of the last three centuries civil and criminal law responses to deceptively induced sex, from seduction to procurement offences and eventually rape, have been given form and substance by the way marriage was prioritised, and exerted power over, sex. The widespread disapproval of extra-marital sex, and the potential damage caused by engaging in sex of this kind, provided one basis on which to limit the range of deceptions that would be held by law to compromise sexual consent. It also shaped interpretations of what made deceptive sex wrongful and injurious. Though the relevant legal responses migrated from the civil into the criminal law sphere, the only substantive innovation in this framework was that the law expanded to take account of certain deceptions that occurred within relations of trust or authority. But rather than reflecting the importance of sexual choice per se, I would suggest that these expansions are better understood as part of the late nineteenth-century protectionist impulse and worries about the reputations of the established professions. It is only since the last couple of decades of the twentieth century, when sex (of certain kinds) has become valued in and of

---

[93] Lesley A. Hall, *Sex, Gender and Social Change in Britain since 1800*, 2nd ed. (Basingstoke: Palgrave Macmillan, 2012), ch. 2; Cheadle, *Sexual Progressives*, p. 99.

[94] Langhamer, 'Love, Selfhood and Authenticity'; Hall, *Sex, Gender and Social Change*, chs. 6–8, 10; Cheadle, *Sexual Progressives*, pp. 178–204; Roger Davidson, *Illicit and Unnatural Practices: The Law, Sex and Society in Scotland since 1900* (Edinburgh: Edinburgh University Press, 2018), p. 165.

[95] Pamela Haag, *Consent: Sexual Rights and the Transformation of American Liberalism* (Ithaca, NY: Cornell University Press, 1999); Cohen, *Regulating Intimacy*.

[96] For a critique, see Chloë Taylor, *Foucault, Feminism, and Sex Crimes: An Anti-Carceral Analysis* (New York: Routledge, 2019). More generally, there is a large and growing literature engaging critically with carceral and governance feminism.

[97] Though, as Murray has argued, marriage's disciplinary power has been widely internalised (Murray, 'Marriage as Punishment', sections IV and V).

itself, that the range of deceptions that might invalidate consent to sex has grown and the scope of the law has become potentially vast.

There are two facets of these developments I want to draw out before moving on to Section 1.5. The first is that, in their differing ways, both sets of legal responses to inducing intimacy – those that focus on sex and those that focus on intimate relationships – now largely embody what I described earlier as the ideal of autonomy. Both aim to protect a conception of freedom that is maximally self-determining, and thus protect unconstrained choice, but while this has mostly worked to curb legal responses in the context of intimate relationships, it has had the opposite effect in the context of sex. This makes sense in light of the account I've offered here; while in the context of intimate relationships, the ideal of autonomy provides some reasons to resist efforts to use law to protect against untrustworthy conduct, especially where this makes the easy dissolution of these relationships more difficult, in the context of sex there are fewer, if any, such concomitant reasons.

But just as we should think critically about the expansion of legal responses to deceptively inducing sex, we should think critically about the retraction of responses to deceptively inducing intimate relationships. The historical disentanglement of sex from marriage is a significant and, in my opinion, mostly welcome development, but there is a risk that it has led us to, as Rachel Fraser puts it, 'confuse[] sex with intimacy, and project[] anxieties proper to the latter onto the former'.[98] Certainly, while calls to impose liability for lying or catfishing (creating and adopting an entirely false persona) on dating apps often focus on the sexual 'gains' secured by these deceptions, they are also interpolated with references to the damage the relationship itself can cause.[99] This might suggest a reduced emphasis on legal responses that focus on sex, but it might also suggest a modest expansion in legal responses that focus on intimate relationships. In concluding this chapter, I want to introduce the final set of overarching concerns which, drawing on the genealogy offered in this book, should be factored in when considering these suggestions. These concerns stem from three senses of public and private.

1.5 Public(s) and Private(s)

Like the other concepts introduced in this chapter, and the cultural trajectories I have outlined, the three senses of public and private I set out in this section underpin the expository and evaluative aims of this book. They do this by providing a lens through which to analyse the historical developments I consider and

---

[98] Rachel Elizabeth Fraser, 'The Erotics of ASMR', *The Oxonian Review*, 8 May 2020.
[99] For example, Adam Lusher, 'MPs Urged to Pass Law against Online "Catfish" Imposters Tricking Women into Sex', *The Independent*, 17 July 2017; Irina D. Manta, 'Tinder Lies' (2019) 54(1) *Wake Forest Law Review* 207–249. This is also clear in the testimony of women who were tricked into sexual and romantic relationships with undercover police officers (https://policespiesoutoflives.org.uk/our-stories).

to engage critically with the contemporary developments I discuss. Two of the senses of public and private are nested within the first, which refers to public (that is, state) and private (that is, non-state) responses to inducing intimacy.[100] The second sense of public and private refers to kinds of interest protected by the state, distinguishing between public (that is, collective) and private (that is, individual) interests. The final sense of public and private refers to kinds of state response and distinguishes between public law (that is, criminal or regulatory law) and private law (that is, civil law) responses.

Since the focus of this book is legal responses to inducing intimacy, it might not be obvious how the first sense of public and private is relevant. One answer is that some of the legal actions featured in this book came into existence and/or disappeared across the modern period, and it is important to try to understand why. As the early development of breach of promise of marriage illustrates, the existence (actual or potential) of extra-legal norms might at certain points in time suggest that legal intervention is unnecessary because these other forms of pressure could be equal, or superior, deterrents.[101] By contrast, legal intervention might seem inappropriate in light of the feeling that collective censure of any kind of would be inappropriate, as was the case when breach of promise of marriage actions were abolished. Though both periods of scepticism reflected worries about encroachment of the public into the private (and vice versa), these worries had quite distinct bases.

The second form of anxiety over encroachment – that legal or perhaps any form of collective censure is inappropriate – points to the other way this first sense of public and private is relevant to this book. As I mentioned at the start of this chapter, a key question in current debates about deceptive sex is whether it is appropriate for legal responses to extend into the potentially wide array of deceptions that occur within 'ordinary' relationships. If, as I have suggested, there is normative force to the longstanding practice of using law to secure certain expectations of trust, which reflect the link between selfhood and intimacy, in this context then it is hard to resist the conclusion that some expansion of this kind is not only predictable but also potentially legitimate. In fact, as I have suggested it might be that some expansion in the realm of intimate relationships is also predictable and potentially legitimate. This does not mean that any legal response must, or should, be as wide ranging as possible, however.

To see why a narrower approach might be desirable, it is helpful to consider the second and third senses of public and private. Thinking about the type of interests protected by law, it is clear that legal responses to inducing intimacy have historically aimed to protect both private (individual) and public (collective) interests. A number of these responses have bolstered the legal and social institution of

---

[100] On the public/private distinction as a communicative phenomenon that establishes fractal distinctions, see Susan Gal, 'A Semiotics of the Private/Public Distinction' (2002) 13(1) *Differences: A Journal of Feminist Cultural Studies* 77–95.

[101] For a discussion of the relationship between individual pressure and social and legal norms, see Dan Threet, 'Mill's Social Pressure Puzzle' (2018) 44(4) *Social Theory and Practice* 539–565.

1.5 Public(s) and Private(s)

marriage at the same time as they protected individuals' reputational and emotional interests, as shaped by this institution. On one level, this is not surprising; though it is now common to think of institutions as facilitating independently conceived ends, they also condition the way we act and make decisions.[102] Recent legal developments in the realm of inducing intimacy tend not to reflect this point, though. If these moves indicate a concern with any collective interest, it is something like the aggregate of each person's individual interest in unconstrained choice.[103] As such, this collective interest has no substantive content that can structure, and constrain, any legal response that serves to protect it.[104]

This development gives rise to particular problems when the legal response in question is some form of public law, such as criminal law. Historically, criminal punishment was usually considered appropriate when the conduct in question was perceived to threaten society or some shared, as opposed to aggregated, interest. This attitude is clearly present in nineteenth-century attempts to criminalise seduction, which I discuss in Chapters 5 and 6. When making their case, advocates of criminalisation couched their pleas in concerns about unmarried mothers, whose abandonment gave rise to social and moral problems, and prostitution, the existence of which posed a perceived threat to both health and morals. And while it is now more commonly accepted that individual interests might legitimately be protected by the criminal law,[105] I would suggest that the situation is different when that interest is effectively untethered from any substantive shared interest, or at least a substantive shared value or social form, that might help give it shape.[106]

There are three difficulties that flow from this situation I want to introduce here, which arise even if a criminal law response is otherwise considered justifiable. The first relates to the fairly uncontroversial desire for prospective clarity regarding the scope of the criminal law. If the range of deceptions that might ground a criminal conviction turns on nothing more than the beliefs of each particular complainant and how, according that complainant, those beliefs were relevant to their decision-making then this prospective clarity is difficult to achieve.[107] The second difficulty relates to the fact that public laws, including

---

[102] Barbara Herman, 'Could It Be Worth Thinking about Kant on Sex and Marriage?' in Louise M. Antony and Charlotte Witt (eds.), *A Mind of One's Own: Feminist Essays on Reason and Objectivity* (Oxford: Westview Press, 1993), p. 59.

[103] On rights individualism and the collapse of a public realm standing above self-interest, see Morton J. Horwitz, 'The History of the Public/Private Distinction' (1982) 130(6) *University of Pennsylvania Law Review* 1423–1428. On liberal conceptions of freedom and the scope of criminal punishment, see Henrique Carvalho, *The Preventive Turn in Criminal Law* (Oxford: Oxford University Press, 2017).

[104] I discuss these points further in Chapter 8.

[105] Farmer, *Making the Modern Criminal Law*, ch. 1, critically analysing this perspective.

[106] On valuing choice with reference to collective values and social forms, see Raz, *The Morality of Freedom*, chs. 14 and 15.

[107] For a critique of some laws that punish the infliction of emotional distress along these lines, see Avlana K. Eisenberg, 'Criminal Infliction of Emotional Distress' (2015) 113 (5) *Michigan Law Review* 607–662.

criminal law, typically focus on the conduct of the defendant and, in contrast to private law, do not always require injury (even if injuries are sometimes presumed in private law).[108] Finally, though complainants' reactions to having experienced a crime are important they are not usually considered determinative; hence, criminal prosecutions are at least purportedly carried out in the public interest and often undertaken by public prosecutors.[109] These points suggest that if it were possible to identify deceptions that could plausibly be described as wrongful and likely to cause harm, there might be at least prima facie good reasons to endorse their criminalisation, and perhaps prosecution, irrespective of particular complainants' experience of being subject to them.[110] Focusing solely on individual, unconstrained choice cannot facilitate the process of identifying such deceptions.

In Chapter 8, I pick up each of these points and suggest that one way they might be addressed is by developing a new framework through which these deceptions might be identified. Building on the insight that sex and intimate relationships both tend to matter in self-constructing terms, I argue that such a framework could and should rest on a contemporary, constructivist account of the links between these forms of intimacy and selfhood. This would provide what Sarah Buss describes as 'a story about why being manipulated and/or deceived is … incompatible with something it makes sense to call "treating autonomous agency with respect"'.[111] As Buss points out, this story is not provided by the concept of bare autonomy. The ideal of autonomy – that unconstrained choice is valuable – cannot in and of itself account for why deciding for oneself is important or make sense of how and why the intuition that it *is* important might need to be cashed out differently in disparate contexts. As I have gestured towards in this section, when this ideal is encoded in law it has the added downside of creating practical problems, too.

In rejecting the ideal of autonomy, the framework I develop embodies something closer to the ideal of authenticity outlined earlier in this chapter. Putting this framework to use in identifying which deceptions should qualify as legally salient therefore involves exploring which sorts of external referents, including social institutions and interpersonal relationships, tend to matter

---

[108] Goldberg and Zipursky, *Recognizing Wrongs*, ch. 6.
[109] Of course, the criminal justice process could be amended (see Duff, 'Torts, Crimes and Vindication'), but this would require taking these points into account. For a critical assessment of restorative justice in practice, see William R. Wood and Masahiro Suzuki, 'Are Conflicts Property? Re-Examining the Ownership of Conflict in Restorative Justice' (2020) 29(6) *Social & Legal Studies* 903–924.
[110] This is similar to the way the Domestic Abuse (Scotland) Act 2018 does not require that the complainer actually experience any of the negative effects outlined in the legislation. See also Gardner and Shute's influential argument that rape should be punished even when it is not harmful in particular cases; see John Gardner and Stephen Shute, 'The Wrongness of Rape' in Jeremy Horder (ed.), *Oxford Essays in Jurisprudence: Fourth Series* (Oxford: Oxford University Press, 2000), pp. 193–218.
[111] Sarah Buss, 'Valuing Autonomy and Respecting Persons: Manipulation, Seduction, and the Basis of Moral Constraints' (2005) 115(2) *Ethics* 195–235 at 207.

in self-constructing terms and when and how they feature in the practices of inducing intimacy. While this provides a general (contestable and revisable) list of deceptions, the framework leaves space for more idiosyncratic deceptions to qualify when their significance has been expressly communicated by one party to the other in advance. This dual approach draws on contemporary accounts and experiences of selfhood by centring the importance of deciding in accordance with one's own values while at the same time recognising the crucial role that culturally sensitive social institutions play in shaping these values. In doing so, it provides a richer account of how selfhood and intimacy are connected and shows how this account can help set the parameters of potentially punitive state responses to the practices of inducing intimacy.

Part I
Marriage

2

Making Marriage

2.1 Scope and Themes

The aim of this chapter is to explore the different ways in which deception, broadly understood, has affected the existence or validity of marital consent (or consent to a civil partnership).[1] The core focus of the discussion is therefore which deceptions have been considered, or suggested to be, legally significant – that is, capable of rendering a purported marriage null – and Sections 2.2–2.7 are organised around the subject matter of these deceptions, categorised by type.[2] In addition to analysing these deceptions by subject matter, this chapter outlines how deception has precluded or vitiated marital consent (and hence made the marriage null) by explaining how misrepresentation, non-disclosure, mistake and ignorance have featured in legal decisions and to what effect.

The fact that the chapter focuses on deception means that I do not discuss impediments to marriage where no element of deception is involved. For example, I do not explore how a purported marriage contracted by someone underage would be void because I have not located cases or commentary concerning deception about the existence of this impediment. Where I have found cases involving an impediment that would make a marriage void in the absence of the deception, such as a prior existing marriage, which *do* feature deception, I concentrate on the difference deception makes. More specifically, I consider how a claim or award of damages would often accompany a declarator of nullity in such cases, providing recognition of the additional harm to the pursuer and/or culpability of the defender.[3] Although nullity of marriage is the area of law most relevant to this chapter, I touch on a few other areas that raise similar issues, namely the torts of deceit (in England) and intentional infliction of emotional distress (in the United States) and the

---

[1] The historically informed nature of this book means that marriage dominates the discussion.
[2] Deception about marital intentions is discussed in Chapter 4 and Part II.
[3] Even when damages were not awarded, declarators of nullity could perform quasi-punitive functions, as two articles from the 1860s which refer to the remedy as a 'penalty' illustrate; see 'The Scotch Marriage Law', *The Glasgow Herald*, 23 October 1863, p. 4 and 'Marriage and Divorce – The Law of England and Scotland' (1861) 35 *The North British Review* 187–218 at 190.

Scottish delict of fraud. I also consider the English law relating to the division of assets when a marriage is null because questions of deception, culpability and harm have arisen in this context too.[4]

Thematically, there are three main points that come through the analysis offered in this chapter. The first is the way that the distinction between void and voidable marriages – marriages that are considered invalid from their inception and marriages that are considered valid and subsisting until a decree annulling them is pronounced, respectively[5] – relates to other legal issues, that is, title to sue and personal bar (and related doctrines). Generally speaking, anyone with an interest in annulling a void marriage can seek to do so but the option of annulling a voidable marriage is reserved to the parties to the marriage. Again speaking generally, personal bar and the doctrines of ratification, insincerity, homologation and approbation – doctrines that can apply to the ability of a party to a marriage to endorse or approve it – are available in relation to voidable but not void marriages.[6] I reflect on the significance of these points in Section 2.8, where I suggest that voidable marriages represent the 'private' side of marriage, and further in Chapter 8, where I discuss the different ways that deception affects consent – rendering it absent or impaired – and the relationship this distinction has to public and private law responses to inducing intimacy.

The second theme is the association(s) between the subject matter of deception and changing ideas about what makes marriage valuable and distinctive. The argument, developed across the rest of the chapter, is that substantive, and often gendered, visions of the meaning and purpose of marriage have shaped, and historically constrained, the range of deceptions that could affect the existence or validity of marital consent. As per the discussion in Chapter 1, I suggest that the significance of marital status for women, particularly women with children, helps explain the individual and collective interests that have been at stake in this area of law historically but that it is possible to detect a more recent shift towards a greater concern for individual choice and transparency in intimate relationships. Other considerations, notably the question

---

[4] Historically, Scots law did not extend the financial consequences of divorce to cases of annulment on the basis that the marriage, if void, never existed; see John C. Gardner, 'A Comparison of the Effects of Decree of Nullity of Marriage in Scotland and England' (1938) *Scots Law Times* 109–110. This is no longer the case; see Family Law (Scotland) Act 1985, s. 17.

[5] D. Tolstoy, 'Void and Voidable Marriages' (1964) 27(4) *Modern Law Review* 385–394; Paul J. Goda, 'The Historical Evolution of the Concepts of Void and Voidable Marriages' (1967) 7 *Journal of Family Law* 297–308. Scots law does not have as many categories of voidable marriage as other jurisdictions; for some reflections on this, see Clive, *Husband and Wife*, Paragraph 01.025 and ch. 7.

[6] For a summary of some aspects of these points in relation to Scots law, see Clive, *Husband and Wife*, ch. 7. On insincerity, an English law term, see *The Church and the Law of Nullity of Marriage: The Report of a Commission Appointed by the Archbishops of Canterbury and York in 1949 at the Request of the Convocations* (London: SPCK, 1955), pp. 19–20. On ratification and approbation in English law, see Law Commission, *Report on Nullity of Marriage* (Her Majesty's Stationery Office, 1970), Paragraphs 11–13.

of what might be called responsibility for knowledge – both the responsibility of the party privy to the relevant information (do they have a duty to share it?) and responsibility of the party who is mistaken or ignorant (are they expected to check?) – have been significant in determining the scope of the law, too.[7] Importantly, these two points are related: the knowledge responsibilities of parties to a marriage are partially undergirded by particular visions of what marriage entails and requires. As such, this chapter aims to show that the relationship between shifts in the meaning of marriage (and anxieties about its significance), as outlined in Chapter 1 but fleshed out in more detail later in this chapter, are capable of being loosely mapped on to a range of changes in the law regarding marital consent and deception.

Finally, this chapter considers the relative prominence of nullity vis-à-vis divorce. Although divorce is not relevant to this book per se, there is a perception that nullity has become largely redundant due to the liberalisation of divorce. Though I do not attempt to offer any substantial commentary on developments concerning divorce, in Section 2.8 I reflect on how the desire for legal recognition of the wrongs and harms associated with deceptively induced intimate relationships has not necessarily abated and note how the liberalisation of divorce might even have enhanced the contemporary relevance of nullity actions. In doing so, I raise questions about whether and how these changes have ramifications for contemporary discussions about how we might use law to respond to deceptively induced intimate relationships, which can no longer easily be confined to marriage or civil partnership.

2.2 Marital Status and Marriage Ceremony or Effects

For centuries, a monogamous conception of marriage has dominated 'Western' societies,[8] and, as such, the existence of a prior, subsisting marriage has been, and still is, an impediment to the formation of any subsequent marriage (and now civil partnership).[9] Irrespective of the parties' knowledge of the impediment, the marriage would be void and, depending on the circumstances, the crime of bigamy might have been committed.[10] Some elements of this offence

---

[7] On how these dynamics played out in a different legal context, see Michelle A. McKinley, *Fractional Freedoms: Slavery, Intimacy, and Legal Mobilization in Colonial Lima, 1600–1700* (New York: Cambridge University Press, 2016), pp. 130–133.

[8] John Witte Jr, *The Western Case for Monogamy over Polygamy* (Cambridge: Cambridge University Press, 2015).

[9] For example, Marriage (Scotland) Act 1977, s. 5(4) (making clear that an existing marriage between the parties who wish to enter a civil partnership will not make the marriage void); Matrimonial Causes Act 1973, s. 11(b); Civil Partnership Act 2004, ss. 3(1)(b) and 86(1)(d).

[10] Fraser, *Husband and Wife*, p. 137; Clive, *Husband and Wife*, Paragraph 07.012. Bigamy is discussed in Chapter 4. Other crimes might be relevant, too. Historically, these included making a false declaration relating to the marriage register or the statutory requirements for marriage, for example, Registration of Births, Deaths and Marriages (Scotland) Act 1854, s. 60; Marriage Notice (Scotland) Act 1878, s. 14; Perjury Act 1911, s. 3 (which does not extend to Scotland or Ireland); Marriage (Scotland) Act 1916, s. 2.

might be missing or insufficiently evidenced, though,[11] so in cases where only one party knew of the subsisting marriage criminal proceedings would not necessarily provide legal recognition of the wrong done to the ignorant or mistaken spouse. Crucially, since the marriage was void, women (and it was most often women) who might have wished to retain the marital status they thought they held, despite the deception, did not have that option. The deceptive spouse would not even be barred by his fraud from seeking a declarator of nullity.[12]

In such circumstances, judges have historically recognised the harm done to the innocent 'spouse' by awarding them damages alongside a decree of nullity and the children of marriages contracted in good faith (either bilateral or unilateral) would also be legitimate, at least by the later nineteenth century.[13] To be clear, I do not want to suggest there was a relationship between the award of damages and the absence of criminal prosecution; more comprehensive work on bigamy would have to be done to investigate this.[14] Rather, I want to draw attention to an important mechanism for recognising the wrongs done, and harms caused, by duplicitous 'spouses' that existed apart from criminal prosecution.

In principle, damages could be awarded or sought whenever a person lied about, or failed to disclose, *any* impediment to a marriage they purported to contract.[15] In practice, however, the only examples I have found relate to prior subsisting marriages,[16] wealth and position[17] and impotence.[18] Textbooks and

---

[11] The tendency in general parlance to conflate marriages void due to prior subsisting marriage and bigamy was noted in *Mendal v. Mendal* [2007] EWCA Civ 437 (at Paragraph 22).

[12] Fraser, *Husband and Wife*, p. 137; Clive, *Husband and Wife*, Paragraph 07.012 cf. Chapter 4 and the discussion of personal bar there. A void marriage is null with or without a court decree, but a decree is often desirable for practical reasons (Clive, *Husband and Wife*, Paragraph 07.004).

[13] Walton, *Husband and Wife*, p. 13; *Steele v. Steele* ('Court of Session', *The Glasgow Herald*, 4 November 1893, p. 4); *Adams v. Adams* ('Court of Session', *The Glasgow Herald*, 19 December 1895, p. 4); *Petrie v. Ross* ('Court of Session', *The Glasgow Herald*, 10 June 1896, p. 9).

[14] In at least one case, a judge who awarded damages along with a declarator of nullity mentioned his intention to pass the papers to Crown Office (the public prosecution service); see *Burke v. Burke* 1983 SLT 331. There are Canadian cases where plaintiffs have sued for the tort of deceit in similar circumstances – these, and the potential for both criminal and civil liability in this context, are discussed in John Murphy, 'Misleading Appearances in the Tort of Deceit' (2016) 75(2) *The Cambridge Law Journal* 301–322.

[15] Clive, *Husband and Wife*, Paragraph 07.076.

[16] *Clark v. Fairweather* (1727) (F. P. Walton (ed.), *Lord Hermand's Consistorial Decisions, 1684–1777* (Edinburgh: The Stair Society, 1940), p. 68); *Morison v. Dunlop* (1756) (Walton (ed.), *Consistorial Decisions*, pp. 93–95); *Ramage v. Mackintosh* (1811) NRS CC8/6/1452; *McCormack v. Shrimpton* (1840) NRS CS46/1840/3/1; *Mackenzie v. Macfarlane* (1889) NRS CS241/2527; *Imrie v. Imrie* ('Court of Session', *The Scotsman*, 21 October 1903, p. 7); *Polack v. Shiels* 1912 2 SLT 329; *Burke v. Burke* (1983).

[17] *Jamieson v. Jeffrey* (1783) NRS CC8/6/684. As discussed in Section 2.4, the attempt to annul the marriage on this basis was unsuccessful.

[18] *Paterson v. Cumming* (1815) NRS CC/8/6/1572 (though the ground of the action was impotence, the pursuer sought damages and solatium on the basis of the injury she suffered by his 'improper and deceitful conduct', which may refer to her presumption that he was not impotent and/or his pretending to be wealthy); *Young v. Young* (1892) NRS CS46/1892/5/86; *Duguid v. Duguid* (1909) NRS CS256/176. Impotence is discussed in Section 2.6.

treatises typically concentrated on the first category, referring, for example, to the right of a 'woman entrapped into a marriage with a man already married' to damages as 'reparation for the grievous injury she sustained'.[19] Within the cases, different features of the interactions between the parties are stressed, from misrepresentation by the already-married 'spouse', sometimes accompanied by an especially clear intention to dupe their partner, to the false belief or assumption on the part of the innocent 'spouse' that their partner was free to marry in the absence of information to the contrary.

As for the nature or basis of the damages, these were sometimes awarded simply for the entrapment of the pursuer into a void marriage.[20] In one case, however, the damages were awarded for the 'deep injuries done to her [the pursuer's] person and feelings'.[21] In line with this reference to injured feelings, the damages sought or awarded were sometimes accompanied by a claim for, or award of, solatium.[22] Though the meaning of solatium is not always clear, it can be described as money awarded separately from 'damages claimable from actual loss', which is given as a 'rude attempt to soften ... the loss represented by the grief and anguish naturally arising from the wrongful proceedings on which the action is founded'.[23] Put differently, solatium might be awarded in the absence of pecuniary loss or physical and what we would now call psychiatric injuries.[24]

Of course, multiple injuries and/or losses could coexist in a single case, such as in the most recent case of this genre I have found, from 1983.[25] The case is notable for the fact that the defender tried to argue that the amount of damages should be reduced because of the pursuer's 'contributory negligence', that is, her failure to realise that he was still married. His somewhat audacious claim was that the pursuer should have realised the truth, even though he told her (and her mother) that he had divorced his wife and remained living with her for the sake of their children. The judge rejected this argument and, in awarding damages and solatium, explained that these remedies were given for the entrapment, the pursuer's distress on learning the truth and her belief that her marriage prospects were adversely affected by having a young child with the defender.[26]

---

[19] Fraser, *Personal and Domestic Relations*, p. 82.
[20] *Clark* v. *Fairweather* (1727); *Paterson* v. *Cumming* (1815) (an impotence case); *Mackenzie* v. *Macfarlane* (1889).
[21] *McCormack* v. *Shrimpton* (1840).
[22] Ibid.; *Mackenzie* v. *Macfarlane* (1889).
[23] John Guthrie Smith, *A Treatise on the Law of Reparation* (Edinburgh: T. & T. Clark, 1864), p. 10.
[24] A modern text describes solatium as having traditionally being considered 'compensation for wounded feelings (distinct from psychiatric injury)' but mentions an alternative theory, that is, that it might be compensation for the infringement of a right per se; see Whitty, 'Overview of Rights of Personality', Paragraph 3.5.2. For a short discussion of these points, and their relationship to criminal punishment, see Kennedy, 'Comparing Criminal and Civil Responsibility'.
[25] *Burke* v. *Burke* (1983).
[26] Ibid. at 334. On contributory negligence and the tort of deceit, see Murphy, 'Misleading Appearances', and on contributory negligence in the contemporary Scots law of delict, see Law Reform (Contributory Negligence) Act 1945.

This last point – that a woman's future might be damaged by an extra-marital pregnancy and birth – connects the wrong of entrapment into a void marriage with the delict of seduction. The action of seduction, discussed in Chapter 5, enabled a woman who had sex on a false promise of marriage to seek damages from her lover on the basis that she had been ruined, and pursuers in these cases fairly often had children with their seducers. In fact, the link between the two actions was drawn by one solicitor, who in 1830 suggested that higher damages would usually be awarded for the void marriage because a woman lured into a void marriage might be free of the 'blame' that would always to some extent attach to a woman who was merely seduced.[27] In other words, the bigamist who ruined the woman who thought she was his wife committed 'a double and peculiarly aggravated crime'[28]: he both tricked her into an 'immoral' sexual act and denied her the marital rights and status she thought she enjoyed.

This double association helps explain why it is not clear that damages for being tricked into a void marriage depended on purportedly marital sex having occurred. In at least one case, a woman sought a declarator of nullity and damages on the basis that she had entered a 'pretended marriage through the false representations of the defender that he was a free man and capable of marrying her' while at the same time stressing that no 'carnal knowledge' had ever occurred.[29] One prominent jurist even suggested that a person duped into a void marriage by an already-married 'spouse' should receive patrimonial rights as if the impediment did not exist.[30] As noted earlier, however, this was not the generally accepted position in Scots law and the argument did not receive judicial approval when made in court.[31] Nevertheless, the suggestion clearly signalled that the wrong was as much about deceiving a woman about her marital

---

[27] Lothian, *Consistorial Actions*, p. 185. It is important to note that this solicitor was writing before actions for seduction became common in Scotland (see Chapter 5, where the 'culpability' of seduced women is also discussed).

[28] Ibid.   [29] *Ramage* v. *Mackintosh* (1811).

[30] Walton, *Husband and Wife*, p. 13, referring to the views of the judge and jurist Patrick Fraser, who eventually became a lord of session (Hector L. MacQueen, 'Fraser, Patrick, Lord Fraser (1817–1889), jurist and judge', *Oxford Dictionary of National Biography* (2004), www-oxforddnb-com.ezproxy.is.ed.ac.uk/view/10.1093/ref:odnb/9780198614128.001.0001/odnb-9780198614128-e-10119).

[31] *Wright* v. *Sharp* (1880) 17 SLR 293. The court held that even if the rule were correct, it would not apply in a case involving a small sum of money. It appears a 'spouse' ignorant of a prior subsisting marriage could sue for damages under the English tort of deceit, at least until the early twentieth century. A statement to this effect appears in the 1909 edition of Courtney Stanhope Kenny's *Outlines of Criminal Law* (Cambridge: Cambridge University Press, 1909) but not in subsequent editions. The change might be explained by the fact that the power to award permanent maintenance following a decree of nullity was introduced in 1907; see Matrimonial Causes Act 1907, s. 1. If the 'spouse' had died, the 'widow' might historically have been able to obtain economic relief via a claim of breach of promise of marriage; see Susie Steinbach, *Promises, Promises: Not Marrying in England 1780–1920* (PhD dissertation, Yale University Proquest Dissertations Publishing, 1996), www.proquest.com/dissertations-theses/promises-not-marrying-england-1780-1920/docview/304306821/se-2, pp. 5, 16.

status as it was about effecting her sexual ruin. In this sense, the suggestion gelled with a judgment delivered earlier in the century, according to which a woman was due aliment for having falsely been led by the defender to believe that she was his wife.[32]

Assuming both parties were free to marry, a marriage might nevertheless be void due to deception about the nature of the ceremony. I have not found many cases like this, but they might arise where, for example, someone mistakenly believed that they were undergoing a betrothal, rather than marriage ceremony.[33] Annulling a marriage due to such a fundamental error has not generated much controversy, and contemporary legislation provides that errors about the nature of the ceremony or relationship make a marriage or civil partnership void.[34] Cases involving deception as to the *effect* of the marriage have proved more controversial. Though deceptions of this kind have not typically rendered a marriage void, there has been at least one exception. *Lendrum* v. *Chakravarti*[35] involved a young woman who married an Indian man, knowing that he intended to return to India, with her, after the marriage. After moving to India and spending an unhappy time there, the young woman returned to Scotland and sought to annul their marriage. The grounds of her claim were that she had been induced to give a 'pretended consent' by 'false and fraudulent representations and personation'. More specifically, she argued that the defender had led her to believe that, as a Brahmo, he was entitled to marry her and that she would become 'his proper wedded wife'. In reality, the marriage appeared (the judge agreed) to be invalid in 'British India', although it was valid in Scotland and likely elsewhere.

The judge rejected the argument based on personation, holding that this required a person to 'disguise himself as another'.[36] The judge also rejected the argument about false representations concerning the defender's ability to marry and the pursuer's status following the marriage. One reason for this outcome was that the pursuer had not made out her claim of fraud, having failed to prove the falsity of the defender's assertions regarding his faith or her reliance on them. She had also not ruled out the possibility that he had innocently misunderstood the law governing marriage. More importantly, the judge held that fraud would not set aside a contract of marriage where 'valid consent' had

---

[32] The decision to award aliment was ultimately overruled, but this outcome seems to be partly attributable to badly drawn arguments, which suggested that the pursuer's complaint was that the defender had tricked *the world*, rather than her, into thinking they were married; see *Campbell* v. *Sassen* (1826) 2 W & S 309; *Sassen* v. *Campbell* (1824) General Collection, Paper 114.
[33] For example, 'Didn't Know She Was Being Married', *Dundee Courier*, 28 May 1921, p. 5 (the Lord Chancellor (the case concerned a marriage contracted in Cape Town) disbelieved the pursuer, who said that her husband had induced her to sign a document which she understood to relate to engagement only). There are more examples drawn from English law in Law Commission, *Report on Nullity of Marriage*, Paragraph 62 and Joseph Jackson, 'Consent of the Parties to Their Marriage' (1951) 14(1) *Modern Law Review* 1–26.
[34] Marriage (Scotland) Act 1977, s. 20A(5)(a); Civil Partnership Act 2004, s. 123(2)(a).
[35] 1929 SLT 96.
[36] Ibid. at 100. Impersonation is discussed in Section 2.3.

been given. In other words, he held that fraud per se did not preclude marital consent and that the option to reduce a marriage contract, which would exist in other contractual contexts, did not exist.[37] Ultimately, the judge did find for the pursuer but on the bases of error on her part, induced by the defender,[38] and a want of *consensus in idem* (meeting of the minds). Although the pursuer had been warned her marriage might be invalid in India, the judge concluded that she had honestly (and mistakenly) believed that the contract would be valid. He also held that the defender was presumed in law to know the law of his own country; so though he had not necessarily acted fraudulently, he was deemed to know that the marriage would be invalid.

The case attracted criticism for what it implied – that an innocently induced error about the validity of a marriage in another jurisdiction would render an otherwise valid marriage null if the parties happened to go and to live there[39] – and, less than a decade later, the judgment was not followed in the very similar case of *MacDougall* v. *Chitnavis*.[40] The pursuer in this case had also married an Indian man and then moved to India with her husband and their baby. On arrival, the defender's family refused to recognise the pursuer as his wife and tried to convert her to Hinduism. When she refused, marital relations effectively ceased. Mirroring the arguments offered in *Lendrum* v. *Chakravarti*, the pursuer sought to annul her marriage on two grounds. The first ground was that the 'only consent given by her was to a marriage which would confer on her the status of the lawful wife' and since the 'pretended marriage did not do so there was no *consensus in idem* and no real consent'.[41] Second, she argued that she had 'consented under essential error induced by the false and fraudulent misrepresentations of the defender'.[42] The second ground was not supported by the facts, and the first was rejected because, in the judge's view, it amounted to an attempt by the pursuer to set a condition on her marital consent, that is, that if she thought she would not be recognised as the defender's wife in India she would not have gone through the ceremony of marriage.[43] In the judge's opinion, consent to marriage was absolute and not conditional[44] so its validity could not turn on 'such a fortuitous circumstance as the determination to live in any particular country'.[45]

---

[37] This was at least partly down to the fact that Scots law did not unequivocally recognise a category of voidable marriage.

[38] This aspect of the judgment is a little confusing, given that the judge found that the pursuer had not relied on the defender's representations. It might be that the judge felt her mistake was caused by the defender's conduct but not his representations.

[39] 'Indian-Scottish Marriage Case', *The Scotsman*, 21 December 1928, p. 7.

[40] 1937 SLT 40.   [41] Ibid. at 40.

[42] Ibid. at 42. There was also a suggestion that the defender lacked capacity to marry the pursuer, but this is not relevant to the present discussion.

[43] Ibid. at 43.

[44] This was an old idea, mentioned by Stair, for example; see Stair; More, *Institutions* (vol. 1), p. 24.

[45] At 43. This was affirmed on appeal and *Lendrum* v. *Chakravarti* explicitly overruled; see *MacDougall* v. *Chitnavis* 1937 SC 390 at 402. When, in 1970, the Law Commission considered whether mistake as to effect of marriage should be capable of nullifying marriage, they

There are two features of these cases worth drawing out. The first is that they illustrate two of the ways that deception, broadly understood, might be considered to affect consent: (i) a mismatch between the object of consent as it exists in the mind of one party and as it exists in the mind of the other, or indeed as it exists in reality, might mean there is no consent in fact and potentially in law (ii) agreement that is obtained by fraud might constitute consent in fact but the circumstances render the consent impaired and potentially legally ineffectual.[46] Second, they illustrate the judicial practice of restricting the scope of marital consent so that even where the parties, or one of them, clearly imposed conditions on their consent, these conditions would not make any difference in law. The exclusion of these conditions was partly down to assumptions about what marriage entails and what marriage partners can reasonably expect from each other, that is, a legally valid if otherwise deeply undesired relationship. There is also a sense, however, that the nature of marriage – its status as a public institution with significant consequences – meant that the validity of marital consent could not turn on events that are matters of chance, such as coming to live in another country.

2.3 Personal Identity

Traditionally, mistake as to the identity of the person has been a basis on which to pronounce a marriage void.[47] Yet from the outset of the period of this study, the parameters of this rule were tightly drawn. Indeed, early texts state that the range of relevant impersonations was limited to persons known by the pursuer by 'sight, hearsay or reputation'.[48] Later texts draw the limits of legally significant impersonation slightly differently, stipulating that the mistake must have led one party to marry someone other than the person whom they had agreed to marry, and this remains the contemporary position, at least in Scotland.[49]

One reason for these restrictions is suggested by another feature of traditional accounts of the relationship between impersonation and marital consent, that is, the fact that supervening consent could render the marriage

---

concluded there was no way this could work – allowing courts to decide on a case-by-case basis would 'clearly go too far' and a test like 'fundamental' mistake was too vague to be practical; see Law Commission, *Report on Nullity of Marriage*, Paragraphs 67–68.

[46] These differences can be seen in relation to sexual consent in Part II.

[47] In this respect, and in some others, such as use of the concepts of essential error, implied conditions and *consensus in idem*, there are some similarities between the law of marriage and contract law more generally (on which, see William W. McBryde, *The Law of Contract in Scotland*, 3rd ed. (Edinburgh: W. Green & Sons, 2007)). The question of whether and to what extent marriage was, or is, regarded as a contract like any other is not within the scope of this book.

[48] John C. Barry (ed. & trans.), *William Hay's Lectures on Marriage* (Edinburgh: The Stair Society, 1967), p. 49. Without much explanation, this text suggests that if the impersonation was of someone unknown (including fictional, presumably) then, according to this view, the case should be classified as one of deception, rather than mistake (p. 51).

[49] For example, Paton, *Hume's Lectures*, p. 24. Marriage (Scotland) Act 1977, s. 20A(5)(b) – the same formulation applies to civil partnership; see Civil Partnership Act 2004, s. 123(2)(b).

valid, even though the mistake meant that the purported marriage was initially void.[50] In other words, if the mistaken party was happy to 'retain'[51] the spouse they were not expecting, this would mean the marriage was good. The potential to render such a marriage valid meant that it was possible to hold that a man should be prevented from annulling his marriage when matters were 'not entire' or, to use less coy language, when the parties had had sex. If sex had occurred, then a 'strong case of fraud' would have to be proved before a man could be rid of a woman about whose identity he had been mistaken.[52] This rule is reminiscent of the desire to encourage marriage, which is discussed in Chapter 4, and it coheres with the worries about sexual ruination expressed in the cases of prior subsisting marriage discussed earlier. Bolstering the need for a strong case of fraud, if the mistake arose from the fault or negligence of the man, then the marriage would likely stand. Again, the reasoning here is gendered and protectionist: 'by his failing to make due inquiry, an irreparable wrong would be committed if the marriage were annulled'.[53]

A more recent gloss on the restrictions regarding impersonation suggests that when the parties see one another frequently prior to marriage, physical identity alone matters. By this view, if a woman marries 'the man (viewed as a physical entity, a bag of living cells) with whom she went through the process of courtship and engagement she has no relief merely because she was in error as to his attributes, whether these be name, nationality, fortune, fame, character or anything else'.[54] Indeed, even if the couple had never met in person, so long as the 'bag of cells' behind the communications showed up to the wedding there would be no impersonation capable of voiding the marriage.[55] This perspective recognises the (perhaps unlikely) possibility that a genuine emotional connection might be forged despite wholesale identity deception,[56] but it discounts a number of reasons why people tend to fall in love with particular 'bags of cells' in the first place by ignoring the possibility that the attributes of a romantic partner might be highly relevant to that process (not to mention the attribute of honesty).[57]

It is therefore perhaps not surprising that courts have come to hear cases dealing with a wider array of deceptions about the self. Some of these are

---

[50] Stair speaks of this as ratification, and Hay speaks of it as consenting to the marriage after the true identity is discovered; see Stair; More, *Institutions* (vol. 2), p. 937; Barry, *Hay's Lectures*, p. 51; Paton, *Hume's Lectures*, p. 24. See also Clive, *Husband and Wife*, Paragraph 07.062.
[51] Stair; More, *Institutions* (vol. 1), p. 26. [52] Paton, *Hume's Lectures*, p. 24.
[53] Fraser, *Husband and Wife*, p. 233; Stair; More, *Institutions* (vol. 2), p. 937.
[54] Clive, *Husband and Wife*, Paragraph 07.034. [55] Ibid.
[56] The relationship between feigning external aspects of the self and feigning emotion arose in dramatic contexts, too; see William D. Brewer, *Staging Romantic Chameleons and Imposters* (New York: Palgrave Macmillan, 2015), pp. 64–69. Emotional authenticity is discussed in more detail in Chapters 3–5.
[57] Even in the modern era, having reasons for loving is recognised – these reasons do not necessarily imply the process of falling is fully voluntary or completely calculated; see Troy Jollimore, 'Love as "Something in Between"' in Grau and Smuts (eds.), *Oxford Handbook of Philosophy of Love*, pp. 149–166.

discussed in Sections 2.4–2.7, but here I consider a pair of cases which illustrate both the parameters of the law's conception of impersonation and the desire to expand these, as well as providing some insight into why this desire has been resisted. In the first case, *Wilson* v. *Horn*, a young woman with substantial pecuniary assets responded to a matrimonial advertisement in *The Scotsman* newspaper, which had purportedly been placed by a young English gentleman with a large country estate. In their communications, the defender claimed his name was Walter Erby Hamilton, that he was a man of independent means, that he had succeeded to a large estate from his deceased father and that his mother was a wealthy lady who was dying of cancer. When the couple met in person, he was staying in one of Aberdeen's finer hotels, he dressed well, and he acted like a gentleman, taking the pursuer to concerts and theatres. After about ten days, the defender proposed and the pursuer accepted, without having contacted her family. The couple were then married via a private ceremony (at the defender's suggestion) and lived together as husband and wife.[58] Unfortunately for the pursuer, it then became clear that the defender was actually Walter Horn, an absconding bankrupt of low station who had recently attempted to entice another woman to marry him in a similar way.

On discovering this, the pursuer sought a declarator of nullity on three grounds: that she had been induced to marry under essential error by the defender's false and fraudulent representations and personation; that the defender was a different person from the person whom she had believed in good faith she was marrying; and that the defender falsely and fraudulently personated and pretended to be Walter Erby Hamilton for no reason other than to induce the pursuer to marry him and she had thereby been so induced.[59] The decree in the pursuer's favour stated that she had been 'circumvented and induced to enter into a pretended marriage … by means of false, fraudulent representations and personation used by the defender towards her',[60] suggesting that the decision rested on the first ground.

In the aftermath of the case, the question it raised – that is, 'can a woman obtain a declarator of nullity of marriage on the ground that the marriage was induced by grossly fraudulent statements by the man as to his fortune and social position?' – was debated on more than one occasion, attracting large audiences and ending in victory for the sides opposing a remedy in such circumstances.[61] Furthermore, the judgment itself was criticised for potentially opening the flood gates. As one publication put it, '[t]here must be many cases where women have been tricked into marriage by plausible scoundrels or victimised by needy adventurers'.[62] But the main complaint made by the author

---

[58] 'Sequel to a Matrimonial Advertisement', *Edinburgh Evening News*, 20 February 1904, p. 6; *Wilson* v. *Horn* (1904) NRS CS46/1904/3/25.
[59] *Wilson* v. *Horn* (1904). [60] *Wilson* v. *Horn* (1904) 11 SLT 702.
[61] 'Joint Legal Debate in Glasgow', *The Scotsman*, 11 February 1905, p. 8; 'Aberdeen Juridical Society', *Aberdeen Press and Journal*, 6 February 1906, p. 4.
[62] 'News', *Aberdeen Daily Journal*, 23 February 1904, p. 4.

of the piece was that the pursuer was at fault for having been 'silly enough to reply to a matrimonial advertisement'. Accordingly, the moral of the story was taken to be that people contemplating marriage should 'make themselves absolutely certain of the character, antecedents, and exact position of the person they propose to marry'.[63]

It is important to recognise that these comments were made at a time when marriage agents and lonely hearts advertisements were both treated with suspicion and frowned upon.[64] From their inception in the late seventeenth century onwards, these advertisements were understood – like all advertising – to involve exaggeration, and even deception. On top of this, from the later nineteenth century, these advertisements were known to be used in the perpetration of financial fraud.[65] Against this backdrop, sympathy for the dupes of romance fraud was typically limited.

A dearth of sympathy is readily apparent in the second case, *M'Leod* v. *Adams*, which involved a fugitive deserter from the Highland Light Infantry who, to conceal his identity, pretended to be a sergeant of the Black Watch. In this guise, and wearing a military medal, the defender met the pursuer on a train, where he gave her a false name and told her that he was the son of an oil merchant, that he was formerly a well-paid private detective, and that he had £100 in the bank. After the defender mentioned that he was looking for lodgings, the pursuer agreed to take him in. Just a few days later, the defender had convinced the pursuer to go through an irregular marriage with him and to transfer all her savings to him.[66]

Like *Wilson* v. *Horn*, this case ended in a favourable outcome for the pursuer, but the judgment rested on different foundations. In fact, the judge explicitly declined to follow *Wilson* v. *Horn*, insofar as that case might stand for the proposition that using a false name and presenting false attributes comprised personation.[67] Instead, the judge granted the annulment on the basis that the defender had lacked an intention to marry the pursuer, which could be inferred from his apparently purely financial motives and his plan

---

[63] Ibid.

[64] Marriage agents, and later agencies, were seen by some as sordid and lax about marriage registration requirements; see Gordon, 'Myth and Reality' at 519–521. In Scotland, contracts made with marriage brokers were considered illegal; see Laura J. MacGregor, 'Pacta Illicita' in Kenneth Reid and Reinhard Zimmermann (eds.), *A History of Private Law in Scotland: Volume 2: Obligations* (Oxford: Oxford University Press, 2000), pp. 129–156.

[65] Francesca Beauman, *Shapely Ankle Perferr'd: A History of the Lonely Hearts Advertisement* (London: Vintage, 2012); Angus McLaren, *The Trials of Masculinity: Policing Sexual Boundaries, 1870–1930* (Chicago: University of Chicago Press, 1999), ch. 2. On advertising, see Anat Rosenberg, *The Rise of Mass Advertising: Law, Enchantment, and the Cultural Boundaries of British Modernity* (Oxford: Oxford University Press, 2022). I have found news stories criticising marriage advertisements and warning of their dangers from as early as 1877 ('Matrimonial Advertisements', *The Evening Telegraph*, 28 June 1877, p. 2 (reporting a story from that day's *Glasgow News*)).

[66] 'Marriage after Meeting in Train', *Dundee Evening Telegraph*, 3 March 1920, p. 1.

[67] *M'Leod* v. *Adams* 1920 1 SLT 229 at 232.

to abscond as soon as he could.[68] This meant that he could theoretically distinguish the case from situations where one party to a marriage, who coveted the fortune of the other, made exaggerated statements about his position in life to induce the marriage.[69] In these cases, there might be an intention to take up the position of husband even though there was also deception motivated by economic gain.

This second decision was clearly aimed at reining in the first, which had suggested both that *any* false representations that induced a marriage could render it void and that personation could be interpreted generously.[70] One reason the judge was keen to bring this decision under control was that it might lead to (unspecified) 'most dangerous and unsettling' consequences. Another was that marrying an unknown man in a 'rash and unseemly' way, and without the input of relatives, showed both recklessness and a 'failure to appreciate the sanctity and permanent character of the marriage tie'.[71] Responding to these worries, the judge suggested that only two scenarios would potentially constitute personation in the eyes of the law. The first was when a courtship had been pursued via correspondence and a third party turned up pretending to be the correspondent. The second was when one party impersonated someone famous or well-known who was known and identifiable to the dupe.[72] Restricting personation to these two situations would not only preserve a greater number of marriages than a more permissive conception of personation,[73] it also reflected a strongly held sense of the meaning and value of marriage and a clear (and stringent) account of the responsibilities of individuals seeking to enter this institution.[74]

2.4 Wealth, Appearance, Class, Character and Disposition

As is now apparent, personal identity has often been defined narrowly in law and in such a way that excludes features considered to be attributes. Furthermore, deception about most – but as Sections 2.5–2.7 will show, not

---

[68] Ibid. See Chapter 4 for more discussion of this kind of reasoning.
[69] *M'Leod* v. *Adams* (1920) at 232.
[70] The notion that deception about one's name constitutes deception as to one's identity in the context of impersonating someone whom the dupe planned to marry was adopted elsewhere; see Jackson, 'Consent of the Parties' at 19, referring to an 1869 Australian case. The importance of, and difficulty in maintaining, the distinction between identity and attributes is discussed in relation to deceptive sex in Chapter 7.
[71] *M'Leod* v. *Adams* (1920) at 231.   [72] Ibid.
[73] On efforts to hold people married wherever possible, see Chapter 4.
[74] It is perhaps significant that the judge, Lord Sands, referenced Biblical figures, beyond those of Leah, Rachel and Jacob mentioned by Stair, in his judgment. On Lord Sands' use of scripture in his judgments, see 'The Judgments of Lord Sands: Their Lighter Side' (1939) 55 *The Scottish Law Review* 137–142. According to the Canonists, errors about condition, family or fortune did not affect the validity of marriage even if they were produced by 'disingenuous representations' because the law presumed caution about matters affecting lifelong happiness; see McKinley, *Fractional Freedoms*, p. 117.

all – attributes has usually not provided the deceived party with a ground for legal relief.[75] One reason for this restriction has already come up in the context of impersonation, that is, the responsibility of spouses-to-be to obtain accurate information about their intended wife or husband. Just as people were expected to guard against most personal identity errors, even in the face of potential difficulties,[76] people were expected to take responsibility for ascertaining the true character, wealth, appearance, class and disposition of their potential spouses, even though courtship practices did not always provide opportunities for, or encourage, candour in this context.[77]

For example, in one late eighteenth-century case, counsel for the defender successfully undermined the pursuer's attempt to nullify her marriage on the basis that her husband had lied about his wealth and position by explaining that the principle underlying the law was as follows: two persons 'contracting this bargain' were to 'examine well and be perfectly informed of one another's character and situation before concluding the transaction'.[78] Similarly, more than a century later, a judge refused an action for annulment even though the bride had told 'certain fairy tales' about her age, marital history and father's position. Commenting on the aptness of the outcome, the judge explained that the pursuer 'must take his chance if he is not careful to ascertain the truth'.[79] In the same vein, a legal treatise published at the end of the nineteenth century described persons about to marry as being put on their inquiry, adding that they were presumed to have satisfied themselves regarding matters they deemed important.[80]

---

[75] Some jurisdictions have allowed annulments based on deception about attributes not covered in this chapter, for example, race in the context of pre–civil rights era United States (see Hasday, *Intimate Lies and the Law*) and religion and ancestry at a time when these were considered critically important to decisions to marry in this jurisdiction (see Joanna L. Grossman, 'Annulments Based on Fraud: What Is the "Essence" of Marriage?' Part One (2010), https://supreme.findlaw.com/legal-commentary/annulments-based-on-fraud-what-is-the-essence-of-marriage.html; and errors as to the character, attributes or quality of a person (which included prostitution, priesthood, fortune and status) in the context of the Napoleonic France (see Emily Latham, 'Recognizing Error and Fraud in the Contract of Marriage' (2006) 66(2) *Louisiana Law Review* 563–607). German Protestant Ecclesiastical law apparently used to allow annulment for error regarding the 'gross moral defect' of serious crime (see Fraser, *Husband and Wife*, p. 453) and the question of annulment for criminal record arose in France, too; see E. G. L., 'Mistake or Fraud as a Ground for Annulling Marriage in Louisiana' (1919) 28(3) *The Yale Law Journal* 272–278 at 273–274.

[76] Lawrence M. Friedman, *Personal Identity in the Modern World: A Society of Strangers* (Lanham: Rowman & Littlefield, 2022).

[77] 'On the Art of Puffing', *Caledonian Mercury*, 8 October 1781, p. 1; 'Matrimonial Blunders', *Southern Reporter*, 6 November 1873, p. 3; 'The Mistakes of Matrimony', *Edinburgh Evening News*, 16 March 1898, p. 2; 'Lovers' Little Deceits', *Perthshire Constitutional & Journal*, 29 March 1916, p. 3.

[78] *Jamieson v. Jeffrey* (1783).

[79] *Bruce v. Bruce* (1919) NRS CS46/1919/4/71. The pursuer did get relief, however – he obtained a divorce on the ground of infidelity.

[80] Walton, *Husband and Wife*, p. 88.

2.4 Wealth, Appearance, Class, Character & Disposition

Though these arguments and remarks are important, they were in a sense supplementary because the main reason deception about such attributes held no legal consequences is that the attributes were not central to the conception of marriage which permeated the law. According to this conception of marriage, errors of fortune or quality were errors about 'accidentals' – issues that were incapable of either undermining the benefits marriage supposedly brought or affecting the offspring of the marriage.[81] Although disposition, appearance, rank and wealth were recognised as considerations that bore on actual decisions to marry,[82] the reasons for choosing to marry presumed by law were 'purely *personal* – resting on personal preference and attachment, excluding all reference to considerations of wealth, rank, or fortune'.[83]

To better understand this view, it is important to see how it depends on the uneasy distinction between personal identity and attributes identified in Section 2.3. Indeed, the author who penned it added that 'it was not wealth or rank [a woman] married, but the man himself', implying a clear distinction between the two. But it is also crucial to see how this view resonates with the idea that marriage created a new and meaningful (and highly gendered) component of selfhood: the status of wife. In light of this reality, it was not entirely glib to say that when a wife 'obtain[ed] a husband, and the rights guaranteed by law to a wife, she obtains all that the law holds she had bargained for'.[84] As one English judgment put it, 'the passion which leads to marriage is apt to overleap these distinctions [of age, rank and condition], and that marriage levels them all, both in legal and moral consideration'.[85]

Nevertheless, the notion that individual decision-making *should* matter to law – especially in a jurisdiction like Scotland where consent alone made marriage[86] – was sufficiently compelling that arguments to this effect were made in court. The clearest example I have found is *Jamieson v. Jeffrey*,[87] a case that is significant in two regards. First, the pursuer sought a declarator of nullity but her action was brought with the concourse of the procurator fiscal. The procurator fiscal is an officer at whose instance criminal proceedings were (and still are) brought, who was able to prosecute in his own name but was obliged to refrain from doing so when he suspected that a complaint tended to vindicate a private interest more than the public interest. In such circumstances, he would instead offer his concurrence to the victim, who sued both for their own remedy and to help repress crime.[88] The fact that the procurator fiscal was involved therefore signals that the conduct

---

[81] Barry, *Hay's Lectures*, pp. 51–52.
[82] 'On Self-Appreciation', *The Scots Magazine*, 1 October 1823, p. 436; 'Conventional Lies', *Mid-Lothian Journal*, 16 August 1895, p. 3.
[83] Fraser, *Husband and Wife*, p. 156 (emphasis original). [84] Ibid.
[85] *Sullivan v. Sullivan* (1818) 161 ER 728 at 731.
[86] This point is discussed in greater detail in Chapter 4. [87] *Jamieson v. Jeffrey* (1783).
[88] George Watson (ed.), *Bell's Dictionary and Digest of the Law of Scotland*, 7th ed. (Edinburgh: Bell & Bradfute, London: Butterworths, 1890), p. 859.

was considered criminal,[89] which is significant because, unlike other cases where criminality was mentioned (e.g., *Wilson v. Horn*), the summons does not mention that the defender obtained any money or property from the pursuer.

Second, the pursuer argued that her marriage should be annulled because the defender had assumed the character of a wealthy farmer. Importantly, her counsel argued that fraudulent and false representations precluded consent altogether (and thus the contract was void), rather than merely impairing consent (making the contract voidable). The strategy he used was to compare fraud to force or fear, admitting that consent given under fraudulent representations 'do's [sic] not admit of such striking marks of the want of Consent' as apparent consent given under force or fear but urging that to the 'Examining mind' apparent consent obtained by fraud must appear 'directly opposite to the Idea of Consent either in the Eye of the Law or common sense'. In both cases, a woman gave her hand to a man to whom 'had she been perfectly her own Mistress she never would have given it'.[90] Given the discussion earlier, it is not surprising that this argument was unsuccessful. Even when a deception was purportedly the cause of the pursuer's decision to marry (another way the argument was framed) and even if she would have refused to marry had she had been aware of the truth, the pursuer could have no relief. As Sections 2.5–2.7 demonstrate, the only time such arguments would succeed is when the subject matter of deception concerned conditions that were implied by the conception of marriage countenanced by law. Though this conception has a long history, I aim to show that it was shaped by changing social and cultural conditions.

2.5 Pregnancy, Paternity and Pre-marital Chastity

Despite the significance of women's chastity across most of the modern era, undisclosed, pre-marital unchastity and even pregnancy by another man at the time of marriage were not grounds on which a marriage could be annulled for much of this time. One eighteenth century author had suggested that pregnancy involving an outside party could annul a marriage but only in the case of a pregnant bride. According to this view, the groom's having impregnated another woman could not ground an annulment because male unchastity was less heinous and because it could not be presumed that a woman

---

[89] The summons concluded for both £100 damages for the pursuer and a fine of £50 to be paid to the procurator fiscal 'to deter others from the like fraudulent practices in time coming'.
It is notable that the summons also argues that it is only in the more civilised stages of society that rank and fortune entered the considerations of those entering marriage contracts, giving rise to the possibility of such frauds. In addition to appealing directly to changing mores about marriage, this argument mimics those found in cases where the court was asked to punish conduct that had not previously been punished; see Chloë Kennedy, 'Declaring Crimes' (2017) 37(4) *Oxford Journal of Legal Studies* 741–769.
[90] *Jamieson v. Jeffrey* (1783).

would refuse a man she knew was unchaste.[91] Nevertheless, this position was not endorsed by jurists in the century that followed.[92]

It was not that there were no arguments for allowing an annulment in such circumstances. One such argument was that chastity was harder to verify than other spousal qualities.[93] It was therefore hard to blame a man who did not discover unchastity in his bride before marriage and the same might be said for undisclosed pregnancy, at least if the pregnancy were not easily detectible.[94] Another argument for allowing relief in cases of undisclosed pregnancy concerned the wife's condition and likely future conduct. Whereas chastity concerned only past behaviour and did not necessarily prevent a woman from being a faithful wife, or giving her husband 'pure offspring', pregnancy, so the argument went, affected a woman's condition at the time of marriage and cast doubt on her capacity to be chaste and faithful.[95] These speculations about post-marital behaviour do not appear to have been particularly persuasive, even at the time, but the suggestion that pregnancy affected a woman's condition carried a little more weight, at least in some jurisdictions. For example, French courts construed concealed pregnancy as 'error dans le persone' and thus annulled a marriage on that basis, and both the Prussian and Austrian Codes provided relief in these circumstances, too.[96]

Yet on what appears to be the first occasion the point was raised in a British court the judge refused to annul a marriage on the basis of concealed pregnancy by another man.[97] The crux of the judgment was that there was no authority for the claim, but the judge also issued some practical and principled warnings about expanding the law. For instance, he was not convinced that treating unchastity resulting in pregnancy differently from unchastity per se was justifiable, and he raised questions about how the law would deal with applications from men who had pre-marital sexual relationships with the women they'd married and how it should respond when the fraud was

---

[91] Lord Bankton, as discussed in many texts. See, for example, William W. McBryde, 'Error' in Reid and Zimmermann (eds.), *History of Private Law*, pp. 72–100. Around 200 years later, the Law Commission would decline to follow the New Zealand approach of allowing an annulment when a woman other than the wife was pregnant with the husband's child at the time of the marriage; apparently, there was 'no analogy' between the cases; see Law Commission, *Working Paper No 20 Nullity of Marriage* (1968), p. 10; Law Commission, *Report on Nullity of Marriage*, Paragraph 75.
[92] Lothian, *Consistorial Actions*, p. 30; Fraser, *Personal and Domestic Relations*, p. 232; Walton, *Husband and Wife*, pp. 89–90.
[93] Fraser, *Personal and Domestic Relations*, p. 231, discussing the views of Voet.
[94] In an unusual paternity case, a husband and wife tried to pin responsibility for the child on a third party, but the judge struggled to believe that the husband remained ignorant of his wife's condition until the birth of her child; see *Reids v. Mill* (1879) 16 SLR 338.
[95] Fraser, *Husband and Wife*, p. 452.
[96] Ibid. According to Fraser, the Prussian courts held that a man was entitled to declare a marriage void on the basis of lack of chastity – the Prussian Code allowed annulment for errors concerning the person of the future spouse or personal qualities usually presupposed in contracting marriage.
[97] *Moss v. Moss* [1897] P 263.

not discovered for years, perhaps after the birth of more children.[98] Referring to American judgments on these topics, he surmised that any extension of the law which did not rest on a sound basis would develop in 'several directions', giving rise to 'many doubts and much confusion'.[99] As one textbook writer cautioned, this jurisprudence was a 'labyrinth' through which the practitioner would struggle to find a path.[100]

At the time the case was decided, that is, at the end of the nineteenth century, the Scots law position was thought to be the essentially the same.[101] Nevertheless, in 1914, in *Stein* v. *Stein*, a court awarded a declarator of nullity to a man who married a woman whom he did not know was four months pregnant with another man's child. The legal basis of the pursuer's claim was that he had contracted while in error about an essential matter, rather than an accidental quality, and that this error had been induced by the defender fraudulently concealing her condition. If it were necessary to show error personae, the pursuer felt he had accomplished this too because he had believed he was marrying a woman capable of fulfilling what he called the 'primary function of marriage', that is, the begetting of children.[102] In response to these arguments, the court held that a duty of disclosure arose whenever a woman knew or suspected she was pregnant with another man's child and knew or suspected that her husband-to-be was unaware of this.[103]

This judgment rested on three justifications: an analogy with identity, the unique nature of the fraud, and the severity of its likely consequences. Starting with the identity analogy, the court held that a mistake about pregnancy, which meant the difference between a woman who is 'single in every sense of the word' and a woman who is 'integrally united with another living human being'[104] was as close to an error about identity as possible while remaining outside that category. As for the nature of the fraud, as has already been noted, the difficulty of ascertaining the existence of a pregnancy arguably distinguished this kind of deception from others and so did the presumption that the marriage would not have gone ahead had the truth been known.[105] Finally, deception of this kind left the husband with the unenviable choice of revealing the truth and facing 'constant humiliation and ignominy' or saving his reputation but at the risk of being held to be the child's legal father.[106]

The judges clearly felt this combination of factors merited distinctive treatment and they seemed confident that they could cordon these cases off from those they felt did not deserve a remedy. Nevertheless, the substance

---

[98] Ibid. at 277–278.   [99] Ibid. at 278.   [100] Ibid.
[101] F. P. W., 'Notes on Decided Cases' (1897) 9(4) *Juridical Review* 458–460.
[102] *Stein* v. *Stein* 1914 SC 903, fn. 1 (opinion of the Lord Ordinary, reporting the case to the Inner House).
[103] Ibid. at 906. In a later case, discussed below, the court regarded the distinction between fraudulent misrepresentation and error induced by fraudulent concealment as unimportant for the law's purposes; see *Lang* v. *Lang* 1921 SC 44 at 49.
[104] Ibid. at 907.   [105] Ibid. 908.   [106] Ibid.

2.5 Pregnancy, Paternity and Pre-marital Chastity

of subsequent claims shifted over time. For example, in a case brought the following year, a man obtained a declarator of nullity on the basis that his wife was pregnant by another man at the time of the marriage and he did not know this. Prior to marriage, however, the defender had told him she was pregnant with a different child by the same man and the pursuer had agreed to marry her.[107] The case therefore cast doubt on the presumption that a man would not marry a woman if he knew she was pregnant by another man.

Furthermore, by 1918 the court had begun to hear actions involving deception about paternity. In these cases, the pursuer knew the defender was pregnant at the time of the marriage; indeed, the belief that she was pregnant with the pursuer's child is allegedly what caused the marriage in the first place.[108] The boundaries of the law had therefore begun to expand and the court had to decide how to handle cases where a pursuer appeared to have continued in the relationship upon discovering the truth, concluding that such actions amounted to forgiveness of the injury and homologation of the contract.[109] On top of this, in a few cases the parties had married after knowing each other a very short period of time[110] – a fact which implied little of the caution that was desired of those entering the married state.

Perhaps unsurprisingly, just six years after undisclosed pregnancy by another man had been incorporated into the law of nullity the decision that had brought about the change was overruled.[111] Describing the extension of the law to include paternity cases as 'insidious',[112] the court held that the reasons underpinning the judgment in *Stein* v. *Stein* were unconvincing. More specifically, one judge described the idea that pregnancy altered the identity of a woman as 'fanciful and unsound'[113] and several of them pointed to the difficulty of keeping the law contained.[114] Importantly, the judges recognised that if fraud regarding *any* matter were allowed to affect the existence of marriage, the number of annulments would potentially be large. As the most senior judge on the bench put it: 'fraud, whether in concealment or in

---

[107] *Munro* v. *Munro* ('An Unhappy Cromarty Wedding', *The Aberdeen Journal*, 15 July 1916, p. 4).
[108] *Wilkie* v. *Wilkie* ('Court of Session', *The Scotsman*, 15 June 1918, p. 3); *Gardner* v. *Gardner* (1919) NRS CS46/1919/9/7; *Bell* v. *Bell* ('Cardenden Miner Gets His Marriage Annulled', *Dundee Courier*, 20 March 1920, p. 7); *Alexander* v. *Alexander* 1920 SC 327. The decree was refused in the first case because the judge was satisfied the pursuer was the father.
[109] *Alexander* v. *Alexander* 1920 SC 327; General Collection, Paper 44.
[110] For example, in one case the parties married just six days after meeting (*McCulloch* v. *McCulloch* (1919) NRS CS255/1310) and in another they reportedly married less than two months after meeting (*Bell* v. *Bell* (1920)).
[111] This attracted criticism regarding the 'unusual' level of inconsistency across the judgments, which was liable to shake public faith in courts and judges; see 'End of the Stein Interregnum' (1920) *Scots Law Times* 129–130.
[112] *Lang* v. *Lang* (1921) at 57. It was so insidious that the unreported cases in note 108 appear not to have been noticed.
[113] Ibid. at 50 (Lord President Clyde).
[114] Lord Dundas (at 57 and 58), Lord Salvesen (at 60) and Lord Mackenzie (at 60). The Lord Justice Clerk (Dickson) also considered that marriages could not be voidable (at 55).

misrepresentation, covers a field as extensive as human duplicity. Further, to rest the limitations of its scope on the interpretation by Courts of law of such generalities as the good sense of mankind, or the interest of the public ... is to introduce into marriage law a flood of uncertainty and insecurity'[115] – phenomena that were undesirable given the need of people to regulate their lives and make plans.[116]

Another issue that is important in appreciating this episode in the law's development is the occurrence of the First World War. This period saw a rise in irregular marriage and bigamy, both of which caused anxiety,[117] and, as one article commenting on the swift reversal of the *Stein* decision noted, actions for both declarators of marriage and nullity had 'been very numerous' 'as a direct result of the war'.[118] It is probably no coincidence that complaints about the lack of legal remedy for men who unwittingly married women pregnant by other men were also made in 1945.[119] The Second World War was similarly disruptive and, to make the perceived deficiency of the law worse, legalisation allowing annulments under these circumstances in England had been passed.[120]

The Matrimonial Causes Act 1937 stated that a marriage would be voidable when at the time of marriage the respondent was pregnant by someone other than the petitioner but it stipulated that a decree would not be granted unless proceedings were instituted within a year and the court was satisfied both that the petitioner was ignorant of the pregnancy at the time of the marriage[121] and that no marital intercourse had taken place with the consent of the petitioner since the discovery of the grounds for a decree.[122]

---

[115] Ibid. at 50 (Lord President Clyde). Commentary at the time *Stein* v. *Stein* was decided pointed out the potential for fraud perpetrated by collusion between the parties; see 'Notes from Edinburgh' (1914) 30 *Scottish Law Review* 177 at 184.

[116] 'End of the Stein Interregnum'.

[117] On bigamy, see Chapter 4; on irregular marriage, see Gordon, 'Irregular Marriage and Cohabitation'.

[118] 'Notes from Edinburgh' (1920) 36 *Scottish Law Review* 375–376. Of the thirteen cases concerning deception as to pregnancy or paternity I found, six explicitly mention the war and/or involve parties in the armed forces.

[119] 'Letters to the Editor' (1945) *Scots Law Times* 12.

[120] The Divorce and Nullity of Marriage (Scotland) Bill, as it then was, had borrowed three clauses from the Matrimonial Causes Act 1937, one of which contained this ground of annulment; the others are discussed in the following section. This clause was struck out before the Bill became the Divorce (Scotland) Act 1938 (Hansard, HC, vol. 107, col. 352, 7 December 1937; Hansard, HC, vol. 338, col. 1280, 12 July 1938; 'The Scottish Divorce Bill' (1938) 54 *Scottish Law Review* 38–44 at 43; George A. Montgomery, 'Ninety Years of Progress' (1947) 59 *Juridical Review* 173–184; *Royal Commission on Marriage and Divorce Report 1951–1955* (Her Majesty's Stationery Office, 1956), Paragraph 288).

[121] It therefore did not include paternity cases; see Jackson, 'Consent of the Parties' at 21.

[122] S. 7(1). The English law currently governing nullity of marriage is very similar except that the time limit for raising the action is three years and the remedy is barred if (i) the applicant, knowing the remedy was open to him, acted in relation to the respondent in such a way to lead them to reasonably believe the remedy would not be sought and (ii) it would be unjust to the respondent to make the order; see Matrimonial Causes Act 1973, ss. 12 and 13. A similar

This provision was similar to a clause that had been proposed for inclusion in the Matrimonial Causes Act 1860[123] and follows two strands of the logic exhibited in the *Stein* case: first, when non-disclosure is the basis of the action ignorance (rather than mistake) is potentially the state of mind of the party who has been wronged and, second, the remedy is unavailable if the applicant's conduct implies endorsement of the relationship after the relevant fact – and, under the 1937 Act, its legal significance – has been discovered.

Another important point about the legislation is the way the information whose non-disclosure could ground a remedy was conceptualised. On one view, not being pregnant by another man – or at least being transparent about such a pregnancy – could be considered an implied condition of the marriage contract (along with the other grounds of nullity based on ignorance included in the 1937 Act, which are discussed in Section 2.6). The legislation could therefore be seen as 'a recognition by society of certain conditions which may be implicit in the making of the marriage contract'. Alternatively, the grounds could be considered 'conditions annexed by law on as terms of the marriage contract on the ground of public policy'.[124] I return to these two ways of conceptualising non-disclosure at the end of this chapter and then again in Chapter 8.

2.6 Impotence, Infertility and Disease

In addition to undisclosed pregnancy by another man, the 1937 Act provided that a marriage would be voidable when a person was affected by three other bodily or psychic conditions and their spouse was ignorant of this fact (and the other requirements of the Act, mentioned earlier, were satisfied).[125] The conditions included unsoundness of mind or mental deficiency (within the meaning of the Mental Deficiency Acts 1913 to 1927) or recurrent fits of insanity or epilepsy on the part of either spouse, and infection by the respondent with venereal disease (VD) in a communicable form at the time of marriage.[126] These grounds for annulment had been suggested, along with undisclosed pregnancy by another man,[127] twenty five years earlier by the Royal Commission on Divorce and Matrimonial Causes with the qualification that the epilepsy or recurrent insanity (but not unsoundness of mind) must have been concealed by either the person with the condition,

---

change is discussed in Law Commission, *Report on Nullity of Marriage*, Paragraphs 44–45, 76–86. Similar rules apply to civil partnerships; see Civil Partnership Act 2004, ss. 50 and 51.

[123] 'Notes on Decided Cases' (1897) at 460.

[124] *The Church and the Law of Nullity of Marriage*, pp. 28–29. See also the claim that little objection would probably be taken to the grounds; see Christopher N. Johnston, 'Report of the Royal Commission upon Divorce' (1912–1913) 24(4) *Juridical Review* 274–291 at 286.

[125] S. 7(1).   [126] S. 7(1)(b) and (c).

[127] The Commission justified this ground by the 'gross and fraudulent character' of such cases; see *Report of the Royal Commission on Divorce and Matrimonial Causes* (His Majesty's Stationery Office, 1912), Paragraph 353.

their parents, or any other person with control over the afflicted person who knew of the intended marriage.[128] A similar qualification existed in relation to communicable VD.[129]

When the Commission made its recommendations, it framed these grounds as exceptions to the general rule that a person would have no remedy for being deceived into marriage by fraudulent statements or concealment of facts and characterised their introduction as beneficial to the complaining spouse, potential children of the couple, and to the state and/or morality.[130] In doing so, they explicitly aligned these benefits with what they called 'the eugenic point of view', according to which the prevention of marriage between those 'unfit' to have healthy children furthered the interests of 'the race and the State'.[131] At the time of the Commission's work, eugenic principles were growing in popularity internationally, reaching their apex in the 1920s.[132] This was also a time of intense concern about the spread of VD, with fears over transmission peaking during the First World War and immediately after, when laws governing those carrying and treating VD were proposed and passed.[133]

When the later Matrimonial Causes Act 1965 was passed, this eugenicist slant remained,[134] with a new provision stating that in addition to unsound mind and recurrent attacks of insanity or epilepsy, a marriage could be annulled on the ground of undisclosed mental disorder (within the meaning of the Mental Health Act 1959) of such a kind or to such an extent as made the sufferer 'unfitted for marriage and the procreation of children'.[135] More substantial changes can be seen in the Matrimonial Causes Act 1973, which still includes mental disorder making a person 'unfitted for marriage' as a ground of annulment but no longer refers to the procreation of children.[136]

---

[128] *Report of the Royal Commission*, Paragraph 353. A Scottish case from around this time also raised these points, though they were not directly relevant to the issue to be determined (that is, whether the defender had capacity to consent to marriage). The pursuer clearly felt that the defender's family had breached a duty to reveal her serious mental health problems before he agreed to marry her (*Todd* v. *Taylor* (1909) CS46/1909/3/58).

[129] *Report of the Royal Commission*, Paragraph 353. Non-disclosure, rather than concealment, was the term used in relation to VD. These grounds were all endorsed by the Commission's Minority Report (p. 190).

[130] *Report of the Royal Commission*, Paragraphs 351–353.

[131] Ibid., Paragraph 297.

[132] Philippa Levine and Alison Bashford, 'Introduction: Eugenics and the Modern World' in Alison Bashford and Philippa Levine (eds.), *The Oxford Handbook of the History of Eugenics* (Oxford: Oxford University Press, 2010), pp. 3–24.

[133] Davidson, *Illicit and Unnatural Practices*, pp. 18, 20–21, 32, 178–179. The relationship between VD and sexual consent is discussed in Chapter 7.

[134] This is perhaps unsurprising since the Act (also not applicable to Scotland) was a piece of consolidating legislation (see preamble to the Act).

[135] S. 9(1)(b)(ii), s. 9(2).

[136] S. 12(1)(d). This formulation appeared in the Nullity of Marriage Act 1971 – the relevant provisions of neither Act were, or are, applicable to Scotland. The Civil Partnership Act 2004 is similar, providing that a civil partnership is voidable if at the time the civil partnership was formed either party was suffering from mental disorder of such a kind or to such an extent as to be unfitted for civil partnership and the requirements regarding ignorance, justice and time bar are met (ss. 50(b) and 51).

2.6 Impotence, Infertility and Disease

Prior to this reform, there had been discussions about whether ignorance of a spouse's sterility should be a ground of annulment when that sterility had been caused by medical or surgical treatment before marriage.[137] The proposal was made partly in recognition of the fact that for many people, especially women, procreation of children was one of the fundamental aims of marriage, even if it was not the principal one.[138] The suggestion was rejected, though, due to fears that it would necessarily extend to ignorance of a spouse's 'natural' sterility too, meaning that any childless marriage would be at risk of annulment.[139] There is also no mention of epilepsy in the 1973 Act, which accords with the fact that advances in medicine meant epilepsy could by this time be kept under better control.[140]

In comparison to the other grounds in this section, the ability to annul a marriage due to impotence was much older and its development occurred at common law. Nevertheless, from an early period there was an association between impotence and deception, though it was not clear whether deception was *required* for an annulment based on impotence. On one view, impotence was like bigamy in that it was an impediment which barred the formation of marriage irrespective of the parties' knowledge of, or attitude towards, its existence.[141] One rationale for this perspective was that the sexual capacities of both parties were essential to the marriage[142] because 'commixion of bodies' was necessary to generate the affinity associated with this relationship.[143] Another rationale was that impotence disappointed the purposes of marriage – the desire to have children and the 'lawful enjoyment' of one anothers' persons – thereby causing harm to the spouses[144] and also to society because the parties might be driven to seek sex outside their marriage.[145]

On another view, however, impotence was more like the other grounds discussed in this section in that awareness of the 'defect' made all the difference.[146]

---

[137] *Marriage and Divorce Report 1951–1955*, Paragraph 271.
[138] Law Commission, *Report on Nullity of Marriage*, Paragraph 33.
[139] Ibid., Paragraph 34. This worry seems to be a consequence of the disappearance from the legislation of a concealment or non-disclosure requirement, which might limit the law to cases where the sterile party knew of their condition before marriage.
[140] Ibid., Paragraph 73. Cf. the earlier view that epilepsy merited inclusion because it could be as distressing to the complaining spouse as insanity (*Marriage and Divorce Report 1951–1955*, Paragraph 282).
[141] Barry, *Hay's Lectures*, p. 113; Stair; More, *Institutions* (vol. 1), p. 35; Fraser, *Personal and Domestic Relations*, p. 51 (disagreeing with this view).
[142] Ibid.   [143] Stair; More, *Institutions* (vol. 1), p. 26.
[144] Fraser, *Personal and Domestic Relations*, pp. 50–51. One reason impotence was typically distinguished from sterility was that the validity of marriages between older people, past the age of procreation, was never doubted; see John Erskine, *Principles of the Law of Scotland*, 14th ed. (Edinburgh: Bell & Bradfute, 1870), p. 60. As with so much else, however, there was a suggestion that this rule was gendered and that 'barrenness' in a woman might constitute impotence; see Fraser, *Personal and Domestic Relations*, p. 53; Fraser, *Husband and Wife*, p. 85.
[145] *D v. A* (1845) 1 Rob Ecc 279 (an English case).
[146] Barry, *Hay's Lectures*, pp. 113–115. The modern view is that impotence makes a marriage voidable – this is the only instance of voidable marriage in Scots law and the rule applies

According to one text, a person who was informed about their spouse's condition could not be cheated; in the absence of any fraud, it was open to them to agree to 'an unequal bargain'.[147] An alternative way of supporting this position was to rely on the notion of implied conditions mentioned at the end of Section 2.5. According to this line of thinking, consent to marriage was given under the implied condition of the other party having the potential to copulate[148] so it made sense that entering marriage without knowing that this condition was not satisfied should attract a legal remedy. Furthermore, it made sense that the doctrine of personal bar might apply to prevent someone bringing an action when they were aware of their spouse's condition at the time of marriage.[149] Finally, when an impotent person knew, or was taken to know, about their condition this indicated culpability because it implied that they had withheld information their spouse should have been given.

Each of these facets of the law relating to impotence comes through the cases litigated across the nineteenth and early twentieth centuries. For example, in several cases, the papers state that the pursuer supposed the defender to have had the capacity to engage in sex (though they do not use that language)[150] or – more frequently – that they were not made aware, or were ignorant of, the defender's condition prior to marriage.[151] The defenders' knowledge of their condition is also sometimes mentioned,[152] and their conduct is occasionally described in terms of deceit or entrapment[153] with damages, sometimes alongside solatium, claimed or mentioned in some cases.[154] There is a condemnatory tone across the cases, too, but there is a subtle shift across time towards condemnation of the impotency per se in addition to, or instead of, condemnation of the failure to disclose its existence.

This shift starts to appear from 1890 when the cases begin to exhibit more medicalised language and refer to specific diseases. For example, in a case

only to marriages between people of different sexes; see R. F. Hunter, 'The Voidable Marriage: Impotency and the Law' (2013) 4 *Scots Law Times* 29–33; Marriage and Civil Partnership (Scotland) Act 2014, s. 5(1).

[147] Barry, *Hay's Lectures*, p. 115.
[148] Fraser, *Personal and Domestic Relations*, p. 52; Fraser, *Husband and Wife*, p. 83. This perspective is evident in the judgments of *AB* v. *CB* (1906) 42 SLR 411 (at 413) and *L* v. *L* 1931 SC 477 (at 481).
[149] Fraser, *Personal and Domestic Relations*, p. 55; Fraser, *Husband and Wife*, p. 93. Mere doubts about the potency of a prospective spouse would not bar an action; see *Allardyce* v. *Allardyce* 1954 SLT 334. Delay or acquiescence might also bar an action, at least by the late nineteenth century; see Walton, *Husband and Wife*, p. 6.
[150] *Paterson* v. *Cumming* (1815); *Baird* v. *Hard* (1859) NRS CS228/B/21/32.
[151] *Reid* v. *Reid* (1879) NRS CS247/5174; *Gordon* v. *Merricks* (1885) NRS CS46/1885/5/65; *Young* v. *Young* (1892); *Spiers* v. *Spiers* (1895) NRS CS46/1895/2/103; *Wheelock* v. *Cameron* (1889) NRS CS46/1889/12/17; *Guest* v. *Lauder* (1909) NRS CS46/1909/10/8; *Thomson* v. *Thomson* (1914) NRS CS255/487.
[152] *Reid* v. *Reid* (1879); *Spiers* v. *Spiers* (1895); *Wheelock* v. *Cameron* (1889); *Duguid* v. *Duguid* (1909).
[153] *Paterson* v. *Cumming* (1815); *AB* v. *CB* (1884) 11 R 1060 (this appears to be the same case as *Gordon* v. *Merricks* (1885)); *Spiers* v. *Spiers* (1895); *Duguid* v. *Duguid* (1909); *G* v. *G* (1922) 60 SLR 125.
[154] *Paterson* v. *Cumming* (1815); *Young* v. *Young* (1892); *Duguid* v. *Duguid* (1909).

from that year, the parties were advised by a medical professor not to live together as man and wife after the wife's genital irregularity was discovered. There is no suggestion that the woman knew before marriage that her genitals were unusual or that this would cause difficulties for penile penetrative sex; the key point is that the parties' marriage was condemned, despite the love the husband continued to declare for his wife.[155] In a case four years later, the defender's impotence was inferred from his sexual abstinence, which one judge related to his 'confessed' history of 'the vice of self-abuse',[156] rather than virtue and morality.[157] A second judge referred to the potential future marriage of the defender without disclosing his sexual difficulties as a 'wicked and abominable act',[158] but there is also a sense in the judgments that the impotence itself was shameful and potentially blameworthy. This attitude is evident in other cases[159] and was in keeping with cultural and medical perceptions of impotence at the time, according to which certain sexual activities, including masturbation, contributed to a new form of pathologised masculinity – the 'undersexed weakling' – and disease was a punishment for indiscretion.[160]

It is possible to map these attitudes on to rules concerning to whom an action of nullity was available and when. Throughout the period, the action was restricted to the parties to the marriage (which made impotence atypical if it was an impediment rendering the marriage void),[161] but during the nineteenth century, the remedy was thought to be available only to the 'aggrieved' party.[162] At this time, as the previous discussion has outlined, an annulment was essentially a remedy for the person who had not been informed of their spouse's impotence before marriage, and it was often delivered along with condemnation of the defender for the deception and/or the 'defect' itself.

---

[155] *Gourlay* v. *Gourlay* (1890) NRS CS46/1890/9/33. In another case, a man was advised not to marry due to a spinal cord injury and prompted outrage when he ignored this advice (*Spiers* v. *Spiers* (1895)).

[156] Similar language – of admitting self-abuse – appears in *Young* v. *Young* (1892).

[157] *AB* v. *CB* (1884) at fn. 8 (Lord Young, at advising).

[158] *AB* v. *CB* (1885) 22 SLR 461 (Lord Bramwell at 468).

[159] For example, *Duguid* v. *Duguid* (1909), concerning a man allegedly 'addicted to masturbation' and described as a case of 'sexual perversion'. A pervert referred to someone who wilfully engaged in 'deviant sexual practices', as opposed to 'inverts' who could not help themselves; see McLaren, *Trials of Masculinity*, p. 212.

[160] McLaren, *Trials of Masculinity*, ch. 6. Though the focus in this section is male impotence, numerous cases involved alleged female impotence, and these also acquired a medicalised tenor in the last decade of the nineteenth century; see, for example, *Gibson* v. *Morrison* (1891) NRS CS46/1891/12/47; *Robinson* v. *Walker* (1900) NRS CS46/1900/2/27; *AB* v. *CB* (1906) 8 F 603; *Wilkie* v. *Wilkie* (1907) NRS CS46/1907/5/89; *Syme* v. *Pirie* (1909) NRS CS46/1909/6/66. On supposed sexual disorders of women at this time, see, for example, Peter Cryle and Lisa Downing, 'Feminine Sexual Pathologies' and the associated special edition of the *Journal of the History of Sexuality* (2009) 18(1).

[161] Paton, *Hume's Lectures*, p. 78; Lothian, *Consistorial Actions*, p. 188; *F* v. *F* 1945 SC 202.

[162] Paton, *Hume's Lectures*, p. 157; Fraser, *Personal and Domestic Relations*, pp. 52, 58; Fraser, *Husband and Wife*, pp. 80, 83; Walton, *Husband and Wife*, p. 2.

By the end of the century, however, it was suggested that the rule restricting relief to the potent spouse was lacking not only in authority but also in reason.[163] It was not until the 1930s, however, that a court decided that the impotent spouse might bring an action of nullity of marriage, a possibility that was confirmed in 1945.[164] It is notable that the judgments in these cases do not turn solely on questions of legal authority, referring to matters of public policy and principle too. The public policy in question was the desirability of preserving a marriage where 'one of the essential conditions of the bond is not capable of fulfilment',[165] and the principled question was why an impotent spouse should be denied the remedy when *both* parties to a sexless (judging by the law's conception of sex) marriage were aggrieved and the condition of impotency was 'not voluntary'.[166] As these comments illustrate, in the first few decades of the twentieth century, beliefs about impotency had changed to become less morally charged and the expectation of sexual satisfaction within marriage had gained prominence.[167] There was also a sense that a marriage afflicted by impotence was more likely to fall apart.[168]

Ironically, these changes in the law, which cohered with growing cultural acceptance of a desire for mutual satisfaction in marriage, somewhat pulled focus from the wrongs and harms associated with failing to disclose impotency before marriage – behaviour that respected neither this desire nor the importance of informed decision-making. By making it easier to terminate marriages that were not satisfying to either party or both, the courts at the same time effaced, or at least reduced, the capacity of the law of nullity to recognise the wrongs and harms associated with deceiving another into a marriage. To be clear, the existence of impotence and the failure to disclose impotence before marriage are separable matters but focussing on the former had the practical effect of eclipsing the latter.

The potential for this was clear in another, earlier, dispute, which concerned the question of whether the pursuer was barred from seeking a declarator of nullity because she knew her husband was impotent before marriage. As one judge pointed out, a case like this was 'devoid of the element of injury which is inflicted on the spouse who enters into a marriage in ignorance of the other party's impotence'[169] but, as another observed, 'considerations of health and family life might render it unjust to refuse a decree'.[170] In the case that decided that the remedy was open to either spouse, the most senior

---

[163] George Joseph Bell (rev. by William Guthrie), *Principles of the Law of Scotland*, 10th ed. (Edinburgh: T. & T. Clark, 1899), Paragraph 1524.
[164] The action might still be barred if the pursuer had fraudulently claimed to be potent; see *SG v. WG* 1933 SC 728 at 734. The position is similar in English law; see *Harthan v. Harthan* [1949] P 115 but cf. *Morgan v. Morgan* [1959] P 92.
[165] *SG v. WG* (1933) at 735.   [166] *F v. F* (1945) at 208.
[167] Angus McLaren, *Impotence: A Cultural History* (Chicago: University of Chicago Press, 2007), pp. xvii, 150–153, 164, 169.
[168] Ibid., p. 158.   [169] *L v. L* (1931) (Lord Blackburn at 483).   [170] Ibid. (Lord Morison at 484).

judge conflated the two issues, suggesting that 'to treat the potent spouse as alone aggrieved is to imply that the impotent spouse is in some sense a defaulter',[171] who has failed to implement their contract. This was to miss the possibility that the relevant grievance might be deception about impotence, rather than impotence per se.

2.7 Gender, Sex and Sexuality

As with the requirement for monogamy, the requirement that marriage be between a man and a woman has a long history. Indeed, for most of its existence, the institution of marriage was confined to couples comprised of a man and a woman.[172] Yet as Jen Manion has argued, this restriction could be interpreted in different ways, according to different ideas about gender and how it relates to sex. In their Anglo-American study of 'female husbands', Manion suggests that it was only in the 1880s that sex was emphasised over gender such that those assigned female at birth, but who felt and acted as men, were considered to be 'really' women and therefore incapable of being a woman's husband.[173] It is not that before this time a more laissez faire attitude towards the gender/sex binary or the inherent heterosexuality of marriage prevailed. Rather, social gender could potentially trump biological sex and adopting gender roles and markers, including being married to a woman, could mean a person would be regarded as male even when this interpretation did not align with their anatomical sex.[174] Yet if the validity of this marriage came under scrutiny, such as if the wife claimed she did not realise that her husband was not really a man, it might be nullified.[175]

By the later nineteenth century, sex had eclipsed gender and a person's designation would be dictated by the way their biological features were read. This encouraged a different attitude towards relationships between women and female husbands – indeed, the term 'female husband' lost its purchase as these

---

[171] *F v. F* (1945) (Lord President Normand at 208).
[172] The first country to legally recognise same-sex partnerships was Denmark in 1989, and the first country to legalise same-sex marriage was the Netherlands in 2001; see Joseph Chamie and Barry Mirkin, 'Same-Sex Marriage: A New Social Phenomenon' (2011) 37(3) *Population and Development Review* 529–551. For a social constructivist history of same-sex marriage, see William N. Eskridge Jr, 'A History of Same-Sex Marriage' (1993) 79(7) *Virginia Law Review* 1419–1513. See also John Boswell, *The Marriage of Likeness: Same-Sex Unions in Pre-modern Europe* (London: HarperCollins, 1995).
[173] Jen Manion, *Female Husbands: A Trans History* (Cambridge: Cambridge University Press, 2020), pp. 3, 64, 66, 235, 253, 262.
[174] Ibid., pp. 108–109, 261.
[175] Manion refers to marriages between people assigned female at birth as potentially being 'voided' in the eighteenth century (ibid., pp. 22, 87, 124) and points out that if the wife did not claim ignorance, she would potentially be liable to social and legal sanction (pp. 114, 121). Caroline Derry has argued that cases involving female husbands were dealt with by English law as cases of economic fraud or theft: the women were construed as having deceptively deprived their 'wives' of money or belongings, even when the financial motivation attributed to the case was lacking; see Caroline Derry, *Lesbianism and the Criminal Law: Three Centuries of Legal Regulation in England and Wales* (Cham: Palgrave Macmillan, 2020), ch. 2.

pairings came to be seen as same-sex relationships, which could attain some degree of recognition, so long as they remained informal.[176] Against this, marriages were for differently sexed parties alone, and it was doubtful that a same-sex relationship could even be considered a purported marriage in respect of which a decree of nullity could be issued.[177] The position had changed by the late 1960s, however, when courts in England held that a marriage would be void on the ground that the parties were of the same sex,[178] irrespective of the beliefs or knowledge of the parties.

Beyond any symbolic significance it held, the decision to classify such relationships as void marriages had practical consequences, for it meant financial relief might be available to either party.[179] In 1970, the Law Commission's view was that such relief was not appropriate in the case of same-sex unions because if there were any 'genuine mistake' as to sex then this would likely be discovered immediately after the ceremony, leading the relationship either to end with minimal financial hardship to anyone or to continue as a 'homosexual relationship'.[180] Since no financial relief existed for these unions, the Commission did not see why it should be available simply because the parties had 'succeeded in deceiving someone into celebrating the marriage in the belief that they [were] of opposite sexes'.[181]

The worry animating this position seems to be the threat of couples circumventing the prohibition against same-sex marriage that existed at the time. But there was also a possibility that one party might have 'married' another in ignorance of, or while mistaken about, the sex of their partner. These were precisely the circumstances that arose in a case from 1996 in which the court had to decide whether to bar an application for, or otherwise deny, ancillary relief[182] to a person who had not transitioned sufficiently far from female to male to be able legally to marry a woman *and* who had allegedly not informed his[183] wife of his 'female gender' before or during their seventeen-year marriage.[184] Legally, the case is fairly complex because there were various ways of conceptualising what the appellant had done wrong.

---

[176] Manion, *Female Husbands*, pp. 231–232, noting that this created some space for a woman to 'admit' that she knew what she was getting into when entering the relationship (p. 233).

[177] Law Commission, *Report on Nullity of Marriage*, Paragraph 30.   [178] Ibid.

[179] Financial relief became available to both men and women in 1971, whereas prior to this 'most forms' of financial relief were available to women only; see Law Commission, *Report on Nullity of Marriage*, Paragraph 31.

[180] Law Commission, *Report on Nullity of Marriage*, Paragraph 32.

[181] Ibid. They left open the possibility that financial relief might be appropriate in 'tragic cases' where one party believed at the time of marriage that he or she was of the opposite sex.

[182] The Law Commission suggested that the appropriate remedy in these cases would be an action of deceit by the ignorant spouse; see Law Commission, *Report on Nullity of Marriage*, Paragraph 32. The parties' not being male and female was included in the Nullity of Marriage Act 1971 as a ground on which a marriage would be void (s. 1(c)) and this was carried over into s. 11(c) of the Matrimonial Causes Act 1973 (now amended)).

[183] I use the pronouns used in the judgment; from the report, it appears these are the pronouns the individual would have used, too.

[184] *S-T (formerly J)* v. *J* [1998] Fam 103 at 111.

The application for ancillary relief was initially dismissed because it was held to be against public policy to allow a claim based on the offence of perjury, committed by the false declaration that there was no lawful hindrance to the marriage, because the culpability of the offence was not mitigated by the genuine conviction of the defendant that he was male or by any alleged knowledge of the plaintiff's that the defendant was a woman.[185] On appeal, one judge expressed some concern over this conclusion. He suggested that bigamy – the offence in relation to which refusing ancillary relief had previously occurred[186] – was more closely connected to the claim for financial relief than perjury relating to a pre-requisite for marriage. He made a point of noting that perjury could cover a wide range of statements, expressing unease that a false declaration of bachelorhood (which might conceal only a former, dissolved marriage) might bar a claim for financial relief.[187]

Nevertheless, he accepted that the appellant should be barred from making a claim in light of the *ex turpi* principle (that is, that a criminal shall not reap the fruits of his crime by the judgment of a court) because, in his opinion, the deception struck at the conception of marriage enshrined in law. This conclusion made clear that it was not deception per se that mattered; in fact, the judge cycled through various serious and potentially harmful deceptions which might render the marriage voidable or void (as per Sections 2.2–2.6), before concluding that he would not dismiss a claim for financial relief on the basis of any of them, confining the prohibition to cases of bigamy and same sex unions where the claimant has 'been guilty of deceiving the other'.[188] Only in these cases did he feel the deception went to 'the fundamental essence of marriage … the two vital cornerstones of marriage implicit in the union of one man and one woman'.[189]

The other judges did not bar the claim,[190] with one holding that the perjury in this case was collateral and 'not itself the crime complained of'. Instead, the 'crime' was the deception practised on the plaintiff – conduct which was *not* actually a crime in and of itself.[191] Instead of holding the appellant disqualified

---

[185] The tension in this claim of the defendant's – that the plaintiff must have known he was not a man, but he did not – was noted by Ward LJ (at 133). The initial judgment is outlined at 111–116.
[186] *Whiston* v. *Whiston* [1995] Fam 198, which held that a person who committed bigamy would be barred from applying for financial relief.
[187] Ward LJ at 136–137.
[188] Ibid. at 141. A later decision made clear that the rule, as it applied to bigamy, would only apply to cases where the spouse who was free to marry did not know the other was already married; see *Rampal* v. *Rampal* [2001] 3 WLR 795. The rationale appears to be where there is collusion both spouses are equally culpable; it is not that being transparent about an existing marriage is considered to lack culpability; see Sheren Guirguis, 'Conduct – When Is It Bad Enough?' (2020) 50 *Family Law* 60–67.
[189] Ward LJ at 141.   [190] Sir Brian Neill at 156; Potter LJ at 148–149.
[191] See Potter LJ at 149. This is not to say that other 'misrepresentations' that induced a marriage would not be a crime; for example, a person described as a woman was charged with erasing the Christian name on their ID card with a view to marrying a young woman who was convinced that the accused was a man. After pleading guilty, the accused was fined £4 and made a solemn undertaking not to dress as a man in future ('Woman Posed as Man; Had Fiancee', *Dundee Courier*, 2 June 1948, p. 3). See Manion, *Female Husbands* for crimes used to charge 'women' who presented as men.

from seeking financial relief, they instead took all the circumstances into account when deciding whether and how to exercise their discretion in considering his claim.[192] This allowed them, in confirming that the claim should be dismissed, to take account of the appellant's crime *and* the relationship between his deception and the plaintiff's decision to marry, calling the relationship a 'marriage procured by fraud' and noting how the wider deception – the 'concealment … of his sex at birth, his subsequent history, and the true nature of his anatomy' – had been 'pivotal' to her consent to marry.[193] This was in contrast to the judgment grounded in the *ex turpi* principle, which conceded that the deception was 'as profound a betrayal of trust between two people as can be imagined'[194] and that the damage caused to the plaintiff was 'catastrophic' and traumatising[195] but nonetheless held that the harm done to her was essentially irrelevant. In a judgment grounded in public policy and the *ex turpi* principle, it was considered appropriate for harm to society and the goal of deterring wrongdoing to take centre stage.[196]

Despite significant changes in the law of marriage, such as the legalisation of same-sex marriage and the introduction of civil partnerships for same- and different-sex partners,[197] deception concerning the gender – or, more accurately, gender history – of a spouse remains legally significant. According to the Matrimonial Causes Act 1973 and the Civil Partnership Act 2004, a marriage or civil partnership is voidable when the respondent is a person whose gender at the time of marriage had become the acquired gender under the Gender Recognition Act and the other conditions of the 1973 and 2004 Acts are met.[198] In other words, under this law a marriage or civil partnership is voidable if the respondent is transgender (with a gender recognition certificate) and their partner did not know this before marriage, so long as the claim is brought in time and it would be just to hear, or make, the order.

---

[192] Potter LJ at 149.

[193] Potter LJ at 145. Sir Brian Neill considered the 'grave deception' practised on the 'wife' to be relevant (at 156).

[194] Ward LJ, agreeing with the initial judgment on this point, called the deception 'gross' (at 133).

[195] At 131. There is a short summary of the plaintiff's own account of the harm at 132. The crux of this is the lack of disclosure by the defendant when charged by a vicar to do so and the devastation caused by disclosure of the defendant's 'true gender', including the humiliation and distress caused to the plaintiff's parents.

[196] At 131. See also the quotation from an earlier judgment that the existence of the *ex turpi* principle is not for the sake of the defendant but because the court will not lend their aid to the plaintiff (at 138).

[197] Civil Partnership Act 2004, as amended by The Civil Partnership (Opposite-Sex Couples) Regulations 2019 and the Civil Partnership (Scotland) Act 2020; Marriage (Same Sex Couples) Act 2013; Marriage and Civil Partnership (Scotland) Act 2014. I do not consider the impact of any formal legal relationship on the acquisition of a gender recognition certificate here.

[198] Matrimonial Causes Act 1973, ss. 12(1)(h), 13; Civil Partnership Act 2004, ss. 50(e), 51. There is no similar provision under Scots law. As one commentator pointed out, and as earlier sections have discussed, the concept of voidable marriage does not feature much in Scots law; see Kenneth McK. Norrie, *Professor Norrie's Commentaries on Family Law* (Dundee: Dundee University Press, 2011), pp. 103–107.

2.7 Gender, Sex and Sexuality

This provision has been criticised on two bases. The first criticism is that this is the only provision which requires disclosure of historical facts and refers to a fixed identity group, rather than a state of affairs.[199] These arguments certainly make sense in light of the fact that it is gender history which requires to be disclosed but they overlook how parenthood, to which pregnancy very often leads, is arguably a fixed identity group and they miss how having a chronic and incurable (even if treatable) illness might also be conceived in these terms.[200] Furthermore, the phenomenon of detransitioning casts some doubt on whether being transgender is necessarily a fixed identity.[201] The second criticism is that it is not clear what harm is caused by ignorance of someone's gender history, other than a 'perceived challenge to heterosexual identity and the heterosexual nature of marriage'.[202]

Though there is room to debate how damaging the first of these potential harms is,[203] the possibility that the gender of one's spouse has an impact on one's own identity has been recognised by others who are critical of the way that gender identity features within marriage law but at the same time acknowledge the arguments that marriage is a core social mechanism for shaping identity and that 'erotic identity', as expressed by marriage, is relationally constructed.[204] The relational significance of gender and sexuality within marriage is also apparent in attempts to make the non-disclosure of same-sex attraction relevant to decisions about custody and the division of assets on termination of a marriage.

More specifically, in China some *tongqis* (*tongqi* translates to 'gay man's wife'[205]) who have been duped into marriage with a 'gay' man seeking to pass as heterosexual have agitated for this change to the law. In doing so, they seek recognition of the way they have been tricked and used and the way their expectations of heterosexual marriage, that is, a partner who is different-sex attracted and who will provide romantic love and emotional care, have been dashed. In contrast to *tongqis* who have been appraised of their husbands'

---

[199] Alex Sharpe, 'Transgender Marriage and the Legal Obligation to Disclose Gender History' (2012) 75(1) *Modern Law Review* 33–53 at 43.
[200] See Chapter 8.
[201] Michael S. Irwig, 'Detransition among Transgender and Gender-Diverse People: An Increasing and Increasingly Complex Phenomenon' (2022) 10(107) *The Journal of Clinical Endocrinology & Metabolism* e4261–e4262.
[202] A. N. Sharpe, 'A Return to the "Truth" of the Past' (2009) 18(2) *Social & Legal Studies* 259–263 at 260–261, suggesting that protecting the ignorant spouse against the harms of VD is a public policy interest and concealed pregnancy can perhaps be explained by concern over uncertain paternity and lineage.
[203] See Chapters 7 and 8.
[204] Flora Renz, 'Consenting to Gender? Trans Spouses after Same-Sex Marriage' in Nicola Barker and Daniel Monk (eds.), *From Civil Partnership to Same Sex Marriage: Interdisciplinary Reflections* (Abingdon: Routledge, 2015), pp. 83–94, noting the arguments. The relationship between gender 'deception' and sexual consent is considered in Chapters 6 and 7.
[205] Jingshu Zhu, '"Unqueer" Kinship? Critical Reflections on "Marriage Fraud" in Mainland China' (2018) 21(7) *Sexualities* 1075–1091 at 1076.

sexual preferences before marriage, and are therefore in on the secret, the women who have entered these marriages without this information feel deeply aggrieved and sometimes suffer other, serious harms.[206] The desire for legal reform expressed by these women therefore provides another example of the way that the rules – actual and desired – governing the law of nullity of marriage and the subsequent division of assets have shifted in response to changing conceptions of gender, sex and sexuality and changes in the way they relate to one another and to marriage.

2.8 Conclusions and Contemporary Connections

The development of the law of nullity can be seen as a series of attempts to expand or constrain the scope of this remedy. As understandings and expectations of marriage have changed, and the importance of this relationship as a status and source of self-construction has morphed over time, the law has often changed too (though sometimes only marginally or temporarily). Looking at how these changes have occurred reveals that the basis on which they have been justified has typically been either convention or public policy. As Sections 2.2–2.7 show, these categories are not necessarily mutually exclusive, but a recurring observation in the analysis I have offered, and a point that is noted explicitly at the end of Section 2.5, is that the deceptions capable of grounding an action of nullity have related to information that it is either reasonably safe to assume would typically be important to someone getting married or whose disclosure is thought to serve some collective aim.

Equally important, however, is the fact that the character of marriage as a public institution has set limits on how far judges and legislators have been willing to go in widening the law, despite the lessening significance of marriage culturally and legally over time.[207] Even as concern for individuals has grown and their interests in remaining in happy and honest marriages, rather than marriages per se, have gained prominence,[208] reformers have been cautious

---

[206] Zhu, '"Unqueer" Kinship?', noting that some *tongqis* have campaigned for the legalisation of same-sex marriage in the hope that this would prevent such cases arising. See also Yuanyuan Wang, Amanda Wilson, Runsen Chen, Zhishan Hu, Ke Peng and Shicun Xu, 'Behind the Rainbow, "Tongqi" Wives of Men Who Have Sex with Men in China: A Systematic Review' (2020) 10 *Frontiers in Psychology* 2929, noting that some *tongqis* suffer intimate partner violence, suicide ideation and attempts, depressive symptoms, anal sex coercion and increased risk of catching STDs.

[207] On the cultural significance, see Chapter 1, and as an example of the legal significance, see the abolition of the status of illegitimacy in Scots law (Family Law (Scotland) Act 2006, s. 21); further changes in the regime of marriage and family law are beyond this scope of this book.

[208] Andrew W. Winkler, 'Domestic Relations – Fraudulent Representation of Pregnancy as Grounds for Annulment' (1968) 57(2) *Kentucky Law Journal* 272–277; Latham, 'Recognizing Error and Fraud' at 571; Joanna L. Grossman, 'Annulments Based on Fraud: What Is the "Essence" of Marriage?' Part Two (2010), https://supreme.findlaw.com/legal-commentary/annulments-based-on-fraud-what-is-the-essence-of-marriage-part-two.html.

2.8 Conclusions and Contemporary Connections

about adopting extremely permissive legal tests. For example, in the middle of the twentieth century, a general ground of nullity based on fraudulent or wilful concealment of material facts which, if known to a person, might have caused them to decline marriage was rejected because it posed serious practical problems, including uncertainty and difficulties in application.[209] As Part II shows, similar reform suggestions – and similar practical problems – have arisen in relation to deceptive sex.

In contrast to this 'public side' of marriage, which has helped to keep the scope of the law in check, its 'private side' is evident in the existence of voidable marriages. By creating the opportunity for individuals to decide whether an issue the law deems relevant is in fact important to them, voidable marriages have partially privatised marriage. As the Law Commission put it back in 1970, 'why, if the parties wish their marriage to be valid, should they run the risk of having the marriage impeached by third parties?'.[210] Voidable marriages are also significant because, at least historically, they have been associated with ignorance, as opposed to mistake.[211] This relationship is important because although mistakes can be generated by both misrepresentation and non-disclosure, ignorance more clearly suggests a failure to disclose.

Thinking back to changing conceptions of marriage, if contemporary marriage is considered to be a relationship of confidence – one of transparency and openness – which is what the developments outlined in Chapter 1 suggest, then disclosure duties can easily seem appropriate.[212] In other words, the greater extent to which confidence is the hallmark of a relationship, the more apt duties to disclose appear. With this in mind, the development of duties of disclosure is at least as important as changes in the subject matter of deceptions that can ground an annulment. It suggests both a movement in the presumed nature of the marriage (and, now, civil partnership) towards greater transparency and a concomitant shift in terms of who is 'responsibilised'. Whereas in the past a would-be spouse would be expected to do their due diligence and verify the characteristics and position of their potential partner, in our contemporary context it is expected that individuals will be open about (some aspects of) their personal identity and situation with a potential spouse.

These particularities of voidable marriages should not obscure the importance that deception has played within the law of nullity more generally, though. As the cases of bigamy and some of the impotence cases show, even where deception, broadly understood, has not been required to ground an action of nullity, it has been legally significant in providing the basis of a claim or award of damages. Put differently, even when the existence of an impediment has been sufficient to annul a marriage, the misrepresentation

---

[209] *Royal Commission on Marriage and Divorce Report 1951–1955*, Paragraphs 267–268.
[210] Law Commission, *Report on Nullity of Marriage*, Paragraph 12.
[211] In English law, mistake is now a ground of nullity; see Matrimonial Causes Act 1937, s. 12(1)(c).
[212] Latham, 'Recognizing Error and Fraud' at 596.

or failure to disclose the existence of that impediment has been regarded as culpable and harmful.

These discussions are not solely of historical relevance. Though nullity is seen by some as an archaic remedy that is largely defunct in light of liberalised divorce laws, this view has been challenged. Apart from the fact that divorce is not palatable for some people, particularly those of certain religious faiths, actions of nullity can 'set the record straight, by showing [one has] been tricked into a marriage [one] did not desire'.[213] Ironically, then, the rise of liberal divorce laws, including the move towards no-fault divorce, might make nullity appear a more attractive option to those who want the wrongs they have suffered to be formally recognised.[214]

Of course, annulments are only available in relation to marriages and civil partnerships. This means that significant deceptions which occur at the outset of sexual and/or romantic relationships of other kinds have not been recognised in law. In the wake of the large-scale deceptions practised by undercover police officers against women with whom they had long-term relationships,[215] we might ask whether this is appropriate. In the last few decades, however, the possibility of a remedy for those outside marriage or civil partnerships has emerged. The English tort of deceit, which is usually concerned with economic loss but might extend to physical and mental distress or harm[216] (possibly even in the absence of compensable financial loss),[217] has been used in the context of paternity fraud.[218] Furthermore, the tort of intentional infliction of emotional distress has been used in paternity fraud cases that have arisen in the United States and the possible application of the Scottish delict of fraud has also been discussed in this context.[219]

---

[213] Grossman, 'Annulments Based on Fraud'.
[214] Margaret F. Brinig and Michael V. Alexeev, 'Fraud in Courtship: Annulment and Divorce' (1995) 2 *European Journal of Law and Economics* 45–62; Joanna L. Grossman and Chris Guthrie, 'The Road Less Taken: Annulment at the Turn of the Century' (1996) 40 *The American Journal of Legal History* 307–330. Deceiving someone into marriage (as opposed to using deception to lure them somewhere before coercing them to marry) might even constitute a crime in some jurisdictions; see Patrick Parkinson AM, 'Tricked into Marriage' (2018) 42(1) *Melbourne University Law Review* 117–148.
[215] https://policespiesoutoflives.org.uk/our-stories.
[216] Murphy, 'Misleading Appearances'.
[217] Roderick Bagshaw, 'Deceit within Couples' (2001) 117 *Law Quarterly Review* 571–574 at 573.
[218] *P v. B* [2001] 1 FLR 1041; *A v. B* 2007 WL 919500; *X v. Y* [2015] 3 WLUK 1062. On the rejection of such claims in Australia, see Nick Wikeley and Lisa Young, 'Secrets and Lies: No Deceit Down Under' (2008) 20(1) *Child and Family Law Quarterly* 81–94. In these cases, there is no need for the deception to occur before or at the outset of the relationship, as is the case with the law of nullity. This may be significant because a long relationship of love might imply mutual indulgence of hurt; see Ira Mark Ellman and Stephen D. Sugarman, 'Spousal Emotional Abuse as a Tort?' (1996) 55(4) *Maryland Law Review* 1268–1343 at 1302.
[219] Elaine Sutherland, 'Dad or Undad: Liability for Paternity Fraud' (2015), www.lawscot.org.uk/members/journal/issues/vol-60-issue-08/dad-or-undad-liability-for-paternity-fraud. The impetus for this discussion was the criminal conviction (of fraud) of a couple for deceiving a man into thinking he was *not* the father of his child (*G v. HM Advocate* 2016 SLT 282).

2.8 Conclusions and Contemporary Connections

The stringency of these actions, in terms of their requirements for an intention to inflict injury, and the need for psychiatric injury or shock amounting to physical injury have set the bar high for these latter two remedies, though.[220] And while it is theoretically possible that the tort of deceit might apply to other instances of deceptively induced intimacy (assuming the requirements of a false statement, intention to deceive, knowledge or reckless indifference to the truth, reliance and loss were all met),[221] questions about the suitability and desirability of using this tort in the context of deceptively induced intimacy remain. For example, one commentator has suggested that there is a risk that this area of law could extend to incorporate the nonfulfillment of promises since, as alluded to in Chapter 1, promises are simultaneously statements of present intention.[222] He has also pointed out that it may be difficult to distinguish mental distress caused by the 'mere fact of the defendant's dishonesty' from distress caused by reliance on the false representation.[223] There is also the worry that compensation for spouses (in cases where the parties were married or civilly partnered) might clash with the growth of no-fault initiatives in family law.[224] Finally, the difficulty of deciding which deceptions should be actionable, which has arisen in relation to nullity of marriage, also arises in relation to deceit, albeit cast in a different light because of the additional requirements imposed by these civil wrongs.[225]

In concluding this chapter, I would suggest that these extra-marital developments are significant in and of themselves because of what they imply about changing expectations regarding intimate relationships, but they also speak to some of the challenges of using law to try to provide redress for deception within this context. Nevertheless, there is scope to further consider whether and why legal intervention might be potentially justifiable and desirable in this context. After offering some reflections on the special cases of promises and intentions in Chapters 3 and 4, I return to these questions in Chapter 8.

---

[220] Sutherland 'Dad or Undad'. See also David Crump, 'Rethinking Intentional Infliction of Emotional Distress' (2018) 25(2) *George Mason Law Review* 287–300.

[221] Peter MacDonald Eggers, *Deceit: The Lie of the Law* (London: Routledge, 2009), ch. 1. Where the deception concerns one's own circumstances, the requirement for knowledge or indifference regarding the truth may be easier to meet and reliance might be presumed; see Bagshaw, 'Deceit within Couples' at 572–573.

[222] Bagshaw, 'Deceit within Couples' at 572.   [223] Ibid. at 573.

[224] Darach Macnamara, 'The Tort of Deceit and Family Law – Some Recent Developments' (2001) 9 *Irish Student Law Review* 163–180 at 174. It has since been held that an action for deceit brought by a spouse already engaged in proceedings relating to financial provision following an annulment might constitute an abuse of process; see *FRB* v. *DCA* [2019] EWHC 2816 (Fam). See also Ellman and Sugarman, 'Spousal Emotional Abuse'.

[225] Macnamara, 'The Tort of Deceit' at 178–179.

3

Promising Marriage

3.1 Scope and Themes

Chapter 2 explored when and how deception, understood in its broadest sense, could affect marital consent. In this chapter, I undertake a similar exercise in relation to promises to marry, analysing the circumstances under which a person could justifiably break such a promise on account of their fiancé(e)'s misrepresentation or failure to disclose certain information. In doing so, I show how the range of deceptions that were legally significant was relatively similar in the two contexts, but with slightly more deceptions providing a defence to a charge of breach of promise. To appreciate why breaking a promise to marry required a justification at all, however, it is first necessary to understand the consequences to which a breach of this kind could give rise. As such, in Section 3.2, I outline how breaking a promise to marry could amount to an actionable civil law wrong.

As well as providing a foundation for the analysis of justifications I undertake in Section 3.4, Section 3.2 also explains how breaking a promise to marry was associated with deception. The difficulty of knowing another person's intentions meant that breaking a promise to marry could potentially imply that the promise had been false when it was made. In other words, when a person did not stand by their commitment this raised questions about whether they had ever intended to do so. There might even be clear evidence that the promise was false from the start, such as the fact that the promiser was already married, and knew this, when they made the promise. This relationship between breaking a promise and deception, which caused some confusion, was further complicated by changing cultural expectations of marriage, including those outlined in Chapter 1. As I suggest in Section 3.4, if the statement that was implicitly communicated by a promise of marriage changed over time – from a statement about constancy to a statement about marrying for real love – then this had consequences for any inferences about deception that could be drawn from not going through with the marriage.

Confusion about the relationship between deception and breach of promise also affected how the action was classified, for it was not always clear whether it should be considered a delict, akin to deceit or fraud, or part of the law of contract. In Section 3.2, I show how this classificatory quandary was connected to questions of remedy and the possibility of civil 'punishment'. I also consider the difficulty of distinguishing breach of promise of marriage from the closely related actions of seduction and declarator of marriage in Section 3.3. I cover some of the complexities involved in this task in subsequent chapters, specifically Chapter 4, where I examine declarators of marriage in detail, and Chapter 5, where I analyse the action of seduction. In this chapter, I focus on the apparently distinguishing features of breach of promise of marriage, including the conduct on which this action could be based and the ways in which it could be proved.

My aim in considering these features of breach of promise is not only to clarify its relationship to other legal doctrines. Through tracing changes in the conduct which could ground an action of breach of promise and examining developments in the nature and form of evidence that could be used to prove it, I aim to show that, just like the contracts of marriage discussed in Chapter 4, promises of marriage were inferred, or even imputed, with differing degrees of latitude across the period of this study. These variations reflect different positions regarding when and why individuals should be deemed bound which, in turn, reflect different attitudes towards freedom and obligation and, ultimately, changing views on the disciplinary role of marriage. Uncovering the different ways that obligations were created both demonstrates the nuance that existed in this area of law and provides a new way of understanding its decline. As existing work on breach of promise of marriage has shown, changing gender norms and, relatedly, worries about shrewd and mercenary women making cynical or unfounded claims contributed to the disappearance of the action of breach of promise.[1] Yet two other, crucial, features of the action that contributed to its decline and which are directly relevant to the subject of this book are its relationship to liberty and love.

As I show across the rest of this chapter, the ability to sue another person for breaking their marital engagement was in direct tension with the expectation that marriage should be free – an expectation that was particularly important in Protestant nations such as Scotland[2] – and the expectation that marriage should be for love. The tension with freedom is evident in the dissatisfaction the action of breach of promise elicited at particular moments in time and in the suggestion that, at the very least, its requirements should become more stringent. It is notable that these moments coincide with one of the periods of liberalisation I outlined in Chapter 1, that is, the late nineteenth century.

As for the ideal of love-based marriage, this shows up in litigation concerning defenders who told their fiancées about their changed feelings. Unlike defenders who changed their mind about marrying but kept this fact to themselves,

---

[1] Ginger S. Frost, *Promises Broken: Courtship, Class, and Gender in Victorian England* (Charlottesville: University of Virginia Press, 1995); Saskia Lettmaier, *Broken Engagements: The Action for Breach of Promise of Marriage and the Feminine Ideal, 1800–1940* (Oxford: Oxford University Press, 2010); Steinbach, *Promises, Promises*; Hasday, *Intimate Lies and the Law*, ch. 4.

[2] Fergusson, *Consistorial Law*, p. 168.

these defenders had at least been honest with their partners – a quality that became increasingly important across the modern era as the expectation that marriage should be based on real love grew.[3] Furthermore, in a context where love came to be understood as at least to some extent uncontrollable,[4] the change of heart could not straightforwardly be seen as blameworthy. Yet because the action of breach of promise was predicated on a duty to follow through with a promise to marry except in a small range of circumstances – a duty that was itself grounded in a rival ideal underpinning of marriage, that is, constancy – it could not accommodate a justification based on changed emotions. Paying attention to these aspects of the action of breach of promise is therefore necessary to fully understand its demise, and it also provides important insights about the capacity of law to regulate promises or statements of future intention in the context of intimate relationships today, a point to which I return in Section 3.5 and again in Chapter 8.

3.2 Wrongfully Breaking and Wrongfully Making Promises

In simple terms, the action of breach of promise enabled people (almost always women) to sue their partner for declining to go through with the anticipated marriage. Initially, only damages for pecuniary losses (both actual and anticipated, due to the woman's 'loss of the market'[5]) were recoverable, but in the 1812 case of *Hogg* v. *Gow*, it was decided that solatium was also due.[6] This decision was based on the belief that jilted women would necessarily sustain mental and emotional injuries[7] and that to inflict 'perhaps the severest distress that the human mind can suffer' was a serious wrong (though this wrong might be justified, as discussed in Section 3.4) that deserved a remedy.[8] The judges who ushered in this change associated it with the progress of civilisation.[9] Lord

---

[3] See Chapter 1.   [4] See Chapter 1.
[5] *Grahame and Erskine* v. *Burn* (1685), as discussed in various texts, such as Stair; More, *Institutions* (vol. 1), p. 34.
[6] It has been suggested that damages for non-patrimonial consequences were recognised in a 'roundabout way' in the 1770 case of *Johnston* v. *Pasley*, in which the affront of a letter breaking off the engagement, which had been sent to a friend of the pursuer, was compensated; see John Blackie, 'Unity in Diversity: The History of Personality Rights in Scots Law' in Whitty and Zimmermann (eds.), *Rights of Personality in Scots Law*, pp. 31–146, p. 125.
[7] Injuries were presumed in other jurisdictions too, at least in the nineteenth century; see Alecia Simmonds, '"She Felt Strongly the Injury to Her Affections": Breach of Promise of Marriage and the Medicalization of Heartbreak in Early Twentieth-Century Australia' (2017) 38(2) *The Journal of Legal History* 179–202; Lettmaier, *Broken Engagements*, pp. 21, 48, 68; Anat Rosenberg, *Liberalizing Contracts: Nineteenth Century Promises through Literature, Law and History* (Abingdon: Routledge, 2019), p. 187; Eric Reiter, *Wounded Feelings: Litigating Emotions in Quebec, 1870–1950* (Toronto: University of Toronto Press, 2017), p. 9.
[8] *Hogg* v. *Gow* (1812) Faculty Collection, Paper 16. The quotation is from Lord Meadowbank.
[9] For reflections on breach of promise of marriage as a civilising project in the Australian context, see Alecia Simmonds, '"Promises and Pie-Crusts Were Made to Be Broke" Breach of Promise of Marriage and the Regulation of Courtship in Early Colonial Australia' (2005) 23 *The Australian Feminist Law Journal* 99–120.

Meadowbank, who portrayed the development as in keeping with older authorities, suggested that the 'loss of market', which had been compensable even in 'rude and uncultivated times', was actually caused by the intangible injuries a breach of promise caused. As he put it, a woman whose 'heart is used' would be indisposed to respond to courtship and falling in love again; he even went so far as to say she would be rendered incapable of this by the 'calamity that has sunk [her] mind'.[10] Lord Bannatyne, who did not portray the development as in keeping with established legal doctrine but, at the same time, held that there were no authorities preventing it, suggested that changes in the manners, habits and feelings of both 'mankind' and 'the people of Scotland' justified an award of solatium. The fact that English courts had started to hear breach of promise cases grounded in the failure to implement the promise, rather than specific pecuniary losses that flowed from this,[11] may have been significant, too. Certainly, a sheriff later described *Hogg* v. *Gow* as having been decided 'in the wake of that [the law] of England',[12] and the two countries eventually became outliers in Europe, where there was otherwise a move away from compensating wounded feelings in this context.[13]

Despite the presumption that a jilted woman would suffer injuries, sometimes very serious injuries resulting in 'lunacy or death',[14] the possibility that some women might suffer little or no injury to their feelings existed. For example, a pursuer might take the disappointment 'very coolly'[15] or be judged to have become engaged to please her parents rather than because she was deeply attached to the defender.[16] There was also an entire class of women, women of a 'lower class', who were presumed to marry for pragmatic, rather than emotional, reasons. It was thought that these women could not afford to 'indulge in the luxury of sentiment' but because they married for 'mercenary' reasons their dashed hopes could more easily be valued in economic terms.[17] Further reflecting the gendered nature of this action, men who brought suits were not always awarded damages for injured feelings;[18] furthermore, they could expect to be

---

[10] *Hogg* v. *Gow* (1812).   [11] This occurred in the 1760s; see Frost, *Promises Broken*, p. 15.
[12] *Hewat* v. *Bennet* ('Breach of Promise of Marriage in Perth', *Fife Herald*, 7 January 1858, p. 4).
[13] Vernon Valentine Palmer, 'Moral Damages in the Age of Codification' in Vernon Valentine Palmer (ed.), *The Recovery of Non-Pecuniary Loss in European Contract Law* (Cambridge: Cambridge University Press, 2015), pp. 43–57.
[14] *Forbes* v. *Brown* ('The Perth Breach of Promise Case', *The Glasgow Herald*, 13 June 1870, p. 4), with Sheriff Barclay stating that this was 'not infrequently' the result.
[15] *Spalding* v. *Oman* ('Small Debt Court', *Dundee Courier*, 7 January 1861, p. 3). See also the finding that there should be no large damages when the pursuer had ceased to care for the defender (*Mackay* v. *Scott* ('Blairgowrie Man's Breach', *The Evening Telegraph*, 13 December 1904, p. 5)).
[16] *Hare* v. *Scott* ('Lanarkshire Sheriff Court', *The Glasgow Herald*, 30 August 1870, p. 2).
[17] Fraser, *Husband and Wife*, p. 497.
[18] For example, *Brennan* v. *Jeffs* ('Breach of Promise of Marriage', *Caledonian Mercury*, 14 February 1862, p. 2); *Kerr* v. *Moore* ('Amusing Breach of Promise Case', *Paisley Herald and Renfrewshire Advertiser*, 6 February 1865, p. 2). Sometimes they did not even seek them, for example, *Donald* v. *Lawrie* ('Male Pursuer in Aberdeen Breach Case', *Dundee Courier*, 23 October 1908, p. 7). If men won damages, they would typically be small; see Lettmaier, *Broken Engagements*, pp. 27–28; Rosenberg, *Liberalizing Contracts*, p. 186.

mocked for seeking them during the mid nineteenth century[19] and, by the end of the century, chastised for their unmanliness.[20] Since men generally enjoyed the freedom to seek out and pursue subsequent engagements, they could not easily be said to have suffered a 'loss of market' either.[21]

Reflecting changes in expectations surrounding marriage – specifically, the shift towards a desire for love-based, companionate marriages – by the turn of the century, a judge might consider the loss of a relationship with limited prospects for happiness to cause little injury to a pursuer's feelings.[22] At this time, there was also a slight shift, towards medicalisation, in the way the intangible injuries associated with breach of promise cases were understood. For example, in one case, it was significant that the pursuer did not have to consult a doctor after she was jilted (though she did sustain a 'severe shock and deep injury to her feelings'[23]) and in another the pursuer was rendered unfit for work due to the shock to her nervous system.[24] Nevertheless, even at this time, the disappointment of a broken engagement was considered 'bound' to cause serious shock and impaired health.[25]

As I mentioned in Chapter 1, damages for dignitarian and emotional injuries tend to blur the line between punishment and compensation, especially when these injuries are presumed. In keeping with this, other studies of compensating wounded feelings have pointed out that this practice more closely resembles satisfaction or vindication than *restitutio in integrum* (restitution to the original position).[26] Within the cases I examined, although the possibility that damages might be given partly 'in poenam' (as a punishment) was rejected, at least one judge seemed to think this was an option.[27] Furthermore, the language of punishment appears in other cases[28] and in commentary,[29] and judges

---

[19] *McLeod v. Miller* ('Local Intelligence', *John o'Groat Journal*, 17 February 1843, p. 2; 'Perth', *Dundee Courier*, 3 September 1844, p. 3).

[20] *Longmore v. Massie* (1883) in William Guthrie, *Select Cases Decided in the Sheriff Courts of Scotland* (vol. 2) (Edinburgh: T. & T. Clark, 1894), pp. 450–453; commentary on *Mitches v. Walker* ('Aberdeen, Wednesday, Oct. 29, 1890', *The Aberdeen Journal*, 29 October 1890, p. 4).

[21] *Macdonald v. Cameron* ('An Elgin Breach of Promise', *Dundee Courier*, 21 May 1878, p. 2); *Shaw v. Campbell* ('Amusing Breach of Promise Case in Elgin', *The Aberdeen Journal*, 22 February 1884, p. 7).

[22] For example, *King v. McVey* ('An Airdrie Breach of Promise Case', *The Glasgow Herald*, 1 January 1894, p. 9).

[23] *Bush v. Reith* ('A Boyish Attachment', *The Evening Telegraph*, 3 December 1919, p. 5).

[24] *Crossan v. Cumming* (1963) NRS SC58/22/1963/1. On the medicalisation of breach of promise claims, see Simmonds, '"Promises and Pie-Crusts"'; Lettmaier, *Broken Engagements*, p. 178 and Simmonds, '"She Felt Strongly"'.

[25] *Neill v. Cassidy* ('Scots Girl Wins "Breach" Case', *Dundee Courier*, 24 November 1932, p. 7).

[26] Reiter, *Wounded Feelings*, p. 8.

[27] 'Court of Session' (1812) *Scots Magazine and Edinburgh Library Miscellany* 721–724, discussing *Hogg v. Gow*. On rejecting punishment, see also *Tucker v. Aitchison* (1846) 9 D 21 and *Reid v. Reid* ('The Reid Breach of Promise Case', *The Aberdeen Journal*, 20 January 1909, p. 3).

[28] For example, *Scott v. Rae* ('Breach of Promise of Marriage', *John o'Groat Journal*, 12 February 1863, p. 4); *Longmore v. Massie* (1883); *Shaw v. Campbell* (1884); *Evanton v. Ross* ('Ross-Shire Breach of Promise Case', *Aberdeen Press and Journal*, 1 February 1899, p. 6).

[29] For example, 'Breach of Promise of Marriage Actions', *John o'Groat Journal*, 27 April 1855, p. 3; 'Breach of Promise Actions', *Paisley Herald and Renfrewshire Advertiser*, 15 August 1868, p. 7.

accepted the possibility of 'exemplary damages',[30] though it has been suggested that this meant the reparation should clearly mark the wrong[31] rather than going above and beyond the amount of compensation merited (which is what the term implies in English law).[32]

Either way, the award of solatium complicated the legal classification of breach of promise of marriage actions. Solatium was not, and is still not, typically awarded for breaches of contract,[33] so its provision meant that while 'as a matter of logical analysis' breach of promise actions belonged with other kinds of contract cases, as a matter of form they seemed to fit better with delicts.[34] The ability to seek damages but not the remedy of specific implement, even though the defaulting party could still perform the obligation, was also seen as marking breach of promise of marriage out as unusual.[35] The reason given for denying the remedy of specific implement was that promises of marriage, like contracts involving partnerships or service, involved intimate relationships, and in these circumstances the law would not compel performance when it was disagreeable to either or both of the parties.[36]

In addition to these remedy-related peculiarities, the wrong-making features of breach of promise were also somewhat hybrid. On the one hand, breaking a promise to marry was considered wrongful because it was a form of inconstant behaviour; on the other hand, it was considered wrongful because it could also imply dishonesty. Starting with inconstancy, it is well recognised that abiding by promises is important in any context involving future planning, such as systems of financial credit.[37] By allowing for the compensation of unfulfilled promises of marriage, the action of breach of promise therefore reflected the life-extensive significance that marital status held, especially for women. As one advocate of the action put it, marriage was the 'natural and honourable

---

[30] *Hogg* v. *Gow* (1812). See also *Kand* v. *Forsyth* ('A Fife Breach of Promise Case', *Dundee Courier*, 29 October 1887, p. 3); *Hutton* v. *Peters* ('The Arbroath Breach of Promise', *Dundee Courier*, 22 June 1901, p. 4).

[31] Blackie, 'Unity in Diversity', p. 127, accepting that English authorities were mentioned when the phrase appeared in *Johnston* v. *Pasley*.

[32] Descheemaker, 'Rationalising Recovery'. The action of breach of promise of marriage and the damages awarded for it were clearly considered punitive in the United States; see Harter F. Wright, 'The Action for Breach of the Marriage Promise' (1924) 10(5) *Virginia Law Review* 361–383.

[33] *Mills and Another* v. *Findlay and Another* 1994 SCLR 397; Lettmaier, *Broken Engagements*, p. 49; Steinbach, *Promises, Promises*, p. 118.

[34] David M. Walker, *The Law of Damages in Scotland* (Edinburgh: W. Green & Sons, 1955), p. 563; David M. Walker, *The Law of Civil Remedies in Scotland* (Edinburgh: W. Green & Sons, 1974), p. 986.

[35] Paton, *Hume's Lectures*, p. 30; *Hogg* v. *Gow* (1812); *Sinclair* v. *Smith* ('Law Intelligence', *The Caledonian Mercury*, 18 July 1860, p. 4). On specific implement in Scots law, including the small range of circumstances where it will not be available, see Laura MacGregor, 'Specific Implement in Scots Law' in Jan Smits, Daniel Haas and Geete Hesen (eds.), *Specific Performance in Contract Law: National and Other Perspectives* (Oxford: Intersentia, 2008), pp. 67–93.

[36] *M'Arthur* v. *Lawson* (1877) 4 R 1134.   [37] Steinbach, *Promises, Promises*, pp. 181–183.

profession' by which most women maintained themselves, and they got access to this institution via an offer or promise of marriage.[38]

Given the importance of marriage to women, it made sense that they should have some mechanism through which a marital promise could be secured, even if it could not be forcibly implemented. Culturally, faith in the constancy of one's future spouse was also a potent ideal, a point that is illustrated in the evidence provided in some breach of promise cases.[39] For example, in a letter to her fiancé one pursuer wrote that she had been 'meditating much on the difference between man's affection and the Man Christ', concluding that '[t]he latter never changed, but the former, alas!!'.[40] Defenders could also allude to the power of this ideal and did so when they emphasised how much they relished the feeling of being trusted by their lover[41] and when they explicitly encouraged this trust.[42] In one remarkable set of letters, the defender described how highly he valued his own trust in her – 'I believe in it and rest in it! It sustains me in my daily work, and without it I would not be what I am' – and urged her to trust him in return, writing '[y]ou should expect great things of me. You should trust and rest in me. Let your heart go out to me in its fullest extent and never fear.' Crucially, this was not trust that was to endure only for as long as it proved to be mutually (or even unilaterally) fulfilling: '[i]t is an ever faithful sentiment, and the essence of Divinity, Heaven's best gift to man.'[43]

These exchanges show more than the importance of trust, understood to mean faith in the constancy of one's lover; they also show that the wrong of breach of promise could be seen not as breaking the promise but as making it in the first place.[44] As one judge explained, although the 'technical' injury in breach of promise cases was the broken promise, the core of the misconduct was pretending to be a betrothed suitor and enjoying the privileges of that position. In other words, it was a kind of fraud.[45] This feature of the action

---

[38] 'The Actions for Breach of Promise Bill', *Edinburgh Evening News*, 30 January 1878, p. 4, reporting on a petition presented to parliament by a group of women in response to a bill to abolish actions of breach of promise of marriage.

[39] On historical archetypes of love, see Rosenwein, *Love: A History*.

[40] Unnamed parties ('Court of Session', *The Glasgow Herald*, 21 February 1872, p. 4). See also a young pursuer who claimed not to need money but liked the idea of the love and constancy of the defender (*Mouat v. Nisbet* (1826), mentioned in Mary Prior, *Fond Hopes Destroyed: Breach of Promise Cases in Shetland* (Lerwick: Shetland Times Limited, 2005), pp. 24–28).

[41] *Urquhart v. Ashforth* ('Breach of Promise Case', *Aberdeen Press and Journal*, 25 August 1877, p. 6).

[42] *Mair v. Taylor* ('A Portsoy Breach of Promise Case', *Aberdeen Press and Journal*, 27 March 1879, p. 3).

[43] *Simpson v. Jack* ('Forfarshire Minister's Breach of Promise', *The Evening Telegraph*, 31 May 1888, p. 2).

[44] 'Lots of Young Men Deceitful', *Aberdeen People's Journal*, 29 October 1892, p. 3.

[45] 'Rationale of "Breach of Promise"', *Fife Herald, and Kinross, Strathearn, and Clackmannan Advertiser*, 21 August 1856, p. 2, reporting on a case heard at the Liverpool Assizes. See also Fraser, *Husband and Wife*, p. 488, quoting from an American case where the injury was described as 'violated faith, more resembling in substance deceit and fraud, than a mere common breach of promise'. This perception is evident in the commentary on the action,

caused some confusion,[46] including in a case where this line of thinking was rejected. In this case, the defender had suggested that breach of promise was not part of contract law but was instead based in deceit. The judge rejected this view, interpreting the relevant deceit as being 'pretending an attachment which he [the defender] did not feel' and pointing out that it had not even been insinuated by the pursuer that the defender was insincere when he made his promise. He also suggested that if deceit were the crux of the action, this would require the pursuer to prove the state of the defender's mind when he entered the contract.[47]

Though understandable, I would suggest that this conclusion might reveal a potential source of confusion, namely confusion as to the subject matter of the deception. It seems to me that 'an attachment' could refer either to a subjective, affective state (which is what the judge seems to have had in mind) or to a highly conventional form of relationship. As I show in Section 3.4, honesty about the former – about one's emotions – was important and seems to have become more so over time, destabilising the action of breach of promise in the process. Yet (dis)honesty about the latter – a highly conventional form of relationship – was arguably the basis of the action of breach of promise, insofar as making a promise to marry could be interpreted as holding oneself out to be the kind of person who would see the commitment through no matter what (barring a small number of special circumstances, outlined in Section 3.4). To renege on the promise was therefore to act in a way that proved this implicit assertion to be false. And whereas deception about one's emotions might require proof of an inner state, deception that was proved via inconstant conduct arguably did not.

In some cases, however, it was apparent that the defender had been unquestionably or perhaps, depending on which interpretation of the relevant deception is preferred, doubly deceptive from the outset. That the defender never intended to marry the pursuer could be inferred from the interactions between the parties,[48] and some defenders even admitted their duplicity.[49] But the greatest potential for clearcut deception existed in cases where the defender was already married at the time he promised marriage. In this context, it could be said – as indeed it was said in relation to English law – that the promise was broken as soon as it was made.[50] A question of public policy arose, however, of whether these promises were

---

too, for example, 'Aberdeen, Wednesday, March 23', *The Aberdeen Journal*, 28 March 1883, p. 4; 'A Plea for Breach of Promise' (1890) 3(77) *The Scots Observer* 683–684; 'Love and Lucre: Broken Hearts and How to Mend Them', *Dundee Weekly News*, 21 March 1891, p. 10.

[46] See, for example, 'Legal Puzzles' (1899) 33(392) *Journal of Jurisprudence* 418–424.
[47] *Sinclair* v. *Smith* (1860) D 1475 at 1482.
[48] *Thorpe* v. *Currie* ('Glasgow Sheriff Court', *The Glasgow Herald*, 13 July 1859, p. 3); *Tait* v. *Edgar* ('Glasgow Breach of Promise Case', *Edinburgh Evening News*, 21 July 1902, p. 3).
[49] *Hall* v. *Bryce* ('A Heartless Breach of Promise Case', *Dundee Courier*, 6 March 1877, p. 3); *Wilson* v. *Young* ('The Ayrshire Breach of Promise Case', *Edinburgh Evening News*, 16 July 1896, p. 7).
[50] Lettmaier, *Broken Engagements*, p. 38.

contra bonos mores (against good morals) and therefore void. Initially, it was held that under English law such promises were valid and capable of grounding a breach of promise action when broken, at least when the plaintiff had been ignorant of the existing marriage.[51] To allow the plaintiff to sue when she knew that her purported fiancé was already married was considered to be against public policy because it would interfere with the ability of the defendant to commit to his marriage and might encourage adultery or desertion.[52] By the twentieth century, however, promises made by married men were ruled completely unactionable on the basis that they contradicted public morality.[53] Prior to this, promises made by married men to unsuspecting women were seen as particularly reprehensible. For example, a defendant might plead that he had not falsely presented himself as single in mitigation,[54] and the fact that a defendant was married was otherwise seen as an aggravation.[55]

The story in Scotland was largely the same except that there appears to have been no decision to rule suits against married men unactionable. As such, in one case, it was held that a defender who pretended to be single for several months was guilty of 'very shameful conduct' and should pay 'ample reparation'.[56] In another, the long duration (seven years) of the defender's deception was singled out for criticism, with the judge referring to this conduct as keeping the pursuer in 'a fool's paradise ... only in the end to drop her suddenly to earth' and judging it to be a cruel wrong worthy of substantial damages.[57] To be sure, allegations that the pursuer knew the defender was married were offered as a defence in several Scottish cases,[58] but there is no suggestion that this knowledge, if proved, would preclude the action or the award of damages on the ground of public policy. Instead, the reason knowledge of the pursuer was relevant is likely that when breach of promise of marriage was pled alongside seduction, as it often was, then, at least formally, some form of deception

---

[51] Ibid.; 'Pacta Illicita' (1875) 19(224) *Journal of Jurisprudence* 393–402.
[52] Lettmaier, *Broken Engagements*, p. 38; Steinbach, *Promises, Promises*, p. 129. For one example, see *Spiers v. Hunt* [1908] 1 KB 720.
[53] Steinbach, *Promises, Promises*, p. 267.
[54] *Bedford v. McKowl* ('Court of Common Pleas', *Caledonian Mercury*, 3 March 1800, p. 2).
[55] 'Disgraceful Breach of Promise Case', *Fife Herald, and Kinross, Strathearn, and Clackmannan Advertiser*, 1 December 1864, p. 4.
[56] *Coleman v. Storm* ('A Falkirk Seduction Case', *Dundee Courier*, 30 January 1878, p. 3). See also *Stewart v. Jackson*, where the conduct of the defender, who was married but promised marriage to two other women, was described as 'very base and cruel' ('Heartless Breach of Promise Case', *Edinburgh Evening News*, 22 December 1886, p. 2) and *Watson v. Anderson*, where the married defender's conduct was called 'shameful' ('News of the Day', *Dundee Courier*, 31 October 1888, p. 3).
[57] *McLeod v. Robertson* ('Married Man Makes Love to a Servant', *The Courier*, 14 April 1911, p. 8).
[58] For example, *Hislop v. Affleck* ('An Edinburgh Breach of Promise', *Edinburgh Evening News*, 6 May 1874, p. 2); *Craig v. Langlands* ('The Glasgow Breach of Promise Case', *Edinburgh Evening News*, 22 August 1881, p. 2); *Anderson v. Currie* ('Abandonment of Action for Alleged Seduction', *Edinburgh Evening News*, 20 July 1882, p. 2); *Stewart v. Jackson* (1886); *Buchanan v. Pocock* (1979) NRS SC21/6/1979/6.

was required. This is because seduction, which in Scotland was a separate and separable ground of action available to women,[59] was predicated on fraud.[60]

3.3 The Meaning and Proof of Promises

As with the formation of the marital contract, which I discuss in Chapter 4, the creation of a binding promise to marry could be theorised in different ways with significant practical implications. On one view, promises were acts of will, reflecting the intentions of their makers; on another, they were more flexible and a way of organising relationships between members of society. On this latter view, a binding promise might exist whenever someone raised the expectations of another person, irrespective of whether they had intended to be bound. This position might be qualified by a requirement that such expectations be raised knowingly and/or a requirement that the expectations be reasonable, but its general rationale was that unintended promises led to the same degree of dependence as their intended counterparts and when they were broken they led to the same amount of disappointment.[61]

Another important aspect of the way promises were understood is the perceived need (or lack thereof) for legal intervention. According to some Enlightenment thinkers, notably David Hume, an unreliable person would lose the trust of others and so it was in a person's own interests to stand by even unintended promises. The threat of reputational loss could therefore be expected to keep those otherwise inclined to break their promises in check.[62] Looking at the legal sources, there are clear traces of this line of thought. For example, soon after Scots law began to accommodate actions for breach of promise of marriage per se, Baron David Hume (nephew of the philosopher)[63] raised some doubts about this development, including the fact that it would potentially undermine more informal mechanisms of governance. In his opinion, before the law changed the 'security of parties' had been protected by 'the feeling of honour and character' and 'dread of [the] censure and disapprobation' that would follow a broken promise. He also thought that the 'fear of the inward reproach of having done an injury, for which no suitable amends can be made' would stop people breaking a promise to marry.[64]

By substituting an award of damages for the pangs of conscience and loss of esteem, however, the action of breach of promise risked making broken promises more common. The worry was that a man who paid compensation would be spared the more onerous penalties of social disapprobation and its negative

---

[59] Cf. in England where it was only an aggravation of breach of promise of marriage or a ground of action open to the woman's parents; see Frost, *Promises Broken*, pp. 18, 108, 166.
[60] At least, this was true for much of the history of this action, as discussed in Chapter 5.
[61] This synopsis is based on Melissa J. Ganz, '"The Fidelity of Promising": Egoism and Obligation in Austen' (2022) 73(309) *The Review of English Studies* 344–360.
[62] Ibid.
[63] On some of the links between the jurist and his uncle, see Kennedy, 'Declaring Crimes'.
[64] Paton, *Hume's Lectures*, p. 31.

consequences for self-esteem.[65] Others felt similarly, with one commentator arguing that those who violated promises of marriage were best dealt with by social stigma[66] and another suggesting that 'the horsewhip and the hair-trigger' would be more effective punishments than an award of damages.[67] Like Hume, the second of these two critics felt that degradation of the inconstant lover was the best way to curb the behaviour of which he was guilty, writing: '[m]ake breach of promise of marriage as disgraceful as cheating at play, and you will suppress it more effectually than if you quadrupled the damages'.[68]

Of course, broken promises of marriage did become a routine matter of legal adjudication and so questions about what kind of conduct constituted a promise and by what kinds of evidence it could be proved had to be addressed. On the latter point, parties to the action were not competent witnesses until 1874,[69] five years after they were deemed admissible in England.[70] Before this time, however (and indeed after this time), promises grounding an action of breach of promise could be proved *prout de jure*, that is, by parole evidence (evidence by oath of witnesses), as opposed to by writ or oath of a party.[71] This meant that unlike promises grounding an action of declarator of marriage, which I discuss in Chapter 4, promises that formed the basis of an action of breach of promise could be proved by the circumstances as well as the testimony of neighbours, friends and even family.[72] It is clear that some wished the rules of evidence to be tightened and the suggestion that only promises contained in writing should be actionable was discussed more than once.[73] At the same time,

---

[65] Ibid.   [66] 'Saturday Morning, June 24', *The Glasgow Herald*, 24 June 1865, p. 4.
[67] 'Breach of Promise to Marry' (1869) 105(643) *Blackwood's Edinburgh Magazine* 564–567 at 566. See also the suggestion that in cases of great hardship and cruelty, the wrongdoer should be 'soundly horsewhipped' ('Breach of Promise of Marriage', *Dundee Courier*, 3 March 1877, p. 4).
[68] 'Breach of Promise to Marry' at 566.
[69] Evidence Law Amendment (Scotland) Act 1874 (c. 64, 37 & 38 Vict.), which repealed s. 4 of the Evidence (Scotland) Act 1853 (c. 20, 16 & 17 Vict.). The 1853 Act had made it competent to adduce parties to an action and their spouses (subject to some restrictions) and examine them as witnesses but s. 4 stipulated that they remained incompetent in actions of breach of promise of marriage, declarators of marriage and nullity and some other forms of litigation.
[70] Evidence Act 1851 (c. 99, 14 & 15 Vict.) and Evidence Further Amendment Act 1869 (c. 68, 32 & 33 Vict.).
[71] Watson (ed.), *Bell's Dictionary*, pp. 693, 771, 871. John Guthrie Smith, *Law of Damages: A Treatise on the Reparation of Injuries as Administered in Scotland*, 2nd ed. (Edinburgh: T. & T. Clark, 1889), p. 130. Outside the marriage context, gratuitous promises could not be proved by witnesses (see Erskine, *Principles of the Law of Scotland*, p. 586) and promises generally were to be proved by writing or oath or by witnesses when followed by *rei interventus* or when forming part of a bargain of movables (see George Joseph Bell and William Guthrie, *Principles of the Law of Scotland*, 6th ed. (Edinburgh: T. & T. Clark, 1872), p. 5).
[72] At one point, there was some confusion over whether promises had to be proved in the same way in both contexts, but it was held that they did not; see *Murray* v. *Napier* (1861) 23 D 1243; *Sinclair* v. *Rowan* (1861) 23 D 1365.
[73] For example, 'Saturday Morning, June 24', *The Glasgow Herald*, 24 June 1865, p. 4; 'Sir Fitzroy's Law of Evidence', *John o'Groat Journal*, 29 June 1865, p. 4; 'Promises of Marriage on Stamped Paper', *The Aberdeen Weekly Journal*, 29 November 1893, p. 3; *King* v. *McVey* (1894); Lettmaier, *Promises, Promises*, p. 277.

3.3 The Meaning and Proof of Promises

the practical limitations of this approach did not go unnoticed, specifically, the unlikely prospect of a woman being willing (or indeed able) to request a promise to marry in writing.[74] It was also considered potentially unjust to limit the remedy to promises put down in writing for this would mean that libertines might engage in acts indicating an intent to marry but evade legal consequences so long as they were careful enough to avoid committing themselves on paper.[75]

Yet a more permissive approach to establishing promises brought complexity. As one article put it, '[t]he law has not defined promise, because promise is, perhaps, undefinable'.[76] Judges had to make determinations, though, and the way they did this reflects the different ways of theorising promises outlined earlier and the tension upon which they are based, that is, the tension between respecting the dependencies and expectations that could grow in the absence of explicit promises and preserving the ostensibly precious liberty of marriage.[77]

Starting with the need for an intention to be bound, this was not mentioned often but, crucially, arose in cases heard during the periods of liberalisation that occurred at the end of the eighteenth and nineteenth centuries.[78] For the most part, however, all that mattered was that the conduct of the defender had created the impression that he intended to marry the pursuer,[79] sometimes with the additional qualification that this impression was reasonable.[80] The main issue was therefore how this impression could be established or, put differently, what conduct on the defender's part could make him vulnerable to a finding that he had promised marriage. It quickly became clear that there was no need for a distinct promise to be made; a course of conduct from which it could be inferred that a promise had been made or that an understanding to that effect had arisen was sufficient. Buying marital presents or furnishing a house could therefore potentially substantiate a claim that marriage had been promised.[81] In one case, the judge was keen to emphasise that no precise rule about what sorts of evidence would suffice existed.[82] An issue that cropped up

---

[74] 'Interesting to the Ladies', *Fife Herald, and Kinross, Strathearn, and Clackmannan Advertiser*, 22 June 1865, p. 2; 'The Ladies in the House of Commons', *Paisley Herald and Renfrewshire Advertiser*, 24 June 1865, p. 2.

[75] *Morison* v. *Ferguson* (1859–1860) 2 Scot LJ 1 109.

[76] 'Inferential Promise of Marriage', *The Caledonian Mercury*, 12 August 1862, p. 3.

[77] I discuss a similar tension in Chapter 4, and the theme of implied agreements and conditions arises in Chapters 7 and 8.

[78] *Johnstone* v. *Pasley* (1769) NRS CC8/6/459; *Wyllie* v. *McCreath* ('Court of Session', *The Glasgow Herald*, 22 March 1889, p. 9).

[79] *Morison* v. *Ferguson* (1859–1860); *Spalding* v. *Oman* (1861); *Kerr* v. *Moore* (1865); *Hutton* v. *Verdon* (1901); *Abraham* v. *McLetchy* ('Glasgow Breach of Promise Case', *The Aberdeen Weekly Journal*, 18 July 1885, p. 8).

[80] *Johnstone* v. *Pasley* (1769); *Hogg* v. *Gow* (1812).

[81] *Morison* v. *Ferguson* (1859–1860). On material proof of promises, see Sally Holloway, *The Game of Love in Georgian England: Courtship, Emotions and Material Culture* (Oxford: Oxford University Press, 2019), ch. 6.

[82] *Tucker* v. *Aitchison* (1846).

in a few cases was equality of age and rank between the parties; if the two parties were, roughly speaking, equal then it was easier to convince a fact-finder that a promise to marry had existed.[83]

The issue of how direct and specific a promise of marriage should be to ground an action of breach of promise did not disappear, though. In one case, it was held that actions of declarator of marriage required direct and specific promises but a lower threshold – inferences based on a course of conduct and correspondence – applied in cases of breach of promise.[84] But only a few years later, a sheriff held that the two actions required similarly direct promises and that the only difference was in the form of evidence that was permitted, with only promises proved by writ or oath of the defender being capable of grounding a declarator of marriage. In the judge's view, courtship, no matter how close or long, was not sufficient to bring an action of breach of promise.[85] This decision was overturned on appeal, though, and it was confirmed that if the whole circumstances implied a promise on which the pursuer was entitled to rely then damages would be due.[86] This left the jury with a lot of discretion, and they were encouraged to use their 'common sense' to work out whether events had occurred which 'necessarily implied a promise to marry', such as proclaiming the banns, buying a wedding ring or walking 'as engaged persons did'.[87] It is significant that the Lord Justice Clerk (Moncreiff) invoked common sense multiple times when charging the jury because this locates his directions within a wider set of legal developments in which he played a key part.[88] Even more significantly for present purposes, his directions endorsed a very permissive approach to establishing promises to marry, which drew on convention for support.

This trend continued,[89] despite the admission of the parties as witnesses,[90] with one judge admitting frankly that it was hard to tell where courtship stopped and engagement began.[91] The practice of generously inferring promises also continued to attract criticism until the last decades of the nineteenth

---

[83] *Hewat* v. *Bennet* (1858); *Couper* v. *Cullen* ('Court of Session', *The Glasgow Herald*, 1 April 1874, p. 4). See Chapter 5 for more discussion.
[84] *Murray* v. *Napier* (1861). See Chapter 4 for how this distinction was not always clear.
[85] *Scott* v. *Stewart* ('The Pitlochry Breach of Promise Case', *The Glasgow Herald*, 3 January 1870, p. 5).
[86] [1870] SLR 8 44.
[87] *Asher* v. *Rennie* ('The Asher-Rennie Breach of Promise Case', *The Glasgow Herald*, 27 December 1871, p. 4).
[88] See Chloë Kennedy, '"Ungovernable Feelings and Passions": Common Sense Philosophy and Mental State Defences in Nineteenth-Century Scotland' (2016) 20(3) *Edinburgh Law Review* 285–311.
[89] For example, *Watson* v. *Milne* ('An Aberdeenshire Breach of Promise Case', *Edinburgh Evening News*, 28 April 1876, p. 2); *Simpson* v. *Logan* ('An Aberdeenshire Breach of Promise', *The Aberdeen Weekly Journal*, 18 October 1876, p. 8).
[90] Rosenberg suggests that proof of promises of marriage depended on social courting expectations prior to the English 1869 Act (*Liberalizing Contracts*, p. 186).
[91] *Fletcher* v. *Grant* (1878) General Collection, Paper 22.

century. One particularly controversial development was a scandal involving a minister who had seemingly broken off an engagement with a young parishioner. In line with other cases from around this time, the judge held that an engagement could be proved in various ways, including by a course of conduct alone; the question was whether the evidence could fairly and legitimately be interpreted as implying that a promise had been given.[92] In this case, the minister had engaged in visits, being alone together and kissing.[93] There is a sense from the coverage that a promise was inferred because it seemed like the minister *should* have made a promise to marry[94] and the decision sparked anxiety, with one writer stressing the importance of clearly delineating conduct that could leave a man vulnerable to the 'heavy penalty' doled out in breach of promise cases.[95] At this time, there was also an unsuccessful attempt to abolish actions of breach of promise of marriage.[96] Yet others claimed it would be unjust to allow men to escape liability by tightening up the law because 'the language of the soul [was] told through the eye'. In their view, a man should not be able to get away with raising expectations simply because the words his conduct implied were not actually uttered or written.[97]

By the 1880s, however, there is a notable change in sensibilities. Looking across the cultural sources, there is a sense that the ease with which promises of marriage could be inferred (or imputed) was stultifying the possibility of a fuller array of relationships between the sexes, including friendships.[98] Furthermore, alongside frustration with the limited roles for women that actions of breach of promise both assumed and reified,[99] there was a renewed emphasis on the problems that effectively forcing marriage could be expected to cause, including undermining the possibility of happy, loving and companionate relationships.[100] At around this time, several mock breach of promise trials were held as entertainment, which suggests that the action was losing some of its credibility.[101]

---

[92] *Couper* v. *Cullen* (1874).
[93] 'Action for Breach of Promise of Marriage against a Minister', *Southern Reporter*, 11 December 1873, p. 3.
[94] See also Lettmaier, *Broken Engagements*, pp. 35–36.
[95] 'Pacta Illicita'. See also the perhaps tongue in cheek suggestion that a Lovers' Liability Insurance Company should be established, or a Guild of Young People set up to facilitate friendly relations between the sexes without ulterior motives ('Flirtation', *The Glasgow Herald*, 12 April 1889, p. 16).
[96] Lord Herschell's 1879 Bill – for a list of subsequent legislative attempts, see Wright, 'The Action for Breach of the Marriage Promise', and see Lettmaier, *Broken Engagements*, p. 138.
[97] 'A Wounded Dove's Complaint', *The Glasgow Herald*, 3 April 1874, p. 6.
[98] See a collection of letters to the editor in *The Glasgow Herald*, 18 April 1889, p. 10.
[99] 'Letters to the Editor', *The Glasgow Herald*, 18 April 1889, p. 10; Frost, *Promises Broken*, ch. 9; Lettmaier, *Broken Engagements*, p. 126; Norrie McLeish, *Broken Promises: Scottish Breach of Promise Cases* (Jedburgh: Alba Publishing, 2013).
[100] Frost, *Promises Broken*, pp. 141–142, 173; Reiter, *Wounded Feelings*, pp. 193, 197–198.
[101] 'London Road Literary Society Mock Trial', *Edinburgh Evening News*, 29 April 1887, p. 2; 'Stonehaven – Mutual Improvement Society', *Aberdeen Press and Journal*, 6 February 1888, p. 6; 'Free Lance Mutual Improvement Society', *The Aberdeen Journal*, 17 March 1904, p. 7; 'St Margaret's Temperance Guild', *The Aberdeen Journal*, 10 October 1908, p. 4.

In terms of legal developments, there were more efforts to abolish the action of breach of promise, which attracted news coverage and sparked debates,[102] and the action was subject to criticism more generally.[103] Judicial decisions from this time also reveal some disagreement over the precise contours of the action. For example, one judge decided that evidence of a man courting a woman of a similar age and station with seeming intentions of marriage was not enough to ground a viable case of breach of promise. In his view, a direct and specific promise to marry was required.[104] This decision was overturned on appeal, however, on the basis that the law permitted a promise to be inferred in such circumstances. In the appeal judge's opinion, people did not typically become engaged by using words such as 'I promise to marry'; indeed, in his opinion, such directness should inspire doubt about the speaker.[105] It is clear from the coverage of this decision that conventions concerning engagement were core to the way this action operated. They could even override claims that the relationship was of another kind, such as 'a spiritual union to which the common men and women of the world were strangers'.[106]

By the 1920s, convention still had a role to play and might be used to infer that a promise to marry had *not* been made. For example, a man telling a woman that he would not leave her if anything happened (i.e., if she became pregnant) could not, on its own, be construed as a promise to marry because local custom apparently implied that this statement amounted only to a commitment to admit paternity.[107] There are also some noteworthy additions to the way pursuers' grievances were described at around this time, with humiliation[108] and

---

[102] For example, 'Aberdeen, Wednesday March 28, 1883', *The Aberdeen Journal*, 28 March 1883, p. 4; 'Maryculter – Young Men's Mutual Improvement Association', *The Aberdeen Journal*, 11 January 1884, p. 6; 'Ballater – Mutual Improvement Association', *The Aberdeen Journal*, 7 February 1889, p. 6; 'District Notes', *The Aberdeen Journal*, 11 February 1889, p. 6; 'Ballater – Mutual Improvement Association', *The Aberdeen Journal*, 21 February 1889, p. 7; 'Breaches of Promise of Marriage', *The Evening Telegraph*, 6 May 1890, p. 2; 'Parish Church Literary Society', 2 April 1896, p. 6.

[103] For example, 'Aberdeen, Thursday Feb. 5, 1883', *The Aberdeen Journal*, 5 February 1883, p. 4; 'Our London Correspondence', *The Glasgow Herald*, 22 November 1893, p. 7; 'A Q. C. on Breach of Promise Cases', *The Aberdeen Journal*, 20 December 1890, p. 7.

[104] *Watson v. Allan* ('The Stanley Breach of Promise Case', *Aberdeen Press and Journal*, 1 April 1882, p. 2).

[105] 'Stanley Breach of Promise Case', *The Evening Telegraph*, 12 April 1882, p. 4; 'Multiple News Items', *Dundee Courier*, p. 2. See also two cases where it was held that courtship did not equate to a promise to marry: *Georgeson v. Walterson* ('A Shetland Breach of Promise Case', *The Glasgow Herald*, 22 October 1894, p. 9); *Stuart v. Robertson* ('The Dunfermline Breach of Promise Case', *Dundee Courier*, 16 April 1897, p. 5).

[106] *Ellis v. Kerr* ('The Aberdeen Breach of Promise Case', *Dundee Courier*, 1 August 1889, p. 3). On alternative forms of adult intimate relationships during this era, see Cheadle, *Reimagining Intimacy*.

[107] Other evidence was used to infer a promise, however ('£100 Damages', *The Aberdeen Journal*, 21 July 1922, p. 6).

[108] *Bray v. Ross* ('Aberdeen Pantomime Sequel', *The Aberdeen Journal*, 12 January 1918, p. 4); *McIntyre v. Smith* (1957) NRS SC1/11/1957/14; *Crossan v. Cumming* (1963).

indignity[109] appearing in the cases, perhaps indicating a slight shift in the perceived harms of broken promises. The other area of significant development was in the justifications offered for breaking promises.

3.4 Justifying a Broken Promise to Marry

In certain circumstances, a person accused of breaking a promise to marry could avoid liability by offering a justification for their conduct. Unsurprisingly, given the focus of this book, I am interested in justifications based on information the pursuer did not disclose, or about which they lied, before the engagement. Yet because honesty about emotions is core to understanding the action of breach of promise, as well as its position in the arguments I put forward in Chapters 7 and 8, in this section I also examine how courts and commentators responded to defenders who broke their engagements due to a change of heart. In particular, I am interested in whether being honest with one's betrothed could serve as a justification and what the answer to this question meant for the sustainability of the action of breach of promise.

Beginning with deceptions by the pursuer, the justifications that fall under this heading to some extent mirror the deceptions that could affect the validity of marital consent, as discussed in Chapter 2. But perhaps because there was less at stake in breach of promise actions, the array of qualifying deceptions was wider.[110] As such, a person's lies about their wealth and attributes might justify the decision not to marry them. For example, in one eighteenth-century case, the defender could relevantly plead that her conduct was justified because the pursuer had passed himself off as a pious man in flourishing circumstances when in fact he was an excommunicated, drunken, bankrupt spendthrift.[111] Perhaps making matters worse, he had tailored his deception to her faith, pretending to be an 'Antiburger [sic], one of the strictest sects of Seceders', which was an issue that carried a lot of weight with the defender.

Similar lies, about wealth, that had been told by a male pursuer were brought to the court's attention in a second case[112] but, in another, a defender's mistake about his fiancée's economic situation was held not to justify his conduct.[113] Some years later, a male defender chose to settle a case brought against him by his fiancée, whom he accused of falsely representing her social and financial position.[114]

---

[109] *Bagan v. Clark* ('Couple Not Allowed to Walk Out Together', *The Evening Telegraph*, 23 March 1910, p. 3).
[110] One judge explained the disparity by suggesting that promises of marriage were closer to regular contracts; see *Lang v. Lang* (1921), Lord President Clyde (at 51).
[111] *Thomson v. Wright* (1767) Mor 13915; NRS CS271/63713.
[112] *McLeod v. Miller* (1843).
[113] *Handley v. Halket* ('Breach of Promise Case', *The Glasgow Herald*, 12 December 1871, p. 3).
[114] *Barclay v. Christie* ('Settlement of an Aberdeenshire Breach of Promise', *The Aberdeen Journal*, 20 March 1886, p. 5). Fraudulent representation by a woman of her financial situation was held to be a defence in England; see Law Commission, *Report on Breach of Promise of Marriage* (Her Majesty's Stationery Office, 1969), p. 2.

Expectations of transparency about finances, at least the finances of male suitors, actually provided two discrete opportunities for deception. As well as their potential to induce engagements of marriage, lies about their finances could help a man *escape* an engagement he no longer wanted to keep. For example, on one occasion, a defender apparently tried to manipulate his fiancée into breaking things off by disclosing his allegedly poor circumstances. To bolster his case, he argued that he was doing the right thing by telling her about his circumstances because to conceal them would both be dishonourable and deprive the pursuer of the power of deciding whether she wanted to go through with the marriage.[115] Disclosures of financial stability were therefore both gendered in their significance and double-edged in their operation.

Turning to alcohol usage, there are several cases of male defenders trying to justify their broken engagements with reference to their fiancées' undisclosed relationship to drink.[116] One of these, involving a woman who was apparently a thief and a drunk, ended in no liability for the defender[117] but the others ended with the defenders paying damages and being told they should have checked who they were marrying more carefully.[118] The additional charge of criminality might have tipped the balance in the first case,[119] and the gender of the pursuers in the other cases may have been important, since a female defender's attempt to justify her breach of promise on the basis of her fiancé's drinking was at least initially successful.[120]

Another issue that gained importance from the late nineteenth century was deception relating to matters that had explicitly been highlighted by the defender as being a dealbreaker. So, in another case involving alcohol, the defender's justification was based on his claim that he had told the pursuer that anything in the nature of intemperance would be a total bar to engagement and her denial that she indulged in any such vice. The fact that the pursuer did, in reality, drink meant that, according to the defender, she had wilfully suppressed matters which she knew he considered to be essential.[121] In the end, the pursuer settled so there is no way to know how a court would have viewed the

---

[115] *Croall* v. *Hutchison* ('Breach of Promise of Marriage', *Fife Herald*, 1 August 1844, p. 4).
[116] In the English context, see Steinbach, *Promises, Promises*, p. 159.
[117] *Christie* v. *Fraser* ('Scotch News', *Fife Herald*, 4 June 1863, p. 4).
[118] *Henderson* v. *O'Donnell* ('Sheriff Small Debt Court', *The Glasgow Herald*, 16 October 1866, p. 3); *Millar* v. *Copeland* ('Amusing Breach of Promise Case', *Dundee Courier*, 5 May 1873, p. 3). There is another failed attempt to defend an action on the ground of the pursuer's intemperance, but this does not appear to have involved deception (*Morrison* v. *Tait* (1888), discussed in Prior, *Fond Hopes Destroyed*, pp. 66–67).
[119] See *Tasker* v. *McGregor*, where undisclosed convictions for theft were held to justify a man's breach of promise of marriage ('Comrie Baker Wins Appeal', *The Evening Telegraph*, 8 June 1923, p. 1).
[120] *Lennie* v. *Burnside* ('Edinburgh Man's Breach of Promise Case', *Edinburgh Evening News*, 22 June 1893, p. 2).
[121] *MacDonald* v. *Campbell* ('The Ross-Shire Breach of Promise Case', *The Aberdeen Journal*, 9 December 1898, p. 6).

defender's arguments,[122] but in a similar case the court seemed to suggest stipulations like this could potentially receive legal recognition. Here, the defender claimed that her agreement to marry had been conditional on the defender giving up cigars and alcohol. Complaining that she found out he had been smoking behind her back, the pursuer's plea that 'it spoils love when there is not complete trust and confidence'[123] did not result in a verdict in her favour, but this seems to have been because the condition she had allegedly set was not distinctly enough averred in her condescendence (the facts supporting a summons[124]). In the sheriff's view, the stipulation was so unusual and trifling in relation to such a serious contract that it would have required a very distinct undertaking to become an essential part of the contract.[125]

The requests of these defenders (if they were made) were not totally unpredictable, though, since in Britain the temperance movement had swelled throughout the nineteenth century.[126] The fact that the legal issue was framed in terms of deception about known dealbreakers is also predictable insofar as it gels with attempts to widen the law of nullity of marriage around this time, as explored in Chapter 2, and the waves of liberalisation set out in Chapter 1. Indeed, to the cases just mentioned might be added one from just a few years later where a man was held to be justified in refusing to marry a woman who, unknown to him, was already engaged to another man.[127] In charging the jury, the judge explained that a breach would not be wrongful if something was discovered which made it unreasonable to expect the defender to marry the pursuer *or* if the pursuer's conduct in some other way destroyed the mutual trust and confidence which was the foundation of married life.[128] Together with the counterfactual formulation used by the defender in making his arguments (that is, if he had known the truth, he would not have promised marriage),[129] the case typifies a liberal approach towards protecting marital freedom.

Earlier in the century, courts had accepted the discovery of an undisclosed illegitimate child as a potential justification for breach of promise, which was understandable in light of the parallels between this and the discovery of

---

[122] 'Schoolmaster's Breach of Promise', *Dundee Courier*, 1 February 1899, p. 6.
[123] *Watson v. Kirkland* ('Peculiar Breach of Promise Case', *The Glasgow Herald*, 19 July 1888, p. 2).
[124] Watson (ed.), *Bell's Dictionary*, p. 217.
[125] 'The Glasgow Breach of Promise Case', *The Glasgow Herald*, 23 July 1888, p. 4. See also deception as to age, which was described as too trifling in *Tosh v. Hall* ('Action for Breach of Promise', *The Aberdeen Journal*, 14 August 1886, p. 5).
[126] Henry Yeomans, 'What Did the British Temperance Movement Accomplish? Attitudes to Alcohol, the Law and Moral Regulation' (2011) 45(1) *Sociology* 38–53. See also *Smail v. McNeil*, where the defender claimed that the pursuer was both immoral with other men and professed to be a teetotaller when she was not ((1908) NRS CS250/6564).
[127] Cf. an earlier English case where a pre-existing promise to marry did not justify the breach, *Beachey v. Brown* ('English Cases' (1860) 4(42) *Journal of Jurisprudence* at 321).
[128] *Stroyen v. McWhirter* ('The Farmer's Daughter's Breach of Promise Case', *Edinburgh Evening News*, 24 July 1902, p. 3).
[129] *Stroyen v. McWhirter* (1901) NRS CS240/S/24/2.

a woman's unchastity, which could also justify a breach.[130] But if the pursuer proved that the defender knew she had a child then he would have no defence,[131] and the same was true of prior unchastity.[132] This shows that it was the lack of information which justified the breach. Other instances of 'immoral' conduct clearly involving deception upon which defenders relied for justification as the century wore on included the pursuer's undisclosed divorce,[133] undisclosed prostitution (or keeping a brothel),[134] undisclosed pregnancy by another man,[135] and misrepresentations regarding the paternity of a child.[136]

Yet undisclosed 'immorality' might not provide a justification if it was perceived not to be the pursuer's fault. For example, towards the end of the century, one defender tried to justify his actions on the ground that the pursuer had misrepresented the circumstances of her birth, hiding the fact that she was illegitimate and thereby wilfully suppressing matters on which she knew he was relying. The sheriff held that, as a rule, courts were less inclined to hold faults that were not the pursuer's (here, the 'fault' was the pursuer's parents') as capable of providing the defender with a justification.[137] Importantly, he also refused to accept that the pursuer's conduct was deceptive insofar as describing her family as mother, father, and so on was what she had been told to do since infancy. In the judge's view, her behaviour was not so uncommon as to be 'regarded as a wilful and serious deception'. In other words, convention dictated which misrepresentations or non-disclosures would amount to deception, or at least deception of a sufficiently serious kind.

---

[130] *Sandilands v. King* ('Jury Trials – Friday', *Caledonian Mercury*, 3 April 1858, p. 2), (1858) General Collection, Paper 187; *Fletcher v. Grant* (1878) 6 R 59, (1878) General Collection, Paper 22; *McLean v. MacKay* ('Breach of Promise', *Dundee Courier*, 26 December 1878, p. 3). There are several other cases involving the claim that the pursuer had an undisclosed illegitimate child or was unchaste. On English law, see Lettmaier, *Broken Engagements*, pp. 41–42; Steinbach, *Promises, Promises*, p. 151.

[131] *Peffers v. McKean* ('Sheriff Small Debt Court – Yesterday', *The Glasgow Herald*, 20 September 1860, p. 3); *McKenzie v. Brander* ('Local News', *Elgin Courier*, 20 February 1863, p. 5); *MacKellar v. Hamilton* ('Breach of Promise Case at Greenock', *The Glasgow Herald*, 30 December 1875, p. 4). The pursuer's damages would be reduced, though; see *Morrison v. McIntyre* ('Sheriff Court – Monday', *The Glasgow Herald*, 26 April 1864, p. 3); *Thornton v. Rodger* ('Forfar – £40 Damages for Breach of Promise', *The Aberdeen Journal*, 6 February 1885, p. 6).

[132] *Smith v. Saddler* ('An Alyth Breach of Promise of Marriage Case', *Dundee Courier*, 15 April 1864, p. 4).

[133] *Harris v. Norval* ('Breach of Promise Case', *The Glasgow Herald*, 18 March 1870, p. 6); *Stewart v. White* ('Perth Breach of Promise Case', *The Aberdeen Journal*, 24 March 1905, p. 3).

[134] *Rodger v. McKenzie* ('Singular Breach of Promise Case', *Dundee Courier*, 20 May 1875, p. 3).

[135] *Mushet v. Murray* ('Breach of Promise Case at Lanark', *Edinburgh Evening News*, 18 June 1902, p. 2); *Kinder v. Andrew* ('Glasgow Man Sued for Breach of Promise', *Dundee Courier*, 12 December 1903, p. 4); *Pithie v. Walker* (1920) NRS SC23/23/1920/8 but in this case the defender did not discover the truth in time to include this ground in his defence. In the English context, see Steinbach, *Promises, Promises*, p. 151.

[136] *Wallace v. Brown* ('Dundee Breach of Promise', *Dundee Courier*, 28 January 1904, p. 3); *Henderson v. Allan* ('£100 Claim', *The Evening Telegraph*, 30 May 1924, p. 8).

[137] *Allan v. Aitken* ('Local Breach of Promise Action', *The Glasgow Herald*, 12 July 1882, p. 9).

Beyond 'immorality', the undisclosed poor physical health of a pursuer[138] might be used to try to justify a broken promise if the disease were serious, such as consumption (that is, tuberculosis),[139] scrofula (also tuberculosis)[140] or epilepsy,[141] or if the injury was sufficiently debilitating, such as to impede the fulfilment of wifely duties.[142] Undisclosed illiteracy appears not to have been a justification, though,[143] and the insanity of the pursuer's ascendants did not provide a defence either because it was held that the defender could have discovered this information prior to the engagement.[144] As in the context of nullity of marriage, however, the rhetoric might not have aligned with reality. Certainly, one commentator complained that men had little chance to get to know women before proposing and so might easily be 'swindle[d]' into becoming engaged to someone with consumption, scrofula or insanity in the family.[145]

Finally, the defender's view that the marriage would be unhappy or ill-suited would not justify a breach of promise,[146] though the argument that it would be better to break things off when there was no chance of happiness was made towards the end of the nineteenth century.[147] At this time, incompatibility had started to appear as a more respectable defence,[148] following a cultural

[138] I do not consider the ill health of the defender here, though the question of whether he could rely on this to justify his broken promise was controversial. On the health of the plaintiff in the English context, see Lettmaier, *Broken Engagements*, p. 45.
[139] *McVey v. Savage* ('Scotch News', *Fife Herald*, 19 May 1859, p. 2); *MacLachlan v. Curle* but here the defence was not substantiated ('Glasgow Breach of Promise Case', *The Glasgow Herald*, 1 February 1893, p. 10; 'The Glasgow Breach of Promise Case', *The Glasgow Herald*, 21 February 1893, p. 3).
[140] *Brodie v. Carmichael* ('Breach of Promise Cases', *Dundee Courier*, 22 February 1879, p. 3).
[141] *Mackenzie v. Hughes* ('Aberdeen Breach of Promise', *The Aberdeen Journal*, 29 March 1881, p. 4); *Craig v. Todd* ('Another Edinburgh Breach of Promise Case', *Edinburgh Evening News*, 20 June 1884, p. 3) – the alleged deception by the pursuer is stressed in this case; see also NRS CS244/295.
[142] For example, *McPhedran v. Campbell* ('Inveraray Sheriff Court', *The Glasgow Herald*, 20 July 1860, p. 7), where a fisherman complained that his fiancée was lame and *Pithie v. Walker* (1920), where the defender claimed the pursuer's injured arm meant she was unfit for household duties or to assist him in business. The pursuer's historic rheumatic fever and repressed menstruation were held not to justify a breach of promise in *Allan v. Henderson* ('Glasgow Sheriff Court', *The Glasgow Herald*, 20 December 1880, p. 6).
[143] *McKean v. Kessack* ('An Inverness Breach of Promise Case', *The Glasgow Herald*, 22 November 1883, p. 5; 'Inverness Breach of Promise Case', *Edinburgh Evening News*, 22 March 1884); *Forbes v. Simpson* ('The Elgin Breach of Promise Case', *The Aberdeen Journal*, 25 January 1887, p. 6; 'Elgin – Settlement of the Breach of Promise Case', *The Aberdeen Journal*, 1 March 1887, p. 7).
[144] At least initially; see *Charleson v. Stewart* (1899) NRS CS240/C/19/4. A history of madness does not appear to have provided a defence in English law, either; see Steinbach, *Promises, Promises*, p. 159.
[145] 'The Wigtown Breach of Promise Case', *The Glasgow Herald*, 7 April 1874, p. 6.
[146] It would not even mitigate the breach, according to English law; see Frost, *Promises Broken*, p. 19.
[147] *Thomson v. Walkingshaw* ('A Glasgow Breach of Promise Case', *Edinburgh Evening News*, 5 October 1883, p. 2); *Torrance v. Muir* (1888) NRS CS247/6205, 'Court of Session', *The Glasgow Herald*, 20 June 1888, p. 9; *MacPherson v. Moir* ('The Turiff Breach of Promise Case', *The Aberdeen Journal*, 7 February 1900, p. 4).
[148] Steinbach, *Promises, Promises*, p. 161.

shift in the meaning of integrity (at least, in the context of marital promises) away from constancy and towards sincerity. Since marriage had come to be regarded as a relationship based on love, as outlined in Chapter 1, to marry after one's feelings had changed – after falling out of love – or upon realising that love had never developed was dishonourable; indeed, it was worse than breaking off an engagement. For similar reasons, desiring a loveless marriage showed a lack of self-respect.[149]

There are examples of cases reflecting these cultural shifts within those I have examined, such as defenders telling pursuers that they wished to be honest about their changed feelings[150] and suggesting, or at least acknowledging, that if these women had self-respect they would welcome the end of the engagement.[151] Importantly, the men who acted this way would not necessarily be chastised for their conduct. If they offered to honour the promise despite everything, this might attract a degree of admiration, assuming this offer did not seem hypocritical but, instead, to be based on a sincere hope that things might turn out well. Furthermore, their honesty might be praised. As one judge put it, 'a promise to marry was not a promise to take a lady before a clergyman and tell a pack of lies towards her', adding that marriage was 'based honestly on true affection'.[152] In other words, the expectation that marriage should be based on honesty and sincere love, which was sometimes used to infer that a person lacked the intention to marry,[153] came to affect the action of breach of promise too. It did so by highlighting the difficulties created by a legal doctrine that left no space to change one's mind for what were culturally considered to be the right reasons. I would suggest that it also undermined the assumed relationship between deception and inconstancy upon which the action of breach of promise arguably rested.

As I explained in Section 3.2, one plausible interpretation of what a promise to marry communicated is this: I am the kind of person who will follow through, no matter what (barring a small number of special circumstances). On this view, failing to honour one's promise in the absence of those circumstances could prove the falsity of the implied communication: the deception was proved by the (not) doing. If the implied communication were to change,[154] however, the association between inconstant conduct and deception could break down. More specifically, if the relevant communication were instead 'I am the kind of person who will follow through if I love you', then deciding not to marry would not necessarily imply that the statement was false.

---

[149] Steinbach, *Promises, Promises*, pp. 255–264.
[150] *Reekie* v. *McKinven* ('"Something Died within Me"', *Dundee Courier*, 20 May 1921, p. 5) and the cases discussed later in this chapter.
[151] *Simpson* v. *Jack* (1888); *Ritchie* v. *Robertson* ('The Altyre Breach of Promise Case', *The Aberdeen Journal*, 7 January 1905, p. 7).
[152] *Ritchie* v. *Robertson* (1905). The defender was still found liable by the jury.
[153] See Chapters 2 and 4.
[154] My suggestions here were inspired by Steinbach's observation that if a promise to marry has no future meaning, it is 'merely a statement of current emotion'; see *Promises, Promises*, p. 249.

Even if the communication were instead 'I am the kind of person who will follow through if I love you, and I currently have good reason to think I do and/or will love you', it would be difficult, in the context of a culture which assumed that love was unpredictable and difficult to control, to conclude that this statement was false simply because the maker chose not to marry. To be sure, there might be cases which strongly suggested duplicity from the start, such as where the promise to marry was given under pressure but its maker gave the promisee reason to mistakenly think he wanted to go ahead with the marriage 'in good earnest'.[155] There could also be cases where the defender admitted to stringing the pursuer along after realising that they were not compatible, continuing to send warm and affectionate letters despite this realisation.[156] Any blanket assumption of falsity would be inappropriate, though.

Be that as it may, the action of breach of promise retained its established form and so the standard response to a defender who was honest with the pursuer about his changed feelings was to consider this a constructive breach of promise. Ironically, the fact that marriage was supposed to be based on love underpinned this conclusion – the thinking was that since the only form of marriage that would realistically be contemplated was a loving one (indeed this was the formula of the Church of Scotland), to offer a loveless marriage was simply an attempt to manoeuvre the pursuer into breaking the engagement off herself and thereby avoid liability.[157] Even if the defender made a new offer to marry, the pursuer was under no obligation to accept it. Since such an offer was made after the defender had divulged his true feelings and because it was made under the threat of an award of damages, courts were ready to conclude that it was not bona fide or sincere.[158]

3.5 Conclusions and Contemporary Connections

By the twentieth century, it was acknowledged that some moral duties – those that involved a duty to act from particular dispositions or with particular motives – could not be enforced by law. While the external performance of the duty could be compelled, the disposition or motive could not be. In fact, the very fact of enforcement risked making the disposition or motive impossible.[159] The action of breach of promise of marriage seems to be a prime example of this kind of duty. At least, this is a good description of where

---

[155] The judge singled out this aspect of the case, which implied either imprudence or culpability, as the reason for awarding damages (*Harkins v. McKechnie* ('Glasgow Sheriff Court', *The Glasgow Herald*, 25 May 1864, p. 6)).

[156] *Reid v. Smith* ('Dundee Breach of Promise Case', *Dundee Courier*, 3 May 1878, p. 3).

[157] *Cattanach v. Robertson* (1864) 2 M 839; (1864) General Collection, Paper 149.

[158] *Milne v. Craik* ('The Forfar Breach of Promise Case', *The Glasgow Herald*, 27 February 1874, p. 4); *Pateman v. Watson* ('Court of Session', *The Glasgow Herald*, 17 February 1876, p. 7); *Mearns v. Fraser* ('The Kintore Breach of Promise Case', *The Aberdeen Journal*, 21 February 1893, p. 6); *Dow v. Macleod* ('Affection Lost', *Dundee Courier*, 8 November 1905, p. 4).

[159] Robert A. Moody, 'Law and Morality' (1939) 51 *Juridical Review* 323–343 at 326.

attitudes towards the action ended up. When the action was eventually abolished by statute in 1984,[160] it was considered out of step with modern views because an engagement to marry was considered, at most, a personal and social commitment and because any legal restriction on the freedom to withdraw from marriage was considered undesirable and against the interests of both the individuals and society.[161]

Yet the account I have offered here shows that this change is not simply attributable to the retreat of law from the private sphere or a decline in the significance of trust within interpersonal relationships. Rather, the development of the law relating to breach of promise of marriage is partly a story about changes in the meaning ascribed to trustworthiness and associated shifts in the expectations that we place on others, including lovers. Furthermore, as with the developments examined in Chapters 2 and 4, the reality is that in withdrawing a previously available legal response (or, in the case of the other legal responses, altering their operation), one opportunity for obtaining formal recognition of the harms and wrongs caused by inducing intimacy has been lost. As I have tried to show, the action of breach of promise was strongly connected with deception on both sides: both the promiser and promisee could be deceptive, and the law was attentive to the possibility in both contexts.

Of course, the justifications to an action of breach of promise depended for their existence on the idea that breaking a promise to marry was a serious wrong per se – a view that does not carry weight anymore. But, like the deceptions featured in Chapter 2, they also shine a light on the things people typically expected to know about their partners when entering an intimate relationship, and how these expectations were culturally mediated and reflected in law. Convention also played a major role in the tasks of inferring or imputing promises to marry, just as it did in inferring or imputing marital consent, as I show in Chapter 4. Taken together, the legal actions examined in Part I therefore demonstrate how convention has been used to make the legal responses to deceptively induced intimacy workable and how convention has the capacity both to expand the law's reach (as in the case of inferring or imputing promises or consent to marry) and keep it reined in (as in the case of limiting the range of deceptions that would render an ostensible obligation non-existent or invalid or its non-performance permissible).

The experience of law's engagement with emotional authenticity also suggests that caution is warranted in subjecting promises or statements of future intent, which are liable to change over time, to legal regulation. This is especially so when the subject matter concerns issues about which we might

---

[160] Law Reform (Husband and Wife) (Scotland) Act 1984, s. 1.
[161] Scottish Law Commission, *Report on Outdated Rules in the Law of Husband and Wife* (Her Majesty's Stationery Office, 1983), Paragraphs 2.4–2.5. The action had been abolished in England by the Law Reform (Miscellaneous Provisions) Act 1970, s. 1 because it was considered to rest on social assumptions that were no longer valid; see Lettmaier, *Broken Engagements*, p. 171.

wish to be able to change our minds without risking penalty or about which we might want our partners to be able to express changed views without fear. Nevertheless, there was, for as long as the doctrine of breach of promise of marriage existed, a subset of behaviour that was considered especially wrongful, that is, broken promises that were characterised by deception from the outset. This situation is not unique to the action of breach of promise of marriage, either; even today, contracts that are broken after having been fraudulently induced are regarded as qualitatively different from regular broken contracts.[162] If there were a way of isolating false promises or statements of future intent that were sufficiently wrongful and did not interfere too much with liberties that are generally considered desirable in the contemporary era, a legal response to these might therefore be desirable. It is likely, however, that the falsity of a promise or statement of future intent could not be presumed on the basis of subsequent inconsistent conduct if the opportunity to change one's mind were to be preserved. Ultimately, however, it is only possible to engage with these issues, which I do in Chapter 8, with an account of the complexity and interests at stake such as the one offered in this chapter.

---

[162] Monu Bedi, 'Contract Breaches and the Criminal/Civil Divide: An *Inter*-Common Law Analysis' (2012) 28(3) *Georgia State University Law Review* 559–618.

4

Faking Marriage

4.1 Scope and Themes

This chapter picks up the theme of false emotions and intentions explored in Chapter 3 and considers examples of deceptively induced intimacy which relate to two of the requirements for lawful marriage: the requirement for matrimonial consent, which was often considered to require that the parties seriously and deliberately intended to marry,[1] and the requirement that there be no prior subsisting marriage. The examples fall into three sometimes overlapping categories: situations where a person fakes an intention to marry, or at least acts as if they intended marriage and later denies that they did; situations where a person has an ulterior motive for marrying, such as obtaining an economic advantage; and situations where a person misrepresents or fails to disclose their married status before 'marrying' another person.

Each of these situations involves slightly different considerations, and I analyse them below in relation to the legal responses with which they are associated, that is, marriage constituted by present consent, marriage constituted by a promise to marry followed by sex,[2] and bigamy. Despite their differences, these are all instances of deceptively induced intimacy where the duplicity centres on the nature of the relationship. Where a person fakes an intention to marry, they might lead their partner to believe that they had thereby married them and that they therefore held a status that historically attracted (and still attracts) social and material benefits. The duplicitous 'spouse' might also enjoy the sexual, emotional, practical and other forms of intimacy that often accompany this relationship. The same can be said about situations where an already-married person 'marries' again. Where a person has an ulterior motive, the undisclosed reason for marrying can mar, or sometimes entirely supplant, the sexual and emotional connections their spouse could reasonably expect to exist or be in contemplation. In these cases, the duplicitous spouse might have induced their

---

[1] Stair; More, *Institutions* (vol. 1), Note B, p. xiv; Erskine, *Institute* (1773), p. 85; Paton, *Hume's Lectures*, pp. 26, 50; Fraser, *Personal and Domestic Relations*, pp. 212–213; Fraser, *Husband and Wife*, p. 415; Walton, *Husband and Wife*, p. 79 and subsequent edition; Clive, *Husband and Wife*, Paragraph 05.003.

[2] See Chapter 1 for more on these modes of constituting marriage.

partner to take on a relationship and legal status which they would have rejected if they had known the full picture. They might also have led their spouse to experience the forms of intimacy outlined earlier on an unreciprocated basis when, importantly, they knew about, or could easily have predicted, the asymmetry.

Three core arguments emerge from my analysis of cases that involve these scenarios. The first is that courts faced challenges in inferring or imputing marital consent which arose because both parts of the requirement that the constitution of marriage required marital consent invited controversy. The need for *marital* consent raised questions about the nature and purpose of marriage because, at least in the case of irregular marriage, there was no formalistic way to identify when consent amounted to consent to marriage. It was not possible, for example, to stipulate that marital consent existed when someone consented to enter the relationship created when specific legal formalities had been observed because the constitution of marriage did not depend on such formalities. As Sections 4.2 and 4.3 show, when marital consent was not defined with reference to a particular form or ceremony, it was defined with reference to the substance of the relationship. Then there was the fact that it was up to the law to determine 'what shall import such consent, and what shall be sufficient evidence of it; or, rather, what shall be a sufficient expression of consent to bind the parties'.[3]

As this quotation suggests, there were different ways by which the existence of consent could be inferred, or even imputed; again, these tasks were particularly difficult in the context of irregular marriage because there was no set formula for expressing consent. On top of this, it was not always clear what courts were meant to be doing when they adjudicated the existence of marital consent because it was uncertain whether the conduct which might indicate that marital consent existed (that is, the exchange of present consent or having sex after promising marriage) *created* the marriage or merely gave rise to a 'pre-contract' whose completion depended on judicial intervention.[4] This uncertainty created practical problems but, more importantly for present purposes, it rested on, and reflected, different ways of thinking about the conceptual structure of consent. The idea that courts could convert marital pre-contracts into marital contracts suggested either that the parties' consent to marriage was irrelevant or that the court was professing to consent for them. This arrangement made sense according to an early practice by which courts could compel the marriage of parties who had entered marital pre-contracts, but it did not make sense once this practice had been abolished. At that time, marriage was conceptualised as a voluntary contract, and the link between the parties' conduct and marital consent had to be reconfigured such that consent would be presumed to exist when the parties engaged in the relevant conduct.[5]

---

[3] Fraser, *Personal and Domestic Relations*, p. 91.
[4] *Report of the Royal Commission*, pp. xviii, xix–xx; 'Some Proposals for Reform of Our Marriage Laws' (1889) 5(51) *The Scottish Law Review* 45–55 at 52–53.
[5] 'The Constitution of Marriage' (1859) 3(28) *Journal of Jurisprudence* 188–196.

Crucially, however, this consent could be presumed in two ostensibly different ways. First, consent could be imputed in a way that effectively ignored or overrode the intentions of either one or both of the parties. By this method, 'logic' could be 'saved' even if 'liberty [was] sacrificed'.[6] The alternative was to accept that fact finders must infer the existence of consent from words and actions because intentions can never be discerned directly. On this view, the tests used to presume consent could be considered reliable – that is, capable of detecting instances of subjective consent – so long as they were within the knowledge and control of the parties.[7]

Despite the apparent difference between these two modes of presuming consent, they were similar in that they were both closer to an objective approach to determining the existence of a contract than they were to a subjective approach. Whereas a subjective approach involved trying to assess the congruence between the parties' actual intentions, an objective approach involved looking at the parties' external acts and deciding when it would be equitable to consider them bound. A third approach, so-called evidential objectivism, was concerned with subjective intentions but a combination of 'judicial skepticism' and limitations on proof meant that the legal inquiry was confined to determining the objective meaning of the parties' words and actions.[8] In reality, there was little difference between evidential objectivism and an objective approach – both could be used to bind a party against their will – but the former preserved the belief (or perhaps the delusion) that ascertaining consent is a matter of trying to discern individual intentions and desires. According to evidential objectivism, a person could be bound because the court did not believe that their intentions and actions really differed; by contrast, an objective approach permitted a person to be bound irrespective of any difference between their intentions and actions.[9]

There are traces of all three of these approaches in the cases I analyse below and, unsurprisingly, where there are disparities there is tension. For example, the argument that a party should be barred from advancing a plea or defence due to their iniquitous conduct (i.e., that they were personally barred) might have cohered with either of the two objective approaches to consent, but it did not sit well with the subjective approach that aimed to establish what the parties really thought. Similarly, if the constitution of marriage depended only on consensus between the parties (as per the subjective approach), it seemed odd that a pursuer could seek *either* damages for seduction or a declarator of marriage.[10] Another point of contention was the rule that an undisclosed unilateral reservation (one

---

[6] 'Constitution of Marriage' at 192.   [7] Ibid. at 193.
[8] John MacLeod, 'Before Bell: The Roots of Error in the Scots Law of Contract' (2010) 14(3) *Edinburgh Law Review* 385–417 at 396.
[9] Ibid. at 397.
[10] In an 1854 case, the pursuer was precluded from raising actions of breach of promise of marriage and seduction because the facts and circumstances suggested she was married to the defender, whom she could not sue if she was his wife (see *A v. M* (1865) 4 Scot L Mag & Sheriff

4.1 Scope and Themes

party's uncommunicated lack of intent to marry) would not affect the constitution of marriage.[11] This rule meant that a party could be held by a court to be married despite not wanting, and perhaps never having wanted, to be married.[12] As Sections 4.2 and 4.3 show, both objective approaches to consent are evident in the way this rule operated: judges sometimes claimed they did not believe there was any mental reservation (evidential objectivism) and they sometimes held the reservation to be unimportant in the face of the obligation the would-be spouse had been led to believe existed (an objective approach). The significance of an ulterior reason to marry could be interpreted in diverging ways, too. On one view, it amounted to fraud on the 'innocent' spouse (an objective approach), and on another, it showed that the duplicitous spouse had not intended marriage despite their claim that they had (evidential objectivism).

Taking these features of the law together reveals the second core argument of this chapter, which is that when faced with the challenges involved in determining the existence of marital consent courts tended to respond by furthering the ends of justice, as determined according to prevailing views about the nature and value of marriage. Across each of the issues outlined earlier, there is an overarching sense that two major rationales behind their resolution were a desire to compensate women who experienced deception at the hands of their lovers and a desire to punish men who engaged in this behaviour. Publications from the time certainly portrayed the ease with which couples could be found married as providing redress for women who had falsely been promised marriage or led to believe they were married.[13] This was seen by some as protecting society's interests, too, by ensuring that as many people as possible, particularly those who had procreated, could be ushered into the only relationship that was socially and morally sanctioned.[14] On top

---

Ct Rep 1 at 61) but in most later cases this argument was unsuccessful because the pursuer did not have evidence of the kind she would need to obtain a declarator of marriage (as discussed later in this chapter). Nevertheless, commentators considered it an absurdity, or anomaly, of Scots law that marital status might depend on the contentions the pursuer advanced; see 'Thursday Morning, Aug 11', *The Glasgow Daily Herald*, 11 August 1870, p. 4; 'Marriage Law of Scotland', *Aberdeen Press and Journal*, 4 February 1936, p. 2.

[11] The Roman Catholic Church and some Canon lawyers believed this should affect the constitution of marriage; see *The Church and the Law of Nullity of Marriage*, pp. 9, 26–27 and lectures by one pre-Reformation cleric working in Scotland, which states that undisclosed unilateral reservations affected the constitution of marriage (Barry, *Hay's Lectures*, pp. xxxi, 51, 53).

[12] An 'amusing' song written by the Scottish lawyer, then judge, Charles Neaves warned how easy it was to become married against one's desires in Scotland; see 'The Tourist's Matrimonial Guide through Scotland' in Charles Neaves, *Songs and Verses, Social and Scientific*, 5th ed. (Edinburgh: Blackwood, 1879), pp. 101–104.

[13] 'Commissioners of Supply', *Fife Herald, and Kinross, Strathearn, and Clackmannan Advertiser*, 13 May 1847, p. 3; 'The Marriage and Registration Bills', *The Aberdeen Journal*, 14 March 1849, p. 8; 'Edinburgh', *Caledonian Mercury*, 3 June 1856, p. 2; 'The Yelverton Case – A Defence of Scottish Law', *The Dundee Courier and Argus*, 25 December 1862, p. 3; 'The Marriage (Scotland) Bill' (1938) *Scots Law Times* 91–93; 'The Scotch Marriage Law', *The Glasgow Herald*, 23 October 1863, p. 4.

[14] 'Imperial Parliament', *Caledonian Mercury*, 22 February 1849, p. 1; 'The Scottish Marriage and Registration Bills' (1849) 66(407) *Blackwood's Edinburgh Magazine* 263–276; 'Marriage and

of this, making marriage hard to escape helped prevent the 'heavy burdens on the fund of the poor' that would materialise if mothers were left husbandless.[15] This combination of factors helps explain how compelling marriage could appear appropriate[16] even though it contradicted the widespread belief that marriage was a consensual contract – a contradiction that was particularly glaring when the imposition of marriage was described in terms of punishment and suffering.[17]

Yet if some saw the law as providing relief for women, punishing deserving men and helping secure social order, others thought it had the opposite effects. Rather than thwarting the efforts of duplicitous men, the law could facilitate deception because ordinary people were not familiar with the law and its complexities. Women could therefore believe they were safe when they were not.[18] Conversely, some worried that the laxity (or stringency, depending on one's point of view) of the law could be turned to the advantage of 'undeserving' women.[19] These two points meant that encouraging women to gamble on uncertain relationships could actually risk, rather than protect, women's virtue,[20] a point judges sometimes acknowledged.[21] Finally,

---

Divorce – The Law of England and Scotland' (1861) 35(69) *The North British Review* 187–218 at 190, 206; 'Summary', *The Caledonian Mercury*, 3 January 1863, p. 2.

[15] 'County Meeting', *The Aberdeen Journal*, 5 May 1847, p. 4. The financial obligations created by marriage are beyond the scope of this book, but for an overview of aliment at around this time, see Fraser, *Husband and Wife*, pp. 837–866.

[16] 'Imperial Parliament', *Caledonian Mercury*, 8 March 1849, p. 1; 'Marriage Law Assimilation' (1863) 7(74) *Journal of Jurisprudence* 68–79 at 72–3, 78, disagreeing that marriage should be compelled but noting that this is effectively what happened; 'Mr Campbell Smith and the Law of Marriage' (1864) 8(88) *Journal of Jurisprudence* 201–206 at 205, criticising this feature of the law.

[17] 'Scotch Law of Marriage', *Inverness Courier*, 13 June 1827, p. 4; 'Marriage and Divorce' at 205–206; 'Mr Campbell Smith' at 205; 'Scotch and English Marriages', *Fife Herald, and Kinross, Strathearn, and Clackmannan Advertiser*, 25 May 1865, p. 2.

[18] 'Necessity for a Reform of the Existing Marriage Law of Scotland', *Arbroath Guide and Weekly Advertiser and Reporter*, 2 June 1849, pp. 8–9; 'Imperial Parliament', *The Aberdeen Journal*, 18 July 1849, p. 6; 'The Marriage Law of Scotland. Proposed Changes', *John o'Groat Journal*, 24 August 1865, p. 4; 'Thursday Morning, Aug 11', *The Glasgow Daily Herald*, 11 August 1870, p. 4. In one unusual case, the defender, who was an already-married lawyer, allegedly read the pursuer passages from Erskine's *Institute* outlining the law governing marriage to persuade her that she was safe; see *McLellan v. Miller* (1828) NRS CC8/6/2116; Leneman, *Promises, Promises*, p. 213.

[19] 'The Marriage Law of Scotland – Proposed Amendment', *Caledonian Mercury*, 30 September 1860, p. 2; *Report of the Royal Commission*, p. 272. Based on my research, the number of men trying to trick women greatly exceeded the number of women trying to trap men into marriage. Some of the cases featuring women were discussed in Chapter 2, but there are a handful more. Notably, in two of these, the woman reported having been raped by either the defender or another man; see *McLauchline v. McDonald* (1782) NRS CC8/6/668, Leneman, *Promises, Promises*, p. 105; *Hutchison v. Brand* (1793) NRS CC8/6/913, Leneman, *Promises, Promises*, pp. 105–106.

[20] 'The Marriage Law of Scotland: Proposed Changes'.

[21] Several judges in the 1794 case of *Low v. Allardice* considered that it was not in the interests of female virtue to make marriage too easy to prove (see *Harvie v. Inglis* (1837) 15 S 964, fn. 4), and half a century later, Lord Cockburn expressed a similar view (see *Harvie v. Inglis* (1839) 14 Fac Dec 608 at 614).

imposing marriage on undesiring subjects flew in the face of the cultural ideal of marrying for love, outlined in Chapter 1.[22]

This ideal, whose significance to breach of promise of marriage actions was explored in Chapter 3, is also implicated in 'ulterior motive' cases but with different effects. Whereas men who faked marital intentions could be punished by being held married, those who married for the 'wrong' reasons could be punished by depriving them of the status and concomitant benefits they coveted. As with the imposition of marriage, this practice favoured both 'innocent' individuals, who were spared being shackled to a spouse who appeared to have used them, and the state, whose preferred allocation of resources was preserved and vindicated. This association – between state and individual interests – is clear in the bigamy cases I consider in Section 4.4, too. As an amatory wrong,[23] bigamy historically served to protect the institution of marriage and the state benefits that were associated with it, but it also provided legal recognition of the significance of marriage to individuals and the harms and wrongs they suffered when deceived about its existence.

Bringing the analysis up to the present day, the third core argument of this chapter is that there has been a decline in using the law to protect the interests of individuals across all these areas of law. The move away from imputing or inferring marital consent on the basis of what was perceived to be just and towards a more formalistic notion of marital intention[24] means that the state's interests in avoiding 'sham' marriages are still protected, although they now rest on a different foundation due to changes in the benefits associated with marital status. Yet, at the same time, when the use of marriage as a form of punishment disappeared the protection afforded to the interests of individuals, usually women, who were subject to deceptively induced intimacy declined. In a similar way, the use of bigamy to protect the interests of individuals has declined as the crime has become 'privatised' in ways I outline in Section 4.4 and as its significance to the state – primarily the way it is implicated in migration-related 'fraud' – has eclipsed its potential significance to individuals deceived into false relationships. In Section 4.5, I consider some of the implications these changes hold for contemporary debates, including to what extent legal responses which centre on sex can capture the array of harms and wrongs associated with deceptively induced intimate relationships, before returning to these points in Chapter 8.

---

[22] 'Notes from Edinburgh' (1922) 38 *Scottish Law Review* 18–22 at 20. See also *Dalrymple v. Dalrymple* (1811) 161 ER 665, where Sir William Scott states (at 675) that the practice of compelling pre-contracted parties was discontinued in Scotland due to the 'apparent incongruity of compelling a man to marry against his will, but with a solemn profession of love and affection to the party who compelled him'.

[23] The potential for bigamy to constitute a sexual wrong is considered in Part II.

[24] On some distinctions between equitable standards and formal, highly administrable rules, see Duncan Kennedy, 'Form and Substance in Private Law Adjudication' (1976) 89 *Harvard Law Review* 1685–1778.

4.2 Marriage by Present Consent

The fact that no specific words, acts or procedures were required to constitute marriage by present consent[25] meant that a marriage could historically be established by proof of the verbal or written exchange of consent or, in the case of women, silent acquiescence in the presence of a man accepting her as his wife.[26] It could also be proved by subsequent acknowledgement of the marriage by written or spoken words and by conduct.[27] In fact, the only notable restriction on proof of marriage by present consent was that the parties could not be adduced and examined as witnesses until 1874.[28] Despite the relative latitude in proving consent, however, various features of the law, introduced briefly earlier, affected whether and how a court would hear evidence and shaped the arguments made by counsel.

Starting with personal bar, this rule stipulated that a party could be prevented from maintaining a plea in action or a defence if they were trying to benefit from their own fraud or behave inconsistently despite having initially acted in good faith.[29] Unusually, given the fact that most of those accused of duplicity of unfaithfulness were men, the earliest example of personal bar I have found[30] – from the middle of the eighteenth century – concerns a purportedly delinquent woman, Magdalen Cochrane (sometimes spelled Cochran) or Kennedy. Cochrane claimed that she had been privately married to Captain Campbell, who was deceased at the time of the litigation, while a second woman, Jean Campbell, claimed that she had been married publicly to the captain (referred to as Carrick) after the date of Cochrane's alleged marriage. Had Carrick been alive, and Cochrane's marriage established, it is possible that Campbell might have obtained damages from him; indeed, Campbell's counsel argued that she 'would have been intitled to very large Damages from the Captain, for putting so gross a Cheat upon her'.[31]

As things turned out, Cochrane was Campbell's legal opponent, so Campbell's efforts to preserve her status and potentially that of her children[32]

---

[25] In 1856, legislation introduced a requirement that one of the parties have lived in Scotland for twenty-one days before marriage; see Gordon, 'Myth and Reality'.
[26] Fraser, *Personal and Domestic Relations*, p. 145; Clive, *Husband and Wife*, Paragraph 05.002.
[27] *Report of the Royal Commission*, pp. xvi, 74; Paton, *Hume's Lectures*, p. 43.
[28] Evidence Law Amendment (Scotland) Act 1874 (c. 64, 37 & 38 Vict.). For a critique of the rule excluding parties to the action as witnesses, see 'Amendment of Law of Evidence in Consistorial Actions' (1862) 6(61) *Journal of Jurisprudence* 35–37.
[29] Watson (ed.), *Bell's Dictionary*, p. 800.
[30] The case is discussed in Leah Leneman, 'The Scottish Case That Led to Hardwicke's Marriage Act' (1999) 17(1) *Law and History Review* 161–169; Leneman, *Promises Promises*, pp. 151–155; Dempsey, 'The Marriage (Scotland) Bill'; and Probert, *Marriage Law and Practice*, ch. 2. None of these accounts explores the angles examined here or draws on the Session Papers.
[31] *Campbell v. Cochran* (1747) Kilkerran Collection, vol. 14, Paper 1. As discussed in Chapter 2, a woman might get damages for having been trapped into a void marriage. Carrick might also have been prosecuted for bigamy (see Section 4.4).
[32] It was not beyond contention that any bona fides on Campbell's part would legitimate her children (see Chapter 2).

4.2 Marriage by Present Consent

were directed accordingly. The case reports show that the nub of Campbell's argument was that Cochrane should be barred *exceptione doli et personali exceptione* from proving her marriage. The term *personali exceptione* simply means by personal exception, that is, personally barred,[33] while *exceptione doli* suggests that Campbell was accusing Cochrane of acting in bad faith, either due to her perceived misconduct or the injustice that would follow if her action were allowed to succeed.[34] In essence, her argument was that Cochrane had watched events unfold and done nothing to assert her alleged marriage to Carrick – conduct counsel for Campbell described as 'grossly fraudulent'[35] – so if it were true that Campbell's purported marriage was merely concubinage, it would partly be Cochrane's fault. As such, Cochrane should not have the chance to strip Campbell of her status – 'to declare her to be a Whore'[36] – or jeopardise the legitimacy of her children[37] by declaring them all 'Bastards'.[38]

In response to this argument, counsel for Cochrane tried to defend her silence by pointing out that her actions cohered with the 'easy Belief of a fond Wife to every Thing a Husband could say in Excuse for himself' and explaining that while Cochrane might have pursued a declarator of marriage during Carrick's lifetime if she had won then this would have been 'at the Expence [*sic*] of losing his Affection, and every Thing else valuable in a married State'. By keeping her peace, she had therefore foregone the 'empty title of wife and kept his affection and company when it was possible'.[39] He also pointed out that if Cochrane and Campbell were married, then nothing anyone could do (or not do) via the action before the court could change this fact. Whereas someone might be barred from seeking a divorce if they committed adultery or connived at their spouse's infidelity, this, so the argument went, was because divorce was 'Reparation' for the innocent spouse, who

---

[33] Peter Halkerston, *A Translation and Explanation of the Principal Technical Terms and Phrases Used in Mr Erskine's Institute of the Law of Scotland*, 2nd ed. (Edinburgh: printed for the author, 1829), p. 96.

[34] In Roman law, an *exceptio doli* clause gave a judge equitable discretion to decide the case in accordance with what seemed fair and reasonable, taking account of the misconduct of the plaintiff and the inequity that would flow from the action being permitted to succeed; see Simon Whittaker and Reinhard Zimmermann, 'Good Faith in European Contract Law: Surveying the Legal Landscape' in Simon Whittaker and Reinhard Zimmermann (eds.), *Good Faith in European Contract Law* (Cambridge: Cambridge University Press, 2000), pp. 7–62, p. 16.

[35] *Campbell v. Cochran* (1747).

[36] *Campbell v. Cochran* (1747–1751) Arniston Collection, vol. 31, Paper 1.

[37] *Campbell v. Cochran* (1747) Mor 10456. It is important that Cochrane's alleged fault rested on her *own* pleas. In the 1808 case of *MacLauchlan* (spelled various ways) v. *Couper & Stark*, the male pursuer (who appeared to be motivated by economic concerns) tried to suggest that a female defender should not be allowed to aver that she was married to her co-defender at the time the pursuer claimed he had married her because 'no party can be permitted to found a claim or defence upon his own turpitude'. Counsel for the defenders responded that it was only by joining the pursuer's plea to the defender's that any turpitude arose (NRS CS271/55559).

[38] *Campbell v. Cochran* (1747–1751).   [39] Ibid.

had the choice to condone the wrong.[40] No other human conduct, beyond the grounds of divorce and the decision of how to respond to them, could destroy a marriage that had been constituted.[41]

Ultimately, Cochrane lost her case and not because she was barred from proving it,[42] but the litigation reveals three important points. First, it was not only a duplicitous spouse who could be regarded as culpable for deceptively inducing intimacy. To be sure, part of Cochrane's perceived wrongdoing was her disrespect for the institution of marriage,[43] yet she was also thought to have wronged Campbell herself through her lack of 'Tenderness for the Defender [Campbell]' and 'Regard for her common Justice'.[44] Second, in defending Cochrane's behaviour, her lawyer drew on cultural conceptions of what made marriage valuable, going so far as to suggest that an unofficial (that is, not yet formally recognised by law) marriage was superior to an official one that lacked emotional substance. Finally, the intuitively appealing notion that the wrong done to Campbell should figure in the court's reasoning might have been accommodated by an objective view of contracting, but it did not make sense on a more subjective view, according to which any iniquitous consequences that would arise could have limited relevance in the face of the allegation that Cochrane and Carrick had jointly willed marriage.

The case of Cochrane and Campbell was unusual, though not unique, in that the personal bar in contemplation would have prevented the marriage from being *pursued*, rather than defended.[45] This feature of the case puts it directly at odds with the desire to facilitate the constitution of marriage outlined in Section 4.1, and it was more typical for a defender to be barred from escaping the conclusion that he was married. This is what makes personal bar just one of a wider range of techniques by which marriages were upheld, which can be grouped according to different ways of handling an apparent divergence between the defender's actions and what he claimed were his intentions.

---

[40] *Campbell* v. *Cochran* (1747).   [41] *Campbell* v. *Cochran* (1747–1751).

[42] The House of Lords overturned the Court of Session's decision to bar her (something the Commissary Court had refused to do) with Campbell's consent (*Campbell* v. *Cochran* (1747–1751)).

[43] Handwritten notes describe her conduct as 'lenocinium [connivance at adultery] a crime equally heinous if not more heinous than adultery itself'; see *Campbell* v. *Cochran* (1747).

[44] Ibid.

[45] Counsel for Cochrane thought it was the first time such an objection had been pled; see *Campbell* v. *Cochran* (1747). Despite similar facts (though a different mode of constituting marriage), the point was not raised in *Pennycook and Grinton* v. *Grinton and Graite* (1752) Mor 12677; *Pennycook* v. *Grinton* (1752) Pitfour Collection, Paper 16. Subsequently, the point came up in *Dalrymple* v. *Dalrymple*, when Sir William Scott took *Campbell* v. *Cochrane* to mean that a woman who 'suffer[ed]' another woman to be trepanned into a marriage with her husband' was not personally barred from asserting her marriage ((1811) at 691). The point was also raised in the 1828 'ulterior motive' case *McGregor* v. *MacNeill or Jolly*, discussed later in this chapter, but by 1844 it was 'no longer thought of' (*Robb* v. *Monteith* (1842–1844) General Collection, Paper 128).

4.2 Marriage by Present Consent

Turning to consider some more of these techniques, the idea that it did not matter whether the defender meant something different from what he had led the pursuer to believe (an objective approach) appears in numerous cases, though sometimes followed by the conclusion that in fact both parties *had* intended marriage. For example, in the important early nineteenth-century case of *Dalrymple* v. *Dalrymple*, Sir William Scott held that although a defender could challenge the meaning of the words he had used, he would have to prove that their alternative meaning was fully understood by the other party at the time the contract was formed if he was to escape the finding that he was married. In support of this view, the judge stated that it surely could not be 'represented as the law of any civilized country that in such a transaction a man shall use serious words, expressive of serious intentions, and shall yet be afterwards at liberty to aver a private intention … to avoid a contract which was differently understood by the other party'. To allow this would, in his opinion, open the door to frauds which the 'justice, and humanity, and policy of all law must be anxious to shut out'.[46]

As these assertions make clear, there was at this time some uncertainty over whether unilateral intentions really were irrelevant to the constitution of marriage, and this uncertainty cropped up again throughout the century.[47] Yet there are several cases where the rule was clearly applied.[48] The first of these, decided in the late 1830s, involved Edward Hoggan, a writer to the signet (a lawyer with particular privileges and duties),[49] who had provided Elizabeth Craigie, with whom he was in a relationship and had a child, a document that was supposed to secure her position, at least financially. Importantly, the wording of the document was equivocal and could be interpreted as either a

---

[46] *Dalrymple* v. *Dalrymple* (1811) at 684.

[47] In *Sassen* v. *Campbell*, Lord Succoth is reported to have stated that '[t]o constitute marriage by the law of Scotland consent alone is necessary; but that consent must be deliberately given by both parties eo intuiu [with that intent]' and therefore to have concluded that '[i]f *either* of them have any other purpose in view than that of marriage, and this be clearly established, then the consent will not be of that nature which is required by law'; see *Campbell* v. *Sassen* (1826) 2 W & S 309 at 319 (emphasis added). A decision from 1843 which refers to 'no real intention in *one or* both of the parties to contract actual marriage' goes on to refer to 'the real intention of the *parties*' so the point is clearer here; see *Browne* v. *Burns* (1843) 5 D 1288 at 1294–1295 (emphasis added). A few years later, however, Lord Hope's comments in *Lockyer* v. *Sinclair* that marriage is a '*mutual* contract … to the formation of which the *consent of both* parties must be really, deliberately, definitively, and irrevocably given' (see (1846) 8 D 582 at 605, emphasis original) were interpreted as conflicting with the rule that unilateral reservations were irrelevant, but these comments were later rationalised as having been concerned with *joint* reservations; see Walton, *Husband and Wife*, p. 86. In 1859, the Privy Council declined to comment on the effect of unilateral reservations (see *Bell* v. *Graham* (1859) 15 ER 91), and in *Longworth* v. *Yelverton* (1862) 1 M 161, the Lord Ordinary acknowledged that the doctrine was disputed (see note of the Lord Ordinary (Ardmillan)).

[48] Around the time these cases were decided, there was a series of important cases concerning marriage by promise and sex, which are discussed in Section 4.3.

[49] For details, see Watson (ed.), *Bell's Dictionary*, pp. 1129–1130.

declaration (or promise)[50] of marriage or an attempt to give Craigie access to the annuity payable to the widows' fund of writers to the signet without making her his wife. In the House of Lords, the highest tribunal that heard the case, it was held that Hoggan had really meant to contract marriage but arguments to the effect that it would not matter if he had not, so long as Craigie believed he had, were made.[51] Prior to this, analogous arguments had been made in the Court of Session where counsel for both Hoggan and Craigie accepted that it was irrelevant whether Hoggan had meant to contract marriage; the important point was whether Craigie could plausibly have understood him to have done so.[52] The Lord Ordinary (Fullerton), who first heard the case, even decided that Hoggan was married to Craigie though he believed Hoggan had been trying to deceive Craigie into thinking she was married while leaving himself free.[53]

In a very similar case decided only a few years later – *Hamilton v. Hamilton* – the Court of Session and the House of Lords appeared willing to accept that the deceased (the purported husband) had intended marriage but was compelled to secrecy due to the disapproval of his family and friends. Nevertheless, both the arguments in the Court of Session and the decisions of both courts reveal that *had* the deceased been faking his intention to marry, the marriage would nevertheless have been constituted.[54] Lord Brougham, in the House of Lords, put the point particularly starkly, stating that if a man indicated that he took a woman to be his wife, and she accepted, it would be irrelevant if 'all the while' he had planned only to deceive her (or to defraud anyone else): '[h]e has contracted a marriage with her as completely *as if he had really intended to contract it*, and not merely attempted to compass a fraud.'[55] Subsequent cases indicate that this position was, broadly speaking, held across the nineteenth century and into the twentieth century, with judges commenting that reserved intentions designed to deceive would not preclude a finding of marriage, even when the ultimate conclusion of the judgment rested on a finding that the defender had in fact acted with matrimonial intentions.[56]

---

[50] The Court of Session held the parties to be married on the basis that the document constituted at least a promise to marry and its delivery had been followed by sex. However, many of the parties' arguments and the decisions of the Lord Ordinary (prior to the decision of the Court of Session) and House of Lords (after the decision of the Court of Session) concentrated on whether the writings constituted a declaration of marriage.
[51] *Hoggan v. Craigie* (1839) MacL & Rob 942 at 958, 962–963.
[52] *Craigie v. Hoggan* (1838) 16 S 584; *Hoggan v. Craigie* (1838) General Collection, Paper 135.
[53] The Lord Ordinary's note is replicated in the House of Lords case report.
[54] *Hamilton v. Hamilton* (1839) 2 D 89.
[55] *Hamilton v. Hamilton* (1842) 1 Bell App 736 at 791 (emphasis added).
[56] *Stewart v. Menzies* (1833) 12 S 179; *Fleming v. Corbet* (1859) 21 D 1034; *Leslie v. Leslie* (1860) 22 D 993; *Forster v. Forster* (1869) 6 SLR 519, (1870–75) LR 2 Sc 244; *Duran v. Duran* (1904) 7 F 87 (in this case, the majority of judges did think the defender had not intended to marry the pursuer but had led her honestly to believe he was marrying her); *Petrie v. Petrie's Executrix and Another* 1911 SC 360 (suggesting that the defender may have deceived the pursuer but noting that the law meant he could not avoid marriage by taking 'refuge in seduction by fraud' (at 371)); *Imrie v. Imrie* (1891) 19 R 185; *Brady v. Murray* 1933 SLT 534.

Another line of cases can be described as more subjectivist in tenor in that the arguments and conclusions are more obviously based on scepticism about the possibility that the defender had intended something other than marriage. In the earliest case like this I have found,[57] which is from the middle of the eighteenth century and is unusual in featuring a female defender, counsel for the pursuer claimed that the defence offered by the deceased woman's relatives – that is, that she had been engaged in an indecent affair, which resulted in a child – was simply unbelievable. He admitted that the pursuer was of a lower rank than the deceased but nevertheless urged that unequal matches were not unheard of. By contrast, the idea that the deceased, who was the Countess-dowager of Strathmore, would stoop to be a concubine was 'morally impossible'. Such change in character, from virtue and honour to disgrace, would, he argued, 'look like what is called *Witchcraft*'.[58] Speaking more generally, he pointed out that it was common for 'faithless men' to deny their marriages[59] but unusual for women to do so, adding that the premises of the defence were 'As contrary to good Manners, and the Laws of the Land, as they are to the Doctrines of the Gospel'.[60] These different lines of argument show that counsel for the pursuer was attempting to portray the defence as incredible by comparing it to all the standards he had marshalled in support of his case: those personal to the defender, those disclosed by social practices, and those conveyed by divine revelation. As such, it seems appropriate to characterise his arguments as an example of evidential objectivism in action – the question to be answered was not simply what the countess had intended; the question was what it was appropriate to assume she had meant in light of her past conduct and prevailing norms.[61]

There are examples of cases like this across the period of this study,[62] including further instances of legal actors assigning a marital intent to the defender in light of prevailing norms. For example, in one mid nineteenth-century case, a judge considered that letters from the defender showed 'a kindly feeling and a warm regard to the pursuer … and [were] alike free from the insolence of one who had got quit of a mistress, or the levity of one who desired to renew an illicit connection'.[63] In another case, from the early twentieth century, marital

---

[57] *Forbes* v. *Countess of Strathmore* [1750] 1 Elchies 365; (1751) 6 Paton 684.
[58] *Forbes* v. *Countess of Strathmore* (1749–1750) Drummore Collection, vol. 10, Paper 49.
[59] *Forbes* v. *Countess of Strathmore* (1754–1756) Campbell Collection, vol. 4, Paper 5.
[60] *Forbes* v. *Countess of Strathmore* (1749–1750).
[61] Though this chapter primarily focuses on how the potentially deceptive party's conduct was interpreted, it is important to note that when courts sought to interpret the beliefs of the 'innocent' party, they would also resort to looking at her past conduct and prevailing norms. See, for example, the assessment that 'having regard to her previous history, and to such knowledge she had of his, it is in the highest degree incredible that the pursuer … after twenty years of honourable courtship, knowingly entered into a state, not of marriage but of concubinage' – that she 'merely accepted the position of another mistress, to be cast off at will' (*Petrie* v. *Petrie's Executrix and Another* (1911) at 370).
[62] For example, *MacAlister* v. *Dun* (1759) 2 Paton 29.
[63] *MacDonald* v. *MacDonald* (1863) 1 M 854, note of the Lord Ordinary (Ardmillan).

intention was judged partly by the fervour and affection of the defender's correspondence.[64] An even more glaring example is the 1874–75 case of *Robertson v. Steuart*, in which the same evidence that led the Court of Session to conclude there was marital intention led to the opposite conclusion in the House of Lords. The pre-'marital' relationship between the two parties, who were far apart in terms of rank, was assessed by some of the judges in the Court of Session to be 'a courtship', albeit one that was not 'very delicate or refined',[65] while the dissenting judges and those who later overturned the decision considered the parties' relationship to be immoral, having involved pre-marital sex.[66] The bad reputation of the pursuer's family and the lack of 'romance' and 'sentiment' in the parties' relationship were among the reasons offered for this conclusion,[67] but it was the mode of expression in letters to and from the defender which created the greatest difficulties for the pursuer. In these, he had addressed her as Miss Wilson, rather than Mrs Steuart, and shown what the judges considered to be insufficient regard for her health and not enough enthusiasm on the occasion of their son's birth.

In line with the rule about unilateral reservations, the defender's lack of intention to marry, as the court saw it, only precluded a finding of marriage because the court held that the pursuer had *also* lacked an intention to marry on account of her conduct following the alleged marriage.[68] Though this move was, legally speaking, not novel what is striking about the judgments is that they reveal a patent desire to tighten up the Scots law of marriage. A number of the opinions emphasise the need for clear and unequivocal marital consent,[69] with one of the judges stating that the 'great defence' of Scots law rested on this point.[70] The report of the Royal Commission on the Laws of Marriage,[71] containing various criticisms of the looseness (or stringency) of Scots law, had been published just six years earlier, in 1868, and both its findings and the possibility of law reform are mentioned explicitly in Lord Selborne's House of Lords judgment.[72] Ironically, however, this move to tighten up the law involved its simultaneous loosening in the sense that an increased focus on the parties' intentions made it easier for them to escape the conclusion that they were married by showing that they ostensibly shared a lack of intention to marry. I come back to this point in Section 4.3 but, in concluding this one, I want briefly to explore how this point arose in cases of ulterior motives.

---

[64] *Elliot* v. *Parkinson* (1905) 12 SLT 710.   [65] *Robertson* v. *Steuart* (1874) 11 SLR 427 at 429.
[66] The House of Lords opinions are reported at *Steuart* v. *Robertson* (1875) 2 R (HL) 80.
[67] As Lord Ardmillan put it, '[s]he had not known and loved him in his better days, and then, like an ivy round a tree, clung to him in his ruin' (see *Robertson* v. *Steuart* (1874) at 475).
[68] She had accepted being called Miss Wilson and even referred to herself in this way; she had also registered the child she had with the defender as illegitimate.
[69] This emphasis also comes through in *Davidson* v. *Davidson* 1921 SC 341, where *Robertson* v. *Steuart* was followed.
[70] *Robertson* v. *Steuart* (1874), Lord Ardmillan (at 478).
[71] *Report of the Royal Commission*; Probert et al., 'A Uniform Law of Marriage?'
[72] *Steuart* v. *Robertson* (1875) at 115–116.

The rule that a 'marriage' which *both* parties had contracted in jest or to deceive others (for example, family members or officials) would not constitute a lawful marriage can be seen in cases from at least as early as 1745,[73] and the rule existed in other jurisdictions.[74] These are examples of what in Scots law was a more general commitment to the idea that, at least in some circumstances, there would be no marriage if *both* parties lacked marital intention. Significantly, however, several cases of this kind appear to have involved one party – a man – who had an ulterior motive for marrying. This meant that when the court held that no marriage had been contracted, the effect was to save the 'innocent' spouse from being bound and to deprive the calculating spouse of the 'illicit' benefit he appeared to desire.

To be clear, the formal reason these cases did not result in a finding of marriage was that in the court's view, there was no clear agreement to marry[75] and/or the parties' subsequent conduct suggested that neither of them considered themselves married and, on that basis, that they most likely had not intended marriage. Though it was controversial, courts held that this reasoning could apply in relation to allegations of both regular and irregular marriages,[76] and, as in the case of *Robertson* v. *Steuart*, judges based their assessment of the parties' conduct on conventional assumptions about the nature and value of marriage,[77] such as the occurrence of sexual intercourse[78] and cohabitation.[79] Again as in *Robertson* v. *Steuart*, courts posited (but with some anxiety) a

---

[73] *McNaughton* v. *Clugston* (1745), discussed in Leneman, *Promises, Promises*, p. 61. See also Fraser, *Personal and Domestic Relations*, p. 213; Fraser, *Husband and Wife*, pp. 415–419, 422; and Clive, *Husband and Wife*, Paragraphs 05.003, 07.041–07.043.

[74] Kerry Abrams, 'Marriage Fraud' (2012) 100(1) *California Law Review* 1–68 at 13; Jackson, 'Consent of the Parties'; Law Commission, *Working Paper No 20 Nullity of Marriage* (1968), p. 13.

[75] *Taylor* v. *Kello* (1786) Mor 12687; *Kello* v. *Taylor* (1787) 3 Paton 56; *Lockyer v Sinclair* (1846) at 589.

[76] *Orlandi* v. *Castelli* 1961 SLT 118 and *SH* v. *HK* 2006 SC 129, both discussed later in this chapter, were cases of regular marriage and *Jolly* v. *McGregor*, which involved a clandestine ceremony conducted by a clergyman, was in some subsequent cases, including *Robertson* v. *Steuart* ((1874) 11 SLR 427 at 470), treated as a regular marriage.

[77] An exception perhaps is *Cameron* v. *Malcolm* (1756) Mor 12680, NRS CS271/69676, where the extreme youth of the defender, who was worth a fortune, and the use of threats to secure her 'consent' underpinned the (contentious) decision that there was no marital consent. The case of *Chapman* v. *Niven* is somewhat similar but without the extreme youth. It is perhaps significant that this case occurred during a period marked by a desire to protect women and girls from exploitation ('Court of Session', *The Glasgow Herald*, 17 January 1898, p. 9).

[78] *Jolly* v. *McGregor* (1828) 3 W & S 85; *Lockyer* v. *Sinclair* (1846) at 595–596, 598, 616; *Orlandi* v. *Castelli* (1961) at 119 (this case seems to have involved collusion about the ulterior purpose, so does not appear to be a case of one party deceiving the other); *SH* v. *HK* (2006), expressing ambivalence about the importance of sex in modern marriages (at Paragraph 41). Sex is also significant in some cases that involve a joint lack of marital intention but do not appear to be 'ulterior motive' cases, for example, *MacLauchlan* v. *Dobson* (1796) Mor 12693; see Stair; More, *Institutions* (vol. 1), Note B, p. xiii, and Walton, *Husband and Wife*, p. 80.

[79] *Kello* v. *Taylor* (1787); *Lockyer* v. *Sinclair* (1846) at 595–596; *Orlandi* v. *Castelli* (1961) at 119; *SH* v. *HK* (2006) at Paragraph 55, though noting the difficulty in formulating a prescriptive account of marriage in an age of varied personal relationships.

distinction between the task of retrospectively discovering whether marital intent had existed at the time the alleged marriage was contracted and the unlawful practice of annulling a marriage based on the parties' post-marital conduct or repentance.[80] The idiosyncratic feature of these cases, however, is that the pursuers appeared to be seeking economic gain,[81] sometimes after misrepresenting or not disclosing their own poor financial position[82] or, later, a beneficial migration status.[83]

Furthermore, sometimes the conduct of these men suggested that they were not appropriately attached to their purported spouse. The most blatant example of this occurred when the pursuer in one case, Malcolm McGregor, congratulated his 'wife' for marrying another man, toasted her as this other man's spouse, and even shared a room with them while they slept in the same bed.[84] This behaviour was interpreted as being inconsistent with a belief that the pursuer and defender were married, but it also suggested that he did not care about the defender and was seeking to be declared married to her for the wrong reasons. On this point, it is useful to contrast the pursuer's conduct with the behaviour of Cochrane in the case discussed earlier. While Cochrane was perhaps overly forgiving, her conduct was at least consistent with affection for her husband; conversely, McGregor appeared calculating and cynical, waiting to see whether his 'wife' would in fact acquire her father's wealth before attempting to assert his marital status.[85]

Reflecting this difference, the argument that McGregor's conduct should bar him from seeking the patrimonial claims that would follow from his matrimonial one[86] was partly founded on the contention that 'no Court of Justice would lend itself to [his] base mercenary plans and designs', which '[could not] be visited with too much censure'.[87] Similarly, in the much later, early twenty-first-century case of *SH* v. *HK*, the fact that the defender[88] was held to have formed a sexual relationship with another woman partway through the process of acquiring his desired migration status, and not to have told the

---

[80] *Robertson* v. *Steuart* (1874) at 472; *Jolly* v. *McGregor* (1828) at 115, 190. The same point was made in *Davidson* v. *Davidson* (1921) at 352.
[81] *Jolly* v. *McGregor* (1828) at 100, 169–170. Some cases like the ones analysed here might have ended with criminal prosecution for theft or fraud if the adventurer absconded with his dupe's property. See, for example, 'A Heartless Fellow', *The Glasgow Herald*, 29 October 1890, p. 4; 'Glasgow High Court – Old Court', *The Scotsman*, 30 October 1901, p. 12; 'Love's Deceit', *Daily Record*, 4 March 1910, p. 3; 'Heartless Hoax on Young Woman', *The Evening Telegraph*, 30 January 1928, p. 4.
[82] *Taylor* v. *Kello* (1786); *Lockyer* v. *Sinclair* (1846) at 583. As such, these cases can be read alongside those discussed in Chapter 2.
[83] *Orlandi* v. *Castelli* (1961) at 119; *SH* v. *HK* (2006) at 129. In some US states, marrying for migration status or property (with no intention to fulfil marital obligations) has been a ground of annulment on the basis of fraud in the essentials; see Latham, 'Recognizing Error and Fraud' at 599.
[84] *Jolly* v. *McGregor* (1828). [85] Ibid. at 171. [86] Ibid. at 143. [87] Ibid. at 142–143.
[88] This is a case of declarator of nullity, so the seemingly duplicitous party is the defender and the apparent dupe is the pursuer.

pursuer about this,[89] suggested that he had furtively strung her along for his own benefit. Again, the court's decision that the parties were not married formally rested on a lack of marital consent, and it was accepted that an 'unworthy motive' would not necessarily 'detract from the genuineness of that party's declaration of marital consent'. Nevertheless, one judge explicitly noted that 'evidence of the motive could provide an adminicle of proof that the unworthy person lacked true matrimonial consent'.[90]

It is striking that the apparent deception of the pursuer is overlooked in much of the commentary on this case.[91] In keeping with the rules governing the constitution of marriage, the focus of the discussion is whether the parties intended marriage, what it means to intend marriage in a modern secular legal system, and the best way to handle the perceived abuse of the law of marriage.[92] And while these issues have now been addressed by legislative intervention, the position of the deceived spouse remains something of an afterthought. More specifically, it is now clear that neither joint nor unilateral reservations are relevant to the constitution of marriage,[93] and migration-related 'sham' marriages and civil partnerships are now criminalised in various ways. Yet what these changes mean for the deceived spouse is that they cannot seek to annul their marriage on the basis of a lack of marital intent (though they might seek a divorce) and that the wrong done to them is ensconced within a criminalisation regime that appears to regard the question of whether a 'sham marriage' was collusive as largely irrelevant.[94]

This situation reflects developments elsewhere, such as in the United States where from the middle of the twentieth century, the law's concern with 'sham marriage' shifted away from the contractual connection between the two spouses

---

[89] *SH* v. *HK* (2006) at Paragraphs 18, 20. At first instance, when the parties were found to be married, the judge (Lord Clarke) believed that the defender had not married the pursuer simply for a visa (*SH* v. *HK* 2003 SLT 515 at Paragraph 18).

[90] *SH* v. *HK* (2006), Lord Penrose at Paragraph 35.

[91] An exception is an article by Jane Mair, which hints at the possibility that the defender might have been dishonest with the pursuer and acknowledges the pursuer and her mother's feeling, as expressed in the case report, that the defender had been 'guilty of a deep breach of trust'; see 'A Sham Marriage or a Proper Wedding? Hakeem v Hussain' (2003) 7(3) *Edinburgh Law Review* 404–409 at 409.

[92] Norrie, *Norrie's Commentaries*, pp. 97–101; Clive, *Husband and Wife*, Paragraphs 07.042–07.052.

[93] Marriage (Scotland) Act 1977, s. 20A(4), inserted by the Family Law (Scotland) Act 2006.

[94] Home Office, *Criminal Investigations: Sham Marriage*, version 3.0 (January 2021). The 'deception' provision of the Immigration Act 1971, that is, s. 24A, which was added by the Immigration and Asylum Act 1999, does not specify deceptions and applies to forging papers, making false claims regarding nationality and so on. Research on this topic tends not to focus on whether there has been collusion either; see, for example, Georgie Wemyss, Nira Yuval-Davis and Kathryn Cassidy, '"Beauty and the Beast": Everyday Bordering Discourse and "Sham Marriage" Discourse' (2018) 66 *Political Geography* 151–160 and, in the Canadian context, Grace Tran, '"We're Dating after Marriage": Transformative Effects of Performing Intimacy in Vietnamese "Marriage Fraud" Arrangements' (2021) 44(9) *Ethnic and Racial Studies* 1569–1588.

towards the perceived mis-acquisition of the privileges that attach to the married state. In this context, deception of one spouse by the other becomes irrelevant or only part of the problem.[95] I reflect further on this point in Section 4.5, where I suggest that the difficulties to which this situation gives rise extend beyond what is perceived to be migration-related marriage fraud. Before that, it is necessary to consider the two other legal responses to which faking marriage could give rise.

4.3 Marriage by Promise and Sex

In contrast to marriage constituted by present consent, the prohibition of hearing evidence from parties to an action for declarator of marriage based on promise of marriage followed by sex remained in place until the end of the twentieth century.[96] Additionally, rules governing the way promises to marry could be proved and the use of presumptions about the relationship between such promises and the subsequent sex, discussed later in this section, made this way of constituting marriage fairly complex. As with marriage by present consent, however, these rules and presumptions were not understood or applied in a uniform way and tracing out shifts in their operation makes clear that the practice of inferring or imposing marriage functioned as a remedy and punishment in this context, too, before gradually declining.

Two major controversies that arose in the early period of this study concerned how a promise to marry could be established and by what kinds of evidence. Taking the latter point first, it was generally understood that to ground a declarator of marriage a promise had to be proved either by reference to the oath of the promisor[97] or by the promisor's writing.[98] Nevertheless, a series of cases raised the possibility that a promise to marry might be proved by parole evidence[99] and, importantly, that proof of honourable courtship without any explicit promise to marry might form the basis of a marriage when followed by sex. The rationale behind this development was that 'in reason and justice',[100] acts that implied that a marriage was going to happen were of *equivalent seriousness* to a promise of marriage, even if they did not necessarily imply that a promise existed.[101] This position had the perceived advantage of according with

---

[95] Abrams, 'Marriage Fraud'.
[96] Evidence Law Amendment (Scotland) Act 1874 (c. 64, 37 & 38 Vict.), s. 3; Requirements of Writing (Scotland) Act 1995, s. 11 (now repealed).
[97] A process by which one party referred a fact at issue to their opponent's oath and by which the evidence given, and only this evidence, would be determinative of the issue. In referring the issue to the oath of their opponent, the referrer bound themselves to allow the cause to be decided on this basis; see Watson (ed.), *Bell's Dictionary*, pp. 415–418.
[98] Æ. J. G. Mackay, *Manual of Practice in the Court of Session* (Edinburgh: W. Green & Sons, 1893), p. 469.
[99] The testimony of witnesses under oath; see Watson (ed.), *Bell's Dictionary*, pp. 409, 771.
[100] *Stewart v. Lindsay* (1816–1817) Hume Collection, vol. 126, Paper 53.
[101] For example, the Lord President in *Smith v. Grierson* (1755) in Fergusson, *Consistorial Law*, p. 137 (but making clear that the evidence would need to be *scripto vel juramento* of the defender); interlocutor of the Commissary Court in *Stewart v. Lindsay* (1817) Fac Dec 380 at 382.

4.3 Marriage by Promise and Sex

the realities of respectable relationships, as they were conventionally understood, whose female participants deserved the law's protection. As one lawyer put it, 'scarce ever [was] a *direct Promise* of Marriage … given by the Man in a fair and honourable Courtship of a Woman'.[102] Its downside was considerable legal uncertainty, though. As another lawyer put it, it was 'altogether impossible to distinguish between a courtship of one sort and a courtship of another' and 'impracticable, with any degree of certainty, to judge of the views and intentions of parties from any proof of courtship'.[103] Eventually, when the argument that honourable courtship followed by sex could create a marriage was pled explicitly, in a case reported in 1844,[104] the court held that the earlier cases stood only for the proposition that proof of honourable courtship, which could be established via parole evidence, could bolster proof of a promise to marry, which had to be evidenced by the promisor's oath or writing.[105]

But the job of inferring a promise to marry from the defender's writing or testimony reflected the same competing desires that underpinned the courtship cases. As such, in cases from the mid eighteenth and the early nineteenth century, there is a glaring tension between the desire to insist that only direct promises were clear enough to ground a contract as important and life-altering as marriage[106] and the desire to allow 'virtual promise[s]', such as the one taken to exist in *Stewart* v. *Lindsay*,[107] to qualify. In this case, the defender had directed the pursuer's attention to a passage of the Bible concerning marriage and asked her to read it and discuss it with him; he had also discussed the exciseman's widows fund, of which he was a member, with the pursuer and her mother, making clear to them that he was a subscriber to the scheme.[108] Allowing this behaviour to found the constitution of a marriage was comprehensible on the view that the defender had led the pursuer to believe he intended marriage, but it threatened to stretch the law, encourage women to take chances on shaky relationships, and facilitate 'immoral' relations. Such an expansive conception of promises also threatened to degrade the institution of marriage and cause damage to the individuals who would be forced into marriages in which neither party could have trust in, or have regard for, the other.[109] Similar points were raised in subsequent cases.[110]

---

[102] *Smith* v. *Grierson* (1753–1755) Campbell Collection, vol. 2, Paper 34 (emphasis original). The same argument was made in *Stewart* v. *Lindsay* (1816–1817), and a similar one was made in *Campbell* v. *Honyman* (1827–1830) General Collection, Paper 509 – that in 'honourable courtship parties never dream of precautions against falsehood and desertion'.

[103] *Low* v. *Allardice* (1794) Dreghorn Collection, vol. 79, Paper 11. Similar points were made in *Harvie* v. *Inglis* (1834–1837) General Collection, Paper 238 and *Sim* v. *Miles* (1829) General Collection, Paper 27.

[104] *Robb* v. *Monteith* (1842–1844).   [105] *Monteith* v. *Robb* (1844) 6 D 934.

[106] *Pennycook* v. *Grinton and Graite* (1755) in Fergusson, *Consistorial Law*, p. 105; *Sim* v. *Miles* (1829).

[107] *Stewart* v. *Lindsay* (1817) at 382.   [108] *Stewart* v. *Lindsay* (1817).

[109] *Stewart* v. *Lindsay* (1816–1817).

[110] *Reid* v. *Laing* (1819) NRS CS234/L/10/1; *Sim* v. *Miles* (1829); *Campbell* v. *Honyman* (1830) Fac Dec 838; *Campbell* v. *Honyman* (1827–1830); *Harvie* v. *Inglis* (1837); *Imrie* v. *Imrie* (1891).

Homing in on the point about the pursuer's beliefs, it is clear that the different means by which a party could be bound that arose in the marriage by present consent cases were also important to the law of marriage by promise and sex. As such, in some cases, the court showed concern for the defender's intentions,[111] but in these cases, and in others, the question of what he had led the pursuer to believe generally assumed greater importance, and thus the defender might properly be barred from arguing that he had not intended marriage.[112] This difference is also manifest in two distinct ways a promise to marry followed by sex was considered to constitute marriage: on one view, when sex occurred on the faith of a promise to marry the sexual connection implied the immediate and mutual marital consent of both parties; on the other, when a woman had given up her person on the faith of the promise the man was barred from resiling for equitable reasons.[113] The latter view had affiliations both with the older practice of courts converting marital pre-contracts into contracts and the idea that marriage functioned as a punishment.[114]

Apart from clashing with the vision of marriage as a voluntary undertaking, the doctrines that made it possible to establish marriage on the basis of the pursuer's belief about the prospect of marriage also threatened to eradicate the civil wrong of seduction. Seduction is discussed more fully in Chapter 5 but, in brief, one of the ways it could be committed was by inducing a woman to consent to sex on a false (or at least unfulfilled) promise of marriage. But if marriage could be established by a promise to marry or even honourable courtship, as proved by parole evidence, then this kind of seduction could amount to a case of marriage.[115] And if the defender's true intentions were irrelevant to determining whether a marriage contract existed, then seduction could not be distinguished from marriage by the falsity of the defender's intentions either.[116]

---

[111] *Smith* v. *Grierson* (1755), p. 135; *Stewart* v. *Lindsay* (1816–1817); *Reid* v. *Laing* (1823) 1 Shaw 440, the opinion of the Lord Chancellor; *Campbell* v. *Honyman* (1830) at 845.

[112] *Smith* v. *Grierson* (1755), p. 135; *Smith* v. *Grierson* (1753–1755); *Low* v. *Allardice* (1791–1797), as discussed in Leneman, *Promises Promises*, pp. 21–25; *Low* v. *Allardice* (1794); *Stewart* v. *Lindsay* (1816–1817); *Reid* v. *Laing* (1823), the opinion of the Lord Chancellor; *Reid* v. *Laing* (1819); *Sim* v. *Miles* (1829); *Campbell* v. *Honyman* (1827–1830); *Campbell* v. *Honyman* (1830); *Ross* v. *MacLeod* (1861) 23 D 972 (note of the Lord Ordinary (Kinloch)).

[113] *Pennycook* v. *Grinton and Graite* (1755), p. 103 (first theory); *Smith* v. *Grierson* (1755), p. 135 (first theory); *Smith* v. *Grierson* (1753–1755) (second theory); *Low* v. *Allardice* (1794) (first theory); *Stewart* v. *Lindsay* (1816–1817) (second theory); *Miles* v. *Sim* (1830) Fac Dec 84 at 85–86 (both theories); *Harvie* v. *Inglis* (1834–1837) (both theories); *Mackenzie* v. *Stewart* (1848) 10 D 611 (both theories).

[114] This point was acknowledged in some of the cases, most notably by Lord Kames in *Smith* v. *Grierson* (1755), and other texts noted that the presumption of mutual consent was recommended by equity and the check it gave to perfidy; see Erskine, *Institute* (1785), p. 90. It also arises in various places in the *Report of the Royal Commission*, for example, pp. 118, 123.

[115] This point was acknowledged in some cases, for example, *Stewart* v. *Lindsay* (1816–1817) and *Campbell* v. *Honyman* (1827–1830).

[116] The idea that false promises were the hallmark of seduction comes up in *Pennycook* v. *Grinton and Graite* (1755), p. 105; *Pennycook* v. *Grinton* (1752); *Low* v. *Allardice* (1794); and *Campbell* v. *Honyman* (1827–1830).

These issues were to some extent cleared up in an important case, *Ross* v. *MacLeod*, which was decided in 1861. In this decision, the court (on appeal) held that a promise that could found a declarator of marriage had to be proved by the defender's writing or oath and the Lord President expressed dissatisfaction with loosely inferred, or even conjectured, promises, stating that these were no substitute for 'direct and absolute evidence'.[117] The suggestion that implied promises, or conduct that created the impression that a promise existed, should only ground a claim of damages for seduction and that a declarator of marriage should require formal and express promises had been made by counsel in some of the earlier cases.[118] After *Ross* v. *MacLeod*, however, the claim that a declarator of marriage required 'direct and specific' proof of a promise of marriage appeared in subsequent judgments.[119]

It is crucial to appreciate that this shift occurred just a year after comments by Lord Deas in the 1860 marriage by present consent case of *Leslie* v. *Leslie* that 'consent is not essential to marriage' and that in cases of marriage by promise of marriage followed by sex, the law did not inquire into whether the parties meant marriage and could presume the existence of consent when there was none in fact.[120] Like the case of *Robertson* v. *Steuart*, discussed in Section 4.2, the decision issued in *Leslie* v. *Leslie* immediately preceded a tightening up of the law such that it would become less likely that parties could be found by a court to be married. A controversial example of this occurred in 1862 when in the now (in)famous *Yelverton* case, the Lord Ordinary (Ardmillan) concluded that there was no marriage between the pursuer and defender because, in his opinion, no promise to marry could be found in the letters that passed between them – they were not marked by the 'great propriety and delicacy' and 'consciousness of honourable attachment' that gave the letters in the *Honyman* case 'the fragrance of a pure and virtuous love'. Explaining his decision further, the judge remarked that it was not competent to construe a promise inferentially or conjecturally from the whole story of the parties' relationship, adding that even if it were he would not think such a promise proved.[121]

---

[117] *Ross* v. *MacLeod* (1861) at 982. The other judges were less clearly against inferring promises, but Lord Deas at least noted that the inference in the *Honyman* case might have been 'a right or wrong inference', suggesting he might prefer clearer evidence of the existence of a promise (at 993).

[118] *Sim* v. *Miles* (1829); *Campbell* v. *Honyman* (1827–1830); *Robb* v. *Monteith* (1842–1844).

[119] For example, *Murray* v. *Napier* (1861) at 1244. *Forbes* v. *Wilson* (1868) 6 M 770 confirmed that proof was restricted to the writing or oath of the defender, but the continued restriction on proof, after the enactment of the 1874 Act (s. 3 of which set out that the law relating to proof of a promise of marriage in an action of declarator of marriage based on promise and sex remained in force), seems to have been misunderstood; see *Burns* v. *McNair* ('Paisley', *The Glasgow Herald*, 21 March 1878, p. 3).

[120] *Leslie* v. *Leslie* (1860) at 1012.

[121] *Longworth* v. *Yelverton* (1862) (note of the Lord Ordinary). In the case cited, the Court of Session overturned the Lord Ordinary's decision, but the House of Lords then found there was no marriage (see *Yelverton* v. *Longworth* (1864) 2 M (HL) 49).

This decision illustrates that the difficulties of trying to discover the true intention of the parties at the time they had acted were similar to those that arose in the marriage by present consent cases discussed in Section 4.2. As one critic wrote, 'if a man's consent, however deliberately given, is to be construed by a theory derived from some prior sentiments entertained by him, how in the name of the commonest sense that ever served the purposes of life could a consensual contract ever be made out at all?'.[122] It also attracted criticism on the ground that Major Yelverton had deceived his lover, Theresa Longworth, about his intentions and had been allowed to get away with this. One story, referring to the Major as 'the dwarf Belial – the pygmy Mephistopheles of the nineteenth century', condemned him as a 'man who arranges his amours as he would his betting-book, and who calculates with devilish deliberation the chances of seduction as he would a deal of the cards or a throw of the dice.'[123]

Both these features of the case mark a more general trend towards the undoing of the doctrine of marriage by promise and sex and its disappearance as a form of redress and punishment. A further change that signalled the same thing was the weakening of the two presumptions that underpinned the two different ways by which a promise to marry followed by sex constituted marriage: the presumption that sex following a promise to marry had occurred on the faith of that promise (and thus the man should not be able to resile) and the presumption that a promise to marry followed by sex signalled that the parties intended marriage (and thus that their conduct implied their immediate and mutual marital consent). The idea that these presumptions could not be rebutted was not uniformly held, but it still existed at around the time the *Yelverton* case was decided.[124] After this time, however, it is common to see reference to the possibility that they could both be rebutted,[125] at least by evidence of the woman's true motivations and intentions.[126] This occurred in three cases in which either the woman appeared (due to her actions) not to have intended marriage[127] or she was resisting the presumptions that were supposed to work to her benefit.[128]

---

[122] 'A Common Sense View of the Yelverton Judgment [by an Old Lawyer]', *The Caledonian Mercury*, 11 July 1862, p. 3.

[123] 'The Yelverton Marriage Case [from the Daily Telegraph]', *The Caledonian Mercury*, 9 July 1862, p. 4.

[124] 'Marriage Law Assimilation' at 72.

[125] Report of the Royal Commission, p. 74; Fraser, *Husband and Wife*, pp. 370–371; Walton, *Husband and Wife*, p. 27.

[126] Erskine, *Institute* (1871), p. 139.

[127] *Morrison* v. *Dobson* (1869) 8 M 347; *Maloy and other* v. *Macadam and others* (1885) 12 R 431; *N* v. *C* 1933 SC 492.

[128] *M* v. *Y* (1934) SLT 187. The judge (Lord Moncrieff) clearly considered this to be unnatural behaviour – he referred to the case as 'distasteful' and the pursuer (this is an action for declarator of freedom, that is, to prove that the pursuer was *not* married to the defender, who claimed he was her husband) as 'dishonouring the traditions of womanhood' (at 187). He added that as a 'professing concubine', the pursuer saw the accusation that she was married as 'an affront' – a position that made him feel he was compelled to 'try to form some psychological estimate of her personality and character' before he 'dare[d] accept' her evidence (at 187–188).

Importantly, in three cases from the interwar period, these presumptions are essentially described as legal fictions. In 1921, the notion that sex following a promise of marriage could be presumed to occur on the faith of that promise was deemed an 'artificial presumption',[129] and the idea that the parties intended marriage by these acts was called a 'curious fiction'.[130] Twelve years later, the latter of these two presumptions was described as 'in complete conflict with reality'[131] and as involving an 'element of legal policy'.[132] The fact that at this time it was accepted that men could bring an action of declarator of marriage on this footing[133] also suggests that the gendered social and moral framework that had supported the presumptions by which this area of law operated had begun to crumble,[134] just as it had in relation to the action of breach of promise of marriage.[135] On top of this, the worry that marriages that were essentially coerced would be loveless and unhappy, which had appeared in some of the marriage by present consent cases, began to pop up in respect of this mode of contracting marriage, too,[136] reflecting the shifting expectations of marriage outlined in Chapter 1. Finally, any benefit to the state that might previously have attached to finding parties married easily[137] was beginning to disappear. By the early twentieth century, the challenges of ascertaining marital status were causing difficulty for those administering public funds[138] and, as the provision of state welfare increased, this difficulty became more significant,[139] thus bolstering the case for abolishing irregular marriage.[140]

4.4 Bigamy

This penultimate section brings the historical analysis to a close by showing how the shifting balance between state and individual interests and the turn

---

[129] *X* v. *Y* (1921) SLT 79, Lord Sands (at 81).
[130] *Ross* v. *Reid* ('Claim to Wifehood Fails', *The Courier*, 23 December 1921, p. 5 (also Lord Sands)).
[131] *N* v. *C* (1933), Lord Sands (at 500).   [132] Ibid., Lord President (Clyde) (at 497).
[133] *Lindsay* v. *Lindsay* 1927 SC 395; *Hardie* v. *Boog* (1931) SLT 198.
[134] See also 'Notes from Edinburgh' (1936) 52 *Scottish Law Review* 86–89, which describes this form of marriage as out of step with 'modern social conditions' (at 86).
[135] See Chapter 3.
[136] Counsel in *Reid* v. *Laing* (1819) relied on this point, and some commentary on the *Yelverton* case suggests that instead of being 'tied to a man who must by this time be hateful to her' Theresa Longworth was free and had the sympathy of the masses, adding that it was undesirable to bind those who are 'wholly estranged' from each other with 'indissoluble bonds' (see 'The Yelverton Case', *Dundee Courier*, 30 July 1864, p. 3). Similar sentiments were expressed in 'Summary', *The Caledonian Mercury*, 29 July 1864, p. 2. In Lord Sands' judgment in *Ross* v. *Reid* (1921), he reportedly disagreed that it was always the duty of a man who wronged a woman to enter a union for life and take vows he knew he could not fulfil (to love, honour and cherish) or that to do so would be in the woman's interest.
[137] See Section 4.1.
[138] 'Scotland's Laws on Marriage', *Dundee Courier and Advertiser*, 4 February 1936, p. 10; 'Notes from Edinburgh' (1936) at 87.
[139] Gordon, 'Myth and Reality' at 518–519.
[140] Gordon, 'Irregular Marriage and Cohabitation' at 1066.

towards greater subjectification, which came through in Sections 4.2 and 4.3, also shaped the crime of bigamy.[141] In this respect, the crime of bigamy developed two strands over time – one that focuses on the individual victim(s) and resembles a private wrong and another, which now appears dominant, that focuses on the state's interests in maintaining its preferred regime of marital benefits, often at the expense of the 'spouses' who have been deceived. This section also shows how the crime of bigamy has provided legal recognition of the significance that intimate relationships hold for individuals' sense of self, even if neither the significance nor the level of recognition has been static. The declining capacity of bigamy to provide this recognition is therefore important and stands in stark contrast to the history of bigamy as a sexual wrong, whose trajectory is one of growth rather than decline, as I outline in Part II.

During the period just before the start of this study, bigamy was conceptualised as perjury – the second union involved giving 'contrary oaths'[142] – and a violation of the oath of 'conjugal chastity' made at the first marriage.[143] The crime was also considered to jeopardise the certainty of birth ties, which were seen as central to the family unit and kinship, and thus to the stability of the bonds of society.[144] By the late eighteenth and nineteenth centuries, however, descriptions of the crime also emphasised the wrong done to the second 'wife' and its negative effects on civil order.[145] According to one publication from this time, it was the particular combination of immorality and danger to society – the 'moral guilt' and 'direct social evil' – which made bigamy an appropriate target of criminal punishment. These characteristics gave bigamy the 'character of public crime falling within the sphere of public law',[146] and its 'peculiar wickedness and depravity of heart' were considered to make the crime often worse than offences such as poaching and rioting, which were disorderly and culpable but not so morally heinous.[147]

Given the perceived seriousness of the offence, it is unsurprising that judges were anxious to punish bigamy severely. Unlike their English counterparts, however, judges in Scotland had no statutory authority with which

---

[141] I only outline the components of this offence that are relevant to the discussion.
[142] Olivia Robinson (ed.), George MacKenzie, *The Law and Customs of Scotland in Matters Criminal* (Edinburgh: Stair Society, 2012), pp. 141–142.
[143] William Forbes, *The Institutes of the Law of Scotland* (Edinburgh: Edinburgh Legal Education Trust, 2012), p. 119. A statute of 1551 appears to have conceived of bigamy in these terms and made the crime punishable with the pains of perjury; see David Hume, *Commentaries on the Law of Scotland, Respecting Crimes* (Edinburgh: Bell & Bradfute, 1844), p. 459.
[144] Alexander Bayne, *Institutions of the Criminal Law of Scotland* (Edinburgh: Thomas & Walter Ruddimans, 1730), p. 45.
[145] Hume, *Commentaries*, ch. XX. By this time, most prosecutions were brought under common law and not the statute; see Archibald Alison, *Principles of the Criminal Law of Scotland* (Edinburgh: William Blackwood, 1832), p. 542.
[146] 'ART. II. – A Supplement to Hume's Commentaries on the Law of Scotland respecting Crimes. By Benjamin Robert Bell, Esq., Advocate. Edinburgh, 1844' (1846) 4(8) *The North British Review* 313–346 at 344.
[147] Ibid. at 345.

to impose sanctions of more than a year in prison,[148] and there is a clear sense, particularly in the 1830s and 1840s, that this lower punishment was insufficient.[149] On numerous occasions, Lord Moncreiff, often joined by Lord Cockburn, repeatedly expressed his desire to impose a more serious penalty, ideally transportation.[150] The increased frequency with which bigamy was prosecuted was one argument in favour of stronger penalties, but judges commenting on the gravity of the crime also referred to the disrespect offenders displayed for religion and the sanctity of marriage, the negative impact of their behaviour on society and public morals, the damage caused to the second 'wife', who was deceived, betrayed and deprived of the status she thought she enjoyed[151] and (less frequently) the cruel desertion and/or deception of the lawful wife.[152] In respect of the wrong to the second 'wife', if the conduct of the accused was particularly duplicitous – if he had courted his dupe under a false name and/or falsely claimed to have a particular occupation, for example – this could be noted and condemned by the judge.[153]

[148] On the English experience, see Rebecca Probert and Liam D'Arcy-Brown, 'The Transportation of Bigamists in Early-Nineteenth-Century England and Wales' (2019) 40(3) *The Journal of Legal History* 223–252.

[149] Changes in population size and demographic were likely important, as references to itinerant workers and Irish migrant offenders suggest; see, for example, Alison, *Principles*, p. 543; *Frederick MacGregor* ('Inverness Justiciary Court', *The Elgin Courier*, 16 April 1847, p. 3); *John Beever* ('Circuit Court of Justiciary at Perth', *Fife Herald, and Kinross, Strathearn, and Clackmannan Advertiser*, April 28 1853, p. 3); *John McIntyre* ('Court of Justiciary, Aberdeen', *Montrose, Arbroath, and Brechin Review*, 25 April 1856, p. 3). On anti-Irish sentiment and changes in counterfeit currency offences around this time, see Chloë Kennedy, 'Counterfeit Currency and Commercialising Scotland' in A. M. Godfrey (ed.), *Miscellany Eight* (Edinburgh: Stair Society, 2020), pp. 285–317.

[150] *John McLeod* ('Circuit Court of Justiciary', *The Caledonian Mercury*, 27 September 1834, p. 4); *Alexander Craig* ('Perth Circuit Court of Justiciary', *Fife Herald, and Kinross, Strathearn, and Clackmannan Advertiser*, 3 May 1838, p. 4); *Charles Hendley* ('High Court of Justiciary', *The Scotsman*, 15 December 1841, p. 3); *Colin Campbell* ('Circuit Court of Justiciary', *Inverness Courier*, 24 April 1844, p. 3); *George Booth* ('Circuit Court of Justiciary', *The Aberdeen Herald*, 27 April 1844, p. 3). The first sentence of transportation that appears in this study is James Purves in 1848 ((1848) J. Shaw 124).

[151] For example, in *Henry Rose*, Lord Cowan stated that 'the essence of bigamy' is (in addition to the breach of the first vow) that 'the second female … is betrayed into a position the consequences of which will remain with her through life' ('Dundee Circuit Court of Justiciary', *The Dundee Advertiser*, 12 September 1866, p. 3); in *William Webster*, Lord Neaves described the crime as 'doing injury to the woman whom the law did not recognise as his wife at all' ('Dundee Circuit Court', *Dundee Courier*, 13 September 1867, p. 2); in *James Muir*, Sheriff Cowan told the accused he had 'not only trifled with her affections, but had destroyed her happiness, possibly for life' ('Paisley – Sheriff Court', *The Glasgow Herald*, 27 April 1883 p. 6); and in *Joseph Ellison*, Sheriff Lyell said it was 'cruel and callous to make a woman believe she was a wife when she is not' ('Glasgow Bigamy Cases', *Edinburgh Evening News*, 26 March 1915, p. 5).

[152] See Probert and D'Arcy Brown, 'The Transportation of Bigamists' for a discussion of many of these factors in that context.

[153] For example, *Thomas McPhail* ('Glasgow Bigamist Gets 18 Months', *Dundee Evening Telegraph*, 15 February 1923, p. 6); *Thomas Fawcett* ('Alleged Use of a Drugged Cigarette', *The Evening Telegraph*, 9 April 1923, p. 1).

By the last decades of the nineteenth century, however, there is a noticeable scaling back in terms of the seriousness with which bigamy is regarded, with an article from 1897 suggesting that it was 'rarely demonstrated that any real injury has been done' and that lawyers sought, and imposed, serious punishments merely from habit.[154] It is true that there seem to be more incidences of second 'spouses' either knowing about the existing marriage or forgiving its existence (and the secrecy) on discovery,[155] and there are examples of judges claiming not only that this should mitigate punishment, as they had done in the first half of the century, but that the gravamen of the crime was missing, rendering the offence a 'technical' crime only.[156] Even though this general trend towards greater leniency is gender-neutral, it is important that these latter cases – the ones where judges regarded the informed 'spouse' of the bigamist as essentially unharmed – involved married women (that is, female bigamists). This cohort, who quite often reported that their lawful husband had deserted or abused them, appears to have been treated more favourably in other respects, too. For example, while as a matter of formal law knowledge of the existing marriage would render *both* parties to a bigamous marriage guilty by the doctrine of art and part liability (complicity),[157] almost all the cases I studied in which this doctrine was applied involved men 'marrying' women they already knew were married. When the roles were reversed, the woman was seldom charged alongside her 'spouse'.

The relative leniency of the late, as compared to mid-, Victorian era, can be contrasted with the experience during the two World Wars and their aftermath, when judges and prosecutors emphasised that bigamy cases were on the rise and stressed that the offence was serious.[158] These developments to some extent reflect the experience in England, where prosecutions spiked at these times and judges condemned the offence strongly.[159] Representing another

---

[154] 'A Wise Decision', *Dundee Courier*, 25 November 1897, p. 4.
[155] This claim is based on the cases found via my searches, rather than exhaustive quantitative analysis.
[156] *Elspeth Bain* ('High Court of Justiciary', *Edinburgh Evening News*, 8 November 1880, p. 3). See also *Christina Davidson and William Gillespie* ('Sheriff Criminal Court', *The Glasgow Herald*, 13 February 1883, p. 3).
[157] Hume, *Commentaries*, p. 462.
[158] For example, *John Walden Prior* ('Three Years for Bigamy', *Aberdeen Journal*, 24 July 1917, p. 6); *Charles Stanley Morse* ('"One of the Worst Cases of Bigamy"', *Dundee Evening Telegraph*, 4 March 1941, p. 3); *Robert Reid Storrar Balmain Thomson* ('Too Many Soldier-Bigamists', *Dundee Courier*, 22 March 1941, p. 2). An annual report of the Prison Commissioners for 1916 recorded a rise in bigamy cases despite a drop in crime overall ('Crime in Scotland in 1916', *Aberdeen Journal*, 18 July 1917, p. 2). In 1943, in response to a rise in bigamy arrests, the Glasgow Presbytery passed an overture to the General Assembly asking that members of H. M. Forces produce certificates stating that they were free to marry (see 'To Prevent Bigamy', *Aberdeen Journal*, 3 March 1943, p. 4). See also 'Bigamy in Forces Alarms Ministers', *The Evening Telegraph*, 20 November 1943, p. 5, which reports a rise in charges during wartime years.
[159] David J. Cox, '"Trying to Get a Good One" Bigamy Offences in England and Wales, 1850–1920' (2012) 1 *Plymouth Law & Criminal Justice Review* 1–32; Langhamer, 'Trust Authenticity and Bigamy', p. 164.

swing in the pendulum, from the 1970s onwards, there has generally speaking been a decline in terms of the perceived seriousness of bigamy – as a crime committed against individuals – and uncertainty over how to categorise the crime in light of its capacity to function as an offence against the public register or welfare system, a sexual wrong against the unsuspecting 'spouse', or a more general fraud against them which, latterly, has been recognised (though not always) as causing significant psychological and emotional damage,[160] especially when the deception has lasted a long time.[161]

Certainly, women who have experienced bigamy are clear about their trauma. As the victim in a case involving extensive deception which included her purported husband's life history, the existence of double lives and growing financial debt put it: 'I just feel totally humiliated. I feel like I have completely no identity. I don't know who I am or who I have been for the past six years.'[162] These comments not only speak to the severity of her experience but also its significance in self-constructing terms: with the loss of the relationship she thought she had, this woman describes losing her sense of self. Another point that appears important to some women is that their 'spouse' was acting in bad faith from the start; for these women, the fact that the deception existed from the outset is particularly damaging.[163] Both these features of bigamy are reflected in comments made by a relationship counsellor who recently explained that '[e]motionally, bigamy is fairly devastating … I think it's actually abuse. You have entered into a lie in the most profound way', adding that the bigamist denied their second partner 'the choice, because probably they wouldn't have chosen to enter into a marriage with someone if they knew they already had another spouse'.[164]

When it comes to the law, however, these experiences now receive minimal recognition. In the early 2000s, the knowledge or forgiveness of the second 'spouse' was important, determining whether a custodial sentence would be given[165] or shortened.[166] Indeed, if this 'spouse' had not been duped, then there was thought to be no 'public interest' in incarceration.[167] This is a

---

[160] G. H. Gordon, *The Criminal Law of Scotland* (Edinburgh: W. Green & Sons, 1967), pp. 951–952; R. D. Leslie, 'Polygamous Marriage and Bigamy' (1972) 17 *Juridical Review* 113–123; Keith Soothill, Elizabeth Ackerley, Barry Sanderson and Moira Peelo, 'The Place of Bigamy in the Pantheon of Crime' (1999) 39(1) *Medicine, Science and Law* 65–71.

[161] For example, Rebecca Sherdley, '14 Years Living with a Bigamist', *Nottingham Evening Post*, 5 March 2004.

[162] Deborah McAleese, 'My Sham Life with a Bigamist Husband', *The Belfast Telegraph*, 30 September 2008 (reporting the views of the victim).

[163] Andy Carswell, 'Bigamy Wife Speaks of Betrayal', *Bucks Free Press*, 9 October 2008; 'Paedophile Jailed for Bigamy', *Press Association National Newswire*, 21 December 2006.

[164] Richard Ault, 'Dozens of People Caught Hiding Secret Spouses in West Yorkshire', *Yorkshire Live*, 17 January 2021.

[165] Dan Bridgett, '"Wife" Saves Bigamist from Prison', *The Evening Standard*, 30 July 2001; 'Bigamy Case Is Adjourned', *The Citizen*, 16 April 2002.

[166] Mike Slingsby, 'A Bigamist Walked Free from Court after the Wife He Had Deceived Said She Was Willing to Forgive Him', *Manchester Evening News*, 10 February 2006.

[167] 'Bigamist Walks Free from Court', *Sunday Mercury*, 6 October 2002.

significant departure from the historical position in that while the punishment might have been lighter in such cases, there remained a public interest in maintaining the institution of marriage or a communal standard of conduct. Another consequence of the modern practice of tying the legal response to the reaction of any *particular* victim is that the fate of the bigamist became a matter of luck, as one judge pointed out.[168]

At around the same time, however, the focus of the law shifted to tackling the kind of marriages I described earlier as 'ulterior motive' cases. The first indication of this shift I have detected was in 1996, when an English court issued a fifteen-month sentence (reduced to nine months on appeal) because the parties intended to commit migration-related fraud on the state and the court accepted that it was important to deter those seeking to avoid immigration controls and those who furthered this purpose by marrying for money.[169] Soon after this, a 'spokesman [sic] from the Metropolitan Police' stated that the main reason for prosecuting bigamy was to 'stop marriage for British citizenship and marriage for the sole purpose of social security fraud',[170] and there is then a run of cases where the question of whether the couple had married for love, rather than financial gain or with fraudulent intent, was significant to the court's determinations.[171]

It is telling that the first prosecution for 'bigamy' under the Civil Partnership Act of 2004 was lauded as a sign that the law took same-sex relationships seriously at the same time as it was criticised for the perceived severity of the sentence.[172] In attracting strong condemnation, the case bucked a trend towards treating cases where the only deceived party was the duped 'spouse' as insignificant.[173] This trend mirrors the developments explored in Section 4.2 in that the state's interest in maintaining the regime of benefits it attaches to marriage seems to have eclipsed the interpersonal harms and wrongs involved in deceptive marital relationships. Furthermore, the modern law of bigamy reflects the modern law governing the (ir)relevance of unilateral reservations

---

[168] 'Gaywood Bigamist in Wedding Sham', *Lynn News and Advertiser*, 12 February 2008 (Judge Peter Thompson).

[169] *R v. Cairns* [1997] Cr App R (S) 118. In early nineteenth-century England, mercenary motives or abandoning the second 'spouse', thereby raising the suspicion that the marriage was not 'genuine' as well as invalid, were aggravations; see Probert and D'Arcy-Brown, 'The Transportation of Bigamists'.

[170] Maria Barrett, 'Crime of Passion That Is Still Doubly Shocking', *The Scotsman*, 20 January 1997.

[171] For example, Karon Kelly, 'Bigamist Trapped by Plea for Help', *The Journal*, 19 March 2004, in which the judge (Guy Whitburn) noted that marrying for reward to facilitate the entry of a 'foreign national' to the county would demand a custodial sentence. After a spate of cases across 2008, 2009 and 2010, a bigamist in 2014 presented himself as the victim of a 'African' scheming wife and described his own motive as love ('Bigamist "Duped by His Third Wife"', *York Press*, 7 February 2014).

[172] 'Strike Up the Band', *The Guardian*, 10 August 2007.

[173] In 2005, a victim of bigamy who felt she received neither justice nor sufficient support set up a website to offer support and advocate for more prosecutions and heavier sentences (Liz Trist, 'Bigamy Victim Is Anxious to Help', *Express and Echo*, 16 February 2005).

4.5 Conclusions and Contemporary Connections

to the validity of marriage in that the crime of purporting to enter either a marriage or civil partnership does not, at least on its face, take account of situations where one party has been deceived by the other.[174]

4.5 Conclusions and Contemporary Connections

There are some important general conclusions to draw out of this chapter, which relate to the trajectory of development across the different areas of law studied, the way the legal doctrines within these areas of law operated and the ambit and focus of these legal responses to deceptively induced intimacy.

Broadly speaking, the pattern of development suggests that punitive and quasi-punitive legal responses to the conduct examined in this chapter reached their apex during the second and third quarters of the nineteenth century. At this time, judicial comments and changes in legal doctrine and sentencing practices suggest that a person (almost always a man) who engaged in deceptive or unfaithful conduct relating to the constitution of marriage was most likely, at least in principle, to suffer for his behaviour. Following this, the overall direction of development is away from using marriage as kind of remedy, or even punishment, and towards leniency in the law of bigamy. There were periods of renewed commitment to taking bigamy seriously that, broadly speaking, track the culturally informed account of sex and marriage offered in Chapter 1 and the experience elsewhere in Britain. Yet at the same time, a sense that the emotional authenticity of a relationship could equal or outstrip its legal validity appears to have made the wrongfulness, or at least the harmfulness, of the crime less clear-cut. Again, this tracks the account offered in Chapter 1.

This decline in legal responses appears to have been facilitated by – or at least to correlate with – a greater concern with subjectivity within these areas of law, as demonstrated by an increasing concern with individuals' intentions, in the case of marriage, and victims' reactions to being wronged, in the case of bigamy. There is a certain irony to this in that the turn towards subjectivity might be expected to have had the opposite effect insofar as the more the law is concerned with individuals' experiences and their mistaken beliefs, the more it might be expected to take account of the wrongs and harms they suffer on account of those experiences and beliefs.

One reason why this might not happen in practice is the high degree of legal certainty that public laws require vis-à-vis private laws. In the case of marriage, the state's (and indeed other people's) interest in knowing when

---

[174] In Scotland, the common law offence of bigamy was abolished by the Marriage and Civil Partnership (Scotland) Act 2014 (s. 28(3)), and it is now an offence to purport to enter a marriage with someone knowing that either or both parties are already married or civilly partnered (see Marriage (Scotland) Act 1977, s. 24 (A1)) and to purport to register a civil partnership knowing that either or both parties are already married or civilly partnered (see Civil Partnership Act 2004, s. 100(1)).

a marriage exists does not sit easily with subjective tests of constitution. The historical evidence also suggests that tests that purport to establish the individual parties' intentions end up collapsing into objective tests because convention is used to determine the meaning of the parties' conduct or words. The attempt to respect individual experiences and beliefs can therefore be self-defeating.[175] Aiming to establish individuals' intentions retrospectively also leads to the challenge of isolating these from after-the-fact regrets. In the case of bigamy, there is a further difficulty with prioritising the individual victim's response, which is that this contributes towards the uneven treatment of offenders on a potentially arbitrary basis.

Nevertheless, the retraction of legal responses that aim to address the wrongs or harms done to individuals who have been deceived does not mean that these experiences are less damaging than they were in the past (though they might be) or that the desire for legal acknowledgement of this has fully abated. In the case of marriage and civil partnership, the state still attaches benefits to this status and while this situation, and the migration-related regime with which it is allied, can be critiqued,[176] the reality is that individuals might be duped by a spouse (or 'spouse') in pursuit of these benefits – or indeed without those motivations – with limited or no legal recognition of this experience.[177] Furthermore, as the experience of the women who had long-term relationships with men who were undercover police officers[178] shows, the devastating effects of a relationship that is based on a fundamental lie are not confined to marriages and civil partnerships. The question, to which I return in Chapter 8, is whether there is a way for the law potentially to accommodate this reality but avoid some of the difficulties demonstrated in this chapter.

---

[175] As Chapters 7 and 8 show, this issue affects sexual consent, too.

[176] Helena Wray, *Regulating Marriage Migration into the UK: A Stranger in the Home* (London: Routledge, 2011); Nadine El-Enany, *Bordering Britain: Law, Race and Empire* (Manchester: Manchester University Press, 2020).

[177] A recent news report suggests that police officers in England and Wales recorded 599 offences of bigamy in the 10 years up to and including 2021 and that 10.8 per cent of the cases investigated in the 5 years prior to the article resulted in someone being charged or summonsed to appear in court. Of the 'completed cases', 82.4 per cent 'went unpunished' due to problems with evidence, including victims not wanting to press charges or because further investigation or prosecution was not deemed to be in the public interest; see Richard Ault, 'Hundreds of Bigamists Accused of Hiding Secret Spouses', *WalesOnline*, 23 June 2022. In another report, one victim suggested that the number of cases of bigamy was likely to be higher than those reported due to what she perceived to be a reluctance on the part of prosecutorial authorities to shoulder the cost of investigating and prosecuting the case, especially when it has a transnational aspect; see Nathan Clarke, 'Bigamy Victim Says It's a "Business"', *Birmingham Live*, 3 July 2022. Data suggests that bigamy and its statutory replacement are very rarely used in Scotland, for example, a freedom of information request in 2018 revealed that that between 2013–14 and 2016–17, there were no prosecutions under s. 24 of the 1977 Act and that there was one prosecution for bigamy in 2014–15, which did not result in a custodial sentence: www.gov.scot/publications/foi-18-02743. The 'Criminal Proceedings in Scotland' statistical bulletins covering the years 2017–2021 do not mention these offences: www.gov.scot/collections/criminal-proceedings-in-scotland.

[178] See Chapters 1 and 2 as well as Chapters 6–8.

4.5 Conclusions and Contemporary Connections

The other important point these women's experiences highlight is how these damaging effects are not confined to sexual violation, either. As one of the women, Donna McLean, has explained, the deception damaged her sense of stability, and the physical intrusion she experienced was conjoined with an exploitation of emotional intimacy.[179] Furthermore, the sexual wrongs were not committed or experienced in isolation. As she put it: 'I did not consent to being a sexual experiment. I did not consent to being a mistress. I did not consent to being fucked all over the world by a man who did not exist.'[180] So while the scope of legal recognition for the sexual wrongs involved in inducing intimacy has expanded somewhat, as Part II shows, we can ask not only whether this, or any greater, expansion is justifiable but also how well these laws can capture the full range of wrongs and harms involved in this conduct.

---

[179] Donna McLean, *Small Town Girl: Love, Lies, and the Undercover Police* (London: Hodder & Stoughton Ltd, 2022), p. 128.
[180] Ibid., p. 127.

Part II
Sex

5

Eliciting Sex

5.1 Scope and Themes

This first of three chapters examining legal responses to deceptive sex considers the civil wrong (delict) of seduction – an action that was predicated on, among other things, a man obtaining a woman's sexual consent by deception.[1] Unlike in England,[2] Australia[3] and the United States,[4] women in Scotland could bring actions of seduction in their own name from the start of the period with which this book is concerned.[5] In fact, despite other changes in relation to the courts that would hear seduction actions[6] and the actions that would typically be brought alongside them,[7] this feature of the law remained unchanged. As such, throughout its history, the Scottish action of seduction provided legal recognition of the wrong committed against seduced women, rather than the losses suffered by her parents or employer because of her seduction, as was the case elsewhere. These two features of seduction – that it involved deceptively induced sexual consent and that it provided a remedy to the victim of this conduct – explain its place within this book: it is the earliest example of a modern

---

[1] I build up a definition of the action through examining its operation in the following sections.
[2] Frost, *Promises Broken*; Steinbach, *Promises, Promises*, p. 133; Fraser, *Husband and Wife*, p. 501; Arthur Thomson Glegg, *A Practical Treatise on the Law of Reparation* (Edinburgh: W. Green & Sons, 1892), p. 99; Walton, *Husband and Wife*, pp. 297–298; David M. Walker, *The Law of Delict in Scotland* (vol. 2) (Edinburgh: published under the auspices of the Scottish Universities Law Institute by Green, 1966), pp. 701–702.
[3] Alecia Simmonds, 'Courtship, Coverture and Marital Cruelty: Historicising Intimate Violence in the Civil Courts' (2019) 45(1) *Australian Feminist Law Journal* 131–157 at 145.
[4] Haag, *Consent*, pp. 4–5; Stephen Robertson, 'Seduction, Sexual Violence, and Marriage in New York City, 1886–1955' (2006) 24(2) *Law and History Review* 331–373. Both these works outline how seduction eventually became a woman's action in some states.
[5] Fraser, *Personal and Domestic Relations*, p. 198.
[6] Seduction actions were heard in the Commissary Court (Leneman, *Promises, Promises*) then the Court of Session and Jury Court (while it lasted) and Sheriff Court. When the Jury Courts Abolition Act 1830 passed, all issues that must have been tried by jury were directed to be tried by jury in the Court of Session. For more detail, see Mackay, *Manual of Practice*, p. 326.
[7] From declarators of marriage to actions for breach of promise of marriage. I explore this development more in Section 5.3, but it has to be understood in light of the history of breach of promise of marriage (see Chapter 3) and irregular marriage (see Chapter 4).

law recognising the injuries suffered by a person[8] whose sexual consent was induced by deception.

In Section 5.2, I outline what these injuries were considered to be, showing how they reflected the significance of staying within a range of conventionally dictated relationship parameters associated with 'moral' forms of intimacy. In line with the cultural framework set out in Chapter 1, these 'moral' forms of intimacy were marriage and relationships where the promise of marriage existed and the harms, which were deeply gendered, included the reputational, affective and material detriment women were assumed to suffer if they were cheated out of a marriage. I also consider why damages were considered the appropriate redress for these harms, as opposed to criminal punishment, examining calls that were made to criminalise seduction so as to identify the foundation on which they rested and why (in Scotland) they were resisted. This discussion helps illustrate the relevance of the different senses of private and public outlined in Chapter 1. In particular, I show how linking these harms to collective interests could bolster the case for a public law response while a feeling that the injured women should have control over initiation of the action suggested that a private law response was more appropriate. Though these points are important, I nevertheless suggest that damages, or perhaps simply a verdict of the civil court, could serve some of the functions of punishment; this point to some extent complicates the distinctions between public and private law responses in the ways I alluded to in Chapter 1 and come back to in Chapter 8.

Turning to the association between deception and seduction, in Section 5.3, I explain how the wrong of seduction was not, or at least not wholly, about having sex with a woman who 'belonged' to another man – her father, for example; rather, it was about luring a woman into having 'immoral' sex by engaging in deception of certain kinds.[9] More specifically, as I argue in this chapter and indeed in the rest of this part of the book, the deceptions that attracted legal censure reflected a concern with protecting the special status of marriage and discouraging sex that occurred outside either this relationship or a relationship that could reasonably be expected to lead to marriage. Even though the line between deceptions that bore on these protected relationships and deceptions that were to be expected in the course of 'immoral' relationships could be difficult to draw, the former were, broadly speaking, the only deceptions deemed legally relevant. As such, the so-called line-drawing problem – the difficulty of distinguishing deceptions that should 'count' for law

---

[8] As I explain in Section 5.2, I have found no male pursuers despite the formal gender neutrality of the action, but it can still be considered a predecessor of contemporary gender-neutral deceptive sex offences in some senses.

[9] Fraser, *Personal and Domestic Relations*, p. 198. I am not concerned here with claims by wronged spouses, including enticing one's spouse away, even though the action available – including to husbands – in such circumstances was sometimes referred to as seduction; see Walker, *The Law of Delict*, p. 702. For a brief overview, see Blackie, 'Unity in Diversity', section 2.2.4(d)(iii).

and those that should not – which has afflicted later legal responses to deceptive sex[10] did not really arise.

A line-drawing problem that did arise, however, was the challenge of distinguishing deception from two other forms of misconduct that sometimes accompanied it: abuse of authority or trust and the use of physical force or its threat. In Section 5.2, I explain why this challenge arose, and in Sections 5.4 and 5.5, I show how the boundaries between deception and these other forms of misconduct were not always clear in practice. At this point, I identify two important effects of these blurred boundaries: first, the action of seduction sometimes incorporated conduct that was not strictly speaking deceptive and, second, the action of seduction ran up against the criminal offences of rape and having sex with a girl under the age of legal consent. Despite the overlap and crossover, there was, in principle, a significant difference between sex that took place with impaired consent (that is, seduction) and sex that took place forcibly and against the complainer's will (that is, rape) and there was also an important difference between sex that took place with impaired consent (that is, seduction) and sex that took place with consent that was legally invalid (that is, sex with an underage girl). By recognising the wrongfulness of all three forms of sex but striving to maintain distinctions between them, the law at this time preserved a space for thinking about consent as something other than a binary,[11] that is, as something that was present and fully effectual or either absent, as in the case of rape, or irrelevant, as in the case of young girls. In the case of seduction, consent was considered to be present but illegitimately obtained.

As I explore in Section 5.6, the idea that consent might be scalar, as opposed to binary, has started to attract some support again in recent years. This means that tracing the decline of seduction is significant for a couple of reasons, beyond the importance of appreciating the action on its own terms. First, it helps reveal what is at stake in adopting different positions with respect to the possibility of scalar consent. Second, and relatedly, it demonstrates how the disappearance of seduction has contributed towards contemporary challenges in responding to deceptive sex. In addition to these points, the way the wrong(s) and harms of seduction were conceptualised provides a good illustration of the temporal complexities affecting the operation of consent in this context, namely, how far back in time the law should look and the difficulty of pinpointing the precise moment of wrongdoing. I return briefly to these complexities in Section 5.6 and then again in Chapters 6–8.

5.2 The Wrongs and Harms of Seduction

Trying to work out what was the wrong, or what were the wrongs, of seduction is not easy. Deception is mentioned in many texts – for example, as one author

---

[10] See Chapters 7 and 8.
[11] On this space and its disappearance in the United States, see Haag, *Consent*, especially pp. 24, 53; Murray, 'Marriage as Punishment' at 19–20.

put it, 'the wrong consists, in the words of Scripture, in "having dealt deceitfully with her"'[12] – but the reason such deception was considered wrongful appears quite unfamiliar to modern eyes. Unlike most contemporary accounts of deceptive sex, according to which deception is wrong because of the way it interferes with autonomy, the wrong of deception according to the action of seduction was that it corrupted the duped woman's mind (and, subsequently, her body and reputation). By inducing a woman to trust him, the seducer convinced his victim to engage in sex outside marriage, an act that was generally considered to be immoral and which was socially, if not legally, proscribed. The fact that seduction involved inducing a woman to *choose* to engage in this proscribed behaviour meant it could be described as the rape of a woman's mind.[13] Moreover, because it was possible to achieve this corrupting effect in different ways, such as by abusing one's authority or by using threats and coercion, the action of seduction was not always exclusively concerned with deception. This idea – that seduction involves temptation or trickery, but potentially also coercion, which results in the victim being led away from the 'correct' path – has a long and diverse history, extending beyond sex to include decisions made in political and religious contexts, too.[14]

In the case of sex, even though legal writings often emphasised deception as the main mode of corruption, these texts were not always clear about exactly what conduct was required. Early works referred to enticement as well as to fraudulent abuse[15] and, as Sections 5.3–5.6 show, uncertainty over which behaviours would amount to seduction endured across the modern period. Importantly, however, this confusion was not static. Deception, specifically deception pertaining to the promise or prospect of marriage, dominated for the bulk of the nineteenth century and abuse of trust or authority, as well as physical violence and its threat, appeared in the later eighteenth and nineteenth centuries. It does not seem to be a coincidence that false marital promises were the main concern at a time when the disciplinary power of marriage was culturally[16] and legally[17] at its strongest or that the action would expand to accommodate more forms of misconduct at times when the liberty of subjects and, latterly, the protection of women were pressing worries.[18] In keeping with the overarching arguments of this book, studying the action of seduction and its changing contours therefore shows that the protection of autonomy and paternalistic attempts to secure women's welfare both tend to cause the legal

---

[12] Guthrie Smith, *Law of Reparation*, p. 51.
[13] Katie Barclay, 'From Rape to Marriage: Questions of Consent in Eighteenth-Century Britain' in Anne Greenfield (ed.), *Interpreting Sexual Violence, 1600–1800* (London: Pickering & Chatto, 2013), pp. 35–44.
[14] Toni Bowers, *Force or Fraud: British Seduction Stories and the Problem of Resistance, 1660–1760* (Oxford: Oxford University Press, 2011).
[15] Blackie, 'Unity in Diversity', section 2.2.4 (b)(ii). [16] See Chapter 1.
[17] See Chapter 4, particularly the practices of holding parties to be married against their will.
[18] See Chapter 1 and the periods of liberalisation and worries about protecting women set out there.

5.2 The Wrongs and Harms of Seduction

responses to inducing intimacy to expand. It is only in the case of protecting autonomy that greater state intervention appears ironic on account of the way it simultaneously protects and circumscribes freedom to choose.

A further consequence of the fact that seduction was understood as leading someone off the 'right' path is that although seduction constituted a wrong committed by the seducer, it also operated as a kind of 'defence' for the seduced. To see how this might be the case, it is important to bear in mind that seduction was a legal action between the seducer and the woman he seduced. The theoretical underpinning to this arrangement is that within Scotland unmarried women were, in principle, free agents, seen as capable of voluntarily choosing to engage in pre-marital sex. If a woman made this choice freely, she would be condemned because this kind of sex was considered immoral. If, however, she was led into the decision by another who used illegitimate means, she could avoid some of the blame that would otherwise be directed at her.[19] This point is expressed well in an early seduction case in which the court rejected the argument that there could be no action by the 'less guilty' against the 'more guilty' of the two parties because both of them were 'guilty of a sin in the sight of God'.[20] In the court's view, the fact that the defender was the 'more guilty' for corrupting the pursuer's mind meant he should be civilly liable. This perspective prevailed throughout the lifespan of the action, with an early twentieth-century judge explaining that to prove seduction the pursuer had to rebut the prima facie view that 'where a man and a woman commit an act of immorality, both are free and willing consenters'.[21] The idea that a person could be wronged by their own quasi-voluntary actions is what allowed an action of seduction belonging to the woman to exist. By contrast, a strict interpretation of *volenti non fit injuria* (a willing person is not wronged) precluded this possibility.[22]

In line with these arrangements, when a woman was seduced her consent was considered to be impaired, rather than absent.[23] This interpretation also fits with extra-legal conceptions of seduction, according to which resistance was seen as significantly and discernibly different to capitulation or collusion,[24] and it was this distinction which meant that there was formally no crossover between seduction and rape. In Scots law rape was, broadly speaking, defined

---

[19] *McGowan* v. *Fisher* (1797) Campbell Collection, vol. 85, Paper 41.
[20] *Linning* v. *Hamilton* (1748) Mor 13909 at 13913. See also the statement that nothing could excuse a woman for straying from the path of maidenly prudence but that the seduction made her conduct less culpable ('The Action for Seduction – Strathaven Morality', *John o'Groat Journal*, 20 August 1863, p. 3).
[21] *Moar* v. *Glass* (1924) 49 Scot L Rev 237. See also *Walker* v. *Colquhoun* (1828) NRS CS271/67308, where the seduced woman is described as 'more sinned against than sinning'.
[22] This is how the English law of seduction was described; see Walton, *Husband and Wife*, pp. 297–298; Hec Burn Murdoch, 'English Law in Scots Practice III' (1909–1910) 21 *Juridical Review* 148–158 at 151; and W. E. Dodds, 'A Few Comparisons between English and Scots Law. II. The Law of Personal Relations' (1927) 9(1) *Journal of Comparative Legislation and International Law* 40–58 at 57.
[23] Blackie, 'Unity in Diversity', p. 66. [24] Bowers, *Force or Fraud*, p. 11.

as forcible sex against the complainer's will[25] and so was distinguishable from seduction, which was seen as involving the wrongfully corrupted will of the pursuer.[26] As I explain in Section 5.4, however, some cases that appear to have potentially satisfied the definition of rape were pursued as actions of seduction and even deeper confusion arose when the Criminal Law Amendment Act 1885 made it a misdemeanour to unlawfully and carnally know or to attempt to have unlawful carnal knowledge of any girl who was thirteen or older but under the age of sixteen.[27] An early prosecution brought under this section of the Act illustrated the potential for confusion within the criminal law insofar as one judge appeared to think that something akin to seduction or force had to be libelled alongside the words of the statute, 'did attempt to have unlawful carnal knowledge of', and another pointed out that while a physical attempt to have sex with a girl short of force would likely constitute the crime, verbal seduction or an offer of money to have sex might not.[28]

Almost thirty years later, the potential for confusion in the civil law emerged. Specifically, questions arose as to whether having sex with a fifteen-year-old girl in breach of the 1885 Act constituted the civil wrong of seduction per se or, alternatively, whether breaching the statute provided an independent ground for damages.[29] The answer to the first question was negative, largely because the age of marital consent remained twelve in Scotland. This fact meant that the court had to presume that a girl of the pursuer's age was capable of understanding the meaning of the marital contract and its physical consequences (that is, sex) or, in other words, that she was capable of giving intelligent consent to the act of sex.[30] Given this, it would be necessary for the pursuer to prove that the defender had influenced her sexual consent in order to prove that he had seduced her. The court also held that the defender could not otherwise be held civilly liable for his crime, for two reasons. The first was that to found an action of damages for breach of a statutory duty it was essential that the Act should have been passed for the interests or protection of a specific class of people to whom a right of reparation had been given. In the judges' view, the 1885 Act did not meet this criterion, having been passed in the public interest though indirectly benefitting the female sex.[31] The second reason was that, according

---

[25] Discussed further in Chapters 6 and 7.   [26] See also Chapter 6 (Section 6.4).
[27] S. 5(1). The accused had a defence if he could prove he had reasonable cause to believe that the girl was sixteen or older.
[28] *HM Advocate* v. *Charles Kelly* (1885) 5 Coup 722. For a short discussion, see 'Technical Objections and Escape from Justice' (1886) 30(355) *Journal of Jurisprudence* 347–357.
[29] *Murray* v. *Fraser* 1914 SLT 200.
[30] A similar argument was made against making the seduction of girls aged twelve, irrespective of their consent, a felony in 1873 ('Imperial Parliament', *The Aberdeen Journal*, 9 April 1873, p. 3). On the diverging ages of consent to sex inside and outside marriage in England, see Laura Lammasniemi, '"Precocious Girls": Age of Consent, Class and Family in Late Nineteenth-Century England' (2020) 38(1) *Law and History Review* 241–266.
[31] For discussion, including of this case, see 'The Doctrine of Statutory Negligence' (1936) SLT 62–63.

to the court, when an Act created a statutory offence it should include a 'full statement … of all the penal consequences'. Since the Act did not state that one of those consequences was civil liability, 'civil responsibility' could not be read into the Act by implication.[32]

The relationship between the public interest and the interests of a particular class of people, or indeed discrete individuals, was therefore significant to the question of whether civil redress was available. It is also important to understanding why seduction was never criminalised (in Scotland), although the prospect was raised. The possibility that seduction might, or even should, be criminally punished was rooted partly in a feeling that it was at least as bad, if not worse, than other conduct that was criminalised. In the middle of the eighteenth century, for example, one letter to a magazine editor asked why cheating a man out of a small sum of money by fraudulent deceit was a 'felony' but defrauding a woman of the 'inestimable jewel' of her innocence was not.[33]

On one view, seduction was actually worse than property fraud because the injury was greater and longer lasting.[34] Seduction was also seen by some as comparable to physical maltreatment in terms of its cruelty and disagreeableness;[35] in fact, the moral depravity of seduction could be seen as worse than many crimes that were punishable by penal servitude because it killed 'not only body but soul' and seriously injured the interests of the community.[36] These injuries to collective interests were described as equally bad as those caused by rape,[37] and they were especially prominent in calls to criminalise seduction on the basis of its purported association with prostitution.[38] The argument was that a woman ruined by seduction would be more likely to descend into prostitution, and this association between damage to collective interests and criminal punishment cohered with developments in the United States. There, the move towards criminalising seduction occurred when the wrong was associated with public order concerns.[39]

---

[32] *Murray* v. *Fraser* (1914) at 203.
[33] Letter to the editor, *The Scots Magazine*, 1 December 1764, p. 639.
[34] 'Privileged Crimes' (1858) 2(2) *Journal of Jurisprudence* 447–458 at 453.
[35] 'The Lash for Wife-Beaters', *The Glasgow Daily Herald*, 18 September 1869, p. 7.
[36] 'The Action for Seduction'. See also, 'the pollution of her body is perhaps the smallest part of the injury … the corruption of the will … is a far more lasting and incurable evil' (*Walker* v. *Colquhoun* (1828)).
[37] 'Review by Charles Scott of "The Criminal" by Havelock Ellis' (1890) 2(4) *Juridical Review* 381–386.
[38] 'Imperial Parliament', *Elgin Courier*, 23 February 1849, p. 4; 'The Social Evil', *Fife Herald, and Kinross, Strathearn, and Clackmannan Advertiser*, 19 May 1859, p. 4; 'The Contagious Diseases Acts', *The Glasgow Daily Herald*, 22 April 1870, p. 4; 'Letters to the Editor', *The Glasgow Daily Herald*, 3 May 1870, p. 6; 'The Contagious Diseases Acts Commission', *The Glasgow Herald*, 13 November 1871, p. 5.
[39] Haag, *Consent*; Murray, 'Marriage as Punishment' at 12. Simmonds suggests that the criminalisation of seduction in the United States might have inspired the 1887 New South Wales Seduction Punishment Bill; see Simmonds, 'Courtship, Coverture and Marital Cruelty' at 136.

Despite the arguments in favour of criminalising seduction, there were various difficulties with the proposal. First, the wrongdoing usually occurred across an extended period of time and was seldom witnessed. Second, its effects – specifically, the extent to which the victim was deceived – were hard to discern and evidence.[40] On top of this, the action was considered to be personal on account of the facts that it put the woman's character in issue and involved publicising issues she might wish to remain private.[41] Where the action was conjoined to a declarator of marriage, the action was even more clearly personal and thus could only be raised by the pursuer.[42] Finally, as with breach of promise of marriage, some felt that social control, in the form of disapproval, might be a sufficient deterrent. As such, banishing a seducer from society and withdrawing invitations to respectable houses were suggested as solutions to the problem of seduction.[43] It is worth noting that at the time this argument was made, it was thought that some conduct fell between moral and criminal behaviour, such that it would be condemned by a society's 'moral code' but go unpunished by its 'criminal code'.[44] Furthermore, it was believed that this in-between category would grow as society became more civilised.[45] It is therefore not surprising that some thought, or perhaps hoped, that social disapproval would be enough to curb seduction – this would signal that society had advanced beyond the need for punishment of this conduct.

In any case, the language of punishment was sometimes used in relation to the civil wrong. For example, a defender might be 'branded as a fraudulent seducer' and suffer the 'penalties' inflicted on those 'guilty' of this form of misconduct.[46] And while some judges informed juries that damages for seduction were intended to compensate the pursuer, rather than punish the defender[47] (sometimes with considerable regret that punishment was not an option),[48] others proclaimed that 'she [the pursuer] is entitled to reparation, not only as compensation for the injury done to her, but that the wicked arts of the defender may receive some punishment'.[49] Suing the seducer might have functioned similarly to punishment for the women who were injured, too. For example, in a

---

[40] 'Privileged Crimes' at 453–454.
[41] *Bern* v. *Montrose Lunatic Asylum, Montrose* (1893) 20 R 859.
[42] *Borthwick* v. *Borthwick* (1896–1897) 4 SLT 130. In this case, the court suggested that the brother of the deceased could have continued the action of damages for injury to her person or character, but this was because she had raised the action before she died.
[43] 'The Social Evil', *The Aberdeen Journal*, 8 January 1862, p. 7.
[44] 'Privileged Crimes' at 447.   [45] Ibid.
[46] *McGowan* v. *Fisher* (1797). The term punishment and language associated with it is used various other times in these papers.
[47] *Campbell* v. *Beveridge* ('Judgment in the Cardross Case', *Fife Herald, and Kinross, Strathearn, and Clackmannan Advertiser*, 25 July 1861, p. 2).
[48] *Scott* v. *Love* ('Scotch Breach of Promise Case', *The Aberdeen Journal*, 28 March 1885, p. 8).
[49] *Burns* v. *McNair* ('Decision in the Paisley Breach of Promise Case', *Dundee Courier*, 22 February 1878, p. 6). See also the statement that damages were to compensate the pursuer for her injury but to punish the defender to a reasonable extent for his heartless conduct (Guthrie Smith, *Law of Damages*, p. 128).

case involving an action brought by the sister of a woman who drowned herself after being seduced (for the pecuniary loss and injured feelings the sister had suffered) one of the pieces of evidence is a note from the deceased in which she firmly accuses the defender, asking her sister to try to get him punished.[50]

The injuries that could lead to this kind of desperation included the dishonour and wounded feelings the pursuer would likely suffer[51] as a consequence of her ill-treatment and subsequent loss of virtue,[52] so the damages were intended at least partly as a solatium.[53] It was possible that the pursuer's marriage prospects might be reduced as a result of her seduction, so a claim of damages might also be grounded in the losses she would suffer as a consequence.[54] These injuries and losses might arise together in a single case, of course, such as in one nineteenth-century claim that demanded damages and solatium for the loss, injury and damages suffered and to be suffered in the pursuer's health, feelings, character and reputation as well as personally and in her prospects in life.[55] The gendered significance of virtue and marriage helps explains why I have not located any cases involving male pursuers, despite the action being formally gender-neutral.[56] If a man were to sue for seduction, it is highly likely that his claim of loss would not be credited[57] because, in general, he would not suffer either a damaged reputation or fortune.

Yet although the centrality of virtue to a woman's perceived worth was clearly key to the action of seduction, there was some uncertainty over whether loss of virginity was necessary. At least one twentieth-century author thought that it was, describing the pursuer's former status as a virgin as core to the action.[58] At the same time, it was acknowledged even in early cases that both

---

[50] In another note, the deceased woman says that the defender's touching her was against her will (see *Greig* v. *Robertson* (1891) NRS CS247/2272).

[51] These were not inevitable, though. For example, in one case, the pursuer was asked if she had lost the esteem of acquaintances for having a child after being seduced under promise of marriage and she replied that she had not but that the defender had (see *White* v. *Dickson* (1808–1809), as discussed in Leneman, *Promises, Promises*, pp. 120, 126).

[52] See, for example, a pursuer complaining that her chance to establish herself as a respectable matron was ruined (*Turpy* v. *McCandie* (1824–1826), General Collection, Paper 339).

[53] Walker, *The Law of Damages*, p. 562; Walker, *The Law of Civil Remedies*, p. 988. Cf. another text by the same author, which states that the damages were not so much solatium as *compansationem ipsius dotis* (compensation for the dowry); see Walker, *The Law of Delict*, p. 702. This seems to have been the pre-Reformation position; see Blackie, 'Unity in Diversity', pp. 91–92.

[54] Walker, *The Law of Civil Remedies*, p. 988; Leneman, *Promises, Promises*, p. 132.

[55] *AV* v. *CD* ('Glasgow Sheriff Court', *The Glasgow Herald*, 1 April 1865, p. 5).

[56] I did find a few defenders claiming in their defence that they had been seduced by the pursuer, for example, *Wallace* v. *Gossland* ('Widow Suing for Breach of Promise', *The Evening Telegraph*, 17 September 1879, p. 2); *Stewart* v. *Ferguson* ('Breach of Promise Case at Portree', *The Evening Telegraph*, 25 April 1890, p. 2); and *Kidd* v. *Vogel* ('Girl Sues Cupar Butcher', *The Evening Telegraph*, 25 February 1926, p. 6).

[57] Fraser, *Personal and Domestic Relations*, p. 199.

[58] Walker, *The Law of Delict*, p. 702; Walker, *The Law of Civil Remedies*, p. 988. See also Kenneth McK. Norrie, 'The Intentional Delicts' in Reid and Zimmermann (eds.), *History of Private Law*, pp. 477–516, and Elspeth Christie Reid, *The Law of Delict in Scotland* (Edinburgh: Edinburgh University Press, 2022), p. 530.

virgins and widows might be seduced in law,[59] and when the question arose in 1857 the court held that it was not necessary for the pursuer to put in issue that she had previously been of virtuous conduct and untainted character.[60] Subsequent writers also held that it was not necessary to put the pursuer's previous virtuous conduct and untainted character in issue[61] – indeed one explicitly stated that 'seduction does not mean defloration'[62] – but they accepted that it would be more difficult to convince a jury that a woman who had made 'previous slips' had been seduced, and they accepted that such a woman would likely receive reduced damages if she won her case.[63]

Another effect of the requirement of virtue (if not virginity) is that seduction had to be libelled as having occurred only once.[64] For example, in 1871, a court held that it was not possible for a pursuer to allege that she had been seduced by the same man in 1860 and in 1863 because if this were true then she had suffered the requisite fall from virtue at the defender's hands in 1860 and could not suffer it again in 1863.[65] This was one of temporal complexities of seduction, but an even more pronounced difficulty was identifying when the relevant wrongful conduct had occurred. For example, if the defender's inducement took the form of promises to marry, the question arose of how specific and temporally bound the alleged promises had to be. Given that promises could be repeated over a long period of time, and inferred from a pattern of behaviour, the wrong could arguably be considered a course of conduct rather than a discrete incident.[66]

Certainly, it seems that some latitude around dates was permitted,[67] and judges clearly saw the temporally extended process of persuasion as a core part of the seducer's wrongdoing. This latter point was addressed directly in a couple of cases where the sex upon which the claim was founded had occurred in England. Since the seduced woman could not sue for seduction in that jurisdiction, it was necessary for the judge to decide where the wrong had occurred. On both occasions, the judge held that because the processes by which the defender obtained his influence over the pursuer had taken place in Scotland, the action could competently be raised in a Scottish court.[68] These

---

[59] *McGowan v. Fisher* (1797). A number of later cases involve pursuers who were widows.
[60] *Walker v. M'Isaac* (1857) 19 D 340.
[61] Fraser, *Husband and Wife*, p. 505. Cf. the earlier text by Robert MacFarlane and Thomas Cleghorn, *Practical Notes on the Structure of Issues in Jury Cases in the Court of Session: With Forms of Issues* (Edinburgh: T. & T. Clark, 1844–1849), which states that loss of virtue must appear in the issue (p. 378).
[62] Guthrie Smith, *Law of Reparation*, pp. 51–52.
[63] Glegg, *Law of Reparation*, p. 98; Walton, *Husband and Wife*, p. 296; Guthrie Smith, *Law of Damages*, p. 128; Walker, *The Law of Damages*, p. 562.
[64] For an interesting discussion of a similar point in relation to the meaning of 'seduction' in s. 17 of the Children Act 1908, see *R v. Frederick Moon; R v. Emily Moon* [1910] 1 KB 818.
[65] *Hill v. Wilson* (1871) 8 SLR 340; 'Court of Session', *The Glasgow Herald*, 6 February 1871, p. 6.
[66] A similar issue arose in relation to the crime of seducing and debauching young girls; see *John Bell* (1777) NRS JC7/39.
[67] *Sheriff v. Potter* ('The Nurse and the Colonel', *Edinburgh Evening News*, 10 November 1896, p. 4).
[68] *Soutar v. Peters* 1912 SLT 111; *McGahan v. Allison* (1946) NRS SC58/22/1946/7.

judgments illustrate how seduction could not be assessed by reference only to the moment at which sex occurred; the question of whether and why the defender had wronged the pursuer required a much farther-reaching inquiry into the circumstances that led up to the sex. But as Sections 5.3–5.6 show, the question of precisely which circumstances amounted to seduction was not easily answered.

5.3 Promising and Expecting Marriage

In Chapters 3 and 4, I discussed how a man might be found married or liable for breach of promise of marriage if he was considered to have promised marriage to a woman and then not honoured this obligation. In practice, in either of these circumstances a pursuer might bring a claim of seduction alongside the action of breach of promise of marriage or declarator of marriage. An action of seduction could also be brought on its own, though this was less common.[69] In the case of declarators of marriage, the action of seduction operated as a kind of safety net in case the promise of marriage could not be proved in the way that was required to find the couple married.[70] The early examples of this practice suggest that courts reached the conclusion to award damages of their own volition,[71] but that over time seduction was more frequently sought by the pursuer as an alternative, with this becoming routine from the 1780s onwards.[72] By the end of the nineteenth century, however, claims of seduction were usually combined with actions for breach of promise of marriage,[73] which, like declarators of marriage, had slightly different evidentiary requirements from seduction actions, at least for some of the period under consideration.[74] This change in accompanying action might be down to the legal developments relating to marriage outlined in Chapter 4, which generally led to the law becoming more stringent, and/or the fact that non-pecuniary damages for breach of promise of marriage could only be claimed from 1812, as discussed in Chapter 3.[75]

---

[69] It seems to have been possible to do this from the start of the period of this study, since all bar one of the actions raised between 1698 and 1830 and examined by Leneman were not initiated as an action of seduction, which implies that one of them was; see Leah Leneman, 'Seduction in Eighteenth and Early Nineteenth-Century Scotland' (1999) 78(205) *Scottish Historical Review* 39–59 at 40.

[70] See Chapter 4.   [71] Leneman, *Promises, Promises*, p. 120.   [72] Ibid.

[73] Glegg, *Law of Reparation*, p. 98.

[74] That is, until the restrictions on parties in breach of promise actions was lifted (see Chapter 3). The fact that the two actions were often brought together could create some complexity when the pursuer was being examined; see Skinner v. Greig ('Action for Breach of Promise and Seduction', *Fife Herald, and Kinross, Strathearn, and Clackmannan Advertiser*, 12 December 1861, p. 3).

[75] Barclay notes that actions for seduction grew in number prior to actions for breach of promise of marriage; see Katie Barclay, 'Emotions, the Law and the Press in Britain: Seduction and Breach of Promise Suits, 1780–1830' (2016) 39(2) *Journal for Eighteenth-Century Studies* 267–284 at 269.

In both contexts, the crucial question was what kind of conduct could support the seduction claim. It seems reasonably clear that promises of marriage which could not be proved in the way required for either a declarator of marriage or an action of breach of promise of marriage would qualify.[76] In fact, this form of seduction – of promising marriage before sex – was thought to be the most commonly committed.[77] Yet express and direct evidence of the promise could not necessarily be expected, especially if the seducer was trying to evade liability, so certain presumptions might aid the pursuer's case, such as the presumption that her rank and condition of life meant it was unlikely she would be corrupted except on a promise of marriage or 'expectations thereof artfully weighed'.[78] And while it was more typical for a defender to try to rebut this presumption by arguing that the pursuer was of a low station, there is at least one example of a defence lawyer arguing that women of a higher class were more likely to yield to sex without seduction because they were not worn down by mediocre food and hard labour and they had the time and freedom to pursue their desires.[79]

The fact that a direct promise was not required meant that expectations of marriage, at least those deemed reasonable, could ground a seduction claim.[80] Looking at the cases, very early examples of what is often described as seduction involved one defender promising to make the pursuer happy[81] and another asking a minister to 'proclaim them [him and the pursuer]', paying the proclamation dues, and then saying something to the effect that if the pursuer could prove her good reputation, he would honour his promises.[82] It was important to the pursuer's case that the defender's conduct was at least theoretically distinguishable from the kind of flattery or pressure that might occur within 'ordinary' seduction, that is to say immoral sex chosen 'voluntarily'. As one early twentieth-century judgment put it, the popular and legal uses of the term 'seduction' were not identical, since the former could include the most complete consent on the part of the woman.[83] Given the stigma that would attach to a woman who engaged in pre-marital sex, there was a sense

---

[76] Fraser, *Husband and* Wife, p. 505, discussing the relationship between seduction and marriage. Unlike declarators of marriage, which were *alternatives* to damages for seduction, it was possible to find a defender liable for both breach of promise of marriage and seduction – the action of breach of promise did not require that sexual intercourse occur (and, as noted earlier, it was subject to different evidentiary rules).

[77] *Walker* v. *Colquhoun* (1828); *Boyd* v. *Swan* (1898) 14 Scot L Rev 230; Glegg, *Law of Reparation*, p. 96; Walton, *Husband and Wife* (1922), p. 251 (listing this alongside conduct the pursuer believed to be honourable courtship, which is discussed later in this section).

[78] Paton, *Hume's Lectures*, p. 132. Leneman shows the significance of rank to the perceived likelihood that the defender had promised marriage, or that the pursuer would believe he had, and to the likelihood that she would only submit to sex in either of these circumstances (Leneman, *Promises Promises*, pp. 121–126).

[79] *Meikle* v. *McGhie* (1819–1822), discussed in Leneman, *Promises Promises*, pp. 124–125.

[80] *Linning* v. *Hamilton* (1748).   [81] *Hislop* v. *Ker* (1696) Mor 13908.

[82] *Irvine* v. *Hamilton of Grange* (1706), discussed in Walton (ed.), *Consistorial Decisions*, p. 67.

[83] *Cathcart* v. *Brown* (1905) 7 F 951 at 953.

5.3 Promising and Expecting Marriage

that women could not easily succumb to sex of this kind, even if they wanted it, without some degree of persuasion[84] – or, as one defender put it, 'without some sort of solicitation'[85] – and there was a corresponding worry that women would fall for, or pretend to fall for, lies that had no 'colour of truth' in order to 'screen [their] sin'.[86]

Testing for credibility and ensuring that women were not duped by conduct they should have seen through were therefore important not only to ensure that the law did not facilitate false claims but also to ensure that feminine chastity was suitably well guarded. The concern was that if damages for seduction were too easy to win the effect might be to encourage vice, rather than compensate those who were its victims. As such, at least during the later eighteenth and earlier nineteenth centuries, a disparity in rank between the pursuer and the defender was considered a ground on which the woman's suspicion should have been roused. Women therefore made a point of arguing that they were of approximately equal status to the men they were suing, and men would argue the opposite.[87] Furthermore, defence lawyers argued that a man's conduct had to amount to more than mere attention or even indications of attachment because almost no one would have sex without this,[88] and certainly no pure-minded woman would fall for behaviour that was (or at least purportedly was) this anodyne.[89]

Courtship was potentially enough to ground an action of seduction because, when honourable, it was typically considered to be a precursor to marriage; courting a woman could therefore predictably and reasonably raise her expectations of marriage.[90] In fact, in some parts of the country, pre-marital sexual contact was endorsed, including by a girl's family, on the understanding that a marriage would follow.[91] Though these practices attracted disapproval,[92] they add extra weight to the conclusion that focussed attention paid by a man to a woman, including sexual attention, could in some circumstances give rise to reasonable expectations of matrimony. In keeping with this, there are several seduction cases that centred on conduct resembling honourable courtship in

---

[84] Patricia Meyer Spacks, *Privacy: Concealing the Eighteenth-Century Self* (Chicago: University of Chicago Press, 2003), ch. 4.
[85] *Bennet v. Ninian* (1807) Hume Collection, vol. 99, Paper 49.
[86] *Scott v. Stewart* [1870] SLR 8 44 at 45.
[87] For example, *Buchanan v. Macnab* (1785) Mor 13918, discussed in Leneman, *Promises, Promises*, pp. 121–123, Leneman, 'Seduction' at 48–49, 55, and Leah Leneman, '"No Unsuitable Match": Defining Rank in Eighteenth and Early Nineteenth Century-Scotland' (2000) 33(3) *Journal of Social History* 665–682 at 671, 674–675, 677; *McGowan v. Fisher* (1797); *McNeill v. Wilson* (1797) NRS CS271/4258; *Mitchell v. Stirling* (1798) Hermand Collection, vol. 27, Paper 2; *Turpy v. McCandie* (1824–1826); *Stewart v. Menzies* (1837) 15 S 1198.
[88] *Walker v. Colquhoun* (1828).   [89] *Turpy v. McCandie* (1825) NRS CC8/6/1983.
[90] See Chapter 4 for discussion of how courtship might imply a promise to marry.
[91] *Report of the Royal Commission*, pp. xxxii, 171; Barclay, 'Marriage, Sex, and the Church of Scotland' at 171; Katie Barclay, *Caritas: Neighbourly Love and the Early Modern Self* (Oxford: Oxford University Press, 2021), pp. 95–96.
[92] For example, 'Letters to the Editor', *Caledonian Mercury*, 30 July 1863, p. 2.

view of marriage,[93] and the existence of this ground was affirmed on more than one occasion.[94]

Even if it was clear that promises of marriage and honourable courtship could underpin an action of seduction, the question of whether this behaviour needed to be false caused some confusion, just as it did in the context of breach of promise of marriage.[95] For example, various texts and cases suggested that seduction required deception,[96] and thus, in contrast to the action of breach of promise of marriage (at least for much of its development), a woman who knew that her lover was married and was therefore incapable of making honest promises of marriage would not be able to obtain damages for seduction.[97] Yet given the uncertainty concerning the place of deception within breach of promise of marriage, and the frequency with which claims of seduction were coupled to this action, it is unsurprising that some misunderstanding existed. As one author noted, there might have been no *dole* (a corrupt, malicious, or evil intention)[98] at the time the promise was made, if the promise was made bona fide, so the wrong committed at the time of its breach was retroactively held to qualify the promise either at the time the promise was made or when sex occurred.[99]

In the case of courtship, it was simply presumed that when sex had taken place but marriage did not follow the courting had been 'fraudulently conducted' in order to 'obtain possession of the woman'.[100] The use of a fake name alongside other lies about marital status, employment and salary might also be taken as evidence that the defender had deceived the pursuer to get sex[101] but not necessarily.[102] Certainly, in qualifying cases where such lies were used as part of a 'continued system of deception and lying' the conduct of the defender

---

[93] For example, *Farquharson v. Anderson* (1800), discussed in Leneman, *Promises, Promises*, pp. 124, 129; Leneman, 'Seduction' at 50–51, 53, 56; *Bennet v. Ninian* (1807); *Cameron v. Cameron* (1813) NRS CC8/6/1501; *Turpy v. McCandie* (1825); *Robertson v. Henderson* (1833), General Collection, Paper 25, (1833) 12 S 70; *Halliday v. Miller* ('Glasgow Sheriff Court', *The Glasgow Herald*, 27 May 1871, p. 2); *Gray v. Brown* (1878) 5 R 971; *Nicol v. Robertson* ('Court of Session', *The Glasgow Herald*, 24 June 1880, p. 3); *Boyd v. Eadie* (1917) 33 Scot L Rev 1, stressing the need for an intention to marry or conduct from which this could be inferred.

[94] Glegg, *Law of Reparation*, p. 98; Arthur Thomson Glegg, *The Law of Reparation in Scotland* (Edinburgh: W. Green & Sons, 1955), p. 133; *Murray v. Fraser* (1914) at 201.

[95] See Chapter 3.

[96] Paton, *Hume's Lectures*, p. 132; *McNeill v. Wilson* (1797), also discussed in Leneman, *Promises, Promises*, pp. 130–131; *Walker v. Colquhoun* (1828); *AB v. CD* ('Glasgow Sheriff Court', *The Glasgow Herald*, 1 April 1865, p. 5); Fraser, *Husband and Wife*, p. 503; *Cathcart v. Brown* (1905); *Quinn v. McAskill* (1952) NRS SC36/9/1952/19; Walker, *The Law of Damages*, p. 561.

[97] *M'Auley v. Pollok* ('The Action against Sir Hew Crauford Pollok, Bart', *The Aberdeen Weekly Journal*, 14 September 1878, p. 6).

[98] Watson (ed.), *Bell's Dictionary*, p. 339.   [99] Glegg, *Law of Reparation*, pp. 96–97.

[100] *Murray v. Fraser* (1914) at 201.

[101] *Bain v. Gray* ('Breach of Promise Case against a Married Man', *The Aberdeen Weekly Journal*, 20 July 1898, p. 6).

[102] *Moar v. Glass* (1924), where use of a fake name and representations by the defender that he was single were held not to amount to seduction (at 242).

might be more harshly condemned,[103] reflecting the view that a high degree of deceit might constitute an aggravation.[104]

Later developments in the law of seduction, outlined in Section 5.5, cast yet more doubt on the relevance of deception, however, because at this time abuse of authority or trust came to constitute a freestanding ground for the action. When this occurred, it was no longer obvious that even presumed or implied deception was important, or that knowledge of the defender's married status would prove damaging to the case.[105] Despite this, and as I come on to show, there remained ways in which deception was implicated in this new form of seduction. Before this, it is important to consider the other forms of conduct that were not obviously deceptive but which featured in actions of seduction, that is, physical violence and its threat.

5.4 Physical Violence and Its Threat

In formal terms, it was very clear that the legal wrongs of rape and seduction were distinct. This point was argued in court[106] and explained in leading texts,[107] which pointed out that seduction involved consent (albeit impaired consent) and rape did not. Indeed, throughout the period during which seduction was most often litigated, that is, the late eighteenth to the mid twentieth century, rape was generally understood in Scots law to involve forcible sex against the woman's will.[108]

Nevertheless, physical force or its threat featured in a number of seduction cases. Sometimes, the use or threat of force accompanied the behaviour traditionally considered to amount to seduction, such as a promise of marriage. In this context, the force might constitute an aggravation if it were proved.[109] On other occasions, though force is mentioned its existence does not seem to have carried much legal significance.[110] Sometimes, the allegation of seduction

---

[103] *Bain* v. *Gray* ('The Glasgow Breach of Promise Case', *Dundee Advertiser*, 14 October 1898, p. 10).
[104] Fraser, *Husband and Wife*, p. 505. Walker doubts this view because exemplary or punitive damages supposedly have no place in Scots law (see Walker, *The Law of Damages*, p. 563) but in another text he appears to accept that evidence of heartless deception or that the defender deliberately led the pursuer astray might lead to aggravated damages (see Walker, *The Law of Civil Remedies*, p. 988).
[105] *Boyd* v. *Swan* (1898) at 231.
[106] *McNeill* v. *Wilson* (1797); *Walker* v. *Colquhoun* (1828); *Quinn* v. *McAskill* (1952).
[107] Fraser, *Husband and Wife*, p. 503; Glegg, *Law of Reparation*, p. 92; Walker, *The Law of Damages*, p. 561; Walker, *The Law of Delict*, p. 701.
[108] See Chapters 6 and 7.
[109] As noted in *Marshall* v. *Linton* ('Glasgow Sheriff Court', *The Glasgow Herald*, 7 November 1860, p. 6).
[110] In *Skinner* v. *Greig*, the pursuer clearly stated in her evidence that the defender forced her and that she had 'an awful struggle' with him ('Action for Breach of Promise and Seduction', *Fife Herald, and Kinross, Strathearn, and Clackmannan Advertiser*, 12 December 1861, p. 3). In *Brownlee* v. *Wharrie*, the fifteen-year-old pursuer said she 'yielded to force and promise of marriage when her cousin locked her in the drawing room with him' ('Perthshire Breach of Promise Case', *The Evening Telegraph*, 9 January 1886, p. 3; 'Breach of Promise Case in

seemed to involve force alone, as in one case where the pursuer alleged that the defender 'overcame her by violence'.[111] Another cluster of cases involves the use of physical force or its threat in an employment context. As Section 5.5 shows, a separate line of authority developed during the latter portion of the nineteenth century according to which sex that occurred in a relationship of trust or authority might constitute seduction per se, but force was also sometimes alleged against men in such circumstances. For example, there are cases involving employers forcing their way into their servants' rooms by breaking down the door[112] and others where the employer seems to have essentially raped his employee, or at least used physical force and/or threats to enable sex with her.[113] In another case, the judge acknowledged that violence or its threat sometimes featured in actions of seduction.[114]

The reasons why an action of seduction, rather than a criminal prosecution for rape, might have been the response in cases where the conduct at least in principle satisfied the definition of the crime are not entirely clear. In England, class prejudice apparently created problems in securing convictions of married employers accused of raping their domestic servants.[115] In the United States, the crime of seduction was sometimes prosecuted when sexual coercion or violence had been used, especially in the context of relationships,[116] and one of the motivations of the women involved was to try to compel the defendants into marriage.[117] As Chapter 4 showed, in Scotland, the law of irregular marriage could be used to effectively compel marriage in some circumstances, but it is possible that some women brought actions of seduction to pressure the defenders into marriage. For some women who had been raped, marriage or compensation were the most desirable forms of legal redress available, and they might have preferred to pursue these options rather than a criminal conviction even if one were theoretically possible.[118]

Edinburgh', *Edinburgh Evening News*, 9 January 1886, p. 3). In *Laidlaw* v. *Reid*, the pursuer claimed that her alleged fiancé 'forced her against her wishes' ('Innerleithen Widow's Breach of Promise Action', *Edinburgh Evening News*, 13 May 1898, p. 3).

[111] A hearing that appears to be related to this case is reported as concerning reparation for rape (*Armstrong* v. *Thomson* (1894) 2 SLT 70), but the coverage of the case clearly describes the action as seduction (for example, 'Court of Session', *The Glasgow Herald*, 14 November 1894, p. 4).

[112] *Sutherland* v. *Hamilton Hart* (1880) NRS CS46/1880/11/50. This case was covered in newspapers extensively and is discussed in McLeish, *Broken Promises*; *McIntyre* v. *Brewster* ('Perthshire Breach of Promise and Seduction Case', *The Evening Telegraph*, 14 March 1889, p. 3).

[113] *Black* v. *Cotton* ('Aberdeen Sheriff Court', *The Aberdeen Journal*, 24 October 1889, p. 3; 'Serious Charges against an Aberdeen Photographer', *Dundee Courier*, 17 December 1889, p. 3); *Gray* v. *Millar* (1901) 39 SLR 256; *Brown* v. *Harvey* 1907 SC 588; *Scott* v. *Harvey* ('Lochgelly Spirit Merchant Sued for £500', *Dundee Courier*, 2 April 1910, p. 6); *Reid* v. *MacFarlane* (1919) 2 SLT 24.

[114] *MacLeod* v. *MacAskill* 1920 SC 72.

[115] Martin J. Wiener, *Men of Blood: Violence, Manliness, and Criminal Justice in Victorian England* (Cambridge: Cambridge University Press, 2004), pp. 101–102.

[116] Robertson, 'Seduction'; Brian Donovan, 'Gender Inequality and Criminal Seduction: Prosecuting Sexual Coercion in the Early-20th Century' (2005) 30(1) *Law & Social Inquiry* 61–88.

[117] Robertson, 'Seduction'.   [118] Barclay, 'From Rape to Marriage'.

Whatever the cause, the occasional use of seduction to respond to behaviour that looked similar to rape did not jeopardise the definition of seduction, or its association with deception, too much. In particular, on at least two occasions judges insisted on maintaining a distinction between rape, which generally required that the sex be forcible and against the woman's will, and seduction.[119] By contrast, the use of seduction to respond to sex that occurred within relationships of trust or authority expanded the definition of seduction considerably, loosening its link with deception in the process.

5.5 Abuse of Trust and Authority

Early in the development of the law of seduction, the fact that a pursuer was under the guardianship of the defender could constitute an aggravation,[120] and a relationship of trust (and indeed authority) was a feature of at least one case from this era. In this case, the pursuer had been brought to live in the mansion of the defender, her uncle, after her parents had died and this relationship meant that the seduction, which was predicated on a promise of marriage, occurred within a domestic arrangement whereby the pursuer was 'under the protection of the defender, as head and master of the family'.[121] At this time, that is, during the early modern period, the household was expected to be a site of patriarchal order,[122] and so it is not surprising that heads of household attracted special censure when they abused the trust reposed in them.[123] It is also possible to construct an account of the householder's wrongdoing that involves an element of deception on the basis of an implied assertion of trustworthiness.

As I suggested in Chapter 3, if a relationship was widely assumed to entail certain obligations, then entering that relationship might be said to involve an implicit commitment to abide by those obligations and failing to do so might effectively reveal that commitment to be false. In the case of the householder, the implicit assertion would be something like 'I undertake to protect you and your honour', and the falsity of this statement would be revealed by conduct that in fact exposed the pursuer to harm and dishonour. Furthermore, and as confirmed by cases occurring 150 years later, discussed later in this chapter, an explicit statement to 'do her [the pursuer] no harm'[124] might also be construed

---

[119] *Toutt v. Mitchell* ('Master and Servant', *Dundee Courier*, 30 March 1905, p. 6; 'Remarkable Dundee Case', *The Evening Telegraph and Post*, 13 June 1905, p. 4; 'A Dundee Scandal', *Edinburgh Evening News*, 31 January 1906, p. 2); *Kidd v. Vogel* ('Girl Sues Cupar Butcher', *The Evening Telegraph and Post*, 25 February 1926, p. 6; 'Girl's Action Against Cupar Butcher', *The Evening Telegraph*, 17 May 1926, p. 3).

[120] Lothian, *Consistorial Actions*, p. 92. See also, Fraser, *Husband and Wife*, p. 505.

[121] *Linning v. Hamilton* (1748) in Fergusson, *Consistorial Law*, p. 121.

[122] Barclay, *Caritas*, ch. 1; Cynthia B. Herrup, *A House in Gross Disorder: Sex, Law and the 2nd Earl of Castlehaven* (Oxford: Oxford University Press, 2001).

[123] For an interesting argument about the enduring significance of status, see George Letsas, 'Offences against Status' (2023) 43(2) *Oxford Journal of Legal Studies* 322–349.

[124] *Linning v. Hamilton* (1748) Mor 13909 at 13909.

as false on the basis that the defender must have known what would happen to the pursuer if he succeeded in seducing her.

By the end of the nineteenth century, the potential for power disparities between women and the men they would likely encounter had changed, and so had attitudes to the risks these disparities entailed. The later nineteenth century was a period of heightened concern for the sexual integrity of women and girls, a point that is illustrated by the passing of the Criminal Law Amendment Act 1885, discussed earlier and in more detail in Chapters 6 and 7. This Act epitomised the worry that younger women and girls, particularly those who were working class, would be abused by powerful men, yet its implementation revealed a distrust and perhaps even a degree of disdain for this category of victim.[125] At the same time, the increased entry of women into the paid workforce, including workplaces outside the home, created opportunities for sexual abuse in employment relationships beyond that of master and servant.[126] Finally, through a period of transformation that took place between 1860 and 1880, the law of seduction in France developed to distinguish between insidious persuasion or flattery and taking advantage of a power imbalance, the latter of which might arise due to familiarity born of family relations or common residence; superior strength; greater experience, age or wealth; and role or position.[127]

Each of these developments is reflected in the changes that occurred within the Scots law of seduction between 1892 and 1920, during which time cases were brought successfully on the basis of an abuse authority or trust. For example, in some cases, the defender's position as master or employer formed the main plank of the action,[128] often alongside the youth of the pursuer (and sometimes the gap between their ages).[129] In others, familiarity with the pursuer's family and

---

[125] Lammasniemi, '"Precocious Girls"'.
[126] Georges Vigarello, *A History of Rape: Sexual Violence in France from the 16th to the 20th Century* (Cambridge: Polity Press, 2001), p. 137.
[127] Ibid., p. 138. On the difficulty of resisting sex within employee–employer relationships (inside and outside the home) and other relationships of power in the context of rape at the same time, see the discussion of English law in Wiener, *Men of Blood*, pp. 114–115. In 1883, it was (unsuccessfully) suggested by Lord Mount-Temple that a version of what would become the Criminal Law Amendment Act 1885 should contain a clause rendering a guardian, master, manager, foreman, lodger or other person whose lawful commands in service or employment a woman was bound to obey guilty of a misdemeanour if he unlawfully and carnally knew, or attempted to have unlawful and carnal knowledge of, or indecently assaulted such a girl with or without her consent (Hansard, HL Deb., vol. 280, cols. 1382–1410, 25 June 1883; Hansard, HL Deb., vol. 297, cols. 939–953, 28 April 1885 (referring to a slightly amended suggested clause)).
[128] *Brown v. Harvey* (1907); *MacLeod v. MacAskill* (1920).
[129] *Fulton v. Anderson* ('Alleged Seduction Case in Banchory', *Aberdeen Press and Journal*, 12 November 1892, p. 7; 'The Girl's Action against a Married Man', *Dundee Courier*, 26 December 1892, p. 2); *Bowie v. Beaton* ('The Cuminestown Breach of Promise Case', *The Aberdeen Journal*, 22 March 1893, p. 8); *Boyd v. Swan* (1898); *Scrimgeour v. Bell* ('Dundee Seduction Case', *The Evening Telegraph*, 10 March 1898, p. 4); *Gray v. Millar* (1901); *McConnachie v. Kilgour* ('Huntly Photographer Sued', *Aberdeen Daily Journal*, 22 October 1915, p. 7); *Reid v. MacFarlane* (1919).

5.5 Abuse of Trust and Authority

the trust the defender enjoyed as a result of this were key, along with the young age of the pursuer.[130] Even in cases involving an alleged promise of marriage, the defender's position and his age vis-à-vis the pursuer's might be significant. As discussed in Section 5.3, earlier in the century, a disparity of rank between the parties was often taken to imply either that the defender had not promised marriage to the pursuer or that he had not created a reasonable expectation that marriage was in contemplation. By contrast, by the later nineteenth century, similar circumstances could lead a judge to conclude that the defender, who was of 'greater age and experience, presumably better educated, of much better social position, and of much greater means' than the pursuer, should have known that if he 'paid attention to a woman like the pursuer, he would excite hopes and desires which he had no business to excite unless he meant to fulfil them'.[131]

Yet even though the law at this later period sought to protect women from perceived abuses of power, some judicial commentary suggested dissatisfaction with this state of affairs which rested on potentially classist views. The most obvious of example of this occurred in relation to the case just mentioned.[132] According to news reports, the Lord Justice Clerk (Kingsburgh) expressed the view that £300 was a ridiculous sum to award for the seduction of an Aberdeen millworker,[133] prompting an 800-person strong protest organised by the Aberdeen Trades Council,[134] and letters in the press defending the judge's view on various grounds, namely that a millworker's virtue really was worth less than a lady's,[135] that the judge meant that a woman's virtue was priceless,[136] and that the judge was expressing a legal, rather than moral, opinion.[137]

More significantly, for present purposes, is that fact that these developments – towards grounding actions of seduction in an abuse of authority or trust – threatened the association between seduction and deception. In some of the cases, the defender had told or promised the pursuer he would do her no harm,[138] a statement that was held by one judge to be obviously false though only after it was interpreted by another probably to have been made honestly on account of the uncertainty over whether pregnancy would result.[139] But the

---

[130] *Cavan* v. *Saunders* ('A Vanman Sued for Damages', *Dundee Courier*, 25 December 1896, p. 4; '£500 Damages for Seduction', *Dundee Courier*, 15 January 1897, p. 4); *Murray* v. *Fraser* (1914); 1916 1 SLT 300; *Holmes* v. *McMurrich*, referred to in a decision about process [1920] SLR 523.

[131] *Langlands* v. *Wright* ('The Wright Breach of Promise', *The Aberdeen Journal*, 27 July 1888, p. 7).

[132] But see also the comment of a defence lawyer that 'to bring one of those Dundee millworker creatures into Court was altogether too absurd. What damages could this woman have suffered?' (*Brett* v. *Stewart* ('A Simple Young Lad', *Dundee Courier*, 4 May 1904, p. 4)).

[133] 'The Lord Justice-Clerk's Blunder', *Dundee Courier*, 21 March 1889, p. 3.

[134] 'Aberdeen Trades Council and Lord Kingsburgh', *The Aberdeen Journal*, 4 April 1889, p. 6.

[135] 'Gossip from *Truth*', *Dundee Courier*, 4 April 1889, p. 4.

[136] 'Notes from Edinburgh' (1889) 5 *Scottish Law Review* 90 96 at 91–92.

[137] 'Lord Kingsburgh and the Mill Girls', *The Aberdeen Journal*, 23 March, 1889, p. 6.

[138] *Gray* v. *Millar* (1901); *Brown* v. *Harvey* (1907); *Reid* v. *MacFarlane* (1919); *MacLeod* v. *MacAskill* (1920); *Holmes* v. *McMurrich* (1920).

[139] *Murray* v. *Fraser* (1914) at 203.

existence of these statements did not seem to carry much legal weight and not every defender offered such an assurance. Furthermore, the implied (false) assertion of trustworthiness I have suggested might appropriately be considered a feature of early seduction actions of this kind is less clearly applicable in the later cases. The changed context within which these cases occurred in which men were readily suspected of abuses of power means it is less plausible to suggest that taking up the role of, say, employer or head of a household involved implicitly making an assertion about one's trustworthiness. The consequence of these changes is that before the action of seduction waned in use, its conceptual connection to deception had been weakened.

5.6 Conclusions and Contemporary Connections

Following the run of cases involving claims of seduction founded on abuse of authority or trust, seduction actions returned to being based on promises of marriage before petering out during the 1950s. It is possible that the criticism levelled at the later abuse of power decisions contributed to this outcome, since one of the judges described their decision to let the second last of these cases proceed, after a challenge to its relevancy, as 'going almost to the extreme limit of indulgence'[140] and an article analysing this class of cases suggested that the decision probably represented their high-water mark.[141] The change in foundation of the action might also have contributed towards its decline. Many of the reasons for the disappearance of the action of breach of promise of marriage mentioned in Chapter 3 applied equally to seduction, but the concept of ascendency that had been used to describe the power imbalance in a number of the Scottish cases[142] and was also used in the French context,[143] added more fuel to the fire. As one critic pointed out, if the law was to 'recognise the sexes as being on an equal footing', then 'logically' this should signal the end of damages for seduction through which the law recognised 'man's ascendency over woman'.[144]

While these comments perhaps conflate different senses of equality, they do home in on something important about the action of seduction: it was predicated on a set of social relations according to which women were both the gatekeepers of sexual morality and liable to suffer if they failed to discharge this duty. It also recognised, but arguably at the same time reified, the dependence of women on marriage, and therefore upon men, and the greater authority and

---

[140] *MacLeod* v. *MacAskill* (1920) at 75 (Lord Dundas).
[141] 'The Pleader' (1920) 36 *Scottish Law Review* 4.
[142] For example, *Gray* v. *Millar* (1901); *Brown* v. *Harvey* (1907); *Murray* v. *Fraser* (1914 and 1916); *Reid* v. *MacFarlane* (1919). The term was also used in some promise of marriage and courtship cases from the later nineteenth century, for example, *Cathcart* v. *Brown* (1905); *Sword* v. *Fullerton* ('Breach of Promise Suit', *Dundee Courier*, 17 July 1907, p. 5); *Morrison* v. *Sinclair* ('Monikie', *The Courier and Argus*, 17 October 1907, p. 6); and *McGahan* v. *Allison* (1946).
[143] Vigarello, *A History of Rape*, p. 138.
[144] 'Notes from Edinburgh' (1921) 37 *Scottish Law Review* 62–67 at 65.

5.6 Conclusions and Contemporary Connections

trust invested in men in particular contexts. Apart from helping explain why seduction disappeared from use, this point is significant because it highlights how the action was underpinned by a host of beliefs and assumptions about women's agency, the limits of permissible male conduct, and the significance and danger of sex. As many others have shown, beliefs and assumptions about these matters are as important now as they were in the past, although their contents, and therefore the disagreements they spark, have shifted.[145]

In Chapters 6–8, I show how more recent legal responses to deceptive sex also rest(ed) on assumptions about women's agency and the significance and danger of sex and I suggest that this is also true of models for reform that have been put forward. What is particularly important about some of these more recent developments is that they explicitly disapprove of some reform options that avoid the ideal of autonomy, including ones I have suggested, on the basis that they 'impose a particular moral perspective on the world'.[146] There is a certain irony about this criticism, given that the author's own reform proposals are based on the claim that 'sexual penetration is a prima facie wrong'[147] – a contentious position which, if encoded in law, would not only lead to extensive criminalisation but would obviously amount to imposing a moral view on the world (or at least the jurisdiction in question). More importantly, I would suggest that it is probably unavoidable that any attempt to regulate deceptive sex through law involves adopting a moral view on sex and its meaning, with potentially very serious consequences for those who break the law.[148]

The consequences are not so severe when the legal wrong in contemplation is civil rather than criminal, but they remain serious and, as this chapter has shown, capable of serving some quasi-punitive functions.[149] This chapter has also shown that the challenge of working out which form(s) of responsibility are appropriate is not new, though it is arguably complicated by the modern tendency to regard censure falling short of criminal punishment as an inadequate response to social and cultural problems.[150] In the case of seduction,

---

[145] See, for example, Brenda Cossman, *The New Sex Wars: Sexual Harm in the #MeToo Era* (New York: New York University Press, 2021). On the phenomenon of modern 'seduction' and 'pick-up' artists, see Rachel O'Neill, *Seduction: Men, Masculinity and Mediated Intimacy* (Cambridge: Polity Press, 2018).

[146] For example, Jonathan Herring, 'Consent Mistaken' in Criminal Law Reform Now Network (CLRNN), *Reforming the Relationship between Sexual Consent, Deception and Mistake: Consultation Report* (2021), www.clrnn.co.uk/publications-reports, pp. 52–58.

[147] Ibid. See also Michelle Madden Dempsey and Jonathan Herring, 'Why Sexual Penetration Requires Justification' (2007) 27(3) *Oxford Journal of Legal Studies* 467–491. This view would also seem to burden sexual penetrators with special responsibilities vis-à-vis anyone else engaging in sexual conduct.

[148] For some reflections on this point, see Chloë Kennedy, 'Crime, Reason, and History: A Critical Introduction to Criminal Law' in Chloë Kennedy and Lindsay Farmer (eds.), *Leading Works in Criminal Law* (Abingdon: Routledge, 2023), pp. 220–241.

[149] See also, Kennedy, 'Comparing Criminal and Civil Responsibility'.

[150] Kennedy, 'Crime, Reason, and History'; Kennedy, 'Comparing Criminal and Civil Responsibility'.

one factor that suggested civil responsibility was the more appropriate option was the assumption that pursuers should have control over the initiation of proceedings. This assumption was partly procedural – if the action involved a matter of personal status, as it might in cases where the claim of seduction was joined to a declarator of marriage, then it was considered right that the pursuer should be the one to raise it. But it was also based on an understanding that the pursuer should be able to decide whether her sexual experience and, by association, her reputation was discussed in a public forum.

Another important factor that militated against the criminalisation of seduction was the difficulty of clearly identifying and proving when the wrong had been committed. In other words, the greater demands for certainty and clarity made of the criminal law were crucial to the classification of seduction as a civil wrong. I return to this issue in Chapters 6–8, but, for now, it is worth noting that partly due to the seriousness of the consequences, despite its status as a civil wrong, the ambit of seduction remained for much of its history fairly tightly circumscribed. As with the legal responses to deceptive intimate relationships examined in Part I, moreover, the scaffolding required to achieve this result was provided by cultural norms regarding what made sex and intimate relationships valuable. As I argue in more detail in Chapters 7 and 8, the desire to ground the law of deceptive sex in the purportedly morally neutral value of autonomy has the effect that the scope of the law cannot be kept in check by reference to communal assumptions, at least not without some hypocrisy.[151]

Since the effective cessation of seduction claims,[152] the one element of this multifaceted wrong that has been invoked in contemporary litigation is abuse of power in the context of sexual conduct. Even though no further cases involving this species of seduction appear to have been brought after the run of decisions outlined earlier, abuse of power remained part of the definition of the wrong. For example, one author stated that 'it is sufficient that by the abuse of the confidence resulting from a particular relation of the parties, or by the exercise of dominating influence acquired in such a relation, the defender has procured the consent of the pursuer'.[153] Importantly, the modern cases that have drawn inspiration from the action of seduction involve litigants trying to analogise from these abuse of power cases to obtain reparation for sexual relations between a social worker and an adult who was under their care[154] and between an uncle and his niece, who was over sixteen at the time of the sexual conduct.[155]

---

[151] For example, the recommendations made in Mark Dsouza, 'False Beliefs and Consent to Sex' (2022) 85(5) *Modern Law Review* 1191–1217, discussed further in Chapters 7 and 8.

[152] In England, actions for seduction were abolished by s. 5 of the Law Reform (Miscellaneous Provisions) Act 1970, and although there has been no formal abolition in Scotland, it has been said that it is doubtful that a seduction claim would be recognised as relevant now (Reid, *Law of Delict*, pp. 530–531).

[153] Walton, *Husband and Wife* (1922), pp. 251–252.

[154] *Shields* v. *Crossroads (Orkney)* [2013] CSOH 144.

[155] *EA (AP)* v. *GN (A)* [2015] CSIH 26.

5.6 Conclusions and Contemporary Connections

These cases tend to support the conclusion that seduction has ceased to represent a potential legal response to deceptive sex. Instead, as the rest of this part of the book shows, other legal actions have come to fill this space. Crucially, however, these actions are criminal wrongs and, over time, they have come to be structured around a binary conception of consent, such that the sexual activity is either consensual, and thus lawful, or it is not, and thus a crime. And while it would jar with contemporary sensibilities to think in terms of joint liability for engaging in sexual wrongs (as was the case historically in seduction actions), either because this has victim blaming connotations or because the activity to which consent has been deceptively obtained is not considered wrongful per se,[156] there may be benefits to thinking about consent as a scalar concept,[157] or at least in recognising that it can be negatively affected in different ways. Furthermore, a different, narrower, temporal lens has been used in conceptualising these criminal wrongs such that they are incapable of capturing some of the wrongful conduct we might hope they could. I return to these points in Chapters 6–8.

---

[156] Though cf. Dempsey and Herring 'Why Sexual Penetration Requires Justification' and Herring 'Consent Mistaken'.

[157] For some thoughts on this, see Kenneth W. Simons, 'Consent and the Assumption of Risk in Tort and Criminal Law' in Dyson (ed.), *Unravelling Tort and Crime,* 2nd ed., pp. 330–355.

6

Procuring Sex

6.1 Scope and Themes

This chapter and Chapter 7 focus on laws that have been used to criminalise deceptive sex, with this chapter concentrating on offences of procuring sex (or at least sex of certain kinds) and Chapter 7 focussing on rape by deception. The earliest of the procuring offences I discuss, which is sometimes considered to be the predecessor of more recent laws criminalising deceptive sex,[1] was passed in the middle of the nineteenth century. Much like the civil wrong of seduction, this crime involved having sex with a woman whose sexual consent was understood to be compromised, or illegitimately obtained, as opposed to absent. The same is true of the related procuring offences I discuss, which existed across the nineteenth and twentieth centuries. As with seduction, this feature of the procuring offences distinguished them from rape, which required a lack of consent and possibly the use of force,[2] although in practice the relationship between the two categories of crime was sometimes unclear.

The main argument of this chapter is that there are two features of the procuring offences that are core to grasping their operation and significance, both on their own terms and in terms of their contributions to the overarching ambitions of this book. The first feature is the meaning of procuring and, specifically, how this verb could be interpreted in different ways. In Section 6.2, I explore the legal meaning of the verb 'to procure', showing how it was interpreted both in situations involving two parties and in situations involving three or more people. During the course of this discussion, I consider the relationship between procuring generally and procuring via fraud, explaining why the latter was preferred in the context of legal responses to two-party scenarios. I also explain how the meaning of 'to procure' has implications for how the agency and responsibility of the procurer and the person whose actions are procured are conceptualised and argue that this has important consequences for the structure of procuring offences, including the temporal framework they incorporate.

---

[1] Rebecca Williams, '*R v Flattery* (1877)' in Philip Handler, Henry Mares and Ian Williams (eds.), *Landmark Cases in Criminal Law* (Oxford: Hart Publishing, 2019), pp. 147–170, p. 149.
[2] Discussed further in Section 6.4 and Chapter 7.

The second feature of the procuring offences which is key to appreciating their operation and significance is the act that is procured or, put differently, the activity that was regulated via the prohibition of its procurement. To explain how that is the case, in Section 6.3 I examine the act(s) whose procurement was criminalised and demonstrate that for much of their history the procuring offences were directed towards a broad category of conduct designated 'unlawful sex'. I also show how this category incorporated more than the activity with which the procuring offences are associated in most of the scholarship on the history of these crimes, that is, prostitution.[3] This shows that the wrongs and harms to which the offences were addressed were two pronged, incorporating those associated with commercial sex but also those associated with non-commercial sex that was nevertheless considered immoral, according to culturally sensitive standards that track the protected interests I outlined in Chapter 1. Furthermore, as with the legal responses examined in Chapters 2–5, a clear sense of the forms of intimacy that were valued and therefore protected provided a way of limiting the range of deceptions that could trigger a legal response. In this context, the immoral acts whose procurement was criminalised were essentially the inverse of these valued forms of intimacy – they were 'immoral' acts which the law sought to prevent – and their nature affected the array of deceptions that might be prohibited via the procurement-by-fraud offences. In other words, despite the fact that there was no formal limit on the range of deceptions that were criminalised, the nature of the regulated activity – the kind of sex whose procurement was forbidden – had the effect of setting such a limit.

Following this, in Section 6.4, I outline the demise of the procuring offences, as they existed in relation to non-trafficked adults with capacity,[4] paying attention to the relationship between these offences and rape and pointing out how the decline of the former set the stage for the expansion of the latter. As Chapter 7 makes clear, this shift has not only led to an increase in the punitiveness attached to deceptive sex; it has also created another line-drawing crisis whereby courts and commentators struggle to find a way to make the law predictable and defensibly restricted on the basis of a coherent justificatory framework. The problem is that the ideal of sexual autonomy,[5] which has come to dominate much of the scholarship and many of the law reform efforts in this area, cannot provide this. Importantly, this problem also affects suggestions

---

[3] For example, J. R. Spencer, 'Sex by Deception' (2013) 9 *Archbold Review* 6–9; Farmer, *Making the Modern Criminal Law*, ch. 9.

[4] The Sexual Offences Act (2003) contains offences against persons with a mental disorder impeding choice which involve inducing or procuring sexual activity (ss. 34–37) and an offence of inciting a child family member to engage in sexual activity (s. 26). The Sexual Offences (Scotland) Act 2009 contains offences against children and mentally disordered persons, but these are framed differently. Contemporary trafficking laws are largely outside the scope of this book for reasons set out in Section 6.2.

[5] On which, see Chapter 1.

that a resuscitated, or revised, version of the procuring offences might complement, or be preferred over, an expansive offence of rape by deception. As I argue in Section 6.5, there are additional difficulties with these suggestions, which include the possibility of overlap with the crime of rape and the challenge involved in classifying some kinds of deceptive sex as rape and others as procuring sex. Through making these arguments, I seek to show that the procuring offences are therefore worth studying for their own sake but also in order to attain a better understanding of the predicaments involved in attempting to respond to the practices of inducing intimacy via law today.

6.2 The Meaning of 'Procuring'

Even though the term 'procuring' was used in several offences involving procuring sex, its meaning was not immediately apparent[6] and its interpretation generated some disagreement and uncertainty. Importantly, these difficulties arose in relation to both two-party and three-or-more party scenarios, but the former of these are more relevant to this book because they involved one person (almost always a man) procuring sex of a particular kind from another (for much of the history of these offences, a woman) by deception. By contrast, in procuring situations involving three (or more) parties, deception might be used only at the first stage of proceedings, to lure the woman to whichever location was to be the site of the sexual activity. Once there, the woman might engage in the sex 'voluntarily' or the sex might occur after the woman's will was overcome or impeded in some way, such as by intoxication.[7] Two-party scenarios are therefore my main focus, but both scenarios are discussed, where relevant, because the proscription and prosecution of three-party scenarios forced legal actors to consider the meaning of procurement, including procurement by deception, and cases involving three or more parties might in fact involve deception at *both* stages, that is, when the woman was lured to the relevant location and when she ended up having sex of the relevant kind.

The first of the offences that addressed these two situations was introduced via the Protection of Women Act 1849,[8] section 1 of which stated that to better prevent the 'heinous Offence' of procuring the defiling of women, any person who by false pretences, false representations or other fraudulent means

---

[6] During debates over what would become the Criminal Law Amendment Act 1885 (discussed later in this chapter), the Earl of Carnarvon asked whether the term 'procuring' was used in its (unspecified) 'technical sense'; he does not appear to have received a response (Hansard, HC Deb., vol. 279, cols. 1294–1296, 31 May 1883).

[7] For example, *Smyth and Taylor*, a case from 1851 involving a female defendant accused of inducing three young women by false pretences to go to the male defendant's house for the purpose of 'gratifying his filthy propensities'. One of the women was reportedly lured to the house by the offer of doing half a day's washing for a shilling but on arrival was given raw gin and water, which led to her partial stupefaction ('Central Criminal Court, April 10', *The Morning Post*, 11 April 1851, p. 7).

[8] C. 76, 12 & 13 Vict.

procured a woman or child under twenty-one to have illicit carnal connexion with any man was guilty of a misdemeanour and liable to up to two years imprisonment with hard labour. Section 49 of the Offences Against the Person Act 1861[9] essentially replicated this offence, but the penalty was imprisonment for any term up to two years with or without hard labour. The Criminal Law Amendment Act 1885,[10] whose procuring provisions applied throughout the United Kingdom[11] and attracted much more attention than the earlier offences, provided that anyone who by false pretences or false representations procured any woman or girl, not being a common prostitute or of known immoral character, to have any unlawful carnal connexion either within or without the Queen's dominions would be guilty of a misdemeanour and liable to up to two years imprisonment, with or without hard labour.[12] The Act also listed a host of other offences involving women and girl victims, including procuring or attempting to procure any girl or woman under twenty-one years old, who was not a common prostitute or of known immoral character, to have unlawful carnal connexion within or without the Queen's dominions with any other person or persons[13] as well as offences involving the procurement or attempted procurement of any woman or girl to: become a common prostitute within or without the Queen's dominions,[14] leave the United Kingdom with intent that she may become an inmate of a brothel or elsewhere,[15] or leave her usual place of abode (not being a brothel) in the United Kingdom with intent that she may become an inmate of a brothel within or without the Queen's dominions for the purposes of prostitution.[16]

As drafted, it appears that the offences in the Acts of 1849 and 1861 could apply to two-party situations and, as I explain later in this chapter, at least some felt the 1849 Act was aimed at tackling these. But at the same time, the legislation was intended to make it easier to punish those who conspired to bring about unlawful sex and those who assisted in its commission,[17] activities that clearly indicate that three-party scenarios were in contemplation. The fact that people who traded in procuring sex presented a particular worry[18] confirms that the Act was thought to be applicable to three-party scenarios, as does the

---

[9] C. 100, 24 & 25 Vict.   [10] C. 69, 48 & 49 Vict.
[11] For one interpretation of how its introduction fit with the existing law of Scotland at the time, see 'The Criminal Law Amendment Act' (1885) 29(346) *Journal of Jurisprudence* 542–545.
[12] S. 3(2). The offence described in s. 3(1) involved using threats or intimidation to procure or attempt to procure any woman or girl to have unlawful carnal connexion within or without the Queen's dominions and the offence described in s. 3(3) was applying, administering or causing to be taken by any woman or girl any drug, matter, or thing with intent to stupefy or overpower so as thereby to enable any person to have unlawful carnal connexion with such woman or girl. All these offences were subject to the same penalty.
[13] S. 2(1).   [14] S. 2(2).   [15] S. 2(3).
[16] S. 2(4). The twentieth-century legislation criminalising procuring sex by deception is discussed later in this section and in the following sections.
[17] Hansard, HL Deb., vol. 98, col. 1418, 26 May 1848.
[18] Hansard, HL Deb., vol. 100, cols. 380–384, 11 July 1848.

fact that the 1849 Bill initially stipulated that third parties would be punishable only when their acts arose from lucre or financial gain.[19] Furthermore, the new law was criticised for seemingly not applying to the 'actual seducer' (that is, the person who had sex with the woman whose acts were procured).[20] Looking at the 1885 Act, section 2(1) appeared clearly to apply to two-party scenarios since it referred to procuring unlawful sex between a woman under twenty-one and *any* other person, which could presumably include the person having sex with this woman. Yet both this section and the procuring offence involving deception, found in section 3 of the Act, were the subject of litigation concerning whether it was permissible to prosecute someone who procured, or attempted to procure, a woman for himself[21] – litigation that eventually determined that this was permissible.[22] Yet there was an impression, possibly created by the circumstances leading up to the passing of the 1885 Act, which included a report of a House of Lords Select Committee concerning girls decoyed to Belgium and immured in brothels[23] and a series of articles about child prostitution in the *Pall Mall Gazette*,[24] that the mischief at which the 1885 Act was aimed was trafficking and therefore the conduct of third party actors.[25]

Across the period, therefore, the potential for procurement offences to be committed in both two-party and three-party scenarios existed and the possibility for deception in these contexts was well recognised. In fact, there was a strong association between procuring and deception. In the third-party, trafficking context, it was suggested that the very act of procuring implied a certain amount of deception because the majority, if not all, of the girls found in foreign brothels reported having been deceived by false pretences.[26] Procuring for the purpose of being carnally known (likely a three-party scenario), however, might mean *taking* a woman or girl out of her proper custody, rather than persuading her, while procuring in the context of the woman submitting to sexual intercourse implied that the decision to have sex had been induced.[27] Later

---

[19] Hansard, HL Deb., vol. 105, cols. 972–975, 25 May 1849; 'Parliamentary Summary', *Blackburn Standard*, 4 July 1849, p. 2.

[20] 'Provincial News', *Shelborne Mercury*, 17 November 1849, p. 4. I consider the description of this behaviour as seduction in Section 6.3. See also Hansard, HC Deb., vol. 107, cols. 953–955, 25 July 1849.

[21] For example, *Edmund Hope Verney* ('The Charge against Captain Verney', *The Belfast Newsletter*, 7 May 1891, p. 5); *William Hollis* ('The Criminal Law Amendment Act Inadequate', *Leeds Mercury*, 11 May 1887, p. 2); *R v. Williams* (1898) 62 JP 310, 'Procuring' (1898–1899) 6 SLT 158; *R v. Mackenzie and Higginson* (1911) 6 Cr App R 64.

[22] For some discussion, see Laura Lammasniemi, 'Trafficking, Rape, or Deceptive Sex? Historical Examination of Procurement Offences in England' (2023) 32(4) *Social & Legal Studies* 499–518.

[23] Hansard, HL Deb., vol. 280, cols. 755–775, 18 June 1883.

[24] Hansard, HC Deb., vol. 300, cols. 578–590, 30 July 1885.

[25] Lammasniemi associates the 1885 Act procurement offences with the combat of trafficking; see 'Trafficking, Rape, or Deceptive Sex?'. On late Victorian anxiety about organised prostitution, see Farmer, *Making the Modern Criminal Law*, pp. 278–279.

[26] Hansard, HL Deb., vol. 297, cols. 939–953, 28 April 1885 (Earl of Dalhousie).

[27] *R v. Mackenzie and Higginson* (1911) at 66.

6.2 The Meaning of 'Procuring'

decisions would hold that procuring a woman or girl to become a prostitute or otherwise engage in unlawful sex with another person – three-party scenarios – required some fraud or persuasion, or at least the issuing of an invitation when she had no other way to obtain money,[28] but it was two-party scenarios that provoked the most anxiety regarding the requirement for fraud.

Such a requirement appears not to have been initially included in the Bill that would become the 1849 Act;[29] instead, it seems to have been added due to the possibility that the crime might be committed in two-party scenarios. Given that 'to procure' might simply mean to obtain, it was possible that, without any further qualification, the offence might be committed by a man who simply engaged in illicit sex[30] with a woman. And as one member of the House of Lords put it, no legislative measure against 'simple fornication' could have good effects.[31] Furthermore, the parliamentary record shows that a fraud requirement was added to remove a major objection to the Bill,[32] and since the inclusion of a fraud requirement was considered to be an *unwelcome* reduction in the scope of the common law as it applied to third-party procurers,[33] it seems more likely that the addition was down to worries about the law being too expansive in its potential regulation of two-party scenarios.

Another reason to limit the kind of procurement that would attract criminal punishment to procurement by deception was the concern that punishing people who tried to induce a woman to lead an immoral life without using fraud would lead to unlimited and unbounded extortion.[34] The fear of potentially unscrupulous complainants[35] also helps explain the limitation of the earlier procuring offences to women and girls under the age of twenty-one. This limitation, which was also an alteration to the Bill that would become the 1849 Act, as introduced,[36] was possibly included with a view to ensuring that those who claimed they had been deceived were not themselves lying.[37] For example, in the context of a prosecution that appears to have been brought under the 1849 Act, the grand jury were told that they must see reason to suppose that the woman was liable 'by her tender years' to be led astray and that she had been the victim of false pretences, representations or other fraudulent means.[38] This

---

[28] *R v. Christian and Another* (1913) 23 Cox CC 541.
[29] Hansard, HL Deb., vol. 100, cols. 380–384, 11 July 1848.
[30] The meaning of 'illicit' is explored in Section 6.3.
[31] Hansard, HL Deb., vol. 100, cols. 380–384, 11 July 1848.   [32] Ibid.
[33] Hansard, HL Deb., vol. 105, cols. 972–975, 25 May 1849; 'Parliamentary Summary'.
[34] Hansard, HL Deb., vol. 280, cols. 1382–1410, 25 June 1883.
[35] I used the term complainant for the sake of consistency across this part of the book, even where prosecutrix would be a more accurate term.
[36] Hansard, HC Deb., vol. 107, cols. 953–955, 25 July 1849.
[37] At the time the 1885 Act was introduced, the reason given for limiting one of the procuring offences to women and girls under twenty-one was that it was impossible to protect those of mature age from the natural results of their own 'misconduct' (Hansard, HL Deb., vol. 297, cols. 939–953, 28 April 1885).
[38] *Smith and Holdsworth* ('West-Riding Michaelmas Sessions', *Leeds Times*, 22 October 1853, p. 3; 'West Riding Michaelmas Sessions', *Leeds Intelligencer*, 22 October 1853, p. 8).

age restriction was removed from the 1885 Act procuring offence which explicitly required fraud (that is, the offence in section 3(2)), but this prompted the addition of a new requirement, which was also partly motivated by worries about false charges: that the complainant not be a common prostitute or of known immoral character. The thinking was that women of this class would be more likely to make false allegations.[39] This fear of false allegations of deceptive sex was not limited to these statutory developments, either; it also constituted one argument against extending the offence of rape to include error or fraud. According to the advocate who put forward this argument, it is easier to feign having been mistaken than it is to feign having been subject to violence.[40]

Conceptually, the association between deception and procuring in two-party situations was particularly strong, as is shown by examining another area of criminal law where the notion of procuring loomed large – accessorial liability.[41] Unlike three-party situations, where the relationship of accessorial liability exists between the procurer and some agent distinct from the person who does the procured act,[42] in two-party situations the accessorial liability can only exist between the procurer and the person who engages in the procured act (in the context of this chapter, the act of having unlawful sex). One important feature of this arrangement is that it is predicated on the idea that the act which is procured is unlawful *irrespective* of the procuring: the procurer is liable for having procured an act which is itself a crime. While this makes sense if the act which is procured is unlawful sex, as it was for much of the procuring offences' history, it does not make sense if the act that is procured is only unlawful *because of the fact* it has been procured, which, as Section 6.3 shows, is how the law concerning procuring sex developed towards of the end of the twentieth century. In any case, supposing the act is unlawful in and of itself, claiming that its commission was procured, meaning caused, by another person can provide the person who carried that act out with a way of avoiding blame and, potentially, criminal liability.

For this argument to be convincing, however, the procurement must have occurred via the ignorance of the person who has carried out the prohibited act. For example, in a case involving drink driving, the accused was able to argue that the criminal act they committed had been procured by another because their drink had been spiked by that person; in other words, they did not know that their drink had been tampered with. The court held that, in contrast to aiding and abetting, forms of accessorial liability which require a common plan, procuring need not involve a meeting of the minds. In fact, in the court's view, the claim that another person has procured an offence is 'very much stronger' when the person who committed the offence was 'innocent

---

[39] Hansard, HC Deb., vol. 300, cols. 636–794, 31 July 1885.
[40] *HM Advocate* v. *William Fraser* (1847) NRS JC26/1847/592.
[41] The link between these areas was historically noted; see Frederick Mead and A. H. Bodkin, *The Criminal Law Amendment Act, 1885 with Introduction, Notes, and Index* (London: Shaw & Sons, 1885), p. 23.
[42] See *R* v. *Williams* (1898).

6.2 The Meaning of 'Procuring'

of all knowledge of what is happening'.[43] These reflections on the meaning of procuring and the agency of those involved resonate to some extent with how the civil wrong of seduction was conceptualised. As I explained in Chapter 5, seduction involved leading someone off the 'right path', including by deception, and the effect of this seduction was to partially eradicate the responsibility of the seduced person for the joint 'wrongdoing'. As the law regarding procuring as a form of accessorial liability developed, the ignorance of the person procured to commit the prohibited act took centre stage, with courts confirming that a common intention is not required[44] and holding that 'to procure' means to produce by endeavour a course of conduct which the person who carried out the act would not have embarked upon spontaneously of their own volition.[45]

These interpretations of the meaning of 'to procure' involve a strong causal link between the conduct of the procurer and the actions of the person whose acts were procured. Yet because of the equally strong emphasis on intention or effort to bring about the outcome and because of the possibility that procuring unlawful sex might involve two stages (that is, getting the woman to go somewhere and then getting her to engage in the sexual activity), the question sometimes arose of whether liability for procuring sex required that the unlawful sex actually occur. Answering this question involved addressing similar issues of temporality to those involved in the civil wrong of seduction, such as how far back in time to look for evidence that the decision to have sex had come about in an impermissible way and whether the activity known as seduction occurred at the time of sex or some earlier time.

In the context of the procuring offences, before the 1849 Act was passed, it was apparently possible to charge the use of false pretences and representations to solicit a woman, irrespective of whether they were successful.[46] After the legislation passed, decisions indicate that it would be possible to charge individuals with engaging in a false pretence with the intention to procure although no sex had occurred.[47] As for the 1885 Act, it did not specify that it was a crime to endeavour to procure, as well as to procure, unlawful sex by fraud though it explicitly provided that it was an offence to engage in either activity when the procurement involved threats.[48] Nevertheless, it was a crime to attempt to commit the near-identical offence that was included in the Sexual Offences Act 1956 as part of the consolidation of sexual offences that occurred at this time.[49] For

---

[43] *Attorney-General's Reference (No. 1 of 1975)* [1975] QB 773 at 780.
[44] R v. *Millward* (1994) 158 JP 1091. [45] R v. *Broadfoot* (1977) 64 Cr App R 71.
[46] 'Parliamentary Summary'.
[47] *Mears and Chalk* ('Southampton Borough Sessions', *Southampton Herald*, 11 January 1851, p. 6 (described as by false and fraudulent pretences attempting to procure a child under fifteen to have illicit connection with a man unknown); 'Law Courts', *The Examiner*, 25 January 1851, p. 10).
[48] Hansard, HC Deb., vol. 300, cols. 636–794, 31 July 1885.
[49] S. 3 of the Sexual Offences Act 1956 stated (until it was amended in 1995, as discussed in Section 6.3) that it was an offence to procure a woman, by false pretences or false representations to have unlawful sexual intercourse in any part of the world. In Scotland, an almost identical offence existed in the Sexual Offences (Scotland) Act 1976 (s. 2(1)(b)).

example, in a two-party case, the defendant was convicted of attempting to procure a woman to have unlawful sexual intercourse by false pretences although the woman did not believe the lie (that her husband had sent the defendant to have sex with her for money) and therefore did not have sex with him.[50]

To be liable for the full offence, as opposed to its attempt, however, it was necessary for sex to occur, even when the procuring involved two stages. So, in a case involving an advertisement for servants issued in Scotland and unlawful sex that occurred in England, the court held that the offence was not completed until carnal knowledge had been obtained. This was to reject the argument, made by the defence, that the offence was complete as soon as the complainant left with one of the defendants. Instead, the court held that the offence was a continuous one which began in Scotland and was completed in England.[51] Around seventy years later, the issue arose again when an appellant argued that it was a misdirection to tell a jury that 'procured to have sex' meant procured for the purpose of sex such that the occurrence of sex was irrelevant. Though the respondents argued that the essence of the offence was the act of procurement and that one can procure an act that is never committed, the court held that the words used in the statute, that is, 'to have unlawful intercourse', meant liability for the full offence depended on sex taking place.[52]

The relatively stringent interpretation of 'procuring' that emerged as the term's meaning was deliberated over time is illustrated well by the recent decision in *R (Monica)* v. *Director of Public Prosecutions*.[53] This case flowed from the decision not to prosecute one of the undercover police officers mentioned in Chapters 2 and 4 for either rape or, more relevantly for this chapter, procuring sexual intercourse by false pretences or false representations under section 3 of the 1956 Act, which was at that time amended but not yet repealed.[54] The applicant argued that 'procure' was a word in common usage[55] rather than a term of art but, following the interpretation outlined earlier, accepted that 'to procure' means to produce by endeavour, comprising a way of bringing about conduct that a woman would never had embarked upon spontaneously.

In Section 6.3, I consider how this conception of procuring shaped the court's attitude towards the range of deceptions to which the applicant was

---

[50] Maurice Oxley ('Miner Fined £100', *Nottingham Evening Post*, 1 December 1965, p. 6).

[51] *R* v. *Mackenzie and Higginson* (1911). Opinion was divided over whether someone could be prosecuted under s. 49 of the 1861 Act for using false pretences in England if the illicit connection was procured in Belgium. Thomas Snagge, a barrister, reportedly thought the law could not reach such cases, whereas James Fitzjames Stephen thought it might, though he was not sure ('The Protection of Young Girls', *The Leeds Mercury*, 26 August 1881, p. 2).

[52] *R* v. *Johnson* [1964] 2 QB 404.   [53] [2019] QB 1019.

[54] The amendment, discussed further in Section 6.3, was to delete the word 'unlawful' from the phrase 'unlawful sexual intercourse'. The repeal is discussed in Sections 6.4 and 6.5.

[55] Cf. the comment that the term has an 'old-fashioned ring'; see Jennifer Temkin, 'A New Law of Sexual Offences for Scotland: A Comment on the Draft Criminal Code' 2006 *Juridical Review* 29–53 at 46.

subject, but here I want to focus on how it worked to undermine the potential applicability of the section 3 offence in other ways. For example, the court held that there was not enough evidence that the officer had caused or persuaded the applicant to have sex. This was partly because the applicant had been the one to initiate the sexual relationship and partly because the court thought that the false pretence of being an environmentalist activist had provided nothing more than the circumstances for them to meet. As such, the court found it hard to see how bringing about this initial encounter could amount to procurement for the purposes of the section 3 offence given that, at that time, no sexual encounter was (apparently) in contemplation. In the court's view, by the time the sexual relationship was about to start, the police officer's deception was simply 'a continuing part of the background'; it could therefore not amount to a step taken by the officer to secure a particular result.[56]

What this case demonstrates is that the strong causal connection and the strong intention or desire to bring about a particular result that have come to be associated with the term 'procuring' can serve to foreclose liability even when intentional deception plausibly results in a mistake, or lack of information, that was important to a person's decision to have sex. It also shows how two-party scenarios can end up being viewed through a narrow temporal lens, which separates out and renders irrelevant the deceptions that preceded a decision to have sex, even though they may have been highly relevant to the person making the decision at the time they made it. In other words, even though, as I outline in Section 6.3, the nature of the act procured has changed over time from unlawful sex to lawful-but-for-the-deception sex, the structure underpinning the law's treatment of a classic two-party scenario concerning procuring sexual activity appears not to have been abandoned. What I have referred to as the first stage in the context of three-party scenarios – the way in which the complainant ends up in a position to engage in the relevant sexual activity – is ignored and this continues to be the case even when it plausibly had a bearing on the second stage, that is, their decision to have sex.

6.3 The Act Procured and the Forms of Deception

From the outset, the offences of procuring sex were directed at preventing the occurrence of *unlawful* sex. As such, the act procured via deception had to be not merely sexual intercourse but illicit or unlawful sexual intercourse, and this illicit or unlawful sexual intercourse need not have amounted to prostitution.[57] As with the term 'procuring', the meaning of the terms 'illicit' and

---

[56] At 1061. See generally the discussion of 'ground 2' of the judicial review.
[57] The titles used in the legislation reflect this broader remit. The 1849 Act was called the Protection of Women Act and the relevant Part (i.e., Part I) of the 1885 Act was titled Protection of Women and Girls.

'unlawful' was not spelled out in the legislation, and this caused some confusion. For example, during debates concerning the 1885 Act, one member of the House of Lords admitted that he did not understand the meaning of the phrase 'unlawful carnal connection' because, first, the carnal connection had to be unlawful to be punishable and, second, as he understood it, illicit connection was not unlawful in itself. On this view, the appearance of the word 'unlawful' in the offence definition appears circular: if sex is unlawful only because it is declared so by law, then no 'pre-legal' meaning of the term 'unlawful' can be used to identify a category of conduct which might then be made unlawful by legislation. When asked directly whether the word 'unlawful' had any special meaning, the Secretary of State, perhaps somewhat unhelpfully, replied that the words had appeared in earlier legislation and were perfectly well understood.[58] Though no answer appears in the parliamentary record, commentary on the 1885 Act indicates that sexual intercourse was considered to be unlawful when no valid marriage existed between the parties,[59] a position that aligns with the way the legal boundary between licit and illicit sex was set by marriage in other contexts.[60]

Importantly, a close association between prostitution and this wider category of unlawful sex was thought to exist because both were species of immoral sex, that is, sex that was contrary to the 'law of chaste love'. Immoral sex was understood to encompass all sexual practices that weakened the family, interpreted as kinship centred around marital union, and disobedience to the law of morality was thought to produce prostitution. Discouraging unlawful sex and prostitution were therefore essentially two sides of the same coin and pursuing these goals via legislation was seen as a legitimate practice so long as this did not involve conditions of such subtlety or complexity that it was impossible to lay the law down in advance or apply the 'compulsory power of the state' justly.[61]

Given such a broad conception of 'unlawful', it is not surprising that there are examples of prosecutions for procuring offences that were based on cohabitation and adultery. To give an example of the latter, a conviction

---

[58] Hansard, HC Deb., vol. 300, cols. 636–794, 31 July 1885 (Mr McCoan); the Secretary of State was Assheton Cross. A very similar point arose in 1958 when an appellant (unsuccessfully) argued that 'unlawful sexual intercourse' should mean intercourse contrary to some enactment of positive law (see *R v. Chapman* [1959] 1 QB 100).

[59] Mead and Bodkin, *The Criminal Law Amendment Act*, p. 25. The court in *Chapman* (1959) reached a similar conclusion, holding that 'unlawful sexual intercourse' meant intercourse outside the bond of marriage.

[60] Ariela R. Dubler, 'Immoral Purposes: Marriage and the Genus of Illicit Sex' (2006) 115 (4) *Yale Law Journal* 756–812.

[61] 'An Attempt to Determine the Limits within Which Legislation on the Subject of Prostitution Is Legitimate, and the Principles on Which Such Legislation Ought to Be Founded', *The Shield*, 12 August 1871, pp. 610–612. In the United States, a similar view prevailed such that prostitution was seen as hostile to marriage-based family and thus part of a much larger body of sexual practices and relationships that were similarly hostile; see Dubler, 'Immoral Purposes'.

was secured under section 2(1) of the 1885 Act for attempting to procure a woman under twenty-one to have unlawful carnal connection when a private detective, hired by a husband to obtain evidence against his wife for a divorce suit, deliberately tried to get the woman to commit adultery. Though commentators acknowledged that the Act was intended to deal primarily with decoying girls overseas, they praised the conviction as novel and salutary.[62] Compared to adultery, cohabitation was more complex because it did not *necessarily* constitute immoral behaviour in the sense of being opposed to marriage. This point was demonstrated when two men were charged under the 1849 Act with having procured the defilement of a nineteen-year-old woman by making an agreement that she would live with one of the men (with whom she had a child and became pregnant at least once more) for a period of eight months, after which time he would marry her. In other words, the cohabitation was a condition upon which the promise of marriage was to be fulfilled.[63] In a later malicious prosecution suit, the court held that this conduct did not come within the scope of the 1849 Act because the men seemed motivated solely by a desire to bring about a lawful marriage and to make the young woman an 'honest woman' instead of a 'prostitute'.[64] Conversely, cohabitation at the expense of marriage might be a lifestyle opposed to marriage but one that was freely chosen by a woman. This possibility was not totally unthinkable during the decades towards the end of the nineteenth century when, as Chapter 1 outlined, attitudes towards marriage liberalised somewhat. In these circumstances – when a woman voluntarily entered 'concubinage' in preference to marriage – the provisions of neither the 1861 nor the 1885 Act would apply.[65]

Engaging in bigamy or otherwise making a woman mistakenly think she was lawfully married are obvious means by which unlawful sex with a woman could be procured via deception. Accordingly, these forms of conduct featured in discussions about the potential application of the procuring offences, as well as in their actual use. For example, legislators cited mock marriage as the kind of deception by which a woman might sacrifice her virtue by means of deceit[66] and at least one sham marriage was prosecuted under section 3 of the 1885 Act.[67] Since bigamy was a crime that was taken seriously for much of the period of this study,[68] it is possible that the existence and severity of this

---

[62] 'The Criminal Law Amendment Act 1885' (1894–1895) 2 SLT 594. The report does not specify which of the men was convicted.
[63] *R* v. *Cutts* ('Singular Action', *Bell's Life in London and Sporting Chronicle*, 15 March 1857, p. 7).
[64] *Cutts* v. *Shepherd* ('Court of Queen's Bench', *John Bull* (Vol XXXVII), 6 February 1858, p. 96).
[65] 'The Liberty of Unlicensed Marriage', *Manchester Courier and Lancashire General Advertiser*, 2 November 1895, p. 10.
[66] Hansard, HC Deb., vol. 300, cols. 636–794, 31 July 1885; Hansard, HL Deb., vol. 300, cols. 1549–1557, 10 August 1885.
[67] *William Gregory Taylor* ('Police Intelligence', *The Standard*, 26 January 1891, p. 2; 'The Alleged Sham Curate', *Lloyd's Illustrated Newspaper*, 1 February 1891, p. 4).
[68] See Chapter 4.

offence can explain the relatively small number of prosecutions for procuring unlawful sex.[69] This hypothesis was put forward in the middle of the twentieth century by Glanville Williams, who suggested that one reason section 3 of the 1885 Act was little-used was that the offence of bigamy carried a higher penalty – a penalty he described as deserved in (and only in) cases of bigamy whereby the woman was deceived and the conduct 'involves something nearly approaching rape'.[70] In addition to this, he floated the idea that such cases of bigamy were the only circumstances in which the 1885 Act could properly be invoked because the woman would be 'morally innocent'. By contrast, deceptions of other kinds, such as those relating to wealth or status, did not go to the 'regularity' (meaning in accordance with established order) of the 'affair' and thus might not merit criminal punishment.[71] This notion – that the complainant would have to be deceived about the lawfulness of the sex for the 1885 Act to apply – had in fact been suggested during the legislative process, when it was proposed that the application of what would become section 3 of the Act should depend on the woman or girl not knowing that the sexual intercourse was unlawful.[72]

Other deceptions within the same realm of bigamy and sham marriage included impersonating a woman's husband and having sex with her which, as I come on to explain in Chapter 7, was eventually held to constitute rape.[73] As counsel in the Scottish case of *William Fraser*, discussed further in Section 6.4, put it, inducing a woman to have sex by impersonating her husband was similar to bigamy because bigamy involved fraudulent representations by which a woman was induced to give her consent to her supposed husband using the privileges of a husband, which she would not have given if she had known the truth.[74] Unfulfilled promises of marriage were also viewed as plausible candidates for criminal prosecution, but their unclear relationship with deception presented difficulties, just as it had in the context of the actions of breach of

---

[69] In the Scottish case of *Gray* v. *The Criminal Injuries Compensation Board* 1999 SC 137, the possibility was raised that sex following a bigamous marriage might amount to the crime of procuring sexual intercourse by false pretences under s. 2(1)(b) of the Sexual Offences (Scotland) Act 1976 (which actually required that the sex be unlawful – this requirement does not seem to have been removed before the repeal of the provision in 1997 by the Crime and Punishment (Scotland) Act 1997, sched. 3).

[70] Glanville L. Williams, 'Bigamy and the Third Marriage' (1950) 13(4) *Modern Law Review* 417–427 at 424, 426. See also James Fitzjames Stephen, *A Digest of the Criminal Law (Crimes and Punishments)* (F. H. Thomas and Company, 1878, reprint Littleton, Colorado: Fred B. Rothman & Co., 1991) in which the author argues that cases of bigamy involving a deceived woman inflict an injury as cruel and heartless as rape and should be punished accordingly (p. xxx).

[71] Williams, 'Bigamy and the Third Marriage' at 426.

[72] Hansard, HL Deb., vol. 297, cols. 939–953, 28 April 1885 (Earl of Dalhousie).

[73] Even after it was decided that this conduct constituted rape, it might still have fallen under s. 3(2) of the 1885 Act (see Mead and Bodkin, *The Criminal Law Amendment Act*, pp. 32–33).

[74] *HM Advocate* v. *William Fraser* (1847) NRS JC26/1847/592. Lord Cockburn seemed convinced by this analogy, and this was one reason he rejected the argument that impersonating a husband to induce a wife to have sex should be rape (*William Fraser* (1847) Ark 280 at 311).

promise of marriage and seduction.[75] As the 1885 Act was being discussed in the House of Commons Mr Labouchère (famous for the so-called Labouchère amendment to the Act, discussed briefly later in this section) asked for more detail about the meaning of the term 'fraudulent pretence', specifically inquiring as to whether unfulfilled promises might be included and prompting other members of the House to ask whether unfulfilled promises to marry might qualify.[76]

No concrete answer appears to have been given, with the Attorney General (echoing the Secretary of State on the meaning of 'unlawful') simply stating that the words were very well understood in law.[77] But the prospect of criminally prosecuting men for falsely promising marriage before sex was clearly a source of concern because of the prevalence of unfulfilled promises of marriage, which was known to be extensive.[78] As coverage of the Bill's progress at the time pointed out, the clause that became section 3 of the 1885 Act had the potential to be the 'most revolutionary of the old morality' because it might entail the criminalisation of 'fraudulent seduction', which would thereby dispel the notion that 'fraud is no fraud where only a woman is to be ruined'.[79] Despite this worry, or perhaps because of it, I have not found any prosecutions for procuring sex based on a false promise to marry; the closest I have found are cases involving married men representing themselves as single and in a position to marry.[80]

---

[75] See Chapters 3 and 5. Some members of the House of Commons highlighted the potential difference between failing to honour a promise and being false about one's intentions (Hansard, HC Deb., vol. 300, cols. 636–794, 31 July 1885 (a point discussed by Mr Stanley, Mr Bentinck and Captain Price)). The author of a newspaper article about the passing of the Bill suggested that, in accordance with a familiar principle of English law, the false pretence would need to be a misrepresentation of an existing fact and not a 'mere deception about the future' such as a false promise of marriage ('News', *Stamford Mercury*, 14 August 1885, p. 6), but commentary on the Act suggested that it was doubtful that the same was true of false representations (Mead and Bodkin, *The Criminal Law Amendment Act*, p. 32). As late as the early twenty-first century, it was apparently not clear whether the definition of false pretences under the Larceny Act 1916 applied, meaning that only misrepresentations of present facts, rather than, for example, an intention to marry, would be caught (see David Ormerod, *Smith and Hogan Criminal Law: Cases and Materials*, 9th ed. (Oxford University Press, 2005), p. 464). In 1984, the Criminal Law Revision Committee (CLRC) suggested that 'deception' should be substituted for 'false pretences or false representations', which they felt might unnecessarily narrow the provision's scope (see *Fifteenth Report: Sexual Offences* (Cmnd. 9213, 1984), Paragraph 2.106), and, in 1995, the Law Commission noted that the 1989 draft Criminal Code for England and Wales did not define deception but that the offences which later appeared in the Theft Act 1968 defined deception as any deception, reckless or deliberate, by words or conduct as to fact or as to law, including present intentions (see Law Commission, *Consent in the Criminal Law: A Consultation Paper* (Her Majesty's Stationery Office, 1995), Paragraph 6.7).
[76] Hansard, HC Deb., vol. 300, cols. 636–794, 31 July 1885.
[77] Ibid.; the Attorney General was Sir Webster.
[78] Ibid. (Mr Stanley, Mr Gregory and Mr Hopwood). See Chapters 3 and 4.
[79] 'In Committee on the Criminal Law Amendment Bill', *Pall Mall Gazette*, 31 July 1885, pp. 1–2.
[80] Theodore Horas and Laura Horas ('Charges against "Mental Scientists"', *Sheffield Daily Telegraph*, 11 October 1901, p. 7); Ramon Moir Steen ('"Girls Not Safe from You", Judge Tells Man', *Hull Daily Mail*, 15 May 1962, p. 1).

For all the worry that criminalising unfulfilled promises to marry generated, this prospect was perhaps not as concerning as the possibility that unfulfilled promises to pay for sex might be punishable.[81] Unlike women who had sex on a promise of marriage, who respected the institution of marriage even as they acted rashly, women who had sex on a promise of money posed a direct threat to family life, understood as living within the confines of Christian marriage. Moreover, such women knew that the sex in which they engaged was unlawful.[82] Even if the man who did not pay the agreed sum had never intended to pay it, this deception did not relate to the lawfulness of the sex. To criminally prosecute such conduct would therefore amount to favouring prostitution and go against the general aims of the legislation.[83] Technically speaking, a prohibition on prosecuting false promises of payment would go even further than excluding prostitutes from the law's protection and would involve excluding any woman who sold sex, even if she could not be classified as a prostitute.[84]

Finally, procuring or attempting to procure the commission of any act of 'gross indecency' (that is, sexual activity) between men, which was punishable as a misdemeanour by section 11 of the 1885 Act (Labouchère's amendment),[85] can usefully be mentioned alongside the procuring offences that are directly relevant to this chapter. Though this offence did not refer to unlawful sex, it was aimed at censuring and preventing sexual activity that was considered to be immoral and therefore was part of the broader category of which the conduct targeted by the rest of the Act was a part.[86] Similarly, while the offence did not mention deception – and there was perhaps less concern to apply the law only, or primarily, to cases involving deception due to the extreme intolerance of sexual activity between men[87] – it was possible that cases involving

---

[81] Labouchère embellished his question about the meaning of 'fraudulent pretence' by highlighting the possibility that promising to pay a certain amount for sex and then paying less might constitute a false pretence (Hansard, HC Deb., vol. 300, cols. 636–794, 31 July 1885).

[82] This point was made by Lord Bramwell but with reference to paying for sex using a bad note or sovereign (Hansard, HL Deb., vol. 300, cols. 1549–1557, 10 August 1885).

[83] As noted by Sir James; Mr Hopwood also pointed out that if the aim of the Bill was to prevent defilement of women and girls then protection should not be extended to 'common women' anyway (Hansard, HC Deb., vol. 300, cols. 636–794, 31 July 1885).

[84] Hansard, HC Deb., vol. 300, cols. 636–794, 31 July 1885 (Mr Serjeant Simon). This point was not explained further but in the United States judges held that prostitution had two core elements: indiscriminate sex and monetary exchange (see Dubler, 'Immoral Purposes' at 772). On this view, sex with one person for money would not constitute prostitution.

[85] F. B. Smith, 'Labouchère's Amendment to the Criminal Law Amendment Bill' (1976) 17(67) *Historical Studies* 165–173.

[86] Cf. the view that the provision was a complete outlier because it did not aim to protect women and girls or suppress brothels (ibid. at 165).

[87] At least as compared to fornication absent deception. See, for example, the reluctance to describe the conduct 'not to be named amongst Christians', which was labelled the 'foulest' and 'one of the most abominable and filthy crimes it is possible to conceive' (*Lionel Hans Hamilton and Henry Dady* ('The Charge against a Factory Inspector', *Blackburn Standard*, 15 July 1893, p. 5)).

6.3 The Act Procured and the Forms of Deception

deception might arise. Again, however, I would suggest that the subject matter of the deception would likely relate to the nature of the prohibited conduct. For example, in 1931, a person prosecuted as a man was charged with procuring another man to commit an act of gross indecency by convincing that man that he (the accused) was a woman, purporting to marry him (the alleged dupe) and then living as 'man and wife'.[88] This deception, which is how the behaviour was conceived, clearly pertained to the nature of the proscribed act; according to the man whose sexual acts had allegedly been procured, he did not know the truth about his lover and therefore did not know that the sexual activity would amount to 'gross indecency'.[89]

Given the various ways that the unlawful sex requirement shaped and structured the offences of procuring sex throughout much of their history, its removal in 1994[90] appears to have been underexamined. The change was made to align section 3 of the 1956 Act with the newly revised definition of rape,[91] in which the word 'unlawful' had been removed from the phrase 'unlawful sexual intercourse' to make clear that the marital rape exemption would no longer apply. This was seen as necessary because the term 'unlawful sexual intercourse' continued to be interpreted at common law as sexual intercourse occurring outside marriage.[92] The member of the House of Lords who moved for the amendment described the change as modest and did not anticipate that it would give rise to much debate or controversy.[93] It appears that this latter assumption was correct, but arguably the amendment deserved more scrutiny, and it was anything but minor.

For one thing, it altered the conceptual underpinning of the offence in the way outlined in Section 6.2, giving rise to the need for a new and cogent account of why it should be a crime to use deception to procure an act that was of itself not 'unlawful' (that is, immoral or wrong).[94] Furthermore, the change arguably detached the offence from the culturally informed framework that had conditioned and constrained the range of deceptions that would potentially trigger criminal liability. Although there was an isolated suggestion that the 1885 Act had the potential to apply to misapprehensions that were not induced by the defendant but which he knew about and did not remove or to situations where a defendant, knowing he was infected with a 'foul disease', induced a girl who was ignorant of his condition to have sex,[95] this is not how

---

[88] *Austin Hall*, discussed in McLaren, *Trials of Masculinity*, ch. 9.
[89] I have not undertaken extensive research into the operation of section 11 of the 1885 Act because it is not part of the genealogy I seek to construct in this book.
[90] The word 'unlawful' was removed by the Criminal Justice and Public Order Act 1994, sched. 11, Paragraph 1. The word does not seem to have been removed from the equivalent Scottish legislation, as noted earlier.
[91] This change was executed via the Criminal Justice and Public Order Act 1994, Part XI, s. 142.
[92] CLRC, *Fifteenth Report*, Paragraph 2.57.
[93] Hansard, HL Deb., vol. 555, cols. 1589–1655, 14 June 1994 (Lord Lester of Herne Hill).
[94] Cf. Dempsey and Herring, 'Why Sexual Penetration Requires Justification'.
[95] Mead and Bodkin, *The Criminal Law Amendment Act*, p. 34.

the legislation was used. Yet from the mid-1990s it was more common to see the section 3 offence (by then in the 1956 Act) referred to as a kind of 'mop up' provision to deal with a potentially wide range of deceptions,[96] and by the early twenty-first century it was suggested that the section 3 offence might apply to any false pretence that in fact induced consent which would not otherwise be given, possibly with the proviso that the pretence would influence the reasonable woman.[97]

The effects of this development can be seen in the case of *Monica* insofar as the range of deceptions described as potentially triggering liability under section 3 was broad, including the police officer's identity, his political affiliations, and the genuineness of his emotions and/or their relationship. Yet partly due to the stringent interpretation of 'to procure' outlined earlier, which I would suggest tallied with the conceptual underpinnings that predated the change in the act to be procured (from unlawful sexual intercourse to sexual intercourse per se), and partly due to the complexity of determining the authenticity of the officer's emotions and/or their relationship, the decision not to prosecute was upheld. On the latter point, the parties disagreed about whether the emotional connection shared by the applicant and the police officer, and thus their relationship, was genuine or whether, having its roots in considerable deception, it was not. In an era when love is thought to be in at least some ways resistant to reason and volition,[98] this is not surprising. Furthermore, the court regarded the case as very different to cases of breach of promise of marriage because 'the mutual agreement to embark on a sexual relationship occurred in the context of a modern-day relationship', adding that 'such agreements are rarely concluded upon the determination of a clear-cut precondition from which intent to procure could be readily inferred'.[99]

As this case shows, the conceptual underpinnings of the procuring offence, which were indexed to the act being procured, have ramifications for the range of deceptions that can qualify as potentially criminal. The case also shows that the possibility of prosecuting *any* deception comes with a degree of complexity which, in the modern era, cannot be avoided on account of the facts that, first, sexual and romantic relationships are now regarded as idiosyncratic and, second, the factors that go towards their initiation and development are not always straightforwardly truth-apt. Finally, as I explain later in this chapter, the development of the procuring offences complicated their relationship with the offence of rape and their demise has paved the way for the expansion of the more serious offence.

---

[96] For example, the statement that s. 3 should apply to all cases of fraud other than those which constituted rape (*R* v. *Linekar* [1995] QB 250, quoting from the CLRC report (at 255), also mentioned in *R* v. *Elbekkay* [1994] EWCA Crim 1).
[97] Ormerod, *Smith and Hogan*, p. 474.   [98] See Chapter 1.
[99] At 1040. It is important to remember that the 'clear-cutness' of promises of marriage was not the only feature that made them justiciable (see Chapter 3, including a discussion of how justiciable promises of marriage were not in fact always clear-cut).

6.4 The Demise of the Procuring Offences

From at least the introduction of the 1885 Act the relationship between the offences of procuring (unlawful) sex and rape has been uncertain. I discuss the development of rape more fully in Chapter 7, but it is enough for now to say that by the time the 1885 Act was passed it had been held, in an English case, *R* v. *Flattery*, that submitting to 'carnal intercourse' on the belief, induced by the defendant, that it was a medical procedure constituted rape on the ground that the complainant had submitted to surgical treatment and nothing else.[100] There were also conflicting decisions on the question of whether having sex with a woman who believed the defendant was her husband constituted rape.[101] While the 1885 Act cleared up this latter uncertainty, stipulating that 'a man who induces a woman to permit him to have connexion with her by personating her husband ... shall be deemed guilty of rape',[102] it also affirmed that there were two tiers of deceptions, with some being punished worse than the rest, without explaining which deceptions – if any – beyond husband impersonation might constitute rape, rather than the section 3 offence.[103]

Furthermore, in a case reported in 1898, *R* v. *O'Shay*,[104] the court decided that in light of section 3(2) of the 1885 Act, the decision in *Flattery* was no longer sound and that consent was a good defence to a charge of rape, even if that consent had been obtained by fraud, in all cases but that of husband impersonation (which the Act had clearly designated rape). Nevertheless, the possibility that it might be rape for a man to use fraud to induce a woman to consent to a completely different undertaking than the one she expected persisted. For example, in a case involving multiple women and three separate deceptions – the claim to be single and in a position to marry, the claim to have Divine attributes, and the claim that by submitting to sex with the fraudster a woman could ensure her immortal salvation – the last of these deceptions was described as potentially capable of grounding a 'more serious crime' than the section 3 misdemeanour that had been charged because it was doubtful that the woman's submission would amount to consent to what had happened to her.[105]

---

[100] (1877) QBD 410. For more discussion, see Chapter 7.
[101] See Chapter 7.   [102] S. 4.
[103] Commentary on the 1885 Act suggested that this one case of deception that definitely constituted rape – husband impersonation – might also fall under s. 3 (see Mead and Bodkin, *The Criminal Law Amendment Act*, p. 32).
[104] (1898) 19 Cox CC 76.
[105] *Theodore Horas and Laura Horas* (1901). For a discussion of whether analogous practices in Taiwan should be considered rape, rather than a separate less serious offence, and an analysis of the notion that religious beliefs might constitute fraud, see Jianlin Chen, 'Joyous Buddha, Holy Father, and Dragon God Desiring Sex: A Case Study of Rape by Religious Fraud in Taiwan' (2018) 13(2) *National Taiwan University Law Review* 183–237. For a discussion of how a provision of the Hong Kong Crimes Ordinances criminalising procurement of sexual acts through false representation has been used to indict those who procured sexual acts on the pretext of performing luck-improving religious rituals, see Jianlin Chen, 'Lying about God (and Love?) to Get Laid: The Case Study of Criminalizing Sex under Religious False Pretence in Hong Kong' (2018) 51(3) *Cornell International Law Journal* 553–607.

By 1909, the most recent edition of *Russell on Crimes* had concluded that consent or submission obtained by fraud was not a defence to a charge of rape or cognate offences,[106] and in 1923 the court in the case of *R v. Williams*[107] held that *O'Shay* had been wrongly decided. There were two reasons for this conclusion. The first was that the lawyers and judge in *O'Shay* had overlooked section 16 of the 1885 Act, which explicitly provided that the legislation did not exempt anyone from any proceeding relating to an offence that was punishable at common law.[108] The second was that, according to the decision in *Flattery*, in cases such as *Flattery* and others like it there was no consent to the act done, rather than consent that had been fraudulently obtained. This is clear from the way the court in *Williams* quoted as correct the view that it 'is rape although the actual thing that was done [that is, a medical operation] was done with her consent, because she never consented to the act of sexual intercourse'.[109]

The idea that having sex without sexual consent and having sex with sexual consent obtained by fraud are distinct wrongs is one reason a procuring offence, or something like it, was historically considered to be merited. For example, though he was referring to the 'procuring by threats' offence in section 3 of the 1885 Act, one member of the House of Commons stressed that it was essential to keep the offences of rape and procuring sex perfectly distinct from one another.[110] And in the case of *William Fraser*, counsel for the defence argued that the accused's conduct (sex with a woman who thought he was her husband) could not amount to rape because fraud is distinct from the force, or constructive force, whose use would mean that there was no consent that could 'do away with the guilt of rape'.[111] Building on the observation that force and fraud were treated differently in civil law, the advocate suggested that it was even more important to maintain the distinction in criminal law. He based this argument on several sub-arguments: that the 'province of the criminal court' was preserving peace among the lieges by protecting their persons and property, rather than preventing injustice; that violence, stealth and fraud all generate great alarm and terror in the mind of the injured party, but violence also causes bodily hurt or death; that crimes committed by stealth or fraud produce less terror and alarm than crimes of violence; that force is less easily resisted than fraud or stealth; and that fraud and stealth are easier to guard against than violence. On top of these arguments, he suggested that it is impossible to say that the will of an injured party consented to the act in cases of violence because, in these cases, the will has been constrained and

---

[106] As noted by Wiener (*Men of Blood*, p. 121). [107] [1923] 1 KB 340.
[108] Ibid. at 345. [109] Ibid.
[110] Hansard, HC Deb., vol. 300, cols. 636–794, 31 July 1885 (Mr Floyer).
[111] *HM Advocate* v. *William Fraser* (1847) NRS JC26/1847/592. This formulation follows the account of rape offered by the jurist David Hume. On how this, and other points of Scots law, imply that rape could be committed by having sex without consent, even in the absence of force (despite decisions to the contrary), see James Chalmers, 'How (Not) to Reform the Law of Rape' (2002) 6(3) *Edinburgh Law Review* 388–396.

6.4 The Demise of the Procuring Offences

overpowered. By contrast, in cases of fraud, so he argued, the will of the injured party consented to the act even though there was a material error in the mind; in other words, the injured party was a willing agent for a time at least.[112]

It is important to remember that rape was still a capital offence according to Scots law at the time these arguments were offered and the same is true of an earlier English decision in which the court concluded that there was a significant difference between compelling a woman against her will, when abhorrence would naturally arise in her mind, and beguiling her into consent and co-operation.[113] It is understandable that there would be considerable anxiety about expanding the boundaries of a crime that was theoretically punishable by death, yet even after this penalty was removed there was resistance to describing 'consent obtained by fraud [as] no consent'. This objection was rooted in the concern that it was unclear how far this doctrine ought to extend and dissatisfaction with the 'objectionable legal fiction' which it involved.[114] This perspective highlights the changeable way in which the problem to be solved was conceptualised. Though referring to the same deceptions, that is, impersonating a husband during sex and gaining 'consent' to sex through the pretence that the acts constituted medical treatment, this author conceived of the problem as how to deal with consent (he did not specify that it was sexual consent) obtained by fraud, rather than how to deal with acts to which no consent had been given.[115] As Chapter 7 and Section 6.5 show, these different conceptualisations continue to circulate in discussions about criminalising deceptive sex. Almost a century and a half ago, when the problem was being discussed, the solution proposed prior to the enactment of the 1885 Act was to punish some instances of fraudulently obtaining consent to sex not as rape but as a statutory offence of equal severity.[116]

In more recent times, distinguishing between types of fraud in such a way that might justify some constituting rape and others a lesser, or simply different, offence has become more difficult. As the rationale behind rape and other sexual offences between adults with capacity within 'ordinary' relationships has moved towards sexual autonomy,[117] a basis on which to draw this distinction has become more elusive and the notion that some ways of interfering with sexual autonomy are worse than others has become less attractive. So, for example, in the 1980s, the Criminal Law Revision Committee (CLRC) disagreed with

---

[112] *HM Advocate* v. *William Fraser* (1847) NRS JC26/1847/592.
[113] Farmer, *Making the Modern Criminal Law*, p. 273. The English case was *R* v. *Jackson* (1822), as discussed in *HM Advocate* v. *William Fraser* (1847) NRS JC26/1847/592. The case is discussed in Chapter 7.
[114] Fitzjames Stephen, *A Digest of the Criminal Law*, p. xxx.
[115] I explore the characterisation of sex with one's husband as ontologically distinct from sex with a man who is not one's husband in Chapter 7.
[116] Fitzjames Stephen, *A Digest of the Criminal Law*, p. xxx. This was essentially the route taken in *William Fraser* except that capital punishment (still theoretically the punishment for rape) was not applicable, and the development was via the common law (on the historical flexibility of common law of crimes in Scotland, see Kennedy, 'Declaring Crimes').
[117] See Farmer, *Making the Modern Criminal Law*, ch. 9.

the opinion of their advisory board – that sexual intercourse obtained by fraud should not be treated as rape so as not to blur the definition of that crime and because the degree of trauma was unlikely to be the same[118] – but worried about the ease of distinguishing between fraud sufficient to vitiate consent (which is not the same as saying there is no consent but which leads to the same outcome) and therefore capable of constituting rape and other frauds, which would be dealt with by the section 3 offence.[119] Similarly, when the Law Commission looked at sexual offences in the early 1990s, they pointed out the difficulty of determining the meaning of consent and figuring out when, as they put it, 'what appears to be consent is really consent at all; and ... whether certain acts of consent should have legal effect'. They saw the section 3 offence, which they described as applying whether the woman was '"consenting" or no', as existing to mitigate some of the difficulties caused by arguments about the meaning of consent.[120] Just a year later, they floated the idea of abolishing any distinctions based on the nature of the fraud, which would do away with the view that so-called fraud in the factum 'abolish[es] the reality of consent' (and thus might constitute rape) and so-called fraud in the inducement does not (and thus might constitute the section 3 offence), but they thought this would be too radical a change to recommend without a complete review of sexual offences.[121]

Yet when this review occurred in the early twenty-first century, the section 3 offence received little consideration. In their post-review report, the Home Office considered the origins of this offence to lie in the 'white slave trade',[122] which this chapter has shown is only partly the case. Perhaps for this reason or perhaps because of the focus on human trafficking around this time,[123] worries about trafficking were clearly their driving concern. Other than the example of 'sham ... marriage'[124] which, as Chapter 4 showed, was also a growing concern at this time, the examples provided to show why a gender-neutral (though still limited to 'sexual penetration')[125] version of the section 3 offence

---

[118] CLRC, *Fifteenth Report*, Paragraph 2.23.
[119] CLRC, *Fifteenth Report*, Paragraphs 2.24–2.25.
[120] Law Commission, *Consent and Offences against the Person: A Consultation Paper* (Her Majesty's Stationery Office, 1994), Paragraphs 24.1–24.2.
[121] Law Commission, *Consent in the Criminal Law*, Paragraphs 6.15–6.16.
[122] Home Office, *Setting the Boundaries: Reforming the Law on Sex Offences* (2000), Paragraph 2.18.2.
[123] See, for example, Jo Doezema, 'Who Gets to Choose? Coercion, Consent, and the UN Trafficking Protocol' (2002) 10(1) *Gender and Development* 20–27, and Janie A. Chuang, 'Exploitation Creep and the Unmaking of Human Trafficking Law' (2014) 108(14) *American Journal of International Law* 609–649, describing how human trafficking had gained global governmental and advocacy attention in the previous fifteen years.
[124] Home Office, *Setting the Boundaries*, Paragraph 2.18.4.
[125] In 1984, the CLRC did not recommend extending s. 3 of the 1956 Act to protect men (*Fifteenth Report*, Paragraphs 2.106–2.107), and in 1995, the Law Commission thought that the s. 3 offence was limited to 'vaginal intercourse' (presumably meaning penile penetration of the vagina) and so might not extend to anal intercourse with a woman. They suggested that if 'sexual intercourse' included 'buggery' then there was no reason to confine the offence to cases involving woman complainants (Law Commission, *Consent in the Criminal Law*, Paragraph 6.4).

6.4 The Demise of the Procuring Offences

might be worth preserving involve scenarios featuring three or more persons and two stages, such as forced marriage and advertising overseas to recruit waitresses who would really be required to provide sex.[126] Furthermore, there is a telling error at one point in the report, where the text refers to the section 3 offence as 'procuring a woman by false pretences *for* sexual intercourse in any part of the world'[127] – a formulation that lends itself to a trafficking interpretation.

Following this review, however, the section 3 offence was repealed and not replaced and the equivalent Scottish offence, which had been repealed in 1997, was not replaced either.[128] It is possible that the UK government thought that cases of procuring sexual acts by fraud involving adults with full capacity would be caught by the offence of causing a person to engage in sexual activity without consent,[129] as one commentator has suggested.[130] But, as this commentator points out, this provision would only apply to acts that are already deemed non-consensual prior to the defendant causing them. They therefore cannot capture, or explain the wrongfulness of, situations where fraud is used but the conduct does not otherwise satisfy whatever conception of 'non-consensual' is in use.[131] So, for all that the section 3 offence appears to have been little used,[132] its demise has not resulted in a functional replacement and the effect, explored in Chapter 7, has been an expansion in the scope of the crime of rape.

---

[126] Home Office, *Setting the Boundaries*, Paragraph 2.18.6. They also recommended an enhanced penalty in the trafficking context (p. 131).

[127] Home Office, *Setting the Boundaries*, Paragraph 2.18.1 (emphasis added). The provision is later described accurately at Paragraph 2.18.4 as 'procuring intercourse by false pretences'.

[128] Nevertheless, in 2013 an accused was charged with, and pled guilty to, two counts of obtaining sexual intimacy by fraud (Chris Wilson, 'Sex Fraud Woman Put on Probation', *BBC News*, 9 April 2013, www.bbc.co.uk/news/uk-scotland-north-east-orkney-shetland-22078298). This prosecution was at common law and arguably follows in the footsteps of the 1847 case of *Fraser*. In Israel, cases of deceptive sex were initially prosecuted as fraud (that is, obtaining a thing by deceit), but rape became the main charging option in the early twentieth century (Amit Pundik, Shani Schnitzer and Binyamin Blum, 'Sex, Lies and Reasonableness: The Case for Subjectifying the Criminalisation of Deceptive Sex' (2022) 41(2) *Criminal Justice Ethics* 167–189).

[129] S. 4 of the Sexual Offences Act 2003. There is a similar provision in s. 4 of the Sexual Offences (Scotland) Act 2009.

[130] Spencer, 'Sex by Deception'. The court in *R* v. *Dica* considered the s. 4 offence in essence to be the s. 3 offence 'in slightly different terms' ([2004] QB 1257 at 1267). Sexual acts involving deception sometimes have been prosecuted under s. 4, for example, in the case of *Duarte Xavier*, a man impersonated a young woman on online dating services then persuaded some of the men with whom he interacted to engage with him in 'vaginal' sex, which was actually anal sex. On other occasions, men agreed to be fellated by the defendant while blindfolded or unable to see him for another reason. For discussion, see Caroline Derry, 'Sustained Identity Deceptions' in CLRNN, *Reforming the Relationship* (2021), pp. 15–23.

[131] Spencer, 'Sex by Deception' at 7.

[132] Though Catarina Sjölin suggests that there are no recorded statistics to verify this claim ('Ten Years On: Consent under the Sexual Offences Act 2003' (2015) 79(1) *The Journal of Criminal Law* 20–35 at 22).

6.5 Conclusions and Contemporary Connections

The disappearance of the procuring offences that applied in relation to non-trafficked adults with capacity has met with mixed responses. Some argue that the section 3 offence should be resuscitated, making clear that it should apply only to telling 'lies' that induce the complainant to consent when the defendant realised that this would be the effect of the lie, or at least that it might have been.[133] Others suggest that there is no longer a place for an offence of this nature, arguing, among other things, that it would end up covering the same conduct as the non-consensual sex offences, offering a kind of 'rape-lite' and introducing the risk of plea bargaining and convictions of a less serious offence than is warranted.[134] These dangers are real, prompting some advocates of (re)-introducing a freestanding deception-based sexual offence (though with the qualification that the same maximum penalties would be available under the new offence and the corresponding non-consensual sexual offences) to suggest that prosecutorial discretion is an acceptable solution to this problem.[135]

The difficulty is that under contemporary assumptions about what makes deceptive sex wrongful, the same ideal – sexual autonomy – underlies both rape and any potential procurement-style offence. In other words, the ideal of sexual autonomy is what typically underpins the suggestion that it is wrong to use deception to procure an act – sex of some kind – that is not unlawful (that is, immoral or wrong) in itself. And while it is possible to develop the notion of sexual autonomy such that it can be differentiated into strands that are impacted by discrete kinds of misconduct,[136] the question still remains of when it is appropriate to conceptualise what has happened as non-consensual and when it is appropriate to conceptualise it as something akin to fraudulently procured and this problem cannot be avoided by suggesting that it is prosecutors who will undertake this sorting exercise, as opposed to legislators[137] or juries.

---

[133] Spencer, 'Sex by Deception' at 8–9.

[134] Sjölin, 'Ten Years On' at 32. Some proponents of a procurement-style offence specifically envision that this would be an offence 'lighter than rape' (Pundik et al., 'Sex, Lies and Reasonableness' at 168). This view is defended by an argument similar to that offered in the earlier nineteenth-century cases of *William Fraser* (1847) and *Jackson* (1822), that is, that coercive and deceptive sex are discrete wrongs and that the former is worse (Amit Pundik, 'Coercion and Deception in Sexual Relations' (2015) 28(1) *Canadian Journal of Law & Jurisprudence* 97–127).

[135] Recommendation of the CLRNN Committee in *Reforming the Relationship between Sexual Consent, Deception and Mistake: Report* (2023), www.clrnn.co.uk/publications-reports, p. 113. For a discussion of overlaps that have emerged in jurisdictions that have kept a procuring offence alongside the non-consensual sexual offences, see Jianlin Chen, 'Fraudulent Sex Criminalisation in Australia: Disparity, Disarray and the Underrated Procurement Offence' (2020) 43(2) *University of New South Wales Law Journal* 581–614.

[136] For example, Matthew Gibson, 'Deceptive Sexual Relations: A Theory of Criminal Liability' (2020) 40(1) *Oxford Journal of Legal Studies* 82–109.

[137] As proposed by the CLRC due to their desire for prospective clarity and certainty (*Fifteenth Report*, Paragraph 2.25).

6.5 Conclusions and Contemporary Connections

This point is explored further in Chapters 7 and 8 but, as a primer that builds on the insights provided by this chapter, I would suggest that distinguishing between kinds of mistake (or forms of missing information) depends on having a clear sense of what makes sexual activity valuable. For much of the history of the offences of procuring sex, this sense was provided by the requirement that the sex procured be unlawful. This implicitly valued only 'lawful' sex and helped delineate the kind of deceptions that would trigger criminal liability, though not always in a way that made the distinction between the procuring offence and rape clear. If, on the other hand, an attempt to distinguish between kinds of mistake rests on sexual autonomy, understood as permitting every person to select the 'object of consent' themselves, then practical considerations and the realities of proof will tend to push in the direction of relying on conventional norms.[138]

The same applies to efforts to determine the line between liability for a procurement-style offence and no criminal liability. This point is illustrated by one recent attempt to draw this line by relying on a 'reasonable excuse' provision, which would limit liability to cases in which someone engages in deceptive sex without a reasonable excuse.[139] The problem is that the claim that in other contexts 'juries have little difficulty deciding for themselves to the criminal standard whether the excuse put forward by a defendant to account for his or her actions was unreasonable', perhaps helped along by jury directions, sits uneasily with the assertion that 'what matters is the effect on the victim's autonomy and not a third party appraisal of the gravity of the deception'.[140] Rather than claiming that sexual autonomy is paramount, it would be preferable simply to acknowledge that to be workable, not to mention defensible, the ideal of sexual autonomy has to be reined in somehow and that one obvious, though not unproblematic, way to do this is to rely on social norms or conventions.

Relying on different modes of commission either to distinguish cases of non-consensual sex from cases of fraudulently procured sex or to distinguish cases of fraudulently procured sex from deceptive sex that attracts no criminal liability might be tempting, but this option suffers from difficulties too. For example, limiting the relevant offence to instances of 'active deception'[141] or 'lies'[142] (as opposed to failures to disclose) is a strategy that has been rejected by courts[143] and whose feasibility and normative attractiveness has been questioned.[144] For their part, requiring an intention to deceive or manipulate[145]

---

[138] See Chapter 7.
[139] Recommendation of the CLRNN Committee in *Reforming the Relationship* (2023). Examples they offer include defendants who apprehend violence if they were to reveal their age or gender identity (p. 113).
[140] CLRNN Committee, *Reforming the Relationship* (2023), p. 114.
[141] As recommended by Pundik et al., 'Sex, Lies and Reasonableness' at 179.
[142] As recommended by Spencer, 'Sex by Deception' at 8.
[143] *R v. Lawrence* [2020] EWCA Crim 971 (Paragraph 41). See also Chapters 2, 7 and 8.
[144] Alex Sharpe, 'Expanding Liability for Sexual Fraud through the Concept of Active Deception: A Flawed Approach' (2016) 80(1) *The Journal of Criminal Law* 28–44.
[145] As recommended by the CLRNN Committee in *Reforming the Relationship* (2023), p. 115.

and/or knowledge that the relevant deception would matter to the complainant[146] sets the prosecutorial bar high. Indeed, it sets the bar higher than it generally sits in relation to the non-consensual sexual offences[147] and a clear account of why this should be the case is needed, especially if the underpinning wrongs and harms of deceptive sex and the non-consensual sexual offences rest on the same foundation, that is, sexual autonomy. As the example of the case of *Monica* shows, when the bar is set very high with respect to *mens rea*, the offence can become almost unworkable and the same is true if a strong causal connection between the deceptive conduct and the proscribed outcome is required.[148] I would suggest, for the reasons outlined earlier, that the need to rein in the kinds of deception that will trigger liability exists irrespective of these other factors, but that it might be especially pronounced if stringent *mens rea* and causation requirements are rejected, as they might be in view of the difficulties the case of *Monica* highlights. I return to these points in Chapter 8.

---

[146] As recommended by Pundik et al., 'Sex, Lies and Reasonableness' at 180.
[147] See Chapters 7 and 8.
[148] See, for example, the suggestion that a replacement procurement-style offence should require that 'it was the lie that actually induced the complainant to consent' (Spencer, 'Sex by Deception' at 8) and the suggestion of the CLRNN Committee that 'induce' rather than 'influence' should be the test, explaining that the deception must have been one of the factors that 'persuaded' the complainant to engage in the sexual activity (*Reforming the Relationship* (2023), p. 114).

7

Imposing Sex

7.1 Scope and Themes

To conclude this part of the book, this chapter examines how deceptive sex has come to potentially constitute the crime of rape. Starting in the early nineteenth century, I trace how the definition of rape changed to incorporate conduct, specifically deceptive conduct, which did not formerly fall within its purview. As this analysis shows, the change that occurred – towards defining rape in terms of a lack of consent – created the possibility that sexual activity secured by deception might satisfy the offence definition. This development was far from straightforward, however, in part due to the different ways in which consent could be conceptualised and the various means by which deception, broadly understood, could be understood to affect the existence or validity of consent. On top of this, deceptive sex was closely related to crimes other than rape, beyond the procuring offences discussed in Chapter 6, including non-sexual offences against the person (in England) and fraud (in Scotland).

In Sections 7.2–7.5, I explore these developments while simultaneously discussing which deceptions have been held to vitiate, negate, or preclude sexual consent with reference to subject matter. I have two aims in doing this. The first is to demonstrate how the legal doctrinal changes I outline help substantiate the claims I made in Chapter 1 about the rise of the ideal of autonomy and its significance for the laws governing deceptively induced intimacy. The second aim is to argue that these legal doctrinal shifts constitute only half of the story of how and why the scope of rape by deception has developed as it has. The other half of the story is, I suggest, provided by considering the array of deceptions that have been deemed suitable (or, conversely, unsuitable) candidates for prosecution as rape.

More specifically, my argument is that while different legal doctrinal requirements clearly affected the scope of criminalisation, and the question of which offence(s) might apply, in order to fully appreciate the changing scope of rape by deception it is necessary to pay attention to both the range of interests the law has sought to protect and how these are reflected in the range of deceptions that have been prosecuted or considered appropriate targets of prosecution. These deceptions, which I refer to as qualifying deceptions, reveal that the criminal law has been used to protect a range of culturally sensitive interests, which correlate with prevailing notions of what makes sex valuable – marriage for much of the history of this offence and then, later, sexual autonomy – as well as other temporally and socially specific concerns associated with sexual conduct, such as trust in certain professions and worries about the spread of disease.

Paying attention to these points shows that, historically, the range of interests protected by law worked to restrict the range of qualifying deceptions just as much as legal doctrinal features, such as mode of deception (i.e., misrepresentations, false pretences and non-disclosures), *mens rea* requirements and any causal connection that has been required between the deception and outcome (that is, sex). At the same time, the desiderata associated with criminal law as a form of public law – clarity, legal certainty and predictability – which I outlined in Chapter 1, and which featured in Chapters 5 and 6 – have also informed efforts to contain the scope of rape by deception. This chapter therefore amplifies and furthers the two main arguments that cut across Chapters 1–6. First, it shows that both the wrongs of deceptive sex and the responses it has elicited have been shaped by changing social and cultural norms, particularly those concerning the significance of sex for self-construction in its historical and contemporary guises. Second, it demonstrates that a combination of principled and pragmatic stances on the appropriateness of legal intervention, which are informed by expectations of private and public law, have been crucial to developments in this area of law.

I substantiate both of these arguments across Sections 7.2–7.5, which are organised with reference to the main topics and circumstances of qualifying deceptions: deceptions relating to personal identity; deceptions that occur in relationships of trust and authority; deceptions pertaining to disease, fertility and contraception; and deceptions about marital status. After this, in Section 7.6, I reflect on the extent to which the main contemporary assumption about the value of sex – that it is valuable as far as it reflects sexual autonomy – has the capacity to constrain and structure the law, both as it has developed and as some now expect it to be used. In doing so, I highlight some of the difficulties that I perceive with contemporary legal developments and expectations in the law of sexual offences, many of which I introduced in Chapter 1 and which I explore further in Chapter 8. This sets up my ambition, also pursued in Chapter 8, to show how the historically informed insights derived from this chapter and those that preceded it might help us think differently about how to respond to deceptively induced intimacy via law.

7.2 Personal Identity

One of the longest-standing categories of qualifying deception is deception as to personal identity, but at the start of the period with which this book is concerned sex involving deception of this kind would not have constituted rape. This was made clear in the early nineteenth century when an English court held

7.2 Personal Identity

that it would not be rape for a man to have sex with a woman who mistakenly thought he was her husband because in such circumstances the woman would have been beguiled into consenting and co-operating, rather than compelled against her will.[1] In a series of cases involving similar circumstances that followed this decision, juries therefore either acquitted the defendant altogether[2] or else convicted him of the lesser offence of assault.[3]

These early developments should be understood in light of definitions of, and attitudes towards, rape at this time. According to one historian, prosecutions for rape in England began to increase from the 1820s, in part because judges became less tolerant of this type of offending and private settlements started to be regarded less favourably.[4] Yet the penalty for rape at this time was still severe – death – so, as I mentioned in Chapter 6, there was some resistance to expanding the boundaries of the crime, and it continued to be defined as carnal intercourse against the will of the woman, who had resisted the imposition.[5] In the cases of women who had mistaken the defendant for their husband, the women had 'consented' to the sexual intercourse and they had offered no resistance, so what happened was not considered to be against their will.[6]

By contrast, assault in these circumstances did not require resistance and could be committed by fraud – as one judge put it, 'if resistance is prevented by the fraud of the man who pretends to be the husband, that is sufficient'.[7] From a procedural point of view, the possibility of convicting the defendant of assault was facilitated by the fact that whereas previously it had been impossible to combine any lesser charges with rape or sodomy (meaning that juries either had to convict of the capital offence or acquit the defendant altogether), legislation passed in 1837 allowed secondary charges to be brought alongside these felonies. This enabled juries to acquit of the more serious crime and convict the defendant of assault if the evidence supported that course of action.[8]

---

[1] *R v. Joseph Jackson* (1822) 168 ER 911.
[2] *R v. Pearson*, discussed in Wiener, *Men of Blood*, p. 117.
[3] *R v. Saunders* (1838) 173 ER 488; *R v. Williams* (1838) 173 ER 497; *R v. Rackstraw*, discussed in Wiener, *Men of Blood*, p. 117.
[4] Wiener, *Men of Blood*, pp. 86, 92.   [5] Ibid., p. 89.
[6] For example, 'supposing it to be her husband, [the prosecutrix] made no resistance' and 'the crime was not committed against the will of the prosecutrix, as she consented, believing it to be her husband' (*R v. Saunders* (1838) at 489); she had 'allowed the prisoner to have connexion with her believing him to be her husband' and resisted only after she discovered that he was not her husband (*R v. Williams* (1838) at 498). See also the cases of *Giles Simes*, where the grand jury ignored the bill for committing rape after being told by the judge that impersonating the husband of the victim, who had been transported twenty-nine years previously, and sharing her bed did not constitute rape ('County Bench', *Berkshire Chronicle*, 7 March 1863, p. 5; 'Western Circuit', *Reading Mercury*, 7 March 1863, p. 6) and *R v. Barrow*, where in the absence of proof of sleep or unconsciousness at the time the sexual intercourse began a woman was deemed to have consented to sex even though her consent was 'obtained by fraud', that is, she mistakenly believed that the man was her husband ((1865–72) LR 1 CCR 156 at 158).
[7] *R v. Williams* (1838) at 498 (Alderson, B).
[8] 1 Vict. c. 85; Wiener, *Men of Blood*, p. 91. This might, however, lead to charges or convictions of assault when rape would be more appropriate in the eyes of the judge; see, for example, 'Central Criminal Court', *Morning Chronicle*, 11 July 1861, p. 7.

Across the course of the century, however, and particularly after the death penalty for rape was removed in 1841,[9] rape came to be organised around the absence of consent, and consent came to be construed in positive terms – as the presence of assent – rather than negative terms – as the lack of resistance.[10] This transition raised the possibility that deceptive sex might constitute rape for, as Chapter 2 illustrated, in various other areas of law deception (at least deception of certain kinds) worked to preclude or vitiate consent. Yet it was not until the later nineteenth century that a court would determine that it might be rape when a woman mistakenly believed that she was having sex with her husband. The case in which this judgment was reached was *R* v. *Dee*,[11] decided in 1884, which had been preceded seven years earlier by the important decision of *R* v. *Flattery*[12] (discussed in Section 7.3) in which it was held that duping a girl into thinking she was receiving medical treatment but instead engaging in sex to gratify one's lust constituted rape because consent to one act did not amount to consent to the other.

Counsel for the prisoner in *Dee* tried to resist the conclusion that the ratio in *Flattery* might apply by suggesting that this would be to continue a growing tendency to extend the definition of rape beyond its proper limits (that is, sex by force and against the will)[13] and by arguing that even if 'no consent' were the proper test it had not been met on this occasion. Here, so he argued, the woman knew the nature and meaning of sexual connection and had intended to engage in this act.[14] By contrast, counsel on the opposing side argued that the woman had never consented to an act of adultery,[15] which was of course an accurate description of sex with a man other than one's husband, adding that the earlier authorities on husband impersonation had been decided so as to avoid the former penalty attached to rape.

This second line of reasoning was adopted by some of the judges, one of whom asked (rhetorically) whether the 'lawful and marital act' and 'adultery' were not 'wholly different in their moral nature' before determining that the act permitted could not be considered the 'real act' which occurred.[16] Importantly,

---

[9] In England; in Scotland, rape was a capital crime until 1887 (Farmer, *Making the Modern Criminal Law*, p. 274).

[10] For an overview, see Wiener, *Men of Blood*, ch. 3 and Farmer, *Making the Modern Criminal Law*, ch. 9. The cases of *Camplin* (1845) 169 ER 163 and *Fletcher* (1859) 8 Cox CC 131 are often singled out as significant to this shift, and the latter of these was described as adopting the Scottish and American position regarding rape insofar as it was acknowledged in these jurisdictions that *in some circumstances*, such as where the victim was young or incapable of exercising her will, the crime of rape would be committed by having sexual intercourse without consent ('English Cases' (1859) 3(3) *Journal of Jurisprudence* 340–344). On this point regarding Scots law, see Chalmers, 'How (Not) to Reform the Law of Rape'. For an overview of changes in the relationship between violence and non-consent in France during the nineteenth century, see Vigarello, *A History of Rape*.

[11] (1884) 15 Cox CC 579.   [12] (1877) QBD 410.   [13] *R* v. *Dee* (1884) at 581–582.

[14] Ibid. at 583.   [15] Ibid. at 583–584.

[16] May, CJ at 587. See also Murphy, J's view that 'she did not consent to adultery, and this was the act the accused committed' (at 599).

this position was distinguished from an alternative way of describing what had happened, namely that the woman had consented to sexual intercourse but that her consent should not be operative because of the existence of fraud.[17] The latter position was more radical in its potential consequences, insofar as it might allow any kind of fraud to undermine otherwise valid consent to sex. It also missed the way that it was plausible at this time to assert an ontological difference between lawful (moral) and unlawful (immoral) sex, which turned on the existence of a valid marriage.[18]

To make clear that this kind of conduct constituted rape, including in Scotland where the highest criminal court had held the opposite,[19] a provision was added to the Criminal Law Amendment Act 1885, discussed in Chapter 6, which stated that '[w]hereas doubts have been entertained whether a man who induces a married woman to permit him to have connexion with her by personating her husband is or is not guilty of rape, it is hereby enacted and declared that every such offender shall be deemed to be guilty of rape';[20] this was essentially replicated in subsequent legislation.[21] It is worth noticing that this provision, and those that followed it, refer to (im)personation, which might imply an active misrepresentation as to one's identity. By contrast, the earlier cases featured men who entered women's beds and began penetrating their vaginas sexually – an act by which they were deemed to have impliedly adopted the husband's role.[22] Because of this, the conduct of the men in these early cases is better described as failing to disclose their identity or taking advantage of the women's assumptions about who they were. The later legislation also included a causation requirement, stipulating that the impersonation must have induced the woman to have sex, but it was silent as to intention to deceive or knowledge

---

[17] Palles, PB at 594, pointing out the difference.
[18] See also Chapter 6. Palles, CB explicitly tied this view to 'Christian wisdom' and the 'divine institution of marriage' (at 594).
[19] *William Fraser* (1847) Ark 280, discussed in Chapter 6. The provision was used at least once in a case involving the impersonation of a husband who was thought to be deceased (*HM Advocate* v. *Montgomery* 1926 JC 2); an earlier case involving sex with someone mistakenly believed to be the woman's husband does not make clear on what basis the prosecution proceeded (see *Robert Thomson*, 1907 (JC26/1907/133; AD15/07/16)).
[20] S. 4. The addition of this provision was apparently made at the proposal of Mr Thomasson, MP and criticised by his colleague Mr Hopwood, MP, as a clumsy and haphazard way of reforming the law (Hansard, HL Deb., vol. 300, col. 1479, 7 August 1885).
[21] Sexual Offences Act 1956, s. 1(2), retained after the amendment of this Act in 1994 (this did not apply to any sexual acts other than vaginal or anal intercourse (see Law Commission, *Consent in the Criminal Law*, Paragraph 6.4)); Sexual Offences (Scotland) Act 1976, s. 2(2); Criminal Law (Consolidation) (Scotland) Act 1995, s. 7(3). In 1976, Robin Cook had expressed scepticism over the continued relevance of the provision, suggesting that the women of Scotland had more pressing worries than the man next door impersonating their husband in order to fraudulently obtain sexual intercourse, calling this a 'Victorian sex fantasy' (Hansard, HC Deb., vol. 918, cols. 136–155, 25 October 1976).
[22] This point was recognised by Lord Deas in the Scottish case of *HM Advocate* v. *Charles Sweenie* (1858) 3 Irvine 109 at 150–151.

of the mistake (though both or either of these might be implied by the act of impersonation).²³

The possibility that impersonations or mistakes as to identity beyond those involving husbands might ground a charge of rape was a live issue from the very beginning of this line of legal development, as illustrated by the prosecution in 1828 of a man who allegedly had sex with a woman who was living in a state of concubinage and mistakenly believed that the prisoner was the man with whom she was living (her 'paramour'). At this time, however, the more restrictive definition of rape still prevailed and, at least as importantly, the desire to classify sex while engaging in impersonation as rape extended only to cases involving married women who had been deceived into thinking they were having sex with their husbands.²⁴ This was entirely predictable, based on both the ontological distinction between 'moral' and 'immoral' sex described earlier and the concern, demonstrated in Chapters 2–6, that legal responses to inducing intimacy should protect and support only those who sought to engage in the former.

By the 1970s when the issue arose again, however, this position began to appear untenable. At this time, a domestic servant was prosecuted for the rape of his employer on the basis that he had begun to have sex with her while she had mistaken him for her 'de facto husband'.²⁵ Though the applicable law (the Queensland Criminal Code) listed only one form of qualifying impersonation – husband impersonation – it specified that false and fraudulent misrepresentations as to the nature of the act would vitiate sexual consent. The prosecution therefore relied on comments made in earlier decisions to the effect that sexual acts comprised their physical character *and* the identity of the man involved to argue that impersonation in these circumstances ought to be considered rape.²⁶ What is significant about this development is that although

---

²³ An express misrepresentation suggests both intention to induce reliance and knowledge/belief as to the falsity of the representation; see Paula C. Murray and Brenda J. Winslett, 'The Constitutional Right to Privacy and Emerging Tort Liability for Deceit in Interpersonal Relationships' (1986) 3 *University of Illinois Law Review* 779–836 at 805. See also *Papadimitropoulos* v. *The Queen* (1957) 98 CLR 249, which states that where mistake as to identity is not produced by fraud the possibility that the defendant was unaware of the mistake exists (at 260).

²⁴ *Jenkins* ('Assizes', *The Examiner*, 17 August 1828, p. 13). The judge, Mr Justice Park, reportedly stated that in the case of married women fraud ought to be considered equivalent to force.

²⁵ *R* v. *Bongab* [1971–72] PNGLR 433.

²⁶ The prosecution relied on the Australian case of *Papadimitropoulos* v. *The Queen* (1957), discussed in Section 7.5, but the comments derived from the 1888 case of *R* v. *Clarence*, discussed in Section 7.4, in which Wills, J stated that rape was the penetration of a woman's person without her consent, that is, 'where the woman does not intend that the sexual act shall be done upon her either at all, or, what is pretty much the same thing, by the particular individual doing it' (at 34) and Stephen, J considered that the only frauds that vitiated sexual consent (or, as he preferred to describe them, cases where no consent existed) were 'frauds as to the nature of the act itself, or as to the identity of the person who does the act' (at 44). Similar views were in fact offered in the earlier case of *R* v. *Dee* (1884), where Palles, B described the person by whom the sexual act was to be performed as part of its essence (at 594), Lawson, J considered consent as to the person to be essential to sexual consent (at 595) and O'Brien, J stated that consent is not simply consent to the act but to the act of a particular person (at 598).

the doctrinal underpinnings of this argument extended back to the nineteenth century, the argument was only made in the later twentieth century, when attitudes towards at least some kinds of heterosexual sexual activity outside marriage became more favourable.[27] Furthermore, it was only at this time that the decision to continue to apply the law to the exclusion of unmarried women in long-term sexual relationships could be described as potentially 'too restricted'.[28] Contemporaneous academic critiques also complained about this restriction on the range of qualifying impersonations, highlighting the lesser protection unmarried women received vis-à-vis their married counterparts.[29]

Yet even these critiques implied that some limitation on qualifying impersonations should exist. For example, it was suggested that the act of climbing into bed with a woman only constituted fraud (and should preclude the possibility of any honest belief in her consent) because doing so entailed holding oneself out to be a person with whom the woman shared considerable intimacy,[30] such as a friend or lover.[31] In line with this view, when the law did eventually expand to incorporate more forms of impersonation it was in the context of impersonating a boyfriend, and the justification offered was that, in 1994, long term, live-in lovers should be treated the same as husbands.[32] Even twenty years later, when the law of sexual offences was reformed and explicitly oriented towards sexual autonomy in its positive sense – that is, the 'capacity to shape and see through one's choices'[33] – the only impersonation named explicitly was impersonating someone known personally to the complainant. In these circumstances, when the defendant intentionally induced the complainant to 'consent' to sexual activity by engaging in such an impersonation, it will conclusively be presumed that there is no consent and no reasonable belief in consent.[34]

There is no obvious reason why this restriction on qualifying impersonations was imposed,[35] especially in light of the other stipulations of the provision, specifically the need for impersonation (as opposed to the complainant's mistake),

---

[27] See Chapter 1.
[28] Frost, SPJ in *R* v. *Bongab*, referring to his own judgment in that case but defending it on the ground of legal certainty.
[29] Jocelynne A. Scutt, 'Fraudulent Impersonation and Consent in Rape' (1975) 9(1) *The University of Queensland Law Journal* 59–65; Jocelynne A. Scutt, 'A Disturbing Case of Consent in Rape' (1976) 40(3) *The Journal of Criminal Law* 206–208 and 'A Disturbing Case of Consent in Rape (Continued)' (1976) 40(4) *The Journal of Criminal Law* 271–274.
[30] Scutt, 'Fraudulent Impersonation' at 62.
[31] Ibid. at 63; Scutt, 'Disturbing Case (Continued)' at 273. Similarly, in 1982, it was argued that impersonating fiancés and cohabitees should qualify but that a line should be drawn here; see Jennifer Temkin, 'Towards a Modern Law of Rape' (1982) 45(4) *Modern Law Review* 399–419 at 406.
[32] *R* v. *Elbekkay* (1994).
[33] Nicola Lacey, 'Beset by Boundaries: The Home Office Review of Sex Offences' [2001] *Criminal Law Review* 3–14 at 11.
[34] Sexual Offences Act 2003, s. 76(2)(b). The only other circumstance like this involving deception relates to the nature or purpose of the act and is discussed in Section 7.3.
[35] Temkin, 'A New Law of Sexual Offences for Scotland' at 52.

intention and causation, all of which restrict the scope of the law. The parliamentary record merely confirms that the reform would slightly expand the scope of the law but without explaining why the restriction was adopted.[36] Similarly, reform documents pertaining to analogous Scottish legislation[37] explain that the wrong at which the Act is aimed is not simply fraud as to the person with whom complainer is having sex but, rather, being led to believe that one is having sex with someone one knows (but not necessarily someone with whom one is in a relationship).[38] Why this was the targeted wrong is not explained and it is not even clear who falls into the category of persons 'known personally', a problem that is particularly pronounced when it is now possible to get to know someone (personally?) via digitally mediated communication alone.[39]

A further question that has arisen in the contemporary era, with its heightened concern for what I described in Chapter 1 as thin sexual autonomy, is whether it is appropriate for the law to presume that the identity of one's partner has any particular importance in the decision of whether to engage in sexual conduct. At the time the law was reformed, those involved felt confident that 'there can be no doubt in anyone's mind that the activity was non-consensual' when the relevant impersonation occurred.[40] But just five years later, the question was asked of whether the identity of one's partner might *not* be a necessary condition of sexual consent.[41] This point could be made about any legal presumption, at least of a conclusive kind, relating to deception in this context[42] and reflects a highly individualised approach to conceptualising sexual consent.

Assuming that a limit to the range of qualifying impersonations should exist, one argument that has been made in favour of drawing the line at those known personally is that it avoids the challenge of distinguishing identity from attributes.[43] Even assuming it has this benefit, it has the additional

---

[36] Hansard, HL Deb., vol. 646, cols. 1130–1131, 31 March 2003 (Lord Falconer).
[37] Sexual Offences (Scotland) Act 2009, s. 13(2)(e). This section provides that there is no consent when the complainer agrees or submits to sexual conduct because the accused induces this agreement or submission by impersonating someone known personally to the complainer. The Act is silent as to the relationship between this provision and *mens rea* as to consent.
[38] Scottish Law Commission, *Report on Rape and Other Sexual Offences* (Edinburgh: The Stationery Office, 2007), Paragraph 2.76.
[39] David Ormerod and Karl Laird, *Smith, Hogan, and Ormerod's Criminal Law*, 16th ed. (Oxford: Oxford University Press, 2021), p. 815.
[40] Hansard, HL Deb., vol. 646, cols. 1130–1131, 31 March 2003 (Lord Falconer). See also the claim that it is clear that there is no consent to the sexual intercourse in these circumstances (Scottish Law Commission, *Report on Rape*, Paragraph 2.30). In the early 1990s, the Law Commission had a similar view; see Law Commission, *Consent and Offences against the Person*, Paragraph 26.2.
[41] Rebecca Williams, 'Deception, Mistake and Vitiation of the Victim's Consent' (2008) 124 *Law Quarterly Review* 132–159 at 135.
[42] Baroness Noakes made a comment to this effect during the debate on the Sexual Offences Act 2003, asking whether there were not cases where consent would have been given despite the deceit. She suggested that rebuttable presumptions might be preferable; see Hansard, HL Deb., vol. 646, col. 1133, 31 March 2003.
[43] Scottish Law Commission, *Report on Rape*, Paragraph 2.76. See Chapter 2 for how this problem has affected the law of nullity of marriage.

consequence of excluding cases where an individual adopts an entirely false persona, as occurred in the undercover police officer cases. This seems to be undesirable since, as counsel for the petitioner in *R (Monica)* v. *Director of Public Prosecutions* pointed out, deception this extensive prevents a person from choosing whether to have sex with 'the real person, even though the physical being remains the same'.[44] By contrast, opposing counsel maintained that the petitioner had consented to sex with the very same person she had 'known' and with whom she been in a relationship, in essence adopting the view of persons as 'bags of cells' outlined in Chapter 2.[45] Ultimately, the court upheld the decision not to prosecute the undercover officer for rape, and it appears that, to date, the only reported examples of wholesale identity deception that have been prosecuted as sex offences have also involved coercion[46] and/or an ulterior purpose.[47]

Perhaps partly motivated by the worry that wholesale identity deception inevitably collapses into deception about discrete attributes, the argument presented in *Monica* turned on the possibility of distinguishing deception about a person's qualities or attributes – such as their profession, wealth or marital status – from adopting a false persona.[48] A similar attempt to cordon off deception about attributes was made in a case decided four years earlier, *R* v. *McNally*,[49] in which it was successfully argued that deception as to gender (which is how the defendant's presenting as a boy despite being biologically female was portrayed) is unlike deception as to age or marital status. Furthermore, it was successfully argued that deception about these latter attributes could not vitiate sexual consent, with the court holding that unlike deception as to gender, which could potentially vitiate sexual consent, 'some deceptions (such as, for example, in relation to wealth) will obviously not be sufficient to vitiate consent'.[50]

The difference between these deceptions and gender deception, according to the court, is that the gender of one's partner changes the 'sexual nature' of the conduct in which they have engaged, even when this conduct is otherwise exactly as the complainant understood it to be (for example, digital vaginal penetration).[51] Again, as with the expansion of impersonation to incorporate non-marital long-term sexual partners, I would suggest that this development should be read in light of broader cultural changes that have occurred over the late modern period. As the wrongs and harms of rape have become more

---

[44] [2019] QB 1019 at 1023.   [45] Ibid. at 1029.
[46] *R* v. *Jheeta* [2007] EWCA Crim 1699; *R* v. *B* [2013] 2 Cr App R 29. See also the unreported case of *Barker* and other cases in Derry, 'Sustained Identity Deceptions' in CLRNN, *Reforming the Relationship* (2021), pp. 15–23. I consider cases involving so-called gender deception separately, later in this section.
[47] *R* v. *Devonald* [2008] EWCA Crim 527. Deception as to purpose is discussed in Section 7.3.
[48] *R (Monica)* v. *Director of Public Prosecutions* (2019) at 1024; opposing counsel made the contrary argument (at 1023).
[49] [2014] QB 593.   [50] Ibid. at Paragraph 25.   [51] Ibid. at Paragraph 26.

closely associated with sexuality and selfhood, as opposed to respectability and reputation,[52] and as sexual identity has become more clearly articulated as a facet of selfhood,[53] the idea that deception about the gender of one's sexual partner is crucial in a way that other deceptions are not makes a certain kind of sense.[54] In other words, when deception appears to target the sexual orientation of the complainant, it registers as a significant wrong and potential harm. Indeed, when *McNally* was subsequently discussed in *Monica*, both counsel for the petitioner and the court rationalised the special treatment of gender on the basis that the gender of one's sexual partner is a critical aspect of many individuals' sexual identity.[55]

It is important to acknowledge that *McNally* was decided under the general legislative definition of consent, which is agreement by choice with the freedom and capacity to make that choice,[56] and so it is not concerned with the Act's conclusive presumption about identity. It is also essential to place the effort to portray gender as affecting the nature of the sexual activity within the context of a growing tendency to consider cases of deceptive sex under this general definition of consent and the responses to this that have limited this potential use.[57] For now, it is enough to say that the challenges of maintaining the boundary between identity and attributes, and between different attributes, are significant and that the intuition that gender matters to sexual choice in a way that, say, wealth does not is not 'obvious' but is, instead, explicable only in light of sociocultural conditions.

7.3 Relationships of Trust and Authority

The other long-standing category of qualifying deceptions is those perpetrated by people whose position, often their professional position, involves considerable trust and authority. Early cases of this kind involved medical practitioners and, doctrinally, these cases followed a similar trajectory to those involving husband impersonation in that the relevant charge was initially assault and the rationale behind criminalisation was that the victim believed she was being

---

[52] Joanna Bourke, *Rape: A History from 1860 to the Present Day* (London: Virago, 2008), pp. 407–408, 425.
[53] See Chapter 1.
[54] In line with this argument, the suggestion that biological sex is as an essential part of a sexual partner's identity was raised in the 1970s (Scutt, 'A Disturbing Case' at 273). For criticism of *McNally* and decisions in the same vein, see the work of Alex Sharpe, especially *Sexual Intimacy and Gender Identity 'Fraud': Reframing the Legal and Ethical Debate* (Abingdon: Routledge, 2018).
[55] *R (Monica)* v. *Director of Public Prosecutions* (2019) at 1024, 1058.
[56] Sexual Offences Act 2003, s. 74. The general definition of consent in the Scottish legislation is 'free agreement' (Sexual Offences (Scotland) Act 2009, s. 12).
[57] See Kyle L. Murray and Tara Beattie, 'Conditional Consent and Sexual Offences: Revisiting the Sexual Offences Act 2003 after Lawrance' [2021] *Criminal Law Review* 556–574. These responses are considered in Sections 7.4 and 7.5.

7.3 Relationships of Trust and Authority

subject to one act whereas in fact she was subject to another. As such, in 1850, the court in *R v. Case*[58] held that a fourteen-year-old girl might be ignorant of the physical and moral nature, and the consequences, of the 'carnal connexion' she experienced and that she had acquiesced to this conduct solely because she was 'disarmed' by fraud. Although the prisoner had not necessarily misrepresented the mechanics of what he was doing, the girl believed, due to what he had told her, that she was receiving medical treatment that would cure her; she had no idea that what happened was done for his gratification. This mistake as to the nature and purpose of the act was described by the court as equivalent to 'total deception' on the basis that the victim had consented to one thing and the prisoner had done another; he was convicted of assault.

Following this case, the decision in *Flattery* was issued whereby it was determined that conduct similar to that in *Case* was rape. Here, the prisoner professed to give medical and surgical advice and, not intending or believing that his conduct would be of any assistance to the complainant, engaged in sexual intercourse with her for his own gratification. The woman, who was nineteen, was described as having believed, on account of the prisoner's representations, that she was undergoing an operation that would cure her. It was therefore accepted that she did not intend him to have sex with her. In holding that this conduct amounted to rape, the court emphasised that the earlier husband impersonation cases did not apply because those were instances of fraud inducing a woman to submit to sexual connection. By contrast, according to the court, *Flattery* involved consent given to a materially different act, one on which the woman had been prevented by fraud from exercising her judgement and will.[59]

Doctrinally, therefore, this legal development was facilitated by the changing conception of rape mentioned earlier and the feasibility of classifying the case as involving non-consent, rather than fraudulently induced consent. To fully appreciate why such a prosecution might occur and be met with a sympathetic reception, however, it is important to consider the wider context. From the middle of the nineteenth century, concerns about the use of chloroform to rape women began to grow,[60] and doctors were recognised as having a 'unique position of authority over bodies'.[61] More generally, in the 1850s, a doctor violating his duties by disclosing private information became the 'classic example' of a professional person engaging in unlawful breach of confidence.[62]

---

[58] (1850) 169 ER 381. The possibility that a medical man might commit assault by sexually penetrating his unwitting patient while dispensing treatment had been considered in *R v. Stanton* (1844) 174 ER 872, but the bulk of the discussion in this case concerns why this conduct was not rape or assault with intent to commit rape.

[59] Kelly, CB, Field, J and Huddleston, B highlighted the distinction from the earlier cases and Mellor, J mentioned the victim's judgment and will (at 413). Cf. the view of Stephen, discussed in Chapter 6.

[60] Bourke, *Rape: A History*, pp. 54–59; Vigarello, *A History of Rape*, p. 136.

[61] Wiener, *Men of Blood*, p. 116.   [62] Blackie, 'Unity in Diversity', section 2.3.6 (a).

Given the special position of trust and confidence doctors occupied, circumstances where medical men acted in an ungentlemanly manner were particularly shocking and particularly damaging to a profession that generally claimed considerable honour and authority.[63] Accordingly, it is not altogether surprising that the 'fraudulent devices' used by medical men to obtain sexual contact were punished as rape at this time.[64]

In fact, even if the conduct were not classified as rape, there was clearly a strong desire for a criminal law response to this kind of behaviour. In Scotland, following the decision in *William Fraser* – that sex under a mistaken belief that the man was the complainer's husband was not rape[65] – a doctor was prosecuted, in 1882, for leading a woman to believe that he was performing a surgical operation on her when he was actually engaging in sexual intercourse. Accepting that a charge of rape would unlikely succeed, the prosecutor was advised to draw up an alternative charge[66] of fraud; more specifically, of being in practice as a physician and surgeon, advising an unmarried female patient to submit, for her cure, to a surgical operation and then, knowing she submitted to the conduct solely so that an operation might be performed, feloniously leading her to believe that such an operation was occurring while instead fraudulently and deceitfully having carnal knowledge of her person by deceiving her as to the true nature of the act.[67] Letters concerning the accused's bail indicate that the professional ruin he would face if he absconded was considered a tolerably severe punishment.[68]

Medicine was not the only profession whose significance provoked anxiety about misconduct, either. Members of the clergy came under heavy criticism when they were involved in deceptive sex. For example, in 1883, a clergyman of the Church of England was given what the judge described as the maximum sentence, of seven years penal servitude, for bigamy – a crime that, as Section 7.5 shows, was regularly construed as a kind of rape by fraud – and the judge expressed his desire to pass a more severe sentence. He also expressed shock that the defendant had been able to secure another position within the Church after having previously received a sentence of penal servitude for falsely registering the death of a child, stating that in 'any other liberal profession which you might have disgraced you would have been speedily dealt with', citing law, medicine and the army as examples of these professions.[69]

Teachers similarly occupied positions of trust and authority and were prosecuted for rape or sexual assault when they falsely told those in their care, who did not appreciate that the conduct they experienced was sexual, that they were

---

[63] McLaren, *Trials of Masculinity*, pp. 90, 101. [64] Vigarello, *A History of Rape*, p. 136.
[65] See Chapter 6. [66] *Edward Pratt Evett* (1882) NRS AD14/82/41.
[67] *Edward Pratt Evett* (1882) NRS JC26/1882/316. I have paraphrased the charge.
[68] *Edward Pratt Evett* (1882) NRS AD14/82/41.
[69] Hughes ('The Charge of Bigamy against a Clergyman', *Leamington Spa Courier*, 17 November 1883, p. 3).

performing actions which would be to their (the charges') benefit.[70] Again, in this context, the conduct was classified as rape, in *R v. Williams*,[71] because the victim had not consented to the act of sexual intercourse; at the same time, however, the wrong was also described as procuring the girl's consent by misleading her as to the nature of the act. Though 'consent' here could refer to two separate things – the thing done (that is, sexual activity) or the thing the defendant purported to do (that is, creating an air passage to help with the victim's singing) – the point of principle endorsed in the judgment was that the victim had been 'persuaded to consent to what he did because she thought it was not sexual intercourse'. This formulation suggests that the girl *did* consent to the sexual activity but only because she was mistaken about its nature, rather than that she did not consent to the sexual activity at all.[72]

In between these nineteenth- and early twentieth-century cases and the reform of sexual offences in the early twenty-first century, there are few examples of prosecutions of a similar kind, possibly supporting the view that misrepresentations about the purportedly medical nature of conduct are less likely to be plausible in the later twentieth century, except when the victim is young or mentally impaired.[73] Those cases that have arisen, but which have been prosecuted as assaults or indecent assaults, have involved examinations of women's genitals that were unconnected to the reason they sought medical advice;[74] a dental practitioner failing to disclose that she had been suspended before treating patients;[75] examinations of women's breasts carried out by a man whom the women believed had medical qualifications;[76] and bogus medical experiments and treatment involving masturbation, being touched by the defendant and having sex in his presence.[77]

When the law was reformed, the legislation specified that it will conclusively be presumed that there is no consent and no reasonable belief in consent

---

[70] *Hatch* (1859) in which a reverend running a private school told young girls that he was merely checking their health and was charged with sexual assault (Wiener, *Men of Blood*, pp. 115–116) and *R v. Williams* (1923) in which a choirmaster of a church told a girl he would do her no harm and that he was making an air passage to improve her singing; he was convicted of rape.

[71] (1923).

[72] *R v. Williams* (1923) at 346. It is therefore not surprising that rape and the offence under s. 3 of the 1885 Act overlapped (see Chapter 6).

[73] James Chalmers and Fiona Leverick (eds.), *The Criminal Law of Scotland*, 4th ed. (vol. 2) (Edinburgh: W. Green & Sons, 2017), Paragraph 38.10.

[74] *Hussain v. Houston* 1995 SLT 1060, a Scottish prosecution for indecent assault (amended to become assault) in which it was held there was no consent (as opposed to consent obtained by fraud).

[75] *R v. Richardson* [1999] QB 444, involving charges of assault occasioning actual bodily harm in which the argument was rejected that this constituted fraud as to one's identity.

[76] *R v. Tabassum* [2000] 2 Cr App R 328, a prosecution for indecent assault in which the court described the women as consenting to the man touching their breasts but as having done so believing this was for medical purposes; this meant their consent was not 'true consent' – they had consented to the nature of the acts but not their quality.

[77] *R v. Green* [2002] EWCA Crim 1501, a prosecution for indecent assaults.

when the defendant intentionally deceived the complainant as to the nature or purpose of the act.[78] This provision arguably applies to a broader range of scenarios than those that have been prosecuted, theoretically extending to procreation,[79] the expression of love[80] or any other deception that might be described as involving the purpose of the sexual activity. Possibly as a consequence of this, a question that has arisen, which appears to be a novelty, is how to determine whose purpose matters when the purposes of the defendant and complainant differ, in light of the possibility that a sexual act may have more than one purpose.[81] In this context, it might also make sense to ask whether an act can have a purpose distinct from the purpose of the actor.[82] These seem to be questions that might be attributed to more pluralist and individualised conceptions of sexual activity and perhaps of action more generally.

Despite these changes, it seems that the legislation was supposed to capture an array of deceptions similar to those that arose prior to the law's reform.[83] This is suggested by statements in the House of Lords that the conclusive presumptions were based on existing statute and case law and that it was right that new legislation should reflect this position.[84] In a similar way, though the Scottish parliamentary debates reveal some worry that the equivalent provision[85] might apply very broadly, potentially to include deception as to age,[86] the response given was that the section was intended to capture cases of spurious medical exams, conducted for the gratification of the examiner under the pretence that the purpose was medical.[87] This mirrors developments elsewhere, where deceptive sex carried out by those in positions of authority, including but not limited to doctors, continues to be treated as rape or sexual assault.[88]

---

[78] Sexual Offences Act 2003, s. 76(2)(a). [79] Ormerod and Laird, *Smith and Hogan*, p. 815.
[80] For a response to this possible application of s. 76 of the 2003 Act, see Hyman Gross, 'Rape, Moralism, and Human Rights' [2007] *Criminal Law Review* 220–227.
[81] Ormerod and Laird, *Smith and Hogan*, p. 813; Chalmers and Leverick (eds.), *Criminal Law*, Paragraph 38.10.
[82] Queensland Law Reform Commission, *Review of Consent Laws and the Excuse of Mistake of Fact* (2020), Paragraph 6.65.
[83] Such cases might not involve people who are medically qualified or are pretending to be; for example, *Sbano* (2007), which involved a pilot telling a woman that he was administering expensive medical treatment to cure herpes to her via anal sex ('Pilot "Raped Woman in Herpes Treatment Con"', Press Association Regional Newswire – London, 24 April 2007; 'Rape Case against Pilot Collapses', Press Association Regional Newswire – London, 1 May 2007).
[84] Hansard, HL Deb., vol. 649, col. 672, 17 June 2003 (Baroness Scotland).
[85] S. 13(2)(d) of the Sexual Offences (Scotland) Act 2009 provides that there is no consent when the complainer agrees or submits to the conduct because they are mistaken, as a result of deception by the accused, as to the nature or purpose of the conduct.
[86] A worry expressed by Ian Duguid QC (advocate), building on a suggestion from the Faculty of Advocates that a promise to marry might be captured by the provision (Scottish Parliament Official Report, Justice Committee, 18 November 2008).
[87] Scottish Parliament Official Report, Justice Committee, 18 November 2008 (Bill McVicar, the convenor of the criminal law committee of the Law Society of Scotland, passing on what he reported having been told by the team who worked on the Bill).
[88] John F. Decker and Peter G. Baroni, '"No" Still Means "Yes": The Failure of the "Non-Consent" Reform Movement in American Rape and Sexual Assault Law' (2011) 101(4) *The*

In practice, the purpose provision has been quite narrowly construed[89] with the effect that the distinction between the purpose and nature of the act has weakened and the former has at least partially collapsed into the latter.[90] This strict construction can partly be explained by the drastic effects of the conclusive presumptions, which effectively remove from the defendant their only line of defence.[91] But another motivation for – or at least another effect of – taking a narrow view of 'purpose' is the exclusion of certain categories of deception from potential punishment (at least under the conclusive presumption), namely false promises to pay sex workers and misrepresentations or mistakes about marital status.[92] As Sections 7.4 and 7.5 show, the exclusion of these deceptions pre-dates the 2003 Act by a long time, so explaining the narrow interpretation of the 'nature or purpose' provision requires more work than merely pointing to the draconian operation of the legislation. Finally, the narrow interpretation of the 'nature or purpose' provision has arguably contributed towards a greater reliance on the general consent provision,[93] and, as Sections 7.4 and 7.5 show, the reappearance of the threat of expansive criminalisation.

7.4 Disease, Fertility and Contraception

Though now an example of the struggle over the use of the general consent provision, the criminalisation of deception as to disease status, first as a non-sexual offence against the person and then as rape, has a history that stretches back to the nineteenth century. Starting with the 1866 case of *R v. Bennett*,[94] the rule, outlined in Section 7.2, that assault could be committed by fraud because the fraud would vitiate consent was held to apply to a charge of indecent assault. Holding that a thirteen-year-old girl had consented to sexual intercourse with her VD-infected uncle, the court nevertheless found that she had not consented to connection with a diseased man. More specifically, it held that the defendant's having induced his niece to sleep with him, knowing that he was suffering from VD and failing to communicate this to her, resulting in her ignorance, and then transmitting the disease to her constituted assault committed by fraud. Just a year later, another man was convicted of assault inflicting actual bodily harm for similar conduct perpetrated against a

---

Journal of Criminal Law & Criminology 1081–1169; Falk, 'Rape by Fraud'; Jianlin Chen and Bijuan Lu, 'Rape-by-Deception in China: A Messy but Pragmatically Desirable Criminal Law' (2023) 43(2) *Columbia Journal of Gender and Law* 151–210 (discussing a range of other jurisdictions, too).

[89] At least in relation to the 2003 Act. There do not seem to be any reported cases involving the Scottish provision.
[90] Ormerod and Laird, *Smith and Hogan*, p. 812.   [91] *R v. B* (2013) (at 20), following *Jheeta*.
[92] Ormerod and Laird, *Smith and Hogan*, pp. 811–812.
[93] Karl Laird, 'Rapist or Rogue? Deception, Consent and the Sexual Offences Act 2003' [2014] *Criminal Law Review* 492–510; Ormerod and Laird, *Smith and Hogan*, pp. 810–811.
[94] (1866) 176 ER 925.

twelve-year-old girl. Though the girl might have consented to the intercourse (at least in the eyes of the law), she was ignorant that the prisoner was diseased when he was not so ignorant, and it was accepted that she would not have consented had she known the truth; thus, her consent was considered to have been procured by fraud making it 'no consent at all'.[95]

Yet when a similar line of argument was pursued in a civil case, *Hegarty* v. *Shine*,[96] eleven years later, the plaintiff was denied a remedy for assault. The reason offered for this decision was that the rule that consent could be vitiated by fraud (at least in assault cases) could only apply to concealing facts if the relationship between the two parties gave rise to a duty of disclosure. Crucially, in this case the plaintiff was an unmarried woman suing a man with whom she was in a sexual relationship, who had paid her the first time they had sex. For the judges, the immorality of this relationship was the main stumbling block to providing a remedy. While one of them simply stated that to do so would be against policy, morality and decency,[97] the other two held that no duty of disclosure could exist in an immoral relationship because courts of justice were not there to provide remedies for the consequences (in this case, the transmission of syphilis) of immoral acts.[98] This left open the possibility that 'active misrepresentation' might be treated differently.[99]

A fear of lending support to immoral practices is also evident in the leading case of *R* v. *Clarence*, decided in 1888.[100] The crimes of which the prisoner was convicted were unlawfully and maliciously inflicting grievous bodily harm (section 20 of the Offences Against the Person Act 1861) and assault occasioning actual bodily harm (section 47 of the same Act). One of the questions at the core of the case, however, was whether the prisoner's wife submitting to the sexual intercourse which led to her becoming infected with gonorrhoea constituted consent in the eyes of the law, given that the prisoner knew he was suffering from the disease and his wife did not (and would not have submitted if she knew). The repercussions of the decision therefore extended beyond these crimes to reach the offence of rape, which, as noted earlier, had by this time come to be defined around a lack of consent.

In overturning the convictions, the court was moved by several considerations, including the danger that upholding them led logically to criminalising deceptions which affected women who acted in a sexually immoral manner. As Chapter 6 showed, the worry that prostitutes might be protected by the criminal law from deceptive conduct contributed towards the narrowing of otherwise potentially relevant offences of procuring sex, so it is not surprising to find in *Clarence* the view that knowingly giving bad money to a prostitute to procure her sexual consent would not support the conclusion that she did

---

[95] *R* v. *Sinclair* (1867) 13 Cox CC 28.   [96] (1878) 14 Cox CC 145.
[97] Deasy, LJA at 152.   [98] Ball, C and Palles, CB. Only Ball, C referred to the role of courts.
[99] Palles, CB at 150.   [100] (1888) 22 QBD 23.

7.4 Disease, Fertility and Contraception

not consent to that sex.[101] Although deception pertaining to sex work is not directly within the scope of this book, it is worth noting that there remains ambivalence about regarding non-payment by clients as rape, even when it is clear that they never intended to pay.[102] In recent discussions about how the law ought to respond to this conduct the distinction alluded to in Chapter 1, between commercial sex and sex that is perceived to have an affective dimension, appears to carry some weight; as such, deception involving payment has been considered closer to economic fraud.[103] Some sex workers are against regarding deception about payment as rape due to the reality that the criminal justice system generally does not respond well to sex workers and because this conduct is distinct from the physically violent rapes that sex workers unfortunately often suffer.[104]

Returning to *Clarence*, even deceptions that were subject to criminal or civil penalties and whose sanction supported the system of morality that underpinned the law at this time, such as bigamy or false promises of marriage, were considered unsuitable candidates for criminalisation as either assault or rape. The potential fit with these crimes was clear enough, though. In bigamy cases involving deception of the 'wife', for example, sexual intercourse followed either a false representation that the man was capable of marriage or suppression of the fact that he was incapable, and the results were extremely damaging: the unwitting woman was turned into a concubine, her status as a virgin was destroyed and the rights and title of wife were withheld from her.[105] Yet defining bigamy or sex under a false promise of marriage as assault or rape was considered not only inaccurate as a matter of law, partly because it had never been done before[106] but also as a distortion of those terms and a dangerous attempt to use the criminal law to teach morals.[107]

---

[101] Ibid. at 28 (Wills, J); at 43 (Stephen, J).
[102] In *R v. Linekar* (1995), the court held this was not rape on the basis of existing authorities. Other cases involving inducements that were falsely held out have been prosecuted as sexual assaults, potentially on the basis that the purpose of the conduct was false, for example, *R v. Piper* [2007] EWCA Crim 2151 (where the defendant told the complainant he was measuring her to check her modelling potential, but his true purpose was sexual gratification) cf. *R v. M* [2001] EWCA Crim 1563 (where a bogus film director duped women into taking part in improvisations involving sexual conduct, but the deception was characterised as relevant only to luring the women to the location of the sexualised conduct, not to the conduct itself).
[103] Queensland Law Reform Commission, *Review of Consent Laws*, Paragraphs 6.84, 6.92.
[104] Michael McGowan and Christopher Knaus, '"It Absolutely Should Be Seen as Rape" When Sex Workers Are Conned', *The Guardian*, 12 October 2018. Cf. Amber Schultz, 'No Payment, No Consent: Sex Worker Advocacy Groups Say Fraud and Rape Is on the Rise', *Crikey*, 5 August 2020, in which a sex worker says non-payment is rape though of a different kind to women who are 'attacked'.
[105] *R v. Clarence* (1888) at 30 (Wills, J). Bigamy is discussed in Section 7.5.
[106] A point also noted in *Hegarty v. Shine* (1878) (Deasy, LJA at 152).
[107] *R v. Clarence* (1888) at 33–34 (Wills, J). See also the suggestion that the minority judges might have been tempted to give a 'new and strained' 'dangerous' interpretation to the law on account of their indignation at a grave moral offence ('Notes' (1889) 5 *Law Quarterly Review* 218–229 at 219).

These complaints were even more obvious in respect of seduction[108] or 'misrepresentation of a thousand kinds in respect of which it has never yet occurred to any one [sic] to suggest that intercourse so procured was an assault or a rape'.[109] On top of this, one of the temporal issues that affected the law of seduction – that is, whether the wrong could occur more than once[110] – presented even greater challenges in the context of rape or assault. If the wrong of these crimes was either having sex with no consent or obtaining sexual consent by fraud (as opposed to leading someone off the 'right path', which, I suggest, was the wrong of seduction), then every time sex occurred under the relevant mistaken belief or as a result of the relevant fraud a new crime would be committed.[111] Across the course of a void marriage or a relationship predicated on a false promise of marriage, potentially countless offences could therefore be committed.

Beyond its outcome, *Clarence* is significant from a doctrinal perspective because it shows how there were different ways of framing the question of whether the prisoner's wife had consented. One way was to ask whether her consent had been obtained by fraud and so did not amount to consent in law; another was to ask whether sex with a diseased man and sex with a healthy man were acts so essentially different that submission to the former without knowledge of the truth was no consent at all; a third was to ask whether the conduct, which was cruelty that could found a judicial separation, fell outside the consent that was implied by the marital relation.[112] Two of the judges supported the 'different acts' formulation, with one noting that fraud might vitiate consent when it related to the act or the identity of the perpetrator, but preferring to see these as instances of no consent to the act done.[113] By contrast, a judge in the minority, Field J, preferred the third option, suggesting that the prisoner's wife had consented to the act of intercourse and so to 'all natural and ordinary attendant circumstances or consequences of the act' and also those that were 'reasonably within her knowledge and contemplation'.[114] He reasoned that her consent was in fact given on the implied condition that, to her knowledge, the intercourse was of a kind to which she was 'bound' (by marriage) to consent, namely, 'natural and healthy'.[115] In light of this, he thought there was a duty on the prisoner to have communicated his condition to his wife before soliciting intercourse and that concealment in the face of such a duty amounted to a false representation. This opinion was essentially the mirror image of the

---

[108] Ibid. at 32 (Wills, J); at 43 (Stephen, J).
[109] Ibid. at 29 (Wills, J). See also the question 'why should not any other deceit have the same effect [of transforming the conduct into assault]?' in *Hegarty v. Shine* (1878) (Ball, C at 147).
[110] See Chapter 5.
[111] In *Hegarty v. Shine* (1878) Ball, C asked whether 'every separate act of intercourse' would be an assault in the context of a woman living with a man under a distinct and reiterated promise of marriage that was neither fulfilled nor intended to be fulfilled (at 147).
[112] *R v. Clarence* (1888) at 27 (Wills, J). [113] Wills, J (at 27) and Stephen, J (at 44), respectively.
[114] At 58. [115] At 59.

decision in *Hegarty*. Here, a 'legitimate' relationship was considered to give rise to a duty of disclosure whose parameters were set by objectively determined implied conditions.

Fast forwarding more than one hundred years to a case with clear parallels, *R* v. *Dica*,[116] the appellant was convicted of two counts of inflicting grievous bodily harm (section 20 of the 1861 Act) for recklessly transmitting HIV to two women through unprotected sex, knowing that he was infected and without disclosing this fact to them. On appeal, the court held that it was possible to convict on this basis, overruling *Clarence* in that respect,[117] and it offered important remarks on the relationship between concealed information and meaningful consent. Taking a similar position to Field J, the court essentially held that convention determined what the women had consented to. More specifically, it suggested that in long-term relationships if a person concealed their infection, then their partner would have no reason to think they were risking infection; in these circumstances, they did not consent to the risk of transmission.[118] The following year, in another similar case, *R* v. *Konzani*, the court held that that 'on any view, the concealment of this fact [that the appellant was infected with HIV] from her [the complainant] almost inevitably means that she is deceived.'[119] Importantly, this comment confirms that 'deceived' does not necessarily mean mistaken, that is, thinking that one's sexual partner is not infected. The court instead described the women's consent as not being properly informed, holding that it is impossible to give informed consent to something of which one is ignorant.[120] Following this line of thinking, the criminal law might impose a duty to disclose facts which the other person may not have considered, as opposed to a duty merely to correct a mistaken belief, and both of these ways of imposing liability are different from criminalising only so-called active deceptions.

Of course, these cases all involved charges of non-sexual offences against the person. Yet similar logic had been applied to sexual consent by the Law Commission in 1995 when they floated the idea that deceptions beyond the traditional categories (that is, nature of the act and identity of the perpetrator) might have an effect on consent. Crucially, they asked whether deception perpetrated by non-disclosure of 'clearly material facts' about which the other

---

[116] [2004] QB 1257.
[117] It is worth noting that this took place against a general development in the meaning of infliction whereby it was held to require neither an assault nor direct or indirect violence (*R* v. *Dica* (2004) at 1263–1266).
[118] At Paragraph 39. The court also held that *informed* consent to the risk of transmission might provide a defence to the charges.
[119] *R* v. *Konzani* [2005] 2 Cr App R 14 at Paragraph 42.
[120] Ibid. The court also held that concealment is incongruous with an honest belief in consent (at Paragraph 42) though it suggested it might be possible for someone to give informed consent despite their partner acting recklessly and concealing their condition if, for example, they knew the defendant when they were in hospital; at the very least, this might suggest an honest belief in consent (at Paragraph 44).

party was not necessarily mistaken but in respect of which they might have been operating under an unconscious assumption should have such an effect, suggesting that having HIV was the strongest contender but wondering if other matters, including infection with other diseases, should too.[121] They were not necessarily committed to the idea that breaching a duty of disclosure of this kind should amount to rape (by virtue of invalidating sexual consent), leaving open the possibility that it might instead generate liability for an offence of doing an act with consent obtained in this manner which would be an offence if done without consent, or for inducing another, by failing to disclose a material fact, to perform the relevant acts.[122]

Yet over time the possibility that a person who fails to disclose their HIV-positive status might be at risk of prosecution for a non-consensual sex offence has arisen. In 2006, a trial judge held that failure to disclose HIV status would be relevant to the question of whether the defendant's sexual partner had consented, under the general consent provision of the 2003 Act, to the sex in which they had engaged, reasoning that the legislation required a person to be in possession of 'all relevant facts', which included the prospect of sexual transmission of HIV.[123] This decision was overturned due to the court following the earlier decisions relating to the 1861 Act, which held that the conduct did not vitiate sexual consent, and its view that the 2003 Act had not changed this legal position.[124] Nevertheless, since then it has been held that this decision left open the possibility that active deception as to one's HIV-positive status might vitiate consent,[125] and the relevance of the distinction between active deception and non-disclosure has been rejected more generally.[126] Again, I would suggest that this shift is not altogether surprising; if autonomy – or even sexual autonomy – is the dominant interest the law seeks to protect, as the most recent legal reforms imply,[127] then the early post-2003

---

[121] Law Commission, *Consent in the Criminal Law*, Paragraphs 6.29–6.31. There are parallels with gender here insofar as where gender, or gender identity, deception is alleged the deception is liable to be based on an assumption on the part of the complainant; see Gavin A. Doig, 'Deception as to Gender Vitiates Consent' (2013) 77(6) *The Journal of Criminal Law* 464–468.

[122] Law Commission, *Consent in the Criminal Law*, Paragraph 6.32.

[123] *R v. B* [2007] 1 WLR 1567 at Paragraph 8. The Scottish Law Commission thought that deception about being free from HIV would fall under their proposed general definition of consent (Scottish Law Commission, *Report on Rape*, Paragraph 2.74).

[124] The court followed *R v. Dica* (2004) (Paragraphs 14–17). The court also supported the Law Commission's earlier observations that important issues of public health and social policy were involved and that these needed to be debated (Paragraphs 18–20).

[125] *R v. McNally* (2014) at Paragraph 24, recognised in *R v. Lawrance* [2020] 1 WLR 5025 at Paragraph 40. In Canada, non-disclosure of HIV-positive status has been held to invalidate sexual consent when there is a realistic possibility of transmission; see Kyle Kirkup, 'Law's Sexual Infections' (2023) 46(2) *Dalhousie Law Journal* at 16.

[126] *R v. Lawrance* (2020) at Paragraph 41. For academic work arguing that the distinction is hard to sustain in practice and the difference in culpability is less clear than in other contexts, see Sharpe, 'Expanding Liability for Sexual Fraud'.

[127] Scottish Law Commission, *Report on Rape*, Paragraphs 1.25–1.27; Home Office, *Setting the Boundaries*, Paragraphs 2.1.1, 2.7.2.

Act judgments decisions look troubling because they fail to protect informed sexual decision-making.[128]

In more recent years, it has been decided that certain deceptions about the use of condoms, other contraceptive practices and fertility status can found a conviction for rape. Again, culturally speaking, this is not altogether surprising due to the increased importance of sexual autonomy but also growing awareness about so-called stealthing[129] – the removal, non-use of, or tampering with a condom without the other person's knowledge or consent.[130] The case that ushered in these developments was *Assange* v. *Sweden*,[131] in which it was alleged that Wikileaks founder Julian Assange had ignored a woman's express desire that he should wear a condom during sex. Reflecting the multitude of ways such behaviour can be described – a feature of this area of law across its history – the court held that it was open to a jury to conclude that there was no consent under the general definition in the 2003 Act. One way to describe this finding is that the woman had consented to sex with a condom and then he had not worn a condom, or removed or damaged it, without her consent. Something different to what was agreed had therefore occurred. The court also accepted that the alleged conduct could be described as deceptive, but it rejected the idea that it constituted deception as to the nature or purpose of the act, though this is clearly one way the deception could be characterised.[132] It took this view due to the strict construal of the conclusive presumption about deception as to the nature or purpose of the act, outlined earlier,[133] but another reason to reject a 'different acts' interpretation is the considerable complexity of determining precisely where one act ends and another begins: would sex with an expired condom be a different act to sex with one within date, for example?[134]

---

[128] Clark Hobson and José Miola, 'Should We Criminalise a Deliberate Failure to Obtain Properly Informed Consent?' (2021) 21(4) *Medical Law International* 369–392. Cf. Jonathan Rogers, who tries to distinguish sexual autonomy from concerns about pregnancy or sexual health (see 'The Effect of "Deception" in the Sexual Offences Act 2003' (2013) 4 *Archbold Review* 7–9).

[129] An article that drew considerable attention to the phenomenon is Alexandra Brodsky, '"Rape-Adjacent": Imagining Legal Responses to Nonconsensual Condom Removal' (2017) 32(2) *Columbia Journal of Gender and Law* 183–210.

[130] Benita Kolovos, 'Affirmative Consent and "Stealthing" Laws to be Introduced to Victorian Parliament', *The Guardian*, 3 August 2022.

[131] 2001 WL 5077784.

[132] This would depend on seeing the 'something different to what was agreed' as a different *act* rather than, say, the same act but performed in a different way or the same act but under different circumstances. An example of following this approach is the New South Wales Law Reform Committee's recommendation that the Crimes Act 1900 make clear that consent to a particular sexual activity does not imply consent to another and that this applies to sex with and without a condom (see New South Wales Law Reform Commission, *Consent in Relation to Sexual Offences Report* (2020), Paragraphs 5.60–5.81). In Scotland, there has been one conviction for rape by 'stealthing', but it is not clear how the 2009 Act was applied (Annie Brown, 'Former Brad Pitt Body Double Is the First in Scotland to Be Convicted of Rape by "Stealthing"', *Daily Record*, 14 May 2023).

[133] *Assange* v. *Sweden* (2001) at Paragraph 85.

[134] An example mentioned alongside others in the Canadian case of *R* v. *Kirkpatrick* 2022 SCC 33 (at Paragraph 275).

The challenges involved in distinguishing discrete acts and the different ways of conceptualising the issue at stake have shown up cases involving other forms of contraception and fertility status, too.[135] In *R (F)* v. *Director of Public Prosecutions*,[136] the claimant alleged that she had agreed to vaginal sexual intercourse on the basis that her husband would withdraw his penis before ejaculation and that he had deliberately ejaculated inside her. It was argued on her behalf that this constituted deception as to the nature of the act, and thus that the relevant conclusive presumption in the 2003 Act should apply, but it was also argued that he went back on their agreement just before ejaculating.[137] These arguments show the different ways it is possible to describe what happened. There are at least two ways of identifying the wrong – going beyond the scope of what was agreed or deceiving the claimant into thinking he was doing, or would do, what was agreed – and various ways of describing the distinction between what was agreed and what happened – different acts or the same act done in a different way under different circumstances and/or with different potential consequences. The arguments also demonstrate the incomplete overlap that exists between giving a false promise and failing to adhere to a promise, as discussed in Chapters 3 and 5; the claimant's position was that it did not matter what he intended when he penetrated her (and therefore, presumably, whether he misrepresented or failed to disclose his true intentions) and that what mattered was that he went beyond what they had agreed.

Despite this, the court analysed the case as involving deception as to intention, following *Assange* in holding that the conclusive presumption regarding deception as to the nature of the act did not apply.[138] Based on the evidence, the court held that it was plausible to conclude that the claimant's 'consent' to sexual penetration was based on the clear understanding that her husband would not ejaculate inside her vagina; that she had believed that he intended and agreed to withdraw his penis before ejaculation; and that he knew and understood that this was the only basis on which she was prepared to have sex with him. The court also held that the context of their relationship, which revealed his sexual dominance and her unenthusiastic acquiescence to his 'demands', as well as his conduct towards her after the alleged event (which included apologising for 'raping' her),[139] suggested that he had intended that this instance of sexual intercourse would end with him ejaculating in her vagina either from the outset or once penetration began. Importantly, the evidence suggested that he did not disclose this intention to her, knowing that she would never have 'consented' if she knew the truth.[140]

---

[135] Apart from the cases discussed later in this chapter, a man has been convicted of rape for deliberately poking holes in a condom when his sexual partner (who only discovered the holes after sex had occurred) had made plain she did not want the sex to lead to a child. The reporting does not make the legal basis of the decision clear ('Worcester Man Who Raped Woman by Puncturing a Hole in Condom Is Jailed', *Worcester News*, 3 October 2020).
[136] [2014] QB 581. [137] At 583. [138] At Paragraph 23.
[139] At Paragraph 18. [140] At Paragraph 25.

7.4 Disease, Fertility and Contraception

The court described this conduct as 'deliberately ignor[ing] the basis of her consent to penetration' and held that, in law, it would mean that the claimant was deprived of the choice required by the 2003 Act's general definition of consent such that her 'consent was negated'.[141] I would suggest that this conclusion is consistent both with the idea that consent did not exist because the claimant's husband had knowingly breached the parameters of what they had agreed – or, put differently, the conditions she had set on her sexual consent – and with the idea that consent was absent (or perhaps vitiated) because he deceived her as to his intentions – intentions that related directly to an explicit condition she had placed upon her sexual consent – by failing to disclose them. Crucially, in *both* these situations, it would seem reasonable to say that the claimant was deprived of the choice of whether to have the sex to which she had 'consented', but it may be that considering the conduct as deception captures something significant about the wrong of stealthing.[142]

Finally, a controversial decision issued in 2020, *R v. Lawrance*,[143] involved a complainant who alleged that the defendant had assured her he had undergone a vasectomy; that she had agreed to unprotected sex on that basis; that the next morning the defendant admitted he had lied to her; and that the result had been that she became pregnant and had a termination. In this case, the court applied a test established in *Monica* – of whether the deception is closely connected the performance of the act[144] – to conclude that a lie about fertility was not sufficiently connected. According to the court, unlike deceptions about whether ejaculate would enter the vagina the deception perpetrated on the complainant 'related not to the physical performance of the sexual act but to risks or consequences associated with it'.[145] As such, according to the court, she had not been deprived of the freedom to choose whether to have the sexual intercourse that occurred.[146] This decision has met with criticism both for having compounded the existing complexity and uncertainty in this area of law[147] and for the way it has further moved the law away from protecting sexual autonomy.[148]

It is also another example of the malleability of the various formulations that have arisen within the decisions and law reform efforts relating to rape by

---

[141] At Paragraphs 25–26.
[142] Queensland Law Reform Commission, *Review of Consent Laws*, Paragraph 6.135. See also Karamvir Chadha, 'Conditional Consent' (2021) 40(3) *Law and Philosophy* 335–359. Cf. Emily C. R. Tilton and Jonathan Jenkins Ichikawa, 'Not What I Agreed To: Content and Consent' (2021) 132(1) *Ethics* 127–154, which suggests that focussing on the scope of consent means that 'the deception becomes inessential' (at 153).
[143] [2020] 1 WLR 5025.
[144] *R (Monica) v. Director of Public Prosecutions* (2019) 1056, 1058, adopted in *R v. Lawrance* (2020) at Paragraphs 29–35. For an argument locating the development of this test in *McNally*, see Murray and Beattie, 'Conditional Consent and Sexual Offences'.
[145] *R v. Lawrance* (2020) at Paragraph 37.
[146] Ibid. at Paragraph 38.
[147] Ormerod, 'Rape and Deception (Again)'.
[148] Murray and Beattie, 'Conditional Consent and Sexual Offences' (pointing out that law reform efforts were supposed to secure sexual autonomy).

deception. Just as we might ask why sex with a condom can potentially be seen as ontologically distinct from sex without a condom but, presumably, sex with and without procreative potential cannot be so distinguished we might ask why deceptions about some risks and consequences of sex, such as the transmission of HIV, are potentially punishable, as rape, but deception about the risk of pregnancy is not. We might also wonder why the distinction between so-called active deception and non-disclosure has been significant at some times but not others. I return to these questions from a more evaluative perspective in Chapter 8, but here I note the benefit of approaching them, from an interpretive point of view, with reference to social and cultural changes.

For example, the move towards expanding the range of qualifying deceptions can again be seen as reflecting prevailing norms, with the argument that intimate partners deserve 'an honest relationship' being cast in terms of an 'important' if under-recognised 'interest' since the 1980s[149] and of course the general move towards heightened concern for sexual autonomy. Yet providing a legal response to deception relating to procreative potential, at least when the deception implies that the potential does not exist or is extremely unlikely to materialise, might appear unattractive due to a reluctance to consider the birth of a child in a negative light.[150] More generally, the waning significance of the distinction between active deception and non-disclosure can be linked to the same points that underpin the expanding range of qualifying deceptions, namely changing expectations of transparency in relationships and a greater concern for sexual autonomy. More specifically, if sexual autonomy is what matters then *how* an information deficit or mistake comes about is arguably unimportant (though it may matter from a culpability point of view[151]). And if there are now greater expectations of transparency in intimate relationships, including but not limited to marriage, then the traditional justifications for imposing a duty of disclosure, such as the 'legitimacy' of the relationship, might seem unconvincing. Similarly, justifications such as the fact that the relevant information is within the peculiar or exclusive knowledge of the accused[152] are now perhaps less significant than the idea that casual sexual encounters come with expectations that the sex should be safe and that boundaries, explicitly communicated or implicitly agreed via conventions,[153] should be respected.[154]

---

[149] Robert A. Prentice and Paula C. Murray, 'Liability for Transmission of Herpes: Using Traditional Tort Principles to Encourage Honesty in Sexual Relationships' (1984) 11(1) *Journal of Contemporary Law* 67–103 at 74, 92, 102.

[150] In the civil law context, see Murray and Winslett, 'Deceit in Interpersonal Relationships' at 783, 794 and the paternity fraud cases in Chapter 2.

[151] It should not be assumed that non-disclosure cannot involve intention or purpose to deceive, though, as noted in Amanda Clough, 'Conditional Consent and Purposeful Deception' (2018) 82(2) *The Journal of Criminal Law* 178–190 (at 184).

[152] Prentice and Murray, 'Liability for Transmission of Herpes' at 78.

[153] Tilton and Ichikawa, 'Not What I Agreed To'.

[154] Rachel Stonehouse, 'Stealthing: "I Didn't Realise It's Rape until It Happened to Me"' *BBC News*, 27 July 2021. Cf. the view that while infection with an incurable STD might be

7.5 Marital Status

The final category of deceptions I want to discuss, briefly, is those involving marital status. The possibility that deceptions as to marital status, whether they involve falsely purporting to be single or to be married to the deceived person (whether while married to another or not), might qualify is clearly part of the overarching concern with bolstering the institution of marriage and protecting the interests of those who commit to it that prevailed for much of the modern period. And as Chapters 2–6 have shown, these interests were very clearly gendered, with women having the most to lose on account of their greater material and reputational dependency on marriage. It therefore makes sense that the potential for both bigamy and sex following a false promise of marriage to constitute rape by deception was raised in cases involving the failure to disclose disease discussed in Section 7.4.

Yet as the judges were keenly aware, this conduct had never been prosecuted as rape before, and there were practical issues that would affect such a proposal, including the problem of numerous charges of rape racking up across the duration of a single relationship. The general reluctance to expand the scope of a very serious offence no doubt also played a role. Beyond this, the law already provided various opportunities to redress this kind of behaviour, as Chapters 2–5 illustrate. In particular, the crime of bigamy provided an opportunity to punish harshly and explicitly label as rapists the men who made women think they were married to them. In Chapter 6, I mentioned that two prominent jurists, Sir James Fitzjames Stephen and Glanville Williams, held the view, in the 1870s and 1950, respectively, that when bigamy involved deception of the second 'wife' it was tantamount to rape and should receive a severe punishment. This sentiment is also evident in judicial statements and sentencing decisions from the middle of the nineteenth century through to the late twentieth century.[155] The earliest example of bigamy being described as rape by fraud I have found is a Scottish case from 1849[156] and thereafter it is described as such multiple times[157] and also as equivalent to rape.[158] In the

something about which a sexual partner should be expected to speak up this is not true of sterility or birth control other than in the context of continuing relationships where prior representations or conduct have created a particular impression (Murray and Winslett, 'Deceit in Interpersonal Relationships' at 803).

[155] On the 1940s, see Langhamer, 'Trust, Authenticity and Bigamy'.
[156] *David Hunter* ('Lamberton Toll', *Kelso Chronicle*, 27 April 1849, p. 7).
[157] *Thomas Stephenson* ('Bigamy', *Shields Daily News*, 30 October 1882, p. 3); *Hughes* (1883); *Wilson* ('"Salvationist Convicted of Bigamy"', *Dundee Evening Telegraph*, 15 February 1889, p. 3); *Arthur Hyne* ('The Trial of Arthur Hyne', *The Aberdeen Journal*, 14 February 1908, p. 6); *Harry Greenwood* ('Judge on Bigamy – Leniency in Leicester Assize Case', *Nottingham Evening Post*, 27 October 1942, p. 9); *John Thomas Rolls*, ('Airman's "Base Deception" – Bigamous Marriage at Hoole Methodist Church', *Cheshire Observer*, 4 March 1944, p. 3); *R v. Carter* (1968) 52 Cr App R 117.
[158] *William Taylor* ('Central Criminal Court', *Reynolds's Newspaper*, 11 January 1863, p. 6); *Joseph Harris* ('Extraordinary Bigamy Case', *Birmingham Mail*, 29 January 1886, p. 2); *William Day* ('Bogus Millionaire – Remarkable Career of a Bigamist', *Daily Record*, 25 April 1917, p. 6);

wake of the passing of the Criminal Law Amendment Act 1885, a time of great concern for the protection of women, one judge even commented that bigamy was sometimes worse than rape because fraud was used rather than 'mere brute violence'[159] and another asked why the prisoner should not have been indicted for rape.[160] The description of bigamy as rape by fraud or equivalent to rape also appears in parliamentary debates in the 1930s[161] and 1970s[162] and in textbooks from the early twentieth century.[163]

Yet on the few occasions where lawyers have tried to persuade a court that it is rape to have sex following bigamy or some other means of deceiving a woman into a void marriage this argument has not been accepted. In 1957, a man was convicted of rape in Victoria, Australia, for having allegedly tricked a woman who spoke no English into believing that they were lawfully married and subsequently having sex with her. Yet on appeal the High Court of Australia quashed the conviction because the woman's mistake, which the court held was the relevant issue to be considered (and not whether it was produced by fraud), did not go to the nature and character of the act. The court's reasoning was that the physical character of the act and the identity of the man formed its nature and character and that the marital status of the man was merely an inducing cause.[164] It is notable that in resisting the tendency to expand the boundaries of the crime of rape, the court rejected the ontological distinction between marital sex and fornication that had underpinned some of the reasoning in *Dee* and on which the Crown in the case before them had sought to rely. It is possible that the plausibility of a sharp distinction of this kind had come into doubt because of the way that sex within loving, but not necessarily marital, relationships had started to be regarded more positively.[165] Although, as the lawyer for the applicant argued, the distinction constituted a 'great social and moral' difference, it did not constitute an 'essential difference'.[166]

Forty years later in Scotland, where the common law essentially remained as it had been when the case of *William Fraser* was decided, a woman's attempt to obtain criminal injuries compensation for the stress and distress she suffered on learning that the 'husband' with whom she'd had sex was still married to another woman failed because the chairman of the compensation board did not believe that this constituted a crime of violence, specifically rejecting the

---

Frederick Douglas Gomm ('Bigamy Sentences – Judge's Comment to Barrow "Bus Driver"', *Lancashire Evening Post*, 18 January 1844, p. 4); Brynley George Davies ('Bigamist Gets Three Years', *Chelmsford Chronicle*, 10 February 1950, p. 12).

[159] Charles Danks ('Curious Case of Bigamy', *Birmingham Daily Post*, 4 August 1886, p. 7).
[160] Isaac Barron ('Manchester Assizes', *Manchester Times*, 29 January 1887, p. 3).
[161] Cox, 'Trying to Get a Good One', referring to a debate from 1938 (at 18).
[162] Hansard, HL Deb., vol. 380, col. 1381, 14 March 1977, during a debate about the Criminal Law Bill.
[163] Kenny, *Outlines of Criminal Law* (1909).
[164] *Papadimitropoulos* v. *The Queen* (1957) at 260–261.   [165] See Chapter 1.
[166] *Papadimitropoulos* v. *The Queen* (1957) at 250.

argument that it was rape.[167] This was in keeping with the earlier case law, but by this time it obviously seemed sufficiently inappropriate to be open to challenge. In Australia, dissatisfaction with the existing law prompted one of the states, New South Wales, to amend its law, in 1981, such that a person who 'consents' to sexual activity under a mistaken belief that they are married to their partner does not consent.[168] This constitutes a limited change, though, and I would suggest that the reticence with which any expansion in this area has been approached speaks to the tension in contemporary attitudes towards the value of sexual activity. Whereas sexual autonomy is prized highly, and therefore deception of this kind appears heinous, liberty within relationships is also cherished[169] with the consequence that treating bigamy, adultery or fornication as serious sex crimes appears inappropriate.[170] Furthermore, in an age where marriage still enjoys legal privileges but has socially and culturally lost some of its purchase, it is questionable whether this specific form of intimate relationship should be afforded special treatment.[171] Finally, and related to this broader range of intimate relationships, worries similar to those outlined in Chapter 3 in relation to breach of promise of marriage surround the possibility that deception as to relationship intentions might qualify if deception as to marital status does.[172] As per my discussion there, however, were it possible to isolate the cases where it could be proved that the declared or implied intentions were false from the outset then these might be treated differently from what would no doubt be the vast majority of cases in which this could not be proved.[173]

7.6 Conclusions and Contemporary Connections

Viewing the development of the law of rape by deception in the round, the trajectory that emerges is one of some confusion due to changes in the definition of rape, towards a 'no consent' model, and the way this affected both the scope of the offence and its relationship to other, non-sexual offences. On

---

[167] *Grey* v. *Criminal Injuries Compensation Board* (1999) General Collection, Paper 15; 1999 SC 137, unsuccessfully challenging a decision made in 1993.

[168] New South Wales Law Reform Commission, *Consent in Relation to Sexual Offences*, Paragraphs 6.159–6.161.

[169] See Chapter 1.

[170] Ormerod and Laird, *Smith and Hogan*, p. 812, discussing the 'nature or purpose' conclusive presumption, but the dismay would hold more generally. See also Scottish Parliament Official Report, Justice Committee, 18 November 2008.

[171] New South Wales Law Reform Commission, *Consent in Relation to Sexual Offences*, Paragraph 6.162. See Chapter 4 for changes in the seriousness with which bigamy has been regarded over time.

[172] In Israel, at least one man accused of lying about his ethnicity, marital status and relationship intentions has been charged with rape by deception (Jason Koutsoukis, 'Deception Rape Case Sparks Legal Concerns in Israel', *The Sydney Morning Herald*, 22 July 2010).

[173] Jane E. Larson, 'Women Understand So Little, They Call My Good Nature Deceit: A Feminist Rethinking of Seduction' (1993) 93 *Columbia Law Review* 374–472 at 466–467.

top of this, different ways of viewing the relationship(s) between deception, broadly understood, and consent entail different conclusions regarding the applicability of rape, as an offence of 'no consent', to deceptively induced intimacy. If consent is considered absent only when there is a mismatch between the complainant's understanding and what happened to them, then deceptions which constitute inducements to engage in sexual activity whose nature was otherwise understood will not qualify. Similarly, deceptions about the consequences or risks that attach to the activity will not qualify. If, on the other hand, the improper conduct of the defendant is the focus, then deceptions might qualify even if they are not considered to affect the complainant's understanding of the activity to which they have agreed.

If consent is the organising principle of the law, as it is in a number of jurisdictions, these latter forms of behaviour can be classified as rape by holding that they vitiate otherwise valid consent. Alternatively, if consent were not the organising principle in this area of law and rape were instead viewed as a particular kind of wrong that can be perpetrated in various ways,[174] then it would not be necessary to work out the range of qualifying deceptions (and indeed other features of the law) with reference to the consent of the complainant. Instead, the ways of wronging could be considered and assessed on their own terms, albeit with reference to some protected value or interest, such as sexual autonomy, or, as I suggest in Chapter 8, authenticity. In fact, this may be the better approach if there is a desire to move away from, or at least question, the narrow range of deceptions that have traditionally qualified. As a recent study has shown, a variety of deceptions that laypeople considered to be wrongful, including in the context of sex, were nevertheless perceived by them to be compatible with the existence of valid consent.[175] It may be, therefore, that practically as well as conceptually it is preferable to concentrate on what makes certain deceptions wrongful and harmful, rather than on whether they preclude or vitiate consent.

To complicate matters, I would suggest that this is how the relation between deception and consent has worked in the law of rape anyway. In practice, decisions have been made about how to interpret the nature and purpose of the act and which conditions are implied in agreements to have sex, and thus which mistakes can preclude consent, and choices have been made about which frauds might vitiate consent. As I have aimed to show in this chapter, these decisions can usefully be interpreted in light of prevailing notions of what makes sex valuable, and other temporally and culturally variable aims and interests the law has sought to further and protect. The central claim of this chapter can therefore provide an answer to the question of how the notion that deception is considered seriously immoral *because* it invalidates consent can be squared with the idea that only some deceptions should be criminalised (and, I would

---

[174] See, Victor Tadros, 'Rape without Consent' (2006) 26(3) *Oxford Journal of Legal Studies* 515–543.
[175] Roseanna Sommers, 'Commonsense Consent' (2020) 129(8) *The Yale Law Journal* 2232–2324.

add, that only some have been).[176] The answer this chapter suggests is that, in reality, deception has not been seen as immoral because it invalidates consent; rather, it has been seen as invalidating (or precluding) consent because it is (sometimes) immoral. Moreover, this chapter also suggests that the degree of immorality, or wrongfulness, has not been seen as identical across all deceptions or across time and place. In other words, part of what makes deception appear wrongful is the context within which the deception occurs and the activity in relation to which it is carried out.

A further question is whether and how this insight might be used under contemporary conditions. On one view, more pluralist conceptions of what makes sexual activity valuable and an increased concern for sexual autonomy, understood as individual choice, make any attempt to categorise deceptions in terms of their aptness for criminalisation in an objective manner appear unattractive. This is the intuition that underpins quite a lot of contemporary scholarship and many law reform efforts. Yet the main ways forward that have been proposed – of determining the 'object of consent' (and thus whether there has been a mistake) with reference to the complainant's reconstruction of what they agreed to[177] or basing liability on the complainant's account of what was important to their decision-making[178] – suffer from problems, some of which undercut the ambitions they set out to achieve.

As I pointed out in Chapter 5, these proposals are committed to a moral vision of the meaning and value of sex (and, indeed, this vision might be decidedly sex negative), so they cannot rely for much support on the argument that alternative proposals, which involve some reliance on objective categories, are moralised and unattractive for that reason.[179] Furthermore, they tend either to shrug off the significance of evidentiary considerations[180] or else imply that they do not pose any particular challenge in this specific context.[181] This is to ignore both the challenges of proving deception and its effects, which are illustrated

---

[176] Kate Greasley, 'Deception and Power amidst Sexual Activity', *Criminal Justice Theory Blog*, 30 September 2022, https://criminaljusticetheoryblog.wordpress.com/2022/09/30/deception-and-power-amidst-sexual-activity.

[177] Dsouza, 'False Beliefs and Consent to Sex'; Murray and Beattie, 'Conditional Consent and Sexual Offences'.

[178] Herring, 'Consent Mistaken'.

[179] Cf. Rachel Clement Tolley, 'Deception, Mistake and Difficult Decisions' in CLRNN, *Reforming the Relationship* (2021), pp. 90–97.

[180] For example, 'concerns about matters of evidence should ordinarily not shape substantive law' (Mark Dsouza, 'False Beliefs and Consent to Sex' in CLRNN, *Reforming the Relationship* (2021), pp. 24–35).

[181] For example, the claims that evidence should be approached in a broad common sense way is 'merely a reminder of the usual evidential tests which apply in bringing a criminal charge, and in directing a jury' (Murray and Beattie, 'Conditional Consent and Sexual Offences' at 560) and 'these challenges [of a tribunal of fact determining whether something was genuinely a dealbreaker for the complainant and, if so, whether 'she made it relevant to her putative consent'] should not be overstated. A jury can make such findings, as it always does' (Dsouza, 'False Beliefs and Consent to Sex' at 1211).

throughout this book, but also the challenges that affect sexual offence trials generally, including the way they tend to invert the focus of the trial, turning it on to the complainant.[182] It is also to underplay the significance of the fact that purporting to ascertain the complainant's subjective understanding and/or the effect this had on their decision-making turns, in reality, into an exercise in applying what the jury considers to be conventional norms.[183]

Furthermore, if the occurrence of an offence turns on the complainant's reaction to the defendant's conduct, then public law goals like clarity and prospective certainty are ill-served.[184] Lastly, it is not so easy to take account of competing demands, particularly those that relate to collective interests, such as public health goals or combatting discrimination, if the sexual autonomy of individuals is the primary, or even sole, orienting value. If the pursuance of such collective interests is a feature of public law, as I suggested it is in Chapter 1, then it ought to figure in determinations about how the criminal law should be used in this area. As others have pointed out, to decide that the criminal law does not apply to some instances of deceptively induced intimacy is not inconsistent with sexual pluralism; people are still free to decide to have sex how they like, it is just that they cannot always seek criminal recourse if their decision is affected by deception.[185] I expand on all of these points in Chapter 8, where I also make the positive case for how a culturally informed framework, which locates the value of sex and intimate relationships in self-construction, might provide an alternative way forward.

---

[182] Emily Finch and Vanessa E. Munro, 'Breaking Boundaries – Sexual Consent in the Jury Room' (2006) 26(3) *Legal Studies* 303–320.

[183] Dsouza notes that juries will draw inferences based on the evidence before them and 'the jurors' experience of how people normally behave' ('False Beliefs and Consent to Sex' at 1211). Cf. Murray and Beattie, who acknowledge that 'what a jury believes most people would find relevant – may already be a significant limiting factor [in determining the 'premises actually operative in the choice of the complainant' and whether the defendant had a reasonable belief in consent]' ('Conditional Consent and Sexual Offences' at 561).

[184] See also Doig, who calls this a novel approach to liability for rape ('Deception as to Gender' at 468).

[185] Nora Scheidegger, 'Balancing Sexual Autonomy, Responsibility, and the Right to Privacy: Principles for Criminalizing Sex by Deception' (2021) 22 *German Law Journal* 769–783 at 782–783.

8
Inducing Intimacy
A Conclusion

8.1 General Dynamics

Having considered a range of legal actions, spanning different areas of law, it is now possible to identify some general dynamics which underpin the development of legal responses to inducing intimacy. These fall into three categories. The first category, which I refer to as the public(s) and private(s) of sex and relationships, concerns the kind of intimacy that is subject to legal regulation; the interests protected by law; the form of response, that is, state or non-state; and the variety of legal response, that is, public or private law. The second category, which I refer to as the structure of legal responses, includes: the way consent and its relation to deception is conceptualised in law and what this means for the availability of legal responses; the modes of deception targeted by law, including misrepresentations, misleading conduct and non-disclosures; matters relating to culpability, such as intention or purpose to deceive, knowledge or suspicion of the relevant information and its truth status and knowledge or suspicion of its significance to others; any causal connection between the deceiver's conduct and a specific outcome; and issues of temporality, including whether the wrong(s) of inducing intimacy are seen as discrete events or a course of conduct and to what extent the periods before and after the decision to engage in sex or an intimate relationship are deemed relevant. Finally, the third category concerns the substance of deceptions, that is, their subject matter and the general dynamics governing the range of topics about which transparency has been considered significant in law.

Though I discuss each of these categories separately in Sections 8.2–8.4, it is crucial to bear in mind that they are all interrelated. Different legal responses have, and are expected to have, different structural features, and these structures make it more or less likely that deceptions relating to particular topics will fall within the laws' scope. Yet each feature requires interpretation and they can be combined in different ways, meaning that the same deception can fit within what appear to be very distinct structures. In other words, the array of deceptions that are recognised by law at any given time is only partly determined by the doctrinal features that make up the law's structure. The other determining factor is which interests and institutions the law protects, and these are themselves partly the product of social and cultural context. These relationships between the general dynamics therefore suggest that it is seriously limiting to consider just one of the issues, or sets of issues, they raise. When it comes to thinking about legal responses to inducing intimacy, the more holistic the approach the better.

For the sake of clarity, however, I consider each category on its own terms, with two aims in mind. First, I want to give a short summary of how these dynamics have played out over time and across the legal actions considered in this book. This is to provide a succinct account of the overarching narrative that comes through the more detailed analysis offered in Chapters 2–7. Second, I want to think about how this narrative, and the insights it conveys, might usefully be deployed in our contemporary context. In this respect, it is here that I seek to show the association between the interpretive and evaluative aims I set out in Chapter 1, pursuing the latter in relation to current debates and scholarship and making contributions to each of those in the process.

8.2 The Public(s) and Private(s) of Sex and Relationships

In Chapter 1, I introduced a cultural framework rooted in the relationships between sex and marriage and between self-construction and intimacy, and I set out in very general terms how I think that framework underpins the kinds of intimacy that have been regulated by law and the public and private interests the law has protected. The intervening chapters have added more weight to these claims by showing how for much of the modern period the institution of marriage, and the social and legal status it bestowed – particularly on women, shaped the wrongs and harms recognised by law. By shaping the law in this way, marriage and the cultural expectations it carried effectively delineated and structured the legal actions and areas of law which regulated the practices of inducing intimacy, limiting their scope and providing some clarity. For example, changes in generally held expectations of marriage served either to facilitate the expansion or contraction of the ambit of legal responses to inducing intimacy at different points in time and conventional relationship norms provided a basis on which to infer (or impute) the existence of the consent and promises with which the law was concerned.

In terms of the interests these arrangements served, the institution of marriage was thought to promote collective benefits and serve shared values, such as security of kinship relations, the distribution of material resources, and the morality of interpersonal relations, including sexual relations. At the same time, the individual interests protected were economic and reputational security and a sense of what we might now call identity through the ascription of a culturally meaningful role. It seems fair, therefore, to characterise these individual interests as being at least partly rooted in the construction of selfhood. To be clear, in making this assertion I do not claim to speak for how men and women actually felt about themselves – my research would not permit me to do that – but I would be surprised if there were no association between law and phenomenology in this respect.[1]

Across the late modern period, however, particularly during the later twentieth and twenty-first centuries, the interest around which legal responses to inducing intimacy have become organised is individual choice and this has, to a large extent, become decoupled from any collective interest. If there is a collective interest that underlies these developments, it is best described as respect for individual choice, aggregated. Again, this is in keeping with the accounts of contemporary self-construction I outlined in Chapter 1, according to which minimally constrained choice is an important ideal. Yet a concern for aggregated individual choice does not represent a collective interest in the sense of either a substantive institution that is collectively valued or a substantive institution, or social form, whose significance is collectively recognised. Insofar as individual choice might be described as a contemporary social form or institution, it is best described as a procedural one – the interest at play is a desire to secure the conditions by which individual choice might be exercised in as unencumbered a manner as possible. This reveals the extent to which the contemporary concern with individual choice is hostile to any substantive collective interests; indeed, the aim is to detach the processes for securing individual choice from any substantive collective interest. In the context of legal responses to inducing intimacy, the effect has been that those collective interests which remain have become untethered from any substantive framework. They are, for the most part, no longer rooted in social institutions or forms, or conceptions of collective good, that could give them structure and shape.

In the case of sex, this has created some acute problems because the balance in legal responses has shifted from civil law to criminal law. This development makes sense in light of the framework I outlined in Chapter 1 because, according to that framework, sex has acquired a new and heightened cultural significance over the last fifty years or so. As such, criminal law – the most severe form of state regulation – appears to be the appropriate response. Yet as I explained in Chapter 1, and as Chapters 4–7 have demonstrated, criminal law as a form of public law has traditionally depended on the pursuit of collective interests for its justification. The erosion of any link with substantive collective interests therefore poses a challenge in and of itself. Beyond this, as Chapters 2–7 show, shared sources of meaning and value have historically been central to achieving clarity and predictability in the operation of *all* the legal responses to inducing intimacy – civil and criminal – I have examined. It is important not to overstate this point because the historical record shows that there has always been scope for confusion and contestation but at the very least there was a shared substantive foundation on which to draw. The loss of this foundation

---

[1] Sophie Loidolt, 'Order, Experience, and Critique: The Phenomenological Method in Political and Legal Theory' (2021) 54(2) *Continental Philosophy Review* 153–170 at 163.

therefore presents a problem, especially in the case of public laws where clarity and predictability are regarded as particularly important.

On top of this, when legal responses were anchored in a collective interest or institution, such as marriage, it was easier to appeal to other collective interests, beyond marriage, such as public health concerns and worries about abuse of authority, in developing and applying the law. When individual choice is the main, or even sole, interest underpinning the law, however, these 'other' considerations can appear subservient or else disappear from view altogether. For instance, when individual choice reigns it might be assumed that autonomy trumps other interests, such as privacy.[2] Alternatively, it might not be clear that there are interests to be served, beyond exploiting others or taking advantage of naivety or vulnerability, by decentring autonomy.[3] Yet the fact that there is some pushback in academic and judicial circles against the move, or suggested move, towards an autonomy-centred approach to sexual offences suggests there is some awareness of its shortcomings. The challenge is to find other substantive collective interests that can anchor this area of law, but which fit contemporary sensibilities better than the now-outdated notion of marriage that formerly prevailed.

In contrast to how the transition towards individual choice has played out in relation to sex, in the context of intimate relationships the desire for individual choice is in a sense rooted in some substantive collective interests – a shared desire for easy exit from unsatisfying relationships and a degree of permissiveness with respect to more prevalent forms of 'misconduct', such as inconstancy (that is, leaving a relationship due to lack of love) and unfaithfulness (that is, sexual or emotional infidelity). Even if these behaviours, which might involve significant deception if not disclosed, are still frowned upon they are not seen as subjects on which the law should have much to say. This position is reflected in the growth of no-fault family law doctrines; the declining relevance of some legal responses, for example, bigamy; and the disappearance of other legal responses, for example, breach of promise of marriage. These changes all point towards the fact that the capacity of law to recognise the wrongs that may be involved in inducing intimate relationships has shrunk as its capacity to recognise the wrongs of inducing sex has grown. Again, there are signs of dissatisfaction with these developments, however, which manifest in a desire for greater legal recognition of the wrongs involved in inducing intimate relationships. This dissatisfaction also raises the question of whether it might be possible to frame potential legal responses in a way that does not clash too strongly with contemporary sensibilities.

The history presented in this book might call into question the need for, or desirability of, legal responses altogether, though, insofar as it shows that in the

---

[2] For discussion, see Scheidegger, 'Balancing Sexual Autonomy', criticising this position.
[3] J. H. Bogart, 'On the Nature of Rape' (1991) 5(2) *Public Affairs Quarterly* 117–136 at 125, specifically discussing fraud and rape.

past commentators thought that social opprobrium might provide sufficient censure and deterrence of the practices of inducing intimacy whose immorality and undesirability was not in doubt. Yet the possibility that social condemnation might prove a viable alternative to law depends on both a reasonably high degree of consensus regarding the behaviour in question and a social structure in which the estimation of one's peers is extremely significant. In contemporary pluralistic societies, it is not obvious that either of these requirements can be taken for granted. As such, law more readily appears to be the solution to what might otherwise be characterised as social problems; it appears to provide a way of coalescing opinions around a particular viewpoint. Of course, the capacity of law, especially criminal law, to perform this function is open to question, but the likelihood that social interventions might be considered enough seems fairly implausible.[4]

Assuming a legal intervention is sought, the preceding chapters caution against too rigid an adherence to a dichotomised view of public and private law responses because, as I highlighted in Chapter 1, one of this book's contributions is to show how private law actions have fulfilled quasi-punitive functions. Insofar as these actions typically remained under the control of the person who had been wronged, they in some ways foreshadow recent debates about the capacity of civil litigation to improve the experience of sexual violence survivors, either in addition to or as an alternative to criminal justice.[5] Yet it is crucial to bear in mind that, perhaps on account of their quasi-punitive character, these older private law actions were expected to have a clear scope, be predictable in their operation, and depend on relatively stringent forms of proof. Again, fulfilling at least some of these expectations was facilitated by the fact that these laws were indexed to important collective interests. To the extent that the analysis in this book challenges a neat bifurcation of private and public laws, therefore, it at the same time suggests that there is something about the features typically associated with public laws that it is worth trying to preserve, irrespective of whether the law in question is formally public or private. This insight underpins many of the comments I make in Sections 8.3 and 8.4, where I discuss the structure of legal responses and the range of qualifying deceptions.

8.3 The Structure of Legal Responses

The meaning of consent and its relationship to deception are two important features of the laws discussed across the chapters of this book.[6] In the case of marriage, consent has been pivotal to the operation of the law for centuries

---

[4] For reflections on these points, see Kennedy, 'Crime, Reason and History'.
[5] Victorian Law Reform Commission, *Improving the Justice System Response to Sexual Offences* (2021), Paragraphs 11.1–11.43.
[6] For some reflections on the relationships between contract, consent and promises, see Gregory Klass, George Letsas and Prince Saprai (eds.), *Philosophical Foundations of Contract Law* (Oxford: Oxford University Press, 2014).

and deception – which has included misrepresentations, non-disclosures and acting in a misleading manner – has sometimes affected either the existence or the validity of consent. While certain deceptions have rendered an apparent marriage void or voidable, misrepresenting an intention to marry has, conversely, sometimes led courts to infer or impute the existence of marital consent. Yet in both of these contexts, a substantive conception of marriage – a shared sense of what it entailed and what made it valuable – has underpinned legal decisions about whether and when deception would have these effects. To be more specific, an account of the wrongs and harms perpetrated by deception of the relevant kinds, which depended on such a substantive conception of marriage, helped support the conclusion that consent was or was not present or that it was or was not legally effectual in specific circumstances.

In terms of the structure of consent, the previous chapters illustrate its capacity to be scalar in the sense that it might be absent, present but impaired, or present and fully effectual. For example, by providing a remedy when sexual consent was present but impaired the civil wrong of seduction occupied a kind of middle space between sex with which the law had nothing to do – because it was considered to be fully consensual – and sex which would eventually constitute rape because it was considered to be non-consensual. Marital consent had a similar structure in that, like seduction, voidable marriages occupied a middle space insofar as the marriage was considered valid unless and until a decree annulling it was passed. Furthermore, similarly to seduction – an action that could only be brought by the woman wronged – control over whether to annul a voidable marriage rested with the parties alone. By contrast, control over annulling a void marriage – a marriage in which consent is deemed absent – was not so confined; anyone with an interest could sue. As with sexual offences, where the absence of consent always entailed a crime, an absence of marital consent meant that annulment took on more of a public character.

From a contemporary perspective, adopting a scalar approach like this is harder to justify because the ideal of autonomy, whether this is sexual autonomy or autonomy in the context of entering intimate relationships, does not easily allow for distinctions to be drawn between different deceptions or modes of deceiving. Without such distinctions, it is not clear why we should distinguish between deceptions relating to the act, which might mean there is no consent, and deceptions relating to inducements,[7] which might lead to impaired consent.[8] It is not clear why we should distinguish between deception and mistakes, either – another distinction around which separate offences have been proposed[9] – since

---

[7] For example, 'Why assume that *fraud in the inducement* is not a serious matter?' (Williams, 'Deception, Mistake' at 154, citing Alan Wertheimer's *Consent to Sexual Relations* (Cambridge: Cambridge University Press, 2003) approvingly).
[8] See Chapter 6.   [9] See Chapter 6.

8.3 The Structure of Legal Responses

both can impair autonomy.[10] Then there is the point that in the contemporary era, established ways of distinguishing between deceptions, such as trying to isolate deceptions that go to the nature of the act, have proved incapable of doing the work needed to maintain clear and defensible distinctions between legal wrongs or between these wrongs and conduct that will attract no legal response.[11] Lest the possibility of overlapping offences appear as a simple solution, the history presented in this book illustrates the problems to which this gives rise, including a lack of clarity about when each offence ought to apply and why.[12]

Yet even if a better way of distinguishing deceptions is found, as I suggest in Section 8.4 that it might, there are problems with dividing up qualifying deceptions on the basis of kind of wrong – that is, civil or criminal – or nominate wrong – that is, one civil action or crime instead of another. Though I suggest, again in Section 8.4, that it might be possible to distinguish between those deceptions most pertinent to sex and those most pertinent to intimate relationships, the difficulty involved in designating some deceptions within each category as constituting one nominate offence and some another, or indeed designating some as a criminal offence and some a civil wrong, is considerable. At least, there are considerable difficulties when failing to respect autonomy, or something like it, is perceived to be the core wrong involved in this conduct.[13]

Assuming that only one legal response were to apply to deceptive sex and only one were to apply to deceptive intimate relationships, the further question arises of what these legal responses should look like. My approach to answering this question is to begin by analysing the features such a response might have, which I do in the rest of this section, before considering whether and how the range of qualifying deceptions should be limited by subject matter, which I do in Section 8.4. This approach deliberately avoids working with existing doctrinal formulations, instead considering each feature of a potential legal response on its own terms and in light of the lessons imparted by the earlier chapters of this book. It also avoids suggesting conclusively that either civil or criminal responsibility is the better option and whether consent should be used in defining the legal response. As I explained in Chapter 7, there may be good reasons to avoid relying on consent; at the same time, as that chapter shows, it is possible to rely on consent without subscribing to the view that its operation should be underpinned by the ideal of autonomy.

Thinking about the features a legal response to inducing intimacy might have, a good place to start is the proscribed mode(s) of commission. It is clear from earlier chapters that non-disclosure has been a long-standing feature of both civil law responses, such as nullity of marriage, and criminal law responses, such as early rape by deception prosecutions involving mistaken

---

[10] See Chapter 7. [11] See Chapter 7. [12] See Chapter 6.
[13] For some other challenges in distinguishing civil and criminal wrongs, see Kennedy, 'Comparing Criminal and Civil Responsibility'.

identity.[14] This mode of commission has sat alongside other forms of conduct, such as behaving or communicating in such a way as to create – or potentially create – a false impression. Examples from the past include creating the false impression that one is free to marry, that one intends to marry, or that one is married to a specific person.[15] On top of these forms of deception is what is now often referred to as active deception, that is, misrepresentations or lies.[16] Importantly, while all three modes of commission have been part of the law for a long time, the tendency to provide a legal response for non-disclosure can be associated with increasing expectations of transparency between intimate and sexual partners. This change is signalled by the growth of categories of non-disclosure which might ground an annulment, increased expectations of candour about reproductive and health matters in the context of casual sex, and the declining significance of the distinction between active deception and non-disclosure in the law of rape by deception.[17]

These developments are not only comprehensible historically but are also defensible when autonomy, or something like it, is the object of the law's protection. After all, though autonomy, like consent, can be considered a scalar concept,[18] with only some degrees of involuntariness or some kinds of information deficit being sufficiently significant to tip the balance in favour of a legal response, the way this threshold is reached – whether it is by misrepresentation or by failure to disclose – seems unimportant.[19] Furthermore, though both non-disclosure and active deception can result in mistakes, non-disclosure has a certain affinity with ignorance. If the aim of a legal response is to focus on the wrongful conduct and take the focus off the person wronged – ambitions that are particularly important in the context of sexual offences[20] but might apply to legal responses to sexual wrongs more generally – then structuring the law around non-disclosure might therefore be desirable. This is because asking whether a person had certain information, rather than whether they were misled or mistaken, at least theoretically takes the focus off that person: the question is not what they thought or believed but, rather, what information was available to them.

There are downsides to imposing disclosure duties, though. Beyond the fact that it is more onerous to impose disclosure duties than it is to proscribe active deceptions, disclosure duties have a unique relationship to discrimination. For example, if any non-disclosure that might affect another person's

---

[14] See Chapters 2 and 7.   [15] See Chapters 3 and 4.
[16] Examples appear throughout Chapters 2–7.   [17] As discussed in Chapters 2 and 7.
[18] See Luis E. Chiesa, 'Solving the Riddle of Rape by Deception' (2017) 35(2) *Yale Law & Policy Review* 407–460.
[19] For one argument that non-disclosure may be sufficiently wrongful to merit criminalisation, see Wertheimer, *Consent*, ch. 9. On disclosure duties in the context of civil wrongs, see, for example, Deana Pollard Sacks, 'Intentional Sex Torts' (2008) 77(3) *Fordham Law Review* 1051–1093.
[20] See Chapter 7.

decision to have sex could potentially trigger a legal response, then privacy interests are seriously impacted because the amount of information one would have to disclose to avoid violating the duty is potentially vast. Yet this impact would disproportionately affect those who have characteristics that are likely to be perceived as undesirable because they are more likely to have to disclose their secret in order to avoid the risk of liability.[21] Furthermore, the low degree of certainty about when disclosure would be necessary to avoid legal consequences would place an additional burden on people who are already marginalised – the burden of trying to anticipate others' attitudes.[22] These problems suggest that it is extremely important to clearly delineate the range of qualifying deceptions (that is, disclosure duties) in a prospective way, a point I pick up in Section 8.4 where I suggest that this should be done with reference to the subject matter of the deception.

In addition to any circumscription based on subject matter, such duties might be limited by culpability requirements. For example, it might be necessary to prove the alleged wrongdoer's knowledge of the information which forms the basis of the disclosure duty. Historically, awareness of one's infection status was important in cases involving transmission of sexual disease,[23] and it was suggested that whereas liability for mistakes should not depend on such knowledge, liability for fraudulently suppressing the truth should.[24] There is certainly scope for considering whether a person should potentially be liable if they *ought* to have had the relevant knowledge, but this possibility could extend only to information about which it is plausible to make such a claim. In the context of inducing intimacy, it might not make sense to say that a person ought to (or perhaps even can) know whether they really love someone or that they should be sure about their sexual orientation or gender identity. If matters such as these were subject to a disclosure duty – and that question should take into consideration the issues relating to discrimination mentioned above – then it would seem reasonable to limit the scope of that duty to circumstances where it could be shown that such knowledge really existed at the relevant time. Again, looking at the historical examples, it is clear that this kind of bad faith at the time of acting has made a difference in law, even if only at the level of condemnation. For example, instances of breach of promise of marriage where the defender knew he was already married at the time he made the promise were considered more reprehensible.[25]

A further potential culpability requirement is an intention or purpose to deceive. Perhaps unsurprisingly, given the concern for culpability in criminal law, this requirement has most obviously featured in criminal law responses,

---

[21] Tolley, 'Deception, Mistake and Difficult Decisions'.
[22] For the argument that inspired this point, see Hannah Walser, 'Vagueness, Double Consciousness, and the Criminal Law: A Cognitive History' (2023) 10(1) *Critical Analysis of Law* 97–115.
[23] See Chapter 7. [24] *R v. Clarence* (1888) at 28 (Wills, J).
[25] See Chapter 3. See also Scheidegger, 'Balancing Sexual Autonomy' at 772.

including the procuring offences discussed in Chapter 6 and at least some forms of rape by deception (impersonating someone known personally to the complainant and deception as to the nature or purpose of the act).[26] More recently, proposals to amend prosecutorial guidance concerning sexual offences for so-called gender deception include the recommendation that the use of 'deliberate deception' should be a factor taken into account, but this point is merged with a discussion of whether there has been 'active deception', examples of which include making false assertions or lying in response to questions.[27] But as I noted in Chapter 7, an intention or purpose to deceive can coexist with either active deception or non-disclosure, so I would suggest that separating these two points out is worthwhile.

More generally, a requirement of intention to deceive is out of step with the culpability requirements that govern contemporary sexual offences, according to which lack of reasonable belief in consent is enough.[28] Admittedly, it is not altogether clear what a lack of reasonable belief in consent means in this context because it is not altogether clear how deception bears on consent. It might be that the lack of reasonable belief must relate to a mistake made by the other person or to the question of whether they had access to the relevant information; it might also be that a reasonable belief that any such mistake or lack of information would not matter to the complainant exculpates. Whatever the case, intention to deceive constitutes a higher threshold than lack of reasonable belief in consent so the suggestion that it should be a requirement, rather than an aggravation, seems to require some justification. Such a justification might be present if there were no need to prove a causal link between the deception and the relevant outcome, a point discussed in more detail later in this section. An even higher threshold, such as the use of exploitation or coercion, might be justified in light of the wide range of reasons people engage in deceptive conduct, including to avoid the negative effects of marginalisation.[29] In such circumstances, the question of culpability for mere deception would be irrelevant because the relevant wrong – exploitation or coercion – would not have been committed.[30]

Assuming that deception per se – at least deception of specific kinds – is the relevant wrong, however, and that lack of reasonable belief in 'consent' (meaning a lack of reasonable belief that the complainant was not mistaken

---

[26] As discussed in Chapter 7.
[27] www.cps.gov.uk/publication/deception-gender-proposed-revision-cps-legal-guidance-rape-and-serious-sexual-offences.
[28] Sexual Offences Act 2003; Sexual Offences (Scotland) Act 2009. This requirement features in a number of the offences against adults with capacity.
[29] For discussion, see Daniel Silvermint, 'Passing as Privileged' (2018) 5(1) *Ergo* 1–43.
[30] Greasley, 'Deception and Power amidst Sexual Activity'. Cf. the proposed CPS guidance for 'gender deception' sex offence prosecutions, which suggests that where there is evidence of coercion, manipulation or exploitation, it is 'less likely' that the suspect held a reasonable belief in consent (www.cps.gov.uk/publication/deception-gender-proposed-revision-cps-legal-guidance-rape-and-serious-sexual-offences).

8.3 The Structure of Legal Responses

or missing information, or lack of reasonable belief that the mistake or information deficit was unimportant) is the relevant culpability threshold, then it is worth acknowledging the fact that this invites scrutiny of the person wronged. Asking whether the deceiver had good reason to believe that there was no mistake or that the other person had access to the relevant information, or that neither the mistake nor lack of information would matter, involves inquiring into the particularities of the parties' relationship to at least some extent.[31] It also presents opportunities to rely on unfounded assumptions about how people make decisions to have sex, such as the idea that this is generally an unreflective process,[32] or that willingness to have sex is not conditional on expectations that are held by the decision-maker.[33] It also facilitates what might be described as victim blaming for, for example, failing to treat declarations of love with 'a healthy measure of skepticism'.[34] But at least these inquiries and practices would be less commonplace than if the beliefs of the person wronged and/or the effect of these beliefs on their decision-making were the basis on which deceptions were deemed qualifying. Put differently, it is better that these possibilities arise only when determining culpability and not when deciding whether the deception qualifies, too.

This point leads on to another feature of legal responses to inducing intimacy which needs to be considered – the requirement for a causal link between the deception and the outcome, whether that be sex or an intimate relationship. The historical examples show some variation in terms of whether this was required and the significance of the answer to this question. A causal connection was formally required but sometimes presumed in cases of seduction and marriage constituted by a promise to marry followed by sex,[35] and it was sometimes required by the law of nullity of marriage but without much indication of whether and how it was to be proved independently of the alleged mistake.[36] Likewise, the criminal offences of procuring sex and at least one kind of rape by deception – impersonation of someone known personally to the complainant – require (or, in the case of the procuring offences, required) a causal connection. Yet while the causation requirement has been important, and constraining, in some procuring cases, as the discussion of the case of *Monica* in Chapter 6 showed, it does not seem to have attracted much attention in the context of rape by deception.[37]

Nevertheless, this is, at least theoretically, another requirement that invites scrutiny of the person wronged because it raises the questions of whether

---

[31] Kennedy, 'Criminalising Deceptive Sex' at 108.
[32] Dsouza, 'False Beliefs and Consent to Sex' at 1202.
[33] Gross, 'Rape, Moralism, and Human Rights' at 224.
[34] Ibid. See also Chapters 2 and 3 for examples of scorn for those who are deceived.
[35] See Chapters 5 and 4, respectively.   [36] See Chapter 2.
[37] It has been suggested that the Solicitor General did not, at the time the legislation was debated, appreciate that the conclusive presumption in what became s. 76(2)(b) of the Sexual Offences Act 2003 would not apply unless the prosecution established a causal link (Jennifer Temkin and Andrew Ashworth, 'The Sexual Offences Act 2003: (1) Rape, Sexual Assaults and the Problems of Consent' [2004] *Criminal Law Review* 328–346 at fn. 48).

they relied on the deceptive conduct and perhaps also whether the reliance was reasonable.[38] And while a causation requirement limits the scope of both prosecutions[39] and civil actions[40] – a consequence that might be desirable – it creates problems similar to those involved in determining the scope of qualifying deceptions with reference to the beliefs or attitudes of the person allegedly wronged. It directs the inquiry towards the plaintiff or complainant and though this might be understandable in the case of private law, which is often concerned with the effects on the person wronged, public law, including criminal law, regularly focuses on the conduct of the wrongdoer and injury or some effect on the alleged victim is not always required.[41] Moreover, in both cases what is known about the operation of sexual offences and the history of sexual and amatory civil wrongs suggests that causation requirements should be approached with caution because they risk importing problematic classed and gendered assumptions into the law.[42] It would be possible to avoid a causation requirement by following the approach taken in the Fraud Act 2006 whereby false representations, failures to disclose and abuses of position are criminalised when done dishonestly and with intention to make a loss or gain, or expose another to risk of loss, irrespective of whether this conduct caused any loss or gain. It has been suggested that to follow this example in the context of deceptive sex would require strong justification, however,[43] and whether the downsides of a causation requirement I have described could serve as such justification is up for debate. Elsewhere, I have argued that they might, particularly if the range of qualifying deceptions were relatively tightly circumscribed.[44]

Finally, the temporal complexities of consent but also, or perhaps alternatively, the wrongful behaviour with which legal responses to inducing intimacy is concerned must be considered. As earlier chapters illustrated, answers to the questions of how far back and forward in time the law looks and how the legal wrong is conceptualised turn on how and why the conduct regulated by law is considered wrongful. When inducing a relationship by deception is the regulated conduct, as in the case of breach of promise of marriage, the law has taken an expansive temporal view and the wrong is characterised as a course of conduct. Although the broken promise occurred at a specific moment in time, if the promise was made in bad faith then the moment of making the promise, which obviously precedes the breach, would mark the beginning of

---

[38] Sacks, 'Intentional Sex Torts' at 1080.   [39] See Chapter 6.
[40] Sacks, 'Intentional Sex Torts' at 1093.   [41] See Chapter 1.
[42] See also Donald A. Dripps, '"Beyond Rape": An Essay on the Difference between the Presence of Force and the Absence of Consent' (1992) 92(7) *Columbia Law Review* 1780–1809, which suggests that sexual assault law should turn solely on the defendant's conduct and mental state and that the victim's psychology should be irrelevant (at 1797–1798).
[43] Williams, 'Deception, Mistake' at 147. For a critical discussion of the Act itself, see David Ormerod, 'The Fraud Act 2006 – Criminalising Lying?' [2007] *Criminal Law Review* 193–219.
[44] Kennedy, 'Criminalising Deceptive Sex' (on which Section 8.4 draws heavily); Chloë Kennedy, 'Sex, Selfhood and Deception' in CLRNN, *Reforming the Relationship* (2021), pp. 59–69 and www.youtube.com/watch?v=oZPzjBWTbIQ.

a course of wrongful conduct.[45] Likewise, although the harm of seduction was seen as a fall from virtue which occurred at the moment sex took place, the process by which the woman was illegitimately led to experience this fall – including by a relationship based on a false promise of marriage – could be drawn out and the wrong was seen as extending back to its start.[46] Conversely, in the case of criminal deceptive sex the legal response has typically homed in on the moment at which the physical act occurs and excluded deceptions that occurred some time before the sexual activity, which are typically thought to constitute inducements.[47] Furthermore, in the case of deceptive sex that takes place in an intimate relationship there has been an understandable reluctance to consider every sexual act that takes place under a temporally extensive deception as a crime.

Thinking about these points reveals another consequence of the decline of legal responses to inducing intimate relationships. Without these, the temporally extended nature of the wrongdoing that often exists in cases of inducing intimacy, including deceptive sex, is missed when arguably it should be captured. One way to rectify this would be to advocate for a legal response (if one were considered merited and desirable) which specifically addresses deceptively induced intimate relationships, including but not limited to marriages and civil partnerships. In the absence of such a formalised relationship, however, there would need to be some way to identify the start of the relationship; cohabitation or sexual activity would arguably be underinclusive and overinclusive, respectively, but they might be starting points for a discussion about whether such a legal action could be made to work. In the case of deceptive sex, if a legal response focussing on the deceptive relationship did not exist or did not apply, then it seems important that that the law should be able to reflect what has occurred without involving manifold sex offence charges. One way to do this might be to limit the number of charges but recognise the extended nature of the deception by way of an aggravation. Another might be to introduce an offence of chronic sexual violation, distinct from but as serious as rape.[48]

8.4 The Substance of Deceptions

From the previous discussion, and the chapters that have come before this one, it is hopefully clear why it might be desirable to limit the range of qualifying deceptions in some way that does not depend solely on the beliefs of the person wronged and/or the effect of these beliefs on their decision-making. In other words, it is hopefully clear why it might be desirable to eschew the ideal of autonomy. To recap the reasons I have offered, these include: the need for legal clarity and certainty, the need to factor in collective interests, a desire to focus

---

[45] See Chapter 3.   [46] See Chapter 5.   [47] See Chapters 6 and 7.
[48] For discussion, see Tanya Palmer, 'Freedom to Negotiate' in CLRNN, *Reforming the Relationship* (2021), pp. 70–79.

on the conduct of the wrongdoer and a desire to avoid undue scrutiny of the person wronged. A further reason is that it is disingenuous to suggest that it is possible to rule out the influence of convention or collective interests by determining the range of qualifying beliefs with reference to the beliefs of the person wronged and/or the effect of these beliefs on their decision-making. As the history presented in this book shows, when subjective conceptions of consent have been deployed the effect in practice has been that conventional norms and expectations tend to creep in. Importantly, this tendency is not confined to assessing culpability regarding consent; it also affects the determination of whether consent exists in the first place.[49] It would therefore be more upfront to acknowledge the role of convention and have an open discussion about how this should be incorporated into law.

In addition to providing reasons for rejecting the ideal of autonomy, however, the preceding chapters have illustrated the shortcomings of existing alternative ways of distinguishing deceptions. In the context of contemporary sensibilities, using a framework that prioritises marriage – whether it is considered an institution that furthers morality, as in the past, or not – is not appropriate. Limiting the range of deceptions to those that involve or risk physical harm seems underinclusive insofar as it is now broadly accepted that interests beyond physical security and integrity are important in the context of sex and intimate relationships. Drawing the line at deceptions that involve the risk – actualised or otherwise – of reproduction is unsatisfying for similar reasons. Though people's interests in making decisions with access to information regarding reproductive potential are significant and have been underappreciated in recent judgments, such as *Lawrance*,[50] they are also only part of the fuller picture. Likewise, although it may be desirable to distinguish between identity and attributes, there is no good reason why the range of qualifying identity deceptions should be limited to individuals known personally to the person wronged.

As for frameworks based on ontological differences between acts, it is clear that these struggle to do the work that is required of them because in the end everything turns on the way that the relevant act – or its nature or purpose – is construed. Furthermore, varying interpretations on this point can lead to both inconsistency in legal decisions and unsatisfactory distinctions.[51] And while a number of the deceptions that can be classified under this heading have historically been perpetrated by those in positions of trust or authority, in an era when inducing intimacy in 'ordinary' relationships can plausibly be described as sufficiently wrongful and potentially harmful to merit a legal response, the existence of a relationship of trust or authority should perhaps aggravate the case but it should not be a requirement. Similarly, the exclusion of deceptions

---

[49] Sacks, 'Intentional Sex Torts' and Chapters 4 and 7. Cf. Tolley, 'Deception, Mistake and Difficult Decisions' and Williams 'Deception, Mistake' at 149.
[50] Discussed in Chapter 7.   [51] As Chapter 7 clearly shows.

8.4 The Substance of Deceptions

relating to inducements is hard to justify from a contemporary perspective – these 'inducements' might be deeply important either to discrete individuals or to the population in general, so it is not clear why they should be treated differently to deceptions relating to the act or facts (assuming these could be clearly distinguished).[52]

The question is whether it might be possible to come up with a framework that addresses, or at least goes some way towards addressing, all the issues raised in this section and Section 8.3. In my view, the insight that sex and intimate relationships are, and have for a long time been, related to self-construction – one of the major strands of the overarching narrative that cuts across this book – can provide a way forward. More specifically, I think that an account of the way that sex and intimate relationships are generally important to how people form their identities in contemporary societies can be used to construct an argument about when and why deceptively induced intimacy is wrong and potentially harmful, and a way of clearly and defensibly circumscribing the range of qualifying deceptions.

Like frameworks based on the ideal of autonomy, the alternative I propose takes seriously the agent-centred view of sex and intimate relationships that now prevails in many parts of the world and, in this respect, it can be contrasted with frameworks based on encouraging 'moral' sex that prevailed historically, as the previous chapters have shown. Indeed, my alternative is based on the idea that the ground for a deception qualifying is not that it encourages valuable, or discourages non-valuable, forms of sexual activity or intimacy. Instead, according to my framework, deceptions qualify when they involve information that is *generally-speaking* important to people in self-constructing terms, as this process *generally-speaking* occurs via sex and intimate relationships. I therefore do not claim that every person attaches the same significance to this information, or that they should, and I do not claim that they should, or would even be more likely to, make any particular decision if the information were available to them.

These features of my alternative framework are made possible by the fact that it is rooted in the ideal of authenticity. Recalling the discussion in Chapter 1, the ideal of authenticity is concerned with deciding in accordance with one's own values, but it recognises the significance of certain shared norms and horizons of meaning. In fact, it posits that these norms and horizons are required in order to develop and hold personal values. Adopting the framework I propose therefore involves focussing on the social meaning that actions and institutions carry. So while the meaning that actions and institutions hold for individuals does feature in my framework, in contrast to the ideal of autonomy the specific meaning that these actions and institutions holds for any particular individual is not the sole concern.[53]

---

[52] Wertheimer, *Consent*, p. 206.
[53] In this respect, it has an affinity with arguments made by Meir Dan-Cohen in 'Basic Values and the Victim's State of Mind' (2000) 88 *California Law Review* 759–778.

To explain the social meanings involved in my framework, and how they support it, it is necessary to return to two insights introduced in Chapter 1: that under modern conditions individuals participate in their own self-construction and that intimate relationships and sex are sites of such self-construction. More specifically, in scholarship on these topics intimate relationships have been described as 'crucibles of inwardly-generated identity',[54] and sex has been described as a way of defining oneself.[55] Furthermore, and as I come on to explain shortly, some of the consequences of sex can be important in self-constructing terms, irrespective of whether that sex occurs in the context of an intimate relationship.

These links between intimate relationships, sex and self-construction are important because they are not only features of contemporary life but also a source of wrongs and potential harms on account of the fact that self-construction is generally a significant and valuable process that is worthy of respect.[56] Failing to respect this process by, for example, withholding information that is crucial to it, can therefore be described as wrongful. In fact, a specific term – identity nonrecognition – exists to capture the precise wrong, which involves failing to recognise the identities of others and/or the development of these identities.[57] In addition to being wrongful, identity nonrecognition is potentially harmful insofar as it can cause negative effects on a person's self-sentiments, including their sense of self-esteem, self-worth and self-efficacy.[58] Moreover, if the identity nonrecognition – in this context, the deprivation of information that is likely to be significant to a person's self-construction – results in a change to that person's identity then these effects will be even greater. To compound the harm, when the change does not cohere with that person's desired life narrative – the description under which their life has value – the effects are usually worse.[59]

This way of conceiving of self-construction, as a description under which one's life has value, means that the notion of identity involved in identity nonrecognition is not static.[60] Rather, it is a continuous process of integrating

---

[54] Charles Taylor, 'The Politics of Recognition' in Amy Gutmann (ed.), *Multiculturalism and the Politics of Recognition* (Princeton: Princeton University Press, 1994), pp. 25–74, p. 25.

[55] Wendy Doniger, *The Bedtrick: Tales of Sex and Masquerade* (Chicago: University of Chicago Press, 2000), pp. 91–95.

[56] Korsgaard, *Self-Constitution*; Christine M. Korsgaard, *The Sources of Normativity* (Cambridge: Cambridge University Press, 1996).

[57] Taylor, 'The Politics of Recognition'. See also Arto Laitinen, 'On the Scope of "Recognition": The Role of Adequate Regard and Mutuality' in Hans-Christoph Schmidt am Busch and Christopher F. Zurn (eds.), *The Philosophy of Recognition: Historical and Contemporary Perspectives* (Lanham, MD: Lexington Books, 2010), pp. 319–342; Heikki Ikäheimo, 'Recognition, Identity and Subjectivity' in Michael J. Thompson (ed.), *The Palgrave Handbook of Critical Theory* (New York: Palgrave Macmillan, 2017), pp. 567–586.

[58] Neil K. MacKinnon and David R. Heise, *Self, Identity, and Social Institutions* (Basingstoke: Palgrave Macmillan, 2010), p. 114; Arto Laitinen, 'Recognition, Needs and Wrongness: Two Approaches' (2009) 8(1) *European Journal of Political Theory* 13–30.

[59] MacKinnon and Heise, *Self, Identity and Social Institutions*, p. 166.

[60] Cf. Brenda Lyshaug, who argues that the politics of recognition might imply an ossified conception of identity; see 'Authenticity and the Politics of Identity: A Critique of Charles Taylor's Politics of Recognition' (2004) 3 *Contemporary Political Theory* 300–320.

certain data, experiences, statuses and roles into a meaningful autobiography.[61] Importantly, not all data, experiences, statuses and roles are likely to be significant to self-construction; they are not all sufficiently important or enduring to contribute towards this autobiography. Even more importantly – indeed, crucially for present purposes – the particular data, experiences, statuses and roles that *are* likely to be important to self-construction vary across time and place and are roughly generalisable across populations. This means that it is possible to identify 'components' of selfhood that will likely, but not necessarily, be significant to individuals' identities, and hence to identify what information is likely to be important to their decision-making.

By drawing on empirical research and intuitive reasoning I have, in other work, suggested a range of information that is likely to be important to self-construction and might be implicated in deceptions carried out in the context of sex – concentrating on those most closely related to sex per se and its direct consequences – and intimate relationships.[62] On the basis of these suggestions, I came to some conclusions regarding the range of deceptions that might qualify in a legal response to deceptive sex. In summary, I concluded that deceptions about the sexual nature or purpose of an act (that is, that the act is sexual as opposed to, for example, medical or therapeutic and about the body parts or objects involved in the sexual activity) should qualify on the ground that this is baseline information which is required in order to make decisions about sexual activity that accord with one's sense of self. On top of this, I argued that wholesale identity deception of any kind – whether it involves a real or fictional persona – should qualify on the basis that, as Wendy Doniger has observed, 'people in different cultures do not react in the same way to the shock of discovering that their lovers, and hence their selves, are not who they thought they were' but 'surprisingly many do'.[63] Her point is that identity is constructed relationally and that the identity of one's lover is crucial to that process; to this I would add that when the deception involves the identity of someone with whom the deceived is in an existing relationship, sexual or otherwise, the wrong is worse because it shows greater disrespect for the significance that relationship is likely to have for the dialogic formation of identity. The disrespect is more pronounced in the case of long-term partners because these relationships are generally key to identity formation,[64] and, in light of this, I have argued that it would be appropriate for deception involving these existing

---

[61] Taylor, *Sources of the Self*; Giddens, *Modernity and Self-Identity*, pp. 52–58; MacKinnon and Heise, *Self, Identity and Social Institutions*, pp. 96–107; Florian Coulmas, *Identity: A Very Short Introduction* (Oxford: Oxford University Press, 2019); Gerrit Glas, 'Idem, Ipse, and Loss of the Self' (2003) 10(4) *Philosophy, Psychiatry & Psychology* 347–352.
[62] Kennedy, 'Criminalising Deceptive Sex'. See also Kennedy, 'Sex, Selfhood and Deception' and www.youtube.com/watch?v=oZPzjBWTblQ.
[63] Doniger, *The Bedtrick*, p. 91.
[64] Laura K. Soulsby and Kate M. Bennett, 'When Two Become One: Exploring Identity in Marriage and Cohabitation' (2016) 38(3) *Journal of Family Issues* 358–380.

relationships – either pretending to be one of the parties to such a relationship or indeed not to be them – to constitute an aggravation.

Regarding deceptions pertaining to potential pregnancy or disease, I have suggested that these are instances of identity nonrecognition, and thus qualifying deceptions, because of the way becoming a parent,[65] undergoing a termination[66] and contracting certain chronic, if treatable, diseases[67] are known to be connected to self-construction. In my view, deception as to gender can also be viewed as an example of identity nonrecognition because of the way that the gender of one's sexual partner is related to one's sexual identity (and possibly gender identity).[68] Finally, deception relating to an issue that someone has expressly described as important to them, such as when they give explicit conditional consent to sex, seems to me to be a clear example of identity nonrecognition because each individual generates their own narrative under which their life has value. If such deceptions qualified on that basis, the requirement for explicit conditionality would avoid the problems relating to certainty, predictability and undue focus on the person wronged outlined earlier. Furthermore, any worries about underinclusivity would be ameliorated by the existence of the other qualifying deceptions, which might be described as implicit or default conditions through which the law seeks to build in a degree of honesty concerning those matters.[69] In these circumstances, however, it seems fair that there should be no liability if the deceptive party had good reason to think either that their partner knew about the relevant matter or that it would not be important to them.[70]

Against these arguments, there are several countervailing considerations which suggest that a legal response, particularly a public law one, might be

---

[65] Tim Lott, 'Becoming a Parent Is the Greatest Identity Change We Go Through', *The Guardian*, 29 April 2016.

[66] Kathryn Rea Smith, *Experiencing Abortion: A Phenomenological Investigation* (PhD dissertation, Tennessee Research and Creative Exchange, 1998), https://trace.tennessee.edu/utk_graddiss/2514; Siân M. Beynon-Jones, 'Untroubling Abortion: A Discourse Analysis of Women's Accounts' (2017) 27(2) *Feminism & Psychology* 225–242.

[67] Lisa M. Baumgartner, 'The Incorporation of the HIV/AIDS Identity into the Self over Time' (2007) 17(7) *Qualitative Health Research* 919–931; Lisa M. Baumgartner and David N. Keegan, 'Accepting Being Poz: The Incorporation of the HIV Identity into the Self' (2009) *Qualitative Health Research* 19(12) 1730–1743; Abigail Merin and John E. Pachankis, 'The Psychological Impact of Genital Herpes Stigma' (2011) 16(1) *Journal of Health Psychology* 80–90.

[68] Except maybe for those who are asexual or pansexual; see Elizabeth M. Morgan, 'Contemporary Issues in Sexual Orientation and Identity Development in Emerging Adulthood' in Jeffrey Jensen Arnett (ed.), *The Oxford Handbook of Emerging Adulthood* (New York: Oxford University Press, 2015), p. 262.

[69] See Chapter 2 for a discussion of implied conditions of marriage, deception and the law of nullity. See also Tilton and Ichikawa, 'Not What I Agreed To'.

[70] Kennedy, 'Criminalising Deceptive Sex'. In this work, I suggested that this should be a defence, rather than an element of the wrong and I left open the kind of onus that should be imposed (that is, evidential or legal). I did not suggest that there should be no liability when the deceptive party's partner did not care about the relevant information because this would seem to involve the problems caused by determining qualifying deceptions on the basis of the beliefs of the person wronged and/or the effect of these beliefs on their decision-making.

inappropriate in the case of some of these deceptions. For example, potentially negative effects on public health goals[71] and privacy concerns[72] might suggest that legal responses to deception about reproductive or disease status are unjustifiable. Similarly, the sensitivities regarding the potential for transgender people to be liable for failing to disclose their gender history might count against a legal response based on gender deception.[73] In addition to these points, my framework provides another reason why criminal prosecution might be inappropriate in specific cases, namely when the deceiver's conduct can be explained by the disadvantage they face and the state is partially responsible for generating that disadvantage. In such circumstances, if the state's failings and the deceiver's wrong are of a similar kind, then it could be argued that the state loses its moral standing to blame.[74] This might be the case in relation to transgender people who are deceptive about their gender history and those of disenfranchised nationalities who deceive their partners about their nationality.[75] As I mentioned earlier, one attraction of the notion of identity nonrecognition is that it is neutral with respect to the decisions people make regarding the issues that are likely to be generally significant in self-constructing terms. For example, it does not suggest that it is better to want to become a parent than to want to avoid this possibility or that it is more laudable to want to have sex with a person of a different gender than it is to want to avoid this. Instead, identity nonrecognition simply helps us try to identity the sort of information that people are likely to want so they can make a decision either way. Yet identity nonrecognition and the framework I suggest might be built upon it has the capacity to recognise that within any given cultural setting some groups experience discrimination and marginalisation, and it provides a way to take this into consideration.

Although my focus in developing this framework was primarily deceptive sex, it can also help identify issues which might generally be significant in identity-constructing terms but are more directly relevant to intimate relationships – more specifically, their likelihood or quality. The potential for deception about religious or political views to qualify in these terms seems relatively strong, as does deception about sexual orientation if it makes a long-term relationship with the deceived person unlikely. By contrast, intentions regarding having children or a specific kind of relationship seem analogous to promises in the sense that one's intentions may change without this signalling anything

---

[71] Patrick O'Byrne, Alyssa Bryan and Marie Roy, 'HIV Criminal Prosecutions and Public Health: An Examination of the Empirical Research' (2013) 39(2) *Medical Humanities* 85–90.
[72] Scheidegger, 'Balancing Sexual Autonomy'.
[73] For a short discussion, see Kennedy, 'Criminalising Deceptive Sex' and Kennedy, 'Sex, Selfhood Deception'.
[74] Kennedy, 'Criminalising Deceptive Sex' at 103–105. This argument would therefore not extend to civil actions.
[75] Aeyal Gross, 'Rape by Deception and the Policing of Gender and Nationality Borders' (2015) 24 *Tulane Journal of Law & Sexuality* 1–33.

about the truthfulness of any earlier statements. Where it could be proved that such a statement was false at the time it was made there would be a stronger case for the deception qualifying, subject to the proviso that subsequent inconsistent conduct could not be interpreted as proof of earlier deception.[76] I would suggest, however, that deception as to marital or relationship status is probably too widespread and its legal regulation too out of step with contemporary sensibilities to plausibly constitute a qualifying deception, even if there were deception from the outset.[77] In terms of the kind of legal response that might be deployed in this context, irrespective of how far the range of qualifying deceptions might extend it would seem more appropriate that private law be used due to the possibility either that the deceived party might want to forgive and forget or that the deception has become less significant to them over time. In other words, the temporalities of relationships – the fact that they form gradually (though they might be marked with specific 'landmarks') and can last a long time – calls for a different approach to potential legal regulation.

8.5 Concluding Reflections

In this final chapter, I have aimed to show that the empirical research and its interpretation which is showcased in Chapters 2–7 of this book, and which is valuable on its own terms, might provide insights that are useful to those involved in contemporary debates about whether and how to use law to respond to deceptively induced intimacy. I did this with a view to contributing towards these debates but also from a desire to illustrate the value of approaching legal questions and problems by starting with the form of conduct and seeing how law has responded to it, rather than beginning with specific legal actions or areas of law. The benefits of this approach hopefully speak for themselves, but I would say that they include the ability to discern patterns and similarities in terms of the functions law performs, such as the punitive and quasi-punitive functions with which this book is concerned, and in terms of doctrinal features, such as the complexities of consent I have discussed. Observing these patterns and similarities makes it possible to predict challenges that might arise and see more clearly how difficulties might be resolved or at least ameliorated. It also helps guard against the tendency to assume that only one kind of legal response either exists or is possible. Beyond this, looking across legal actions and areas of law can reveal points of substantive similarity that would otherwise be missed. In the case of inducing intimacy, this includes the topics that have formed the basis of qualifying deceptions and the frameworks of meaning within which their significance makes sense. Identifying these both strengthens the argument that cultural and social conditions can help explain the range

---

[76] See Chapter 3 (Section 3.5) and Section 8.3.
[77] There is also the danger, present in the context of legally formal intimate relationships, of clash with 'no-fault' regimes in family law, as Chapter 2 pointed out.

of deceptions that have attracted a legal response and provides a novel foundation for determining what the scope of legal regulation should be.

Similar benefits accrue from examining the law historically. Despite the large time period covered in this book, certain doctrinal and substantive issues have recurred and, as I have argued, there is an enduring core to the way these issues have been worked through which centres on the relationship between intimacy and self-construction. To be clear, the nature of this relationship and the way individual and collective interests have been associated with it has not remained static, but its long-standing status suggests a certain normative significance and provides a fresh perspective from which to consider the challenges our current era presents. This fresh perspective is particularly important given the problems with the ideal of autonomy that are disclosed by taking a historically informed view of these challenges.

On top of exposing these problems, a longue durée perspective shows that the dominance of autonomy is not a matter of inevitability; deciding to stick with it or to pursue an alternative is ultimately a matter of debate and decision. It also makes clear that the decision to prioritise individual interests, which is itself related to the dominance of autonomy, is as contestable and morally charged as the decision to make space for collective interests. It is therefore not the case that calling on objective standards and relying on conventional norms is a uniquely moralised way of engaging with the problem of regulating inducing intimacy through law. And while these standards and norms are in some ways hegemonic, they have the capacity to highlight, and assist in attempts to push back against, legal practices that might further or compound oppression. As Amia Srinivasan has said of sex, '[t]here is nothing else so riven with politics and so inviolably personal'.[78] Placing sex within a series of wider contexts shows this to be true of intimate relationships, too, and, as this book demonstrates, there is much to be gained by remaining cognisant of these points.

---

[78] Amia Srinivasan, 'Does Anyone Have the Right to Sex?' (2018) 40(6) *London Review of Books*.

Bibliography

Ahnert, Thomas and Manning, Susan, 'Introduction' in Thomas Ahnert and Susan Manning (eds.), *Character, Self, and Sociability in the Scottish Enlightenment* (New York: Palgrave Macmillan, 2011), pp. 1–30.

Alexander, Larry and Sherwin, Emily, 'Deception in Mortality and Law' (2003) 22 *Law and Philosophy* 393–450.

Alison, Archibald, *Principles of the Criminal Law of Scotland* (Edinburgh: William Blackwood, 1832).

Ault, Richard, 'Dozens of People Caught Hiding Secret Spouses in West Yorkshire', *Yorkshire Live*, 17 January 2021.

Ault, Richard, 'Hundreds of Bigamists Accused of Hiding Secret Spouses', *WalesOnline*, 23 June 2022.

Bagshaw, Roderick, 'Deceit within Couples' (2001) 117 *Law Quarterly Review* 571–574.

Barclay, Katie, *Love, Intimacy and Power: Marriage and Patriarchy in Scotland, 1650–1850* (Manchester: Manchester University Press, 2011).

Barclay, Katie, 'From Rape to Marriage: Questions of Consent in Eighteenth-Century Britain' in Anne Greenfield (ed.), *Interpreting Sexual Violence, 1600–1800* (London: Pickering & Chatto, 2013), pp. 35–44.

Barclay, Katie, 'Marriage, Sex, and the Church of Scotland: Exploring Non-conformity amongst the Lower Orders' (2019) 43(2) *Journal of Religious History* 163–179.

Barclay, Katie, 'Doing the Paperwork: The Emotional World of Wedding Certificates' (2020) 17(3) *Cultural and Social History* 315–332.

Barrett, Maria, 'Crime of Passion That Is Still Doubly Shocking', *The Scotsman*, 20 January 1997.

Barry, John C. (ed. & trans.), *William Hay's Lectures on Marriage* (Edinburgh: The Stair Society, 1967).

Baumgartner, Lisa M., 'The Incorporation of the HIV/AIDS Identity into the Self over Time' (2007) 17(7) *Qualitative Health Research* 919–931.

Baumgartner, Lisa M. and Keegan, David N., 'Accepting Being Poz: The Incorporation of the HIV Identity into the Self' (2009) 19(12) *Qualitative Health Research* 1730–1743.

Bayne, Alexander, *Institutions of the Criminal Law of Scotland* (Edinburgh: Thomas & Walter Ruddimans, 1730).

Beauman, Francesca, *Shapely Ankle Perferr'd: A History of the Lonely Hearts Advertisement* (London: Vintage, 2012).

Bedi, Monu, 'Contract Breaches and the Criminal/Civil Divide: An Inter-common Law Analysis' (2012) 28(3) *Georgia State University Law Review* 559–618.

Bell, Benjamin Robert, 'ART. II. – A Supplement to Hume's Commentaries on the Law of Scotland Respecting Crimes' (1846) 4(8) *The North British Review* 313–346.

Bell, George Joseph and Guthrie, William, *Principles of the Law of Scotland*, 6th ed. (Edinburgh: T. & T. Clark, 1872).

Bell, George Joseph (rev. by Guthrie, William), *Principles of the Law of Scotland*, 10th ed. (Edinburgh: T. & T. Clark, 1899).

Beynon-Jones, Siân M., 'Untroubling Abortion: A Discourse Analysis of Women's Accounts' (2017) 27(2) *Feminism & Psychology* 225–242.

Blackie, John, 'Unity in Diversity: The History of Personality Rights in Scots Law' in Niall R. Whitty and Reinhard Zimmermann (eds.), *Rights of Personality in Scots Law* (Edinburgh: Edinburgh University Press, 2009), pp. 31–146.

Bogart, John H., 'On the Nature of Rape' (1991) 5(2) *Public Affairs Quarterly* 117–136.

Boswell, John, *The Marriage of Likeness: Same-Sex Unions in Pre-Modern Europe* (London: HarperCollins, 1995).

Bourke, Joanna, *Rape: A History from 1860 to the Present Day* (London: Virago, 2008).

Bowers, Toni, *Force or Fraud: British Seduction Stories and the Problem of Resistance, 1660–1760* (Oxford: Oxford University Press, 2011).

Brake, Elizabeth, 'Love and the Law' in Christopher Grau and Aaron Smuts (eds.), *The Oxford Handbook of Philosophy of Love* (New York: Oxford University Press, 2017).

Brewer, Gayle, 'Deceiving for and during Sex' in Tony Docan-Morgan (ed.), *The Palgrave Handbook of Deceptive Communication* (Cham: Springer International Publishing, 2019), pp. 551–566.

Brewer, William D., *Staging Romantic Chameleons and Imposters* (New York: Palgrave Macmillan, 2015).

Bridgett, Dan, '"Wife" Saves Bigamist from Prison', *The Evening Standard*, 30 July 2001.

Brinig, Margaret F. and Alexeev, Michael V., 'Fraud in Courtship: Annulment and Divorce' (1995) 2 *European Journal of Law and Economics* 45–62.

Brodsky, Alexandra, '"Rape-Adjacent": Imagining Legal Responses to Nonconsensual Condom Removal' (2017) 32(2) *Columbia Journal of Gender and Law* 183–210.

Brown, Annie, 'Former Brad Pitt Body Double Is the First in Scotland to Be Convicted of Rape by "Stealthing"', *Daily Record*, 14 May 2023.

Brunning, Luke and McKeever, Natasha, 'Asexuality' (2021) 38(3) *Journal of Applied Philosophy* 497–517.

Buss, Sarah, 'Valuing Autonomy and Respecting Persons: Manipulation, Seduction, and the Basis of Moral Constraints' (2005) 115(2) *Ethics* 195–235.

Cameron, Anne, 'The Establishment of Civil Registration in Scotland' (2007) 50(2) *The Historical Journal* 377–395.

Carswell, Andy, 'Bigamy Wife Speaks of Betrayal', *Bucks Free Press*, 9 October 2008.

Carvalho, Henrique, *The Preventive Turn in Criminal Law* (Oxford: Oxford University Press, 2017).

Chadha, Karamvir, 'Conditional Consent' (2021) 40(3) *Law and Philosophy* 335–359.

Chalmers, James, 'How (Not) to Reform the Law of Rape' (2002) 6(3) *Edinburgh Law Review* 388–396.

Chalmers, James and Leverick, Fiona (eds.), *The Criminal Law of Scotland*, 4th ed. (vol. 2) (Edinburgh: W. Green & Sons, 2017).

Chambers, Clare, *Against Marriage: An Egalitarian Defence of the Marriage-Free State* (Oxford: Oxford University Press, 2017).

Chamie, Joseph and Mirkin, Barry, 'Same-Sex Marriage: A New Social Phenomenon' (2011) 37(3) *Population and Development Review* 529–551.

Cheadle, Tanya, *Sexual Progressives: Reimagining Intimacy in Scotland, 1880–1914* (Manchester: Manchester University Press, 2020).

Chen, Jianlin, 'Joyous Buddha, Holy Father, and Dragon God Desiring Sex: A Case Study of Rape by Religious Fraud in Taiwan' (2018) 13(2) *National Taiwan University Law Review* 183–237.

Chen, Jianlin, 'Lying about God (and Love?) to Get Laid: The Case Study of Criminalizing Sex under Religious False Pretence in Hong Kong' (2018) 51(3) *Cornell International Law Journal* 553–607.

Chen, Jianlin, 'Fraudulent Sex Criminalisation in Australia: Disparity, Disarray and the Underrated Procurement Offence' (2020) 43(2) *University of New South Wales Law Journal* 581–614.

Chen, Jianlin and Lu, Bijuan, 'Rape-by-Deception in China: A Messy but Pragmatically Desirable Criminal Law' (2023) 43(2) *Columbia Journal of Gender and Law* 151–210.

Chiesa, Luis E., 'Solving the Riddle of Rape by Deception' (2017) 35(2) *Yale Law & Policy Review* 407–460.

Chuang, Janie A., 'Exploitation Creep and the Unmaking of Human Trafficking Law' (2014) 108(14) *American Journal of International Law* 609–649.

Church of England, *The Church and the Law of Nullity of Marriage: The Report of a Commission Appointed by the Archbishops of Canterbury and York in 1949 at the Request of the Convocations* (London: SPCK, 1955).

Clarke, Nathan, 'Bigamy Victim Says It's a "Business"', *Birmingham Live*, 3 July 2022.

Clive, Eric, *The Law of Husband and Wife in Scotland*, 4th ed. (Edinburgh: W. Green & Sons, 1997).

Clough, Amanda, 'Conditional Consent and Purposeful Deception' (2018) 82(2) *The Journal of Criminal Law* 178–190.

Coel, Michaela, 'I May Destroy You', *HBO-BBC* (2020).

Cohen, Jean L., *Regulating Intimacy: A New Legal Paradigm* (Princeton: Princeton University Press, 2002).

Cohen, Rhaina, 'What If Friendship, Not Marriage, Was at the Center of Life?', *The Atlantic*, 20 October 2020.

Coontz, Stephanie, *Marriage, A History: How Love Conquered Marriage* (New York: Penguin Books, 2006).

Cossman, Brenda, *The New Sex Wars: Sexual Harm in the #MeToo Era* (New York: New York University Press, 2021).

Coulmas, Florian, *Identity: A Very Short Introduction* (Oxford: Oxford University Press, 2019).

Cox, David J., '"Trying to Get a Good One" Bigamy Offences in England and Wales, 1850–1920' (2012) 1 *Plymouth Law & Criminal Justice Review* 1–32.

Criminal Law Reform Now Network, *Reforming the Relationship between Sexual Consent, Deception and Mistake: Consultation Report* (2021) www.clrnn.co.uk/publications-reports.

Criminal Law Reform Now Network, *Reforming the Relationship between Sexual Consent, Deception and Mistake: Report* (2023), www.clrnn.co.uk/publications-reports.

Criminal Law Revision Committee, *Fifteenth Report: Sexual Offences* (Cmnd. 9213, 1984).

Crown Prosecution Service, *Deception as to Gender: Proposed Revision to CPS Legal Guidance on Rape and Serious Sexual Offences* (26 September 2022), www.cps.gov.uk/publication/deception-gender-proposed-revision-cps-legal-guidance-rape-and-serious-sexual-offences.

Crump, David, 'Rethinking Intentional Infliction of Emotional Distress' (2018) 25(2) *George Mason Law Review* 287–300.

Cryle, Peter and Downing, Lisa, 'Feminine Sexual Pathologies' and the associated special edition of the *Journal of the History of Sexuality* (2009) 18(1).

Dan-Cohen, Meir, 'Basic Values and the Victim's State of Mind' (2000) 88 *California Law Review* 759–778.

David, Joseph E., *Kinship, Law and Politics: An Anatomy of Belonging* (Cambridge: Cambridge University Press, 2020).

Davidson, Roger, *Illicit and Unnatural Practices: The Law, Sex and Society in Scotland since 1900* (Edinburgh: Edinburgh University Press, 2018).

Decker, John F. and Baroni, Peter G., '"No" Still Means "Yes": The Failure of the "Non-Consent" Reform Movement in American Rape and Sexual Assault Law' (2011) 101(4) *The Journal of Criminal Law & Criminology* 1081–1169.

DeGirolami, Marc O., 'Reconstructing Malice in the Law of Punitive Damages' (2021) 14(1) *The Journal of Tort Law* 193–240.

Del Mar, Maksymilian, 'Philosophical Analysis and Historical Inquiry' in Markus D. Dubber and Christopher Tomlins (eds.), *The Oxford Handbook of Legal History* (Oxford: Oxford University Press, 2018), pp. 3–21.

Dempsey, Brian, 'The Marriage (Scotland) Bill 1755' in Hector L. MacQueen (ed.), *Miscellany Six* (Edinburgh: Stair Society, 2009), pp. 77–78.

Dempsey, Michelle Madden and Herring, Jonathan, 'Why Sexual Penetration Requires Justification' (2007) 27(3) *Oxford Journal of Legal Studies* 467–491.

Derry, Caroline, *Lesbianism and the Criminal Law: Three Centuries of Legal Regulation in England and Wales* (Cham: Palgrave Macmillan, 2020).

Derry, Caroline, 'Sustained Identity Deceptions' in Criminal Law Reform Now Network, *Reforming the Relationship between Sexual Consent, Deception and Mistake: Consultation Report* (2021), www.clrnn.co.uk/publications-reports, pp. 15–23.

Descheemaker, Eric, 'Rationalising Recovery for Emotional Harm in Tort Law' (2018) 134 *Law Quarterly Review* 602–626.

Dodds, W. E., 'A Few Comparisons between English and Scots Law. II. The Law of Personal Relations' (1927) 9(1) *Journal of Comparative Legislation and International Law* 40–58.

Doezema, Jo, 'Who Gets to Choose? Coercion, Consent, and the UN Trafficking Protocol' (2002) 10(1) *Gender and Development* 20–27.

Doig, Gavin A., 'Deception as to Gender Vitiates Consent' (2013) 77(6) *The Journal of Criminal Law* 464–468.

Doniger, Wendy, *The Bedtrick: Tales of Sex and Masquerade* (Chicago: University of Chicago Press, 2000).

Donovan, Brian, 'Gender Inequality and Criminal Seduction: Prosecuting Sexual Coercion in the Early-20th Century' (2005) 30(1) *Law & Social Inquiry* 61–88.

Douglas, Benedict, 'Love and Human Rights' (2023) 43(2) *Oxford Journal of Legal Studies* 273–297.

Dripps, Donald A., 'Beyond Rape: An Essay on the Difference between the Presence of Force and the Absence of Consent' (1992) 92(7) *Columbia Law Review* 1780–1809.

Dsouza, Mark, 'False Beliefs and Consent to Sex' in Criminal Law Reform Now Network, *Reforming the Relationship between Sexual Consent, Deception and Mistake: Consultation Report* (2021), www.clrnn.co.uk/publications-reports, pp. 24–35.

Dsouza, Mark, 'False Beliefs and Consent to Sex' (2022) 85(5) *Modern Law Review* 1191–1217.

Dubler, Ariela R., 'Immoral Purposes: Marriage and the Genus of Illicit Sex' (2006) 115(4) *Yale Law Journal* 756–812.

Duff, R. A., 'Torts, Crimes and Vindication: Whose Wrong Is It?' in Matthew Dyson (ed.), *Unravelling Tort and Crime* (Cambridge: Cambridge University Press, 2014) pp. 146–173.

Duguay, Stefanie, 'Dressing Up Tinderella: Interrogating Authenticity Claims on the Mobile Dating App Tinder' (2017) 20(3) *Information, Communication & Society* 351–367.

E. G. L., 'Mistake or Fraud as a Ground for Annulling Marriage in Louisiana' (1919) 28(3) *The Yale Law Journal* 272–278.

Eisenberg, Avlana K., 'Criminal Infliction of Emotional Distress' (2015) 113(5) *Michigan Law Review* 607–662.

El-Enany, Nadine, *Bordering Britain: Law, Race and Empire* (Manchester: Manchester University Press, 2020).

Ellin, Abby, 'Is Sex by Deception a Form of Rape?', *The New York Times*, 23 April 2019.

Ellman, Ira Mark and Sugarman, Stephen D., 'Spousal Emotional Abuse as a Tort?' (1996) 55(4) *Maryland Law Review* 1268–1343.

Erskine, John, *Principles of the Law of Scotland*, 14th ed. (Edinburgh: Bell & Bradfute, 1870).

Eskridge, William N., Jr, 'A History of Same-Sex Marriage' (1993) 79(7) *Virginia Law Review* 1419–1513.

F. P. W., 'Notes on Decided Cases' (1897) 9(4) *Juridical Review* 458–460.

Falk, Patricia J., 'Rape by Fraud and Rape by Coercion' (1998) 64(1) *Brooklyn Law Journal* 39–180.

Farmer, Lindsay, *Making the Modern Criminal Law: Criminalization and Civil Order* (Oxford: Oxford University Press, 2016).

Fergusson, James, *A Treatise on the Present State of the Consistorial Law in Scotland, with Reports of Decided Cases* (Edinburgh: Bell & Bradfute, 1829).

Ferzan, Kimberly Kessler, 'Losing the Right to Assert You've Been Wronged: A Study in Conceptual Chaos?' in Paul B. Miller and John Oberdiek (eds.), *Civil Wrongs and Justice in Private Law* (New York: Oxford University Press, 2020), pp. 111–130.

Finch, Emily and Munro, Vanessa E., 'Breaking Boundaries: Sexual Consent in the Jury Room' (2006) 26(3) *Legal Studies* 303–320.

Fischel, Joseph J., *Sex and Harm in the Age of Consent* (Minneapolis: University of Minnesota Press, 2016).

Forbes, William, *The Institutes of the Law of Scotland* (Edinburgh: Edinburgh Legal Education Trust, 2012).

Fortenberry, Dennis J., 'Trust, Sexual Trust and Sexual Health: An Interrogative Review' (2019) 56(4–5) *The Journal of Sex Research* 425–439.

Fraser, Patrick, *Treatise on the Law of Scotland as Applicable to the Personal and Domestic Relations* (Edinburgh: T. & T. Clark, 1846).

Fraser, Patrick, *Treatise on Husband and Wife, According to the Law of Scotland* (Edinburgh: T. & T. Clark, 1876).

Fraser, Rachel Elizabeth, 'The Erotics of ASMR', *The Oxonian Review*, 8 May 2020.

Friedman, Lawrence M., *Personal Identity in the Modern World: A Society of Strangers* (Lanham: Rowman & Littlefield, 2022).

Frohock, Fred M., 'Liberal Maps of Consent' (1989) 22(2) *Polity* 231–252.

Frost, Ginger S., *Promises Broken: Courtship, Class, and Gender in Victorian England* (Charlottesville: University of Virginia Press, 1995).

Frye, Brian L. and Romero, Maybell, 'The Right to Unmarry: A Proposal' (2020) 69(1) *Cleveland State Law Journal* 89–104.

Gal, Susan, 'A Semiotics of the Private/Public Distinction' (2002) 13(1) *Differences: A Journal of Feminist Cultural Studies* 77–95.

Galanter, Marc, and Luban, David, 'Poetic Justice: Punitive Damages and Legal Pluralism' (1993) 42(4) *American University Law Review* 1394–1463.

Ganz, Melissa J., '"The Fidelity of Promising": Egoism and Obligation in Austen' (2022) 73(309) *The Review of English Studies* 344–360.

Gardner, John C. and Shute, Stephen, 'The Wrongness of Rape' in Jeremy Horder (ed.), *Oxford Essays in Jurisprudence: Fourth Series* (Oxford: Oxford University Press, 2000), pp. 193–218.

Gardner, John C., 'A Comparison of the Effects of Decree of Nullity of Marriage in Scotland and England' (1938) *Scots Law Times* 109–110.

Gibson, Matthew, 'Deceptive Sexual Relations: A Theory of Criminal Liability' (2020) 40(1) *Oxford Journal of Legal Studies* 82–109.

Giddens, Anthony, *Modernity and Self-Identity: Self and Society in the Late Modern Age* (Cambridge: Polity Press, 1991).

Giddens, Anthony, *The Transformation of Intimacy: Sexuality, Love and Eroticism in Modern Societies* (Newark: Polity Press, 1992).

Gilbert, Andrew, *British Conservatism and the Legal Regulation of Intimate Relationships* (Portland: Hart Publishing, 2018).

Glas, Gerrit, 'Idem, Ipse, and Loss of the Self' (2003) 10(4) *Philosophy, Psychiatry & Psychology* 347–352.

Glegg, Arthur Thomson, *A Practical Treatise on the Law of Reparation* (W. Green & Sons, 1892).

Goda, Paul J., 'The Historical Evolution of the Concepts of Void and Voidable Marriages' (1967) 7 *Journal of Family Law* 297–308.

Goldberg, John C. P. and Zipursky, Benjamin C., *Recognizing Wrongs* (Cambridge, MA: Harvard University Press, 2020).

Goodrich, Peter, *Law in the Courts of Love: Literature and Other Minor Jurisprudences* (London: Routledge, 1996).

Gordon, Eleanor, 'Irregular Marriage: Myth and Reality' (2013) 47(2) *Journal of Social History* 507–525.

Gordon, Eleanor, 'Irregular Marriage and Cohabitation in Scotland, 1855–1939: Official Policy and Popular Practice' (2015) 58(4) *The Historical Journal* 1059–1079.

Gordon, G. H., *The Criminal Law of Scotland* (Edinburgh: W. Green & Sons, 1967).

Greasley, Kate, 'Deception and Power amidst Sexual Activity', *Criminal Justice Theory Blog*, 30 September 2022, https://criminaljusticetheoryblog.wordpress.com/2022/09/30/deception-and-power-amidst-sexual-activity.

Green, Stuart P., *Criminalizing Sex: A Unified Liberal Theory* (New York: Oxford University Press, 2020).

Gross, Aeyal, 'Rape by Deception and the Policing of Gender and Nationality Borders' (2015) 24 *Tulane Journal of Law & Sexuality* 1–33.

Gross, Hyman, 'Rape, Moralism, and Human Rights' [2007] *Criminal Law Review* 220–227.

Grossman, Joanna L., 'Annulments Based on Fraud: What Is the "Essence" of Marriage?' Part One (2010), https://supreme.findlaw.com/legal-commentary/annulments-based-on-fraud-what-is-the-essence-of-marriage.html.

Grossman, Joanna L., 'Annulments Based on Fraud: What Is the "Essence" of Marriage?' Part Two (2010), https://supreme.findlaw.com/legal-commentary/annulments-based-on-fraud-what-is-the-essence-of-marriage-part-two.html.

Grossman, Joanna L. and Guthrie, Chris, 'The Road Less Taken: Annulment at the Turn of the Century' (1996) 40 *The American Journal of Legal History* 307–330.

Guirguis, Sheren, 'Conduct: When Is It Bad Enough?' (2020) 50 *Family Law* 60–67.

Guthrie, William, *Select Cases Decided in the Sheriff Courts of Scotland* (vol. 2) (Edinburgh: T. & T. Clark, 1894).

Guthrie Smith, John, *A Treatise on the Law of Reparation* (Edinburgh: T. & T. Clark, 1864).

Guthrie Smith, John, *Law of Damages: A Treatise on the Reparation of Injuries as Administered in Scotland*, 2nd ed. (Edinburgh: T. & T. Clark, 1889).

Haag, Pamela, *Consent: Sexual Rights and the Transformation of American Liberalism* (Ithaca, NY: Cornell University Press, 1999).

Haag, Pamela, *Marriage Confidential: Love in the Post-Romantic Age* (New York: Harper Perennial, 2011).

Halkerston, Peter, *A Translation and Explanation of the Principal Technical Terms and Phrases Used in Mr Erskine's Institute of the Law of Scotland,* 2nd ed. (Edinburgh: printed for the author, 1829).

Hall, Lesley A., *Sex, Gender and Social Change in Britain since 1800*, 2nd ed. (Basingstoke: Palgrave Macmillan, 2012).

Halperin, David M., 'Is There a History of Sexuality?' (1989) 28(3) *History and Theory* 257–274.

Hammack, Phillip L., Frost, David M. and Hughes, Sam D., 'Queer Intimacies: A New Paradigm for the Study of Relationship Diversity' (2019) 56(4–5) *The Journal of Sex Research* 556–592.

Hasday, Jill, *Intimate Lies and the Law* (New York: Oxford University Press, 2019).

Hawley, Katherine, *How to Be Trustworthy* (Oxford: Oxford University Press, 2019).

Herman, Barbara, 'Could It Be Worth Thinking about Kant on Sex and Marriage?' in Louise M. Antony and Charlotte Witt (eds.), *A Mind of One's Own: Feminist Essays on Reason and Objectivity* (Oxford: Westview Press, 1993), pp. 53–72.

Herring, Jonathan, 'Mistaken Sex' [2005] *Criminal Law Review* 511–524.

Herring, Jonathan, 'Consent Mistaken' in *Criminal Law Reform Now Network, Reforming the Relationship between Sexual Consent, Deception and Mistake: Consultation Report* (2021), www.clrnn.co.uk/publications-reports, pp. 52–58.

Herrup, Cynthia B., *A House in Gross Disorder: Sex, Law and the 2nd Earl of Castlehaven* (Oxford: Oxford University Press, 2001).

Hobson, Clark and Miola, José, 'Should We Criminalise a Deliberate Failure to Obtain Properly Informed Consent?' (2021) 21(4) *Medical Law International* 369–392.

Holden, Katherine, Froide, Amy and Hannam, June, 'Introduction' (2008) 17(3) *Women's History Review* 313–326.

Holloway, Sally, *The Game of Love in Georgian England: Courtship, Emotions and Material Culture* (Oxford: Oxford University Press, 2019).

Home Office, *Setting the Boundaries: Reforming the Law on Sex Offences* (London: Home Office Communication Directorate, 2000).

Home Office, *Criminal Investigations: Sham Marriage*, version 3.0 (January 2021).

hooks, bell, *All about Love: New Visions* (New York: William Morrow, 2003).

Horwitz, Morton J., 'The History of the Public/Private Distinction' (1982) 130(6) *University of Pennsylvania Law Review* 1423–1428.

Hume, David, *Commentaries on the Law of Scotland, Respecting Crimes* (Edinburgh: Bell & Bradfute, 1844).

Hunter, R. F., 'The Voidable Marriage: Impotency and the Law' (2013) 4 *Scots Law Times* 29–33.

Ikäheimo, Heikki, 'Recognition, Identity and Subjectivity' in Michael J. Thompson (ed.), *The Palgrave Handbook of Critical Theory* (New York: Palgrave Macmillan, 2017), pp. 567–586.

Irwig, Michael S., 'Detransition among Transgender and Gender-Diverse People: An Increasing and Increasingly Complex Phenomenon' (2022) 10(107) *The Journal of Clinical Endocrinology & Metabolism* e4261–e4262.

Jackson, Joseph, 'Consent of the Parties to Their Marriage' (1951) 14(1) *Modern Law Review* 1–26.

Jamieson, Lynn 'Personal Relationships, Intimacy and the Self in a Mediated and Global Digital Age' in Kate Orton-Johnson and Nick Prior (eds.), *Digital Sociology: Critical Perspectives* (London: Palgrave Macmillan, 2013), pp. 13–33.

Johnston, Christopher N., 'Report of the Royal Commission Upon Divorce' (1912–1913) 24(4) *Juridical Review* 274–291.

Jollimore, Troy, 'Love as "Something in Between"' in Christopher Grau and Aaron Smuts (eds.), *The Oxford Handbook of Philosophy of Love* (New York: Oxford University Press, 2017), pp. 149–166.

Jones, Timothy Willem and Harris, Alana, 'Introduction: Historicizing "Modern" Love and Romance' in Alana Harris and Timothy Jones (eds.), *Love and Romance in Britain, 1918–1970* (London: Palgrave Macmillan, 2015), pp. 1–19.

Kelly, Karon, 'Bigamist Trapped by Plea for Help', *The Journal*, 19 March 2004.

Kennedy, Chloë, '"Ungovernable Feelings and Passions": Common Sense Philosophy and Mental State Defences in Nineteenth-Century Scotland' (2016) 20(3) *Edinburgh Law Review* 285–311.

Kennedy, Chloë, 'Declaring Crimes' (2017) 37(4) *Oxford Journal of Legal Studies* 741–769.

Kennedy, Chloë, 'Immanence and Transcendence: History's Roles in Normative Legal Theory' (2017) 8(3) *Jurisprudence* 557–579.

Kennedy, Chloë, 'Counterfeit Currency and Commercialising Scotland' in A. M. Godfrey (ed.), *Miscellany Eight* (Edinburgh: Stair Society, 2020), pp. 285–317.

Kennedy, Chloë, 'Sociology of Law and Legal History' in Jiří Přibáň (ed.), *Research Handbook on the Sociology of Law* (Northampton: Edward Elgar 2020), pp. 31–42.

Kennedy, Chloë, 'Criminalising Deceptive Sex: Sex, Identity and Recognition' (2021) 41(1) *Legal Studies* 91–110.

Kennedy, Chloë, 'Sex, Selfhood and Deception' in Criminal Law Reform Now Network, *Reforming the Relationship between Sexual Consent, Deception and Mistake: Consultation Report* (2021), www.clrnn.co.uk/publications-reports, pp. 59–69.

Kennedy, Chloë, 'Sex, Selfhood and Deception', 8 December 2021, www.youtube.com/watch?v=oZPzjBWTbIQ.

Kennedy, Chloë, 'Crime, Reason, and History: A Critical Introduction to Criminal Law' in Chloë Kennedy and Lindsay Farmer (eds.), *Leading Works in Criminal Law* (Abingdon: Routledge, 2023), pp. 220–241.

Kennedy, Chloë, 'Comparing Criminal and Civil Responsibility: Contextualising Claims to Distinctiveness' in Thomas Crofts, Louise Kennefick, and Arlie Loughnan (eds.), *Routledge International Handbook on Criminal Responsibility* (Routledge, forthcoming 2025).

Kennedy, Duncan, 'Form and Substance in Private Law Adjudication' (1976) 89 *Harvard Law Review* 1685–1778.

Kenny, Courtney Stanhope, *Outlines of Criminal Law* (Cambridge: Cambridge University Press, 1909).

Khaitan, Tarunabh, and Steel, Sandy, 'Areas of Law: Three Questions in Special Jurisprudence' (2023) 43(1) *Oxford Journal of Legal Studies* 76–96.

Kirkup, Kyle, 'Law's Sexual Infections' (2023) 46(2) *Dalhousie Law Journal*.

Klass, Gregory, 'Meaning, Purpose, and Cause in the Law of Deception' (2012) 100 *Georgetown Law Journal* 449–496.

Klass, Gregory, Letsas, George and Saprai, Prince (eds.), *Philosophical Foundations of Contract Law* (Oxford: Oxford University Press, 2014).

Klass, Gregory, 'The Law of Deception: A Research Agenda' (2018) 89 *University of Colorado Law Review* 707–740.

Kolovos, Benita, 'Affirmative Consent and "Stealthing" Laws to Be Introduced to Victorian Parliament', *The Guardian*, 3 August 2022.

Korsgaard, Christine M., *The Sources of Normativity* (Cambridge: Cambridge University Press, 1996).

Korsgaard, Christine M., *Self-Constitution: Agency, Identity, and Integrity* (Oxford: Oxford University Press, 2009).

Koutsoukis, Jason, 'Deception Rape Case Sparks Legal Concerns in Israel', *The Sydney Morning Herald*, 22 July 2010.

Lacey, Nicola, 'Beset by Boundaries: The Home Office Review of Sex Offences' [2001] *Criminal Law Review* 3–14.

Laird, Karl, 'Rapist or Rogue? Deception, Consent and the Sexual Offences Act 2003' [2014] *Criminal Law Review* 492–510.

Laitinen, Arto, 'Recognition, Needs and Wrongness: Two Approaches' (2009) 8(1) *European Journal of Political Theory* 13–30.

Laitinen, Arto, 'On the Scope of "Recognition": The Role of Adequate Regard and Mutuality' in Hans-Christoph Schmidt am Busch and Christopher F. Zurn (eds.), *The Philosophy of Recognition: Historical and Contemporary Perspectives* (Lanham, MD: Lexington Books, 2010), pp. 319–342.

Lammasniemi, Laura, '"Precocious Girls": Age of Consent, Class and Family in Late Nineteenth-Century England' (2020) 38(1) *Law and History Review* 241–266.

Lammasniemi, Laura, 'Trafficking, Rape, or Deceptive Sex? A Historical Examination of Procurement Offences in England' (2023) 32(4) *Social & Legal Studies* 499–518.

Langhamer, Claire, 'Love and Courtship in Mid-Twentieth-Century England' (2007) 50(1) *The Historical Journal* 173–196.

Langhamer, Claire, 'Love, Selfhood and Authenticity in Post-War Britain' (2012) 9(2) *Cultural and Social History* 277–297.

Langhamer, Claire, 'Trust, Authenticity and Bigamy in Twentieth-Century England' in Katie Barclay, Jeffrey Meek and Andrea Thomson (eds.), *Courtship, Marriage and*

Marriage Breakdown: Approaches from the History of Emotion (New York: Routledge, 2019), pp. 160–174.

Larson, Jane E., 'Women Understand So Little, They Call My Good Nature Deceit: A Feminist Rethinking of Seduction' (1993) 93 *Columbia Law Review* 374–472.

Latham, Emily, 'Recognizing Error and Fraud in the Contract of Marriage' (2006) 66(2) *Louisiana Law Review* 563–607.

Law Commission, *Working Paper No 20 Nullity of Marriage* (1968).

Law Commission, *Report on Breach of Promise of Marriage* (Her Majesty's Stationery Office, 1969).

Law Commission, *Report on Nullity of Marriage* (Her Majesty's Stationery Office, 1970).

Law Commission, *Consent and Offences against the Person: A Consultation Paper* (Her Majesty's Stationery Office, 1994).

Law Commission, *Consent in the Criminal Law: A Consultation Paper* (Her Majesty's Stationery Office, 1995).

The Laws of Scotland: Stair Memorial Encyclopaedia, reissue (Edinburgh: Butterworths, 2016).

Leneman, Leah, 'Seduction in Eighteenth and Early Nineteenth-Century Scotland' (1999) 78(205) *Scottish Historical Review* 39–59.

Leneman, Leah, 'The Scottish Case That Led to Hardwicke's Marriage Act' (1999) 17(1) *Law and History Review* 161–169.

Leneman, Leah, '"No Unsuitable Match": Defining Rank in Eighteenth and Early Nineteenth Century-Scotland' (2000) 33(3) *Journal of Social History* 665–682.

Leneman, Leah, *Promises, Promises: Marriage Litigation in Scotland, 1698–1830* (Edinburgh: National Museums of Scotland, 2003).

Leslie, R. D., 'Polygamous Marriage and Bigamy' (1972) 17 *Juridical Review* 113–123.

Letsas, George, 'Offences against Status' (2023) 43(2) *Oxford Journal of Legal Studies* 322–349.

Lettmaier, Saskia, *Broken Engagements: The Action for Breach of Promise of Marriage and the Feminine Ideal, 1800–1940* (Oxford: Oxford University Press, 2010).

Levine, Philippa and Bashford, Alison, 'Introduction: Eugenics and the Modern World' in Alison Bashford and Philippa Levine (eds.), *The Oxford Handbook of the History of Eugenics* (Oxford: Oxford University Press, 2010), pp. 3–24.

Loidolt, Sophie, 'Order, Experience, and Critique: The Phenomenological Method in Political and Legal Theory' (2021) 54(2) *Continental Philosophy Review* 153–170.

Lothian, Maurice, *The Law, Practice and Styles Peculiar to the Consistorial Actions Transferred to the Court of Session, by Act 1, Gul. IV. c. 69* (Edinburgh: Adam Black, 1830).

Lott, Tim, 'Becoming a Parent Is the Greatest Identity Change We Go Through', *The Guardian*, 29 April 2016.

Loughnan, Arlie, *Self, Others and the State: Relations of Criminal Responsibility* (Cambridge: Cambridge University Press, 2020).

Lusher, Adam, 'MPs Urged to Pass Law against Online "Catfish" Imposters Tricking Women into Sex', *The Independent*, 17 July 2017.

Lyshaug, Brenda, 'Authenticity and the Politics of Identity: A Critique of Charles Taylor's Politics of Recognition' (2004) 3 *Contemporary Political Theory* 300–320.

MacDonald Eggers, Peter, *Deceit: The Lie of the Law* (London: Routledge, 2009).

MacFarlane, Robert and Cleghorn, Thomas, *Practical Notes on the Structure of Issues in Jury Cases in the Court of Session: With Forms of Issues* (Edinburgh: T. & T. Clark, 1844–1849).

MacGregor, Laura J., 'Pacta Illicita' in Kenneth Reid and Reinhard Zimmermann (eds.), *A History of Private Law in Scotland: Volume 2: Obligations* (Oxford: Oxford University Press, 2000), pp. 129–156.

MacGregor, Laura, 'Specific Implement in Scots Law' in Jan Smits, Daniel Haas and Geete Hesen (eds.), *Specific Performance in Contract Law: National and Other Perspectives* (Oxford: Intersentia, 2008), pp. 67–93.

Mackay, Æ. J. G., *Manual of Practice in the Court of Session* (Edinburgh: W. Green & Sons, 1893).

MacKinnon, Neil K. and Heise, David R., *Self, Identity, and Social Institutions* (Basingstoke: Palgrave Macmillan, 2010).

MacLeod, John, 'Before Bell: The Roots of Error in the Scots Law of Contract' (2010) 14(3) *Edinburgh Law Review* 385–417.

MacNamara, Darach, 'The Tort of Deceit and Family Law: Some Recent Developments' (2001) 9 *Irish Student Law Review* 163–180.

MacQueen, Hector L., 'Fraser, Patrick, Lord Fraser (1817–1889), Jurist and Judge', *Oxford Dictionary of National Biography* (2004), www-oxforddnb-com.ezproxy.is.ed.ac.uk/view/10.1093/ref:odnb/9780198614128.001.0001/odnb-9780198614128-e-10119.

Mair, Jane, 'A Sham Marriage or a Proper Wedding? Hakeem v Hussain' (2003) 7(3) *Edinburgh Law Review* 404–409.

Manion, Jen, *Female Husbands: A Trans History* (Cambridge: Cambridge University Press, 2020).

Manta, Irina D., 'Tinder Lies' (2019) 54(1) *Wake Forest Law Review* 207–249.

McAleese, Deborah, 'My Sham Life with a Bigamist Husband', *The Belfast Telegraph*, 30 September 2008.

McArthur, Neil, 'Is Lying to Get Laid a Form of Sexual Assault?', *Vice*, 5 September 2016.

McBryde, William W., 'Error' in Kenneth Reid and Reinhard Zimmermann (eds.), *A History of Private Law in Scotland: Volume 2: Obligations* (Oxford: Oxford University Press, 2000), pp. 72–100.

McBryde, William W., *The Law of Contract in Scotland*, 3rd ed. (Edinburgh: W. Green & Sons, 2007).

McGowan, Michael and Knaus, Christopher, '"It Absolutely Should Be Seen as Rape" When Sex Workers Are Conned', *The Guardian*, 12 October 2018.

McKinley, Michelle A., *Fractional Freedoms: Slavery, Intimacy, and Legal Mobilization in Colonial Lima, 1600–1700* (New York: Cambridge University Press, 2016).

McLaren, Angus, *The Trials of Masculinity: Policing Sexual Boundaries, 1870–1930* (Chicago: University of Chicago Press, 1999).

McLaren, Angus, *Impotence: A Cultural History* (Chicago: The University of Chicago Press, 2007).

McLeish, Norrie, *Broken Promises: Scottish Breach of Promise Cases* (Jedburgh: Alba Publishing, 2013).

Mead, Frederick and Bodkin, Archibald H., *The Criminal Law Amendment Act, 1885 with Introduction, Notes, and Index* (London: Shaw & Sons, 1885).

Merin, Abigail and Pachankis, John E., 'The Psychological Impact of Genital Herpes Stigma' (2011) 16(1) *Journal of Health Psychology* 80–90.

Moloney, Pat, 'Savages in the Scottish Enlightenment's History of Desire' (2005) 14(3) *Journal of the History of Sexuality* 237–265.

Montgomery, George A., 'Ninety Years of Progress' (1947) 59 *Juridical Review* 173–184.

Morgan, Elizabeth M., 'Contemporary Issues in Sexual Orientation and Identity Development in Emerging Adulthood' in Jeffrey Jensen Arnett (ed.), *The Oxford Handbook of Emerging Adulthood* (New York: Oxford University Press, 2015), pp. 262–279.

Morris, George, 'Intimacy in Modern British History' (2021) 64(3) *The Historical Journal* 796–811.

Murdoch, Hec Burn, 'English Law in Scots Practice III' (1909–1910) 21 *Juridical Review* 148–158.

Murphy, John, 'Misleading Appearances in the Tort of Deceit' (2016) 75(2) *The Cambridge Law Journal* 301–322.

Murray, Kyle L. and Beattie, Tara, 'Conditional Consent and Sexual Offences: Revisiting the Sexual Offences Act 2003 after Lawrance' [2021] *Criminal Law Review* 556–574.

Murray, Melissa, 'Marriage as Punishment' (2012) 112(1) *Columbia Law Review* 1–65.

Murray, Paula C. and Winslett, Brenda J., 'The Constitutional Right to Privacy and Emerging Tort Liability for Deceit in Interpersonal Relationships' (1986) 3 *University of Illinois Law Review* 779–836.

Neaves, Charles, 'The Tourist's Matrimonial Guide through Scotland' in Charles Neaves (ed.), *Songs and Verses, Social and Scientific*, 5th ed. (Edinburgh: Blackwood, 1879), pp. 101–104.

New South Wales Law Reform Commission, *Consent in Relation to Sexual Offences Report* (2020).

Norrie, Alan, 'Criminal Law and Ethics: Beyond Normative Assertion and Its Critique' (2017) 80(5) *Modern Law Review* 955–973.

Norrie, Kenneth McK., 'The Intentional Delicts' in Kenneth Reid and Reinhard Zimmermann (eds.), *A History of Private Law in Scotland: Volume 2: Obligations* (Oxford: Oxford University Press, 2000), pp. 477–516.

Norrie, Kenneth McK., *Professor Norrie's Commentaries on Family Law* (Dundee: Dundee University Press, 2011).

O'Byrne, Patrick, Bryan, Alyssa and Roy, Marie, 'HIV Criminal Prosecutions and Public Health: An Examination of the Empirical Research' (2013) 39(2) *Medical Humanities* 85–90.

Office for National Statistics (2019), Families and Households in the UK: 2018, www.ons.gov.uk/peoplepopulationandcommunity/birthsdeathsandmarriages/families/bulletins/familiesandhouseholds/2018.

O'Neill, Rachel, *Seduction: Men, Masculinity and Mediated Intimacy* (Cambridge: Polity Press, 2018).

Ormerod, David, *Smith and Hogan Criminal Law: Cases and Materials*, 9th ed. (Oxford University Press, 2005).

Ormerod, David, 'The Fraud Act 2006 – Criminalising Lying?' [2007] *Criminal Law Review* 193–219.

Ormerod, David, 'Rape and Deception (Again)' [2010] 10 *Criminal Law Review* 877–881.

Ormerod, David and Laird, Karl, *Smith, Hogan, and Ormerod's Criminal Law*, 16th ed. (Oxford: Oxford University Press, 2021).

Palmer, Tanya, 'Freedom to Negotiate' in Criminal Law Reform Now Network, *Reforming the Relationship between Sexual Consent, Deception and Mistake: Consultation Report* (2021), pp. 70–79, www.clrnn.co.uk/publications-reports.

Palmer, Vernon Valentine, 'Moral Damages in the Age of Codification' in Vernon Valentine Palmer (ed.), *The Recovery of Non-Pecuniary Loss in European Contract Law* (Cambridge: Cambridge University Press, 2015), pp. 43–57.

Parkinson, Patrick, 'Tricked into Marriage' (2018) 42(1) *Melbourne University Law Review* 117–148.

Paton, G. Campbell H. (ed.), *Baron Hume's Lectures, 1786–1822* (Edinburgh: J. Skinner & Co. Ltd., 1939).

Police Spies Out of Lives (2019), 'Our Stories', https://policespiesoutoflives.org.uk/our-stories.

Pollard Sacks, Deana, 'Intentional Sex Torts' (2008) 77(3) *Fordham Law Review* 1051–1093.

Prentice, Robert A. and Murray, Paula C., 'Liability for Transmission of Herpes: Using Traditional Tort Principles to Encourage Honesty in Sexual Relationships' (1984) 11(1) *Journal of Contemporary Law* 67–103.

Prior, Mary, *Fond Hopes Destroyed: Breach of Promise Cases in Shetland* (Lerwick: Shetland Times Limited, 2005).

Probert, Rebecca, *Marriage Law and Practice in the Long Eighteenth Century: A Reassessment* (Cambridge: Cambridge University Press, 2009).

Probert, Rebecca and D'Arcy-Brown, Liam, 'The Transportation of Bigamists in Early-Nineteenth-Century England and Wales' (2019) 40(3) *The Journal of Legal History* 223–252.

Probert, Rebecca, Harding, Maebh and Dempsey, Brian, 'A Uniform Law of Marriage? The 1868 Royal Commission Reconsidered' (2018) 30(3) *Child and Family Law Quarterly* 217–237.

Pundik, Amit, 'Coercion and Deception in Sexual Relations' (2015) 28(1) *Canadian Journal of Law & Jurisprudence* 97–127.

Pundik, Amit, Schnitzer, Shani and Blum, Binyamin, 'Sex, Lies and Reasonableness: The Case for Subjectifying the Criminalisation of Deceptive Sex' (2022) 41(2) *Criminal Justice Ethics* 167–189.

Queensland Law Reform Commission, *Review of Consent Laws and the Excuse of Mistake of Fact* (2020).

Raz, Joseph, *The Morality of Freedom* (Oxford: Clarendon Press, 1988).

Reddy, William M., *The Making of Romantic Love: Longing and Sexuality in Europe, South Asia and Japan, 900–1200 CE* (Chicago: University of Chicago Press, 2012).

Reemtsma, Jan Philipp, *Trust and Violence: An Essay on a Modern Relationship* (Princeton: Princeton University Press, 2012).

Reid, Elspeth, 'Personal Bar: Case-Law in Search of Principle' (2003) 7(3) *Edinburgh Law Review* 340–366.

Reid, Elspeth, 'Protecting Legitimate Expectations and Estoppel in Scots Law' (2006) *Electronic Journal of Comparative Law*, www.ejcl.org/103/art103-11.pdf.

Reiter, Eric, *Wounded Feelings: Litigating Emotions in Quebec, 1870–1950* (Toronto: University of Toronto Press, 2017).

Renz, Flora, 'Consenting to Gender? Trans Spouses after Same-Sex Marriage' in Nicola Barker and Daniel Monk (eds.), *From Civil Partnership to Same Sex Marriage: Interdisciplinary Reflections* (Abingdon: Routledge, 2015), pp. 83–94.

Report of the Royal Commission on Divorce and Matrimonial Causes (His Majesty's Stationery Office, 1912).

Report of the Royal Commission on the Laws of Marriage (London: George E. Eyre & William Spottiswoode, 1868).

Robertson, Stephen, 'Seduction, Sexual Violence, and Marriage in New York City, 1886–1955' (2006) 24(2) *Law and History Review* 331–373.

Robinson, Margaret, 'Polyamory and Monogamy as Strategic Identities' (2013) 13(1) *Journal of Bisexuality* 21–38.

Robinson, Olivia (ed.), George MacKenzie, *The Law and Customs of Scotland in Matters Criminal* (Edinburgh: Stair Society, 2012).

Rogers, Jonathan, 'The Effect of "Deception" in the Sexual Offences Act 2003' (2013) 4 *Archbold Review* 7–9.

Rosenberg, Anat, *Liberalizing Contracts: Nineteenth Century Promises through Literature, Law and History* (Abingdon: Routledge, 2019).

Rosenberg, Anat, *The Rise of Mass Advertising: Law, Enchantment, and the Cultural Boundaries of British Modernity* (Oxford: Oxford University Press, 2022).

Rosenbury, Laura A. and Rothman, Jennifer E., 'Sex in and out of Intimacy' (2010) 59(4) *Emory Law Journal* 809–868.

Rosenwein, Barbara, *Love: A History in Five Fantasies* (Cambridge: Polity Press, 2022).

Rotenberg, Ken J. and Qualter, Pamela, '50 Shades of Trust', *Psychology Today* (24 February 2014), www.psychologytoday.com/us/blog/matter-trust/201402/50-shades-trust.

Royal Commission on Marriage and Divorce Report 1951–1955 (Her Majesty's Stationery Office, 1956).

Rubenfeld, Jed, 'The Riddle of Rape by Deception and the Myth of Sexual Autonomy' (2013) 122(6) *The Yale Law Journal* 1372–1443.

Salmela, Mikko, 'What Is Emotional Authenticity?' (2005) 35(3) *The Journal for the Theory of Social Behaviour* 209–230.

Scheidegger, Nora, 'Balancing Sexual Autonomy, Responsibility, and the Right to Privacy: Principles for Criminalizing Sex by Deception' (2021) 22 *German Law Journal* 769–783.

Schultz, Amber, 'No Payment, No Consent: Sex Worker Advocacy Groups Say Fraud and Rape Is on the Rise', *Crikey*, 5 August 2020.

Scott, Charles, 'Review of "The Criminal" by Havelock Ellis' (1890) 2(4) *Juridical Review* 381–386.

Scottish Government, 'Criminal Proceedings in Scotland' Statistical Bulletins 2017–2021, www.gov.scot/collections/criminal-proceedings-in-scotland.

Scottish Government, 'Prosecution for the Crime of Bigamy under Common Law: FOI Release' (2018), www.gov.scot/publications/foi-18-02743.

Scottish Law Commission, *Report on Rape and Other Sexual Offences* (Edinburgh: The Stationery Office, 2007).

Scottish Parliament Official Report, Justice Committee, 18 November 2008.

Scutt, Jocelynne A., 'Fraudulent Impersonation and Consent in Rape' (1975) 9(1) *The University of Queensland Law Journal* 59–65.

Scutt, Jocelynne A., 'A Disturbing Case of Consent in Rape' (1976) 40(3) *The Journal of Criminal Law* 206–208.

Scutt, Jocelynne A., 'A Disturbing Case of Consent in Rape (Continued)' (1976) 40(4) *The Journal of Criminal Law* 271–274.

Seigel, Jerrold, *The Idea of the Self: Thought and Experience in Western Europe since the Seventeenth Century* (Cambridge: Cambridge University Press, 2005).

Selznick, Philip, *The Moral Commonwealth: Social Theory and the Promise of Community* (Berkeley: University of California Press, 1992).

Sharpe, Alex, 'Transgender Marriage and the Legal Obligation to Disclose Gender History' (2012) 75(1) *Modern Law Review* 33–53.

Sharpe, Alex, 'Expanding Liability for Sexual Fraud through the Concept of Active Deception: A Flawed Approach' (2016) 80(1) *The Journal of Criminal Law* 28–44.

Sharpe, Alex, *Sexual Intimacy and Gender Identity 'Fraud': Reframing the Legal and Ethical Debate* (Abingdon: Routledge, 2018).

Sharpe, A. N., 'A Return to the "Truth" of the Past' (2009) 18(2) *Social & Legal Studies* 259–263.

Sherdley, Rebecca, '14 Years Living with a Bigamist', *Nottingham Evening Post*, 5 March 2004.

Silvermint, David, 'Passing as Privileged' (2018) 5(1) *Ergo* 1–43.

Simmonds, Alecia, '"Promises and Pie-Crusts Were Made to Be Broke": Breach of Promise of Marriage and the Regulation of Courtship in Early Colonial Australia' (2005) 23 *The Australian Feminist Law Journal* 99–120.

Simmonds, Alecia, '"She Felt Strongly the Injury to Her Affections": Breach of Promise of Marriage and the Medicalization of Heartbreak in Early Twentieth-Century Australia' (2017) 38(2) *The Journal of Legal History* 179–202.

Simmonds, Alecia, 'Courtship, Coverture and Marital Cruelty: Historicising Intimate Violence in the Civil Courts' (2019) 45(1) *Australian Feminist Law Journal* 131–157.

Simons, Kenneth W., 'Consent and the Assumption of Risk in Tort and Criminal Law' in Matthew Dyson (ed.), *Unravelling Tort and Crime* (Cambridge: Cambridge University Press, 2014), pp. 330–355.

Sjölin, Catarina, 'Ten Years On: Consent under the Sexual Offences Act 2003' (2015) 79(1) *The Journal of Criminal Law* 20–35.

Slingsby, Mike, 'A Bigamist Walked Free from Court after the Wife He Had Deceived Said She Was Willing to Forgive Him', *Manchester Evening News*, 10 February 2006.

Smith, F. B., 'Labouchere's Amendment to the Criminal Law Amendment Bill' (1976) 17(67) *Historical Studies* 165–173.

Smith, Kathryn Rea, *Experiencing Abortion: A Phenomenological Investigation*, PhD dissertation (Tennessee Research and Creative Exchange, 1998), https://trace.tennessee.edu/utk_graddiss/2514.

Sommers, Roseanna, 'Commonsense Consent' (2020) 129(8) *The Yale Law Journal* 2232–2324.

Sommers, Roseanna, 'You Were Duped into Saying Yes: Is It Still Consent?', *The New York Times*, 5 March 2021.

Soothill, Keith, Ackerley, Elizabeth, Sanderson, Barry and Peelo, Moira, 'The Place of Bigamy in the Pantheon of Crime' (1999) 39(1) *Medicine, Science and Law* 65–71.

Soulsby, Laura K. and Bennett, Kate M., 'When Two Become One: Exploring Identity in Marriage and Cohabitation' (2016) 38(3) *Journal of Family Issues* 358–380.

Sparrow, Robert, and Karas, Lauren, 'Teledildonics and Rape by Deception' (2020) 12(1) *Law, Innovation and Technology* 175–204.

Spencer, J. R., 'Sex by Deception' (2013) 9 *Archbold Review* 6–9.

Srinivasan, Amia, 'Does Anyone Have the Right to Sex?' (2018) 40(6) *London Review of Books*.

Srinivasan, Amia, 'Genealogy, Epistemology and Worldmaking' (2019) 119(2) *Proceedings of the Aristotelian Society* 127–156.

Stair, James Dalrymple and More, John S. (eds.), *Institutions of the Law of Scotland, Deduced from Its Originals, and Collated with the Civil, Canon, and Feudal Laws, and with the Customs of Neighbouring Nations* (Edinburgh: Bell & Bradfute, 1832).

Stark, Findlay, 'Tort Law, Expression and Duplicative Wrongs' in Paul B. Miller and John Oberdiek (eds.), *Civil Wrongs and Justice in Private Law* (New York: Oxford University Press, 2020), pp. 441–462.

Steinbach, Susie, *Promises, Promises: Not Marrying in England 1780-1920* (PhD dissertation, Yale University ProQuest Dissertations Publishing, 1996), www.proquest.com/dissertations-theses/promises-not-marrying-england-1780-1920/docview/304306821/se-2.

Stephen, James Fitzjames, *A Digest of the Criminal Law (Crimes and Punishments)* (F. H. Thomas and Company, 1878, reprint Littleton, Colorado: Fred B. Rothman & Co., 1991).

Stephens, Amber K. and Emmers-Sommer, Tara M., 'Adults' Identities, Attitudes, and Orientations Concerning Consensual Non-Monogamy' (2020) 17 *Sexuality Research and Social Policy* 469–485.

Stewart, Angus, 'The Session Papers in the Advocates Library' in Hector L. MacQueen (ed.), *Miscellany Four* (Edinburgh: The Stair Society, 2002), pp. 199–221.

Stone, Lawrence, *Uncertain Unions: Marriage in England, 1660-1753* (Oxford: Oxford University Press, 1992).

Stonehouse, Rachel, 'Stealthing: "I Didn't Realise It's Rape until It Happened to Me"', *BBC News*, 27 July 2021.

Sutherland, Elaine, 'Dad or Undad: Liability for Paternity Fraud' (2015), www.lawscot.org.uk/members/journal/issues/vol-60-issue-08/dad-or-undad-liability-for-paternity-fraud.

Tadros, Victor, 'Rape without Consent' (2006) 26(3) *Oxford Journal of Legal Studies* 515–543.

Taylor, Charles, *Sources of the Self: The Making of Modern Identity* (Cambridge, MA: Harvard University Press, 1989).

Taylor, Charles, *The Ethics of Authenticity* (Cambridge, MA: Harvard University Press, 1991).

Taylor, Charles, 'The Politics of Recognition' in Amy Gutmann (ed.), *Multiculturalism and the Politics of Recognition* (Princeton: Princeton University Press, 1994), pp. 25–74.

Taylor, Chloë, *Foucault, Feminism, and Sex Crimes: An Anti-carceral Analysis* (New York: Routledge, 2019).

Temkin, Jennifer, 'Towards a Modern Law of Rape' (1982) 45(4) *Modern Law Review* 399–419.

Temkin, Jennifer, 'A New Law of Sexual Offences for Scotland: A Comment on the Draft Criminal Code' (2006) *Juridical Review* 29–53.

Temkin, Jennifer and Ashworth, Andrew, 'The Sexual Offences Act 2003: (1) Rape, Sexual Assaults and the Problems of Consent' [2004] *Criminal Law Review* 328–346.

Thomson, Andrea, '"The Best of Both Worlds"? Young Women, Family and Marriage in 1970s Scotland' in Katie Barclay, Jeffrey Meek and Andrea Thomson (eds.), *Courtship, Marriage and Marriage Breakdown: Approaches from the History of Emotion* (New York: Routledge, 2019), pp. 127–143.

Threet, Dan, 'Mill's Social Pressure Puzzle' (2018) 44(4) *Social Theory and Practice* 539–565.

Tilton, Emily C. R. and Ichikawa, Jonathan Jenkins, 'Not What I Agreed To: Content and Consent' (2021) 132(1) *Ethics* 127–154.

Tobin, Katie, 'What Is 'Consent Theft' and Why Aren't We Talking about it?', *Restless*, 31 March 2021.

Tolley, Rachel Clement, 'Deception, Mistake and Difficult Decisions' in Criminal Law Reform Now Network, *Reforming the Relationship between Sexual Consent, Deception and Mistake: Consultation Report* (2021), www.clrnn.co.uk/publications-reports, pp. 90–97.

Tolstoy, D., 'Void and Voidable Marriages' (1964) 27(4) *Modern Law Review* 385–394.

Toma, Catalina L., Bonus, James Alex and Van Swol, Lyn M., 'Lying Online: Examining the Production, Detection, and Popular Beliefs Surrounding Interpersonal Deception in Technologically-Mediated Environments' in Tony Docan-Morgan (ed.), *The Palgrave Handbook of Deceptive Communication* (Cham: Springer International Publishing, 2019), pp. 583–602.

Tran, Grace, '"We're Dating after Marriage": Transformative Effects of Performing Intimacy in Vietnamese "Marriage Fraud" Arrangements' (2021) 44(9) *Ethnic and Racial Studies* 1569–1588.

Trist, Liz, 'Bigamy Victim Is Anxious to Help', *Express and Echo*, 16 February 2005.

Umbach, Maiken and Humphrey, Mathew, 'Introduction' in Maiken Umbach and Mathew Humphrey (eds.), *Authenticity: The Cultural History of a Political Concept* (Cham: Springer International Publishing, 2018), pp. 1–12.

Varga, Somogy and Guignon, Charles, 'Authenticity', *The Stanford Encyclopedia of Philosophy* (Spring 2020 Edition), Edward N. Zalta (ed.), https://plato.stanford.edu/archives/spr2020/entries/authenticity/.

Victorian Law Reform Commission, *Improving the Justice System Response to Sexual Offences* (2021).

Vigarello, Georges, *A History of Rape: Sexual Violence in France from the 16th to the 20th Century* (Cambridge: Polity Press, 2001).

Wahrman, Dror, *The Making of the Modern Self: Identity and Culture in Eighteenth-Century England* (New Haven: Yale University Press, 2004).

Walker, David M., *The Law of Damages in Scotland* (Edinburgh: W. Green & Sons, 1955).

Walker, David M., *The Law of Delict in Scotland* (vol. 2) (Edinburgh: published under the auspices of the Scottish Universities Law Institute by Green, 1966).

Walker, David M., *The Law of Civil Remedies in Scotland* (Edinburgh: W. Green & Sons, 1974).

Walser, Hannah, 'Vagueness, Double Consciousness, and the Criminal Law: A Cognitive History' (2023) 10(1) *Critical Analysis of Law* 97–115.

Walton, Frederick Parker, *A Handbook of Husband and Wife* (Edinburgh: W. Green & Sons, 1893).

Walton, Frederick Parker, *A Handbook of Husband and Wife According to the Law of Scotland* (Edinburgh: W. Green & Sons, 1922).

Wang, Yuanyuan, Wilson, Amanda, Chen, Runsen, Hu, Zhishan, Peng, Ke and Xu, Shicun, 'Behind the Rainbow, "Tongqi" Wives of Men Who Have Sex with Men in China: A Systematic Review' (2020) 10 *Frontiers in Psychology* 2929.

Watson, George (ed.), *Bell's Dictionary and Digest of the Law of Scotland*, 7th ed. (Edinburgh: Bell & Bradfute, London: Butterworths, 1890).

Wemyss, Georgie, Yuval-Davis, Nira and Cassidy, Kathryn, '"Beauty and the Beast": Everyday Bordering Discourse and "Sham Marriage" Discourse' (2018) 66 *Political Geography* 151–160.

Wertheimer, Alan, *Consent to Sexual Relations* (Cambridge: Cambridge University Press, 2003).

Wheeler, Leigh Ann, 'Inventing Sexuality: Ideologies, Identities and Practices in the Gilded Age and Progressive Era' in Christopher McKnight Nichols and Nancy C. Unger (eds.), *A Companion to the Gilded Age and Progressive Era* (Chichester: Wiley-Blackwell, 2017), pp. 102–115.

Whittaker, Simon and Zimmermann, Reinhard, 'Good Faith in European Contract Law: Surveying the Legal Landscape' in Simon Whittaker and Reinhard Zimmermann (eds.), *Good Faith in European Contract Law* (Cambridge: Cambridge University Press, 2000), pp. 7–62.

Whitty, Niall R., 'Overview of Rights of Personality in Scots Law' in Niall R. Whitty and Reinhard Zimmermann (eds.), *Rights of Personality in Scots Law: A Comparative Perspective* (Edinburgh: Edinburgh University Press, 2009), pp. 147–246.

Wiener, Martin J., *Men of Blood: Violence, Manliness, and Criminal Justice in Victorian England* (Cambridge: Cambridge University Press, 2004).

Wikeley, Nick and Young, Lisa, 'Secrets and Lies: No Deceit Down Under' (2008) 20(1) *Child and Family Law Quarterly* 81–94.

Williams, Glanville L., 'Bigamy and the Third Marriage' (1950) 13(4) *Modern Law Review* 417–427.

Williams, Rebecca, 'Deception, Mistake and Vitiation of the Victim's Consent' (2008) 124 *Law Quarterly Review* 132–159.

Williams, Rebecca, 'R v Flattery (1877)' in Philip Handler, Henry Mares and Ian Williams (eds.), *Landmark Cases in Criminal Law* (Oxford: Hart Publishing, 2019), pp. 147–170.

Winkler, Andrew W., 'Domestic Relations: Fraudulent Representation of Pregnancy as Grounds for Annulment' (1968) 57(2) *Kentucky Law Journal* 272–277.

Witte, John, Jr, *The Western Case for Monogamy over Polygamy* (Cambridge: Cambridge University Press, 2015).

Wood, William R. and Suzuki, Masahiro, 'Are Conflicts Property? Re-Examining the Ownership of Conflict in Restorative Justice' (2020) 29(6) *Social & Legal Studies* 903–924.

Wray, Helena, *Regulating Marriage Migration into the UK: A Stranger in the Home* (London: Routledge, 2011).

Wright, Harter F., 'The Action for Breach of the Marriage Promise' (1924) 10(5) *Virginia Law Review* 361–383.

Zhu, Jingshu, '"Unqueer" Kinship? Critical Reflections on "Marriage Fraud" in Mainland China' (2018) 21(7) *Sexualities* 1075–1091.

Index

abuse of authority or trust, 123, 140, 142, 170
  clergy, 180
  law reforms, 181–183
  medical profession, 2, 179–181
  rape, 178–183
  seduction, 137–140
  teachers, 2, 180–181
accessorial liability, 143
  procuring offences, 150–151
action of breach of promise of marriage, 18, 65–66, 71, 109, 131–132, 140. *See also* breach of promise of marriage
  action for seduction compared, 134–135
  damages for pecuniary losses, 66, 73–75
  deception, relationship with, 79, 84–87
  emotional harm, 66, 69, 73–75, 79
  honourable courtship, 76
  moral duty, 85
  solatium, 66, 69, 73–75, 79
action of declarator of marriage, 5, 74, 109, 131
action of seduction, 5, 121, 123–125, 129, 131, 140, 142. *See also* seduction
  honourable courtship, 133–135
adultery
  deception, 172, 195
  procuring offences, 154
  promises *contra bonos mores*, 71–72
age of marital consent, 126
age of sexual consent, 126
agency, 4, 24, 141
  procuring offences, 144, 151
alcohol abuse, 80–81
annulments, 35, 62, 204. *See also* nullity of marriage
  concealed pregnancy, 44–49
  epilepsy, 49–50
  impotence, 51–55
  infertility, 51
  insanity, 49–50

mental deficiency, 49
  paternity, deception surrounding, 47–48
  pre-marital chastity, 44
  sexually transmitted diseases, 49
  unsoundness of mind, 49–50
  wealth and position, deception around, 41–44
assault
  abuse of authority and trust, 178, 180–181
  actual bodily harm, 183–184
  deception, 185–186
  false promises of marriage, 185
  fraud, 183–184
  indecent assault, 183
  rape, relationship with, 170–171
authenticity, 13, 17, 24, 86, 115, 160, 213
autonomy, 4, 13, 24–25, 125, 175, 204, 206, 212. *See also* sexual autonomy

bigamy, 5, 7, 31–32, 57, 61, 88, 93, 109–115, 195
  damages, 32
  legitimacy of children of marriages contracted in good faith, 32
  marital status and deception, 193–194
  perjury, as, 110
  private wrong, as, 110
  procuring offences, 155–156
  public crime, as, 110
  public interest, and, 113–115
  sanctions, leniency of, 110–112
  social security fraud, 114
  state's interests, 110
biological sex, 55
breach of promise of marriage, 5–7, 22, 64–66, 73. *See also* action of breach of promise of marriage
  abolition of action, 78, 85
  award of damages, 73
  changed feelings, 65, 84–86

Index

cultural shifts, 83–85
degradation of the inconstant lover, 74
intentional deception, 71–73
justifications, 86
   alcohol abuse, 80–81
   incompatibility, 83–84
   undisclosed immorality, 81–83
   wealth and position, 79–80
proving, 74
seduction, 72

causation requirement, 170, 176
   impersonation offences, 173, 176, 209–210
changed feelings, 65, 84–86
chastity, pre-marital, annulments, 44
choice of partner and marriage, 15
civil liability, 127
   seduction, 141
Civil Partnership Act 2004, 58
   bigamy, 114
civil responsibility, 127
   seduction, 141
clarity of law, criminal law, 23, 142, 170, 201
clergy, abuse of authority and trust, 180
cohabitation
   cohabiting as spouses, 8–9
   immoral behaviour, 154–155
   lifestyle choice, as, 155
collective interest, 23, 200–202, 211, 219
   individual choice, relationship with, 201–202
   public law responses to deceptions, 122, 127, 198
companionate marriage, 68, 77
compensation of women, 136, 194. *See also* damages
   punishment of men, relationship with, 10, 68, 91, 128
   seduction, 128
concealed pregnancy, annulments, 44–46
consent
   age of marital consent, 126
   age of sexual consent, 126
   approaches to, 89–91
   consent and deception, conceptualisation of, 199, 203–211
   consent obtained by fraud, 161–164
   deception and validity of marital consent, 29–30
   deceptively induced sexual consent, 121
   different understandings of, 37
   expressing mutual consent to marriage, 8

false promises of marriage, 9–11
formation of marriage, 9
fraud, 37
fraudulently induced consent, 179–180
husband impersonation, 172, 174–175
impaired consent, 123, 125–126
imputed consent, 11, 89–90
legally invalid consent, 17, 21, 123, 188, 196
marriage by present consent, 88, 94–104
objective approaches to consent, 90–91, 97
rape and absence of consent, 171–174
   husband impersonation, 172, 174–175
reasonable belief in, 208–209
sexual consent, 204
subjective approaches to consent, 90–91, 98–99
temporal complexities, 210–211
consent and deception, conceptualisation of, 199, 203–211
contested marriages, 5
contraception and deception, 170, 189, 191–192
contracts of marriage, 35, 65
creation of a binding promise to marry, 73
criminal law, 1–6, 20, 23–24
Criminal Law Amendment Act 1885, 126–127, 138, 147–148
   bigamy, 155–157
   procuring offences, 158
criminal liability, 2, 150, 159, 166–168, 205
criminal responsibility, 2, 150, 159, 166–168, 205
criminalisation and sexual autonomy, 1, 24, 169, 183
   sham marriages, 103
criminalisation of seduction, 122, 127–128, 141–142, 157
culpability requirement, 207–208

damages. *See also* compensation of women; solatium
   bigamy, 32
   nonpecuniary damages, 131
   pecuniary losses, 66
   prior subsisting marriages, 32–33
      entrapment, 33–35
      psychiatric injuries, 33
dating apps, 16, 21
deception, 5
   abuse of authority or trust compared, 123
   action of breach of promise of marriage, relationship with, 79, 84–87

deception (cont.)
  adultery, 172, 195
  assault, 185–186
  bigamy, 193–194
  concept of, 5–7
    distinguishing deceptions, 204–205
    contraception and deception, 170, 189, 191–192
  deceptive intimate relationships, 4, 205
  deceptive sex
    legal responses to, 3–4, 205
    prosecutions for, 2
  deceptively induced sexual consent, 121
  engaging in deceptive conduct, 5
  identity deception, 170
    gender deception, 177–178
    impersonation, 37–41
    mistaken identity, 37–41, 206
    rape, 170–178
  marital status and deception, 193
    bigamy, 193–194
    rape by fraud, 193–194
    rape prosecutions, 194–195
  mistake distinguished, 204
  procuring offences, 148, 155–160
  rape by deception, 5–6, 20, 195, 205
  substance of, 199, 211–218
  use or threat of physical force, 123
  validity of marital consent, 29–30
decrees of nullity, 30, 32, 39, 48, 56, 204
delict, 64
  fraud, 30, 62
  seduction, 5, 9, 34, 121
desertion, 111
  promises *contra bonos mores*, 72
disciplinary role of marriage, 20, 65, 124
disclosure duties, 49, 61, 184, 205–207.
    See also transparency in intimate relationships
  disease status, 187–189
  financial stability, 80
  pregnancy, 46
  same-sex attraction, 59
disease status and deception, 170, 183–189
divorce, liberalisation of, 31, 62

emotional authenticity. *See* authenticity
emotional injuries. *See* psychological and emotional damage
epilepsy, 49–50, 83
estoppel, 11. *See also* personal bar
evidential objectivism, 90–91, 99

expectations of marriage, 60, 64, 200
  seduction, 132–135
extramarital pregnancy, 34, 81–82
extra-marital sex, 20

failure to honour promises, 6
failures to disclose information, 6.
    See also disclosure duties
false emotions, 88
false impression, 206
false pretences, 160, 170
  procuring offences, 146–148, 151–153, 165
false representation, 35
  procuring offences, 151
  wealth and position, 41–44
"female husbands", 55–56
fertility status and deception, 170, 189–191
forfeiture by insincere act, 11
formation of marriage, 31–37, 51
  consent, 9
fornication, 149, 194–195
fraud, 5, 35
  impersonation, 175
  procuring offences, 149–150
fraudulent misrepresentation, 36, 174
fraudulent representation
  personation, 35–36, 39, 42
  wealth and position, 41–44
fraudulent seduction, 128, 157
fraudulently induced consent, 44, 156, 179–180
friendships, 3, 16, 77

gender and sex, 55–60
gender identity, 58–60, 207, 216
gender norms, 65
gender recognition, 58
gender/sex binary, 55–57
good faith promise to marry, 6, 39
gross indecency, procuring offences, 158–159

HIV status, 2, 187–189
honesty, expectation of, 16
honourable courtship, 76
  action of seduction, 133–135
  proving promise to marry, 104–106
Hume, David, 73
husband impersonation. *See also* impersonation
  consent, 172, 174–175
  procuring offences, 156, 161
  rape, 172, 174–175

identity deception, 170
  gender deception, 177–178
  impersonation, 38–41
    marital consent, 37–38
  mistaken identity, 206
    void and voidable marriages, 37–41
  rape, 170–178
identity nonrecognition, 214–215
illegitimacy, 34, 81–82
impaired consent, 30, 37, 123, 125–126, 135, 204–205. *See also* seduction
impersonation. *See also* husband impersonation
  broadness of scope, 38–41, 175–178
  fraud, 175
  husband impersonation
    procuring offences, 156, 161
    rape, 172, 174–175
  marital consent, 37–38, 172
impotence, 32, 51–55, 61
imputing consent, 11, 89–90
inconsistent conduct, 11
individual choice, 4, 18, 30, 197. *See also* autonomy; sexual autonomy
  collective interest, relationship with, 201–202
infertility, 51
innocent misunderstanding, 35–36
insanity, 49, 83
  recurrent insanity, 49–50
intention requirement, procuring offences, 151, 153, 207–208
intentional infliction of emotional distress, 5, 29, 62–63, 207–208
intimacy, expectation of, 16
intimacy, forms of, 1–2, 18–21, 88, 122, 145
intoxication, 146
irregular marriage, 8–9, 48, 89, 109, 136–137

legal certainty, 89, 105, 115–117, 170, 211
legal clarity, 23, 142, 170, 198, 201, 211
legally invalid consent, 17, 21, 123, 188, 196
liberalisation of marriage, 14–18, 65, 75, 155
liberty. *See* autonomy
lies, 5. *See also* deception
love-based marriage, 14–16, 65, 68

marital status and deception, 116, 193
  bigamy, 193–194
  rape by fraud, 193–194
  rape prosecutions, 194–195

marriage. *See also* formation of marriage; sham marriages; void marriages; voidable marriages
  annulments. *See* annulments; nullity of marriage; termination of marriages
  breach of promise of marriage. *See* breach of promise of marriage
  consent and deception, 203
  disciplinary role of marriage, 20, 65, 124
  irregular marriage. *See* irregular marriage
  love-based marriage. *See* love-based marriage
  public institution, as, 55, 60, 200
  punishment, as, 11–12
  status of, 5–6
    prestige and respectability of women, 14
  valuable and distinctive, as, 30
marriage by present consent, 88, 94–104
marriage by promise and sex, 8, 88, 104–109
  presumptions, 108–109
marriage with a 'gay' man, 59
Matrimonial Causes Act 1860, 49
Matrimonial Causes Act 1937, 48
Matrimonial Causes Act 1965, 50
Matrimonial Causes Act 1973, 50, 58
medical profession
  abuse of authority and trust, 2, 179–181
  unlawful breach of confidence, 179
mens rea requirements, 168, 170
mental deficiency, 49
misleading conduct, 6, 10, 199. *See also* deception
misrepresentations, 5, 170, 206. *See also* deception
mutual consent to marriage, 8, 106, 108

non-disclosures, 48–49, 61, 82, 170, 187–189, 204–207
nonpecuniary damages, 131
nullity of marriage, 5, 31–32, 34, 205. *See also* annulments
  legal development, 60–63

objective approaches to consent, 90–91
  marriage by present consent, 97
Offences Against the Person Act 1861, 147
'ordinary' relationships, 2–4, 22, 163, 212

parole evidence, proving breach of promise, 74, 104–106
paternity
  annulments, 47–48
  paternity fraud, 62, 82

pecuniary losses, breach of promise, 66, 73, 129
personal bar, 11, 30, 51–52
  marriage by present consent, 94–96
personation, 35. *See also* fraudulent representation
power dynamic. *See* abuse of authority or trust
pregnancy, 46–49
  concealed pregnancy, 44–46
  extramarital pregnancy, 34, 81–82
procuring offences, 5–6, 20
  accessorial liability, 150–151
  act that is procured, 145, 153–160
  bigamy, 155–156
  consent obtained by fraud, 161–164
  deception, 148
  demise of, 161–165
  false representations, 151
  fraud, 149–150
  gross indecency, 158–159
  impersonating a woman's husband, 156, 161
  intention and effort, 151, 153
  meaning of procuring, 144, 146–153
  prostitution, 146–148
  rape, relationship with, 145–146, 162–164, 166
  sex requirement, 152
  trafficking, 148
  undercover police officers, 152
  unfulfilled promises of marriage, 156–158
  unlawful sex requirement, 153–160
promises *contra bonos mores*, 72
prostitution, 145
  procuring offences, 146–148
  unlawful sex, relationship with, 154–155
Protection of Women Act 1849, 146
prout de jure, proving breach of promise, 74
proving breach of promise, 74–79
proving promise to marry, 105–106, 132
  honourable courtship, 104–106
  parole evidence, 104–106
psychological and emotional damage, 116–117
  bigamy, 112–113
  damages
    breach of promise, 66–69
    prior subsisting marriages, 33
  seduction, 129–130
public policy, 49, 53–54, 57–58, 71–73
public versus private spheres, 199, 200–203
  encroachment of public into private, 22, 60–61, 86
  public law (criminal or regulatory law) and private law responses, 22–24, 122, 202–203
  public/collective and private/individual interests, 22–23, 200–202
  seduction, 122
  state/non-state responses to inducing intimacy, 22
punitiveness element, 11–12, 91–93

rape
  abuse of authority or trust, 178–183
  death penalty, 172
  development of crime of rape, 169–170, 195–198
  identity and deception, 170–178
  marital rape exemption, 159
  procuring offences, relationship with, 145–146, 159, 162–164, 166
  prosecutions, 171
    marital status and deception, 194–195
  seduction distinguished, 135–137
  undercover police officers, 177
rape by deception, 5–6, 20, 195, 205
rape by fraud, marital status and deception, 193–194
redress. *See* compensation of women
romantic love, 59
  love-based marriage, 14–16, 65, 68
  sexual desire, tensions between, 18–21
Royal Commission on Divorce and Matrimonial Causes, grounds for annulment, 49–50
Royal Commission on the Laws of Marriage, 100
rules of evidence, proving breach of promise, 74

same-sex relationships, 55–56
  bigamy, 114
  legalisation of same-sex marriage, 58
  non-disclosure of same-sex attraction, 59
seduction, 5, 7, 9, 72, 121–123, 130–131, 204. *See also* action of seduction
  abuse of authority or trust, 137–140
  corruption, 124–125
  damages, 128, 133
  deception, 123
  enticement, 124
  expectations of marriage, 132–135
  fraudulent abuse, 124
  impaired consent, 125–126
  marriage by promise and sex, 106
  minors, 126
  promising marriage before sex, 131–135, 140

public interest, 127
rape distinguished, 135–137
use or threat of force, 135–137
self-construction and intimacy, relationship between, 12–13, 15, 17, 24–25, 113, 170, 200, 213–217, 219
selfhood and intimacy, relationship between, 4, 12–18. *See also* authenticity; autonomy
sex and marriage, 18–21
sex positivism, 19
sexual autonomy, 4, 175, 192, 204. *See also* autonomy
sexual coercion, 124, 136, 177, 208
sexual consent, 204. *See also* consent
age of sexual consent, 126
sexual desire, romantic love, tensions between, 18–21
Sexual Offences Act 1956, 151
sexuality, concept of, 19, 59–60
sexually transmitted diseases, 49–50, 184, 187–188, 192, 207
sham marriages, 93, 103–104, 155, 164
social gender, 55
social purity movements, 20
solatium, 33, 52, 66–67, 69–70, 129. *See also* damages; psychological and emotional damage
stealthing, 189
subjective approaches to consent, 90–91
marriage by present consent, 98–99

teachers, abuse of authority and trust, 2, 180–181
termination of marriages, 15–16, 54
trafficking, procuring offences, 148, 164
transgender identity, 58–59
deception, 216–217
transparency in intimate relationships, 17, 30, 61, 80, 192, 199, 206. *See also* disclosure duties
trust, expectations of, 1, 17, 22, 70, 170

uncertainty over intentions
marriage by present consent, 97–102
marriage by promise and sex, 107–108

unchastity, 44–46, 82
undercover police officers, 62, 116, 152, 177
unfulfilled promises of marriage
criminalisation, 158
procuring offences, 156–158
unfulfilled promises to pay for sex, 158
unilateral reservations, 90
United States
criminalisation of seduction and public order, 127, 136
intentional infliction of emotional distress, 29, 62
sham marriages, 103
unjustifiable termination of an engagement, 5
unlawful sex, 153
procuring offences, 153–160
prostitution, relationship with, 154–155
unsoundness of mind, 49–50
use or threat of force, 123
seduction, 135–137

validity of marriages, 35–37
venereal disease. *See* sexually transmitted diseases
virtue requirement, 129–131, 139
void marriages, 30–31
mistaken identity, 37–41
same-sex relationships, 55–56
seduction, 33–35
voidable marriages, 30
public/private sphere, 61
seduction, 204

wealth and position, 15, 32, 138, 156, 177
breach of promise of marriage, 79–80
false representation, 41–44
fraudulent representation, 41–44
World War I
bigamy, 48, 112
irregular marriage, 48
sexually transmitted diseases, 50
World War II, 48
bigamy, 112

For EU product safety concerns, contact us at Calle de José Abascal, 56–1°, 28003 Madrid, Spain or eugpsr@cambridge.org